John Milton Among the Neapolitans:
Mansus—Contexts, Texts, Intertexts

John Milton Among the Neapolitans:
Mansus—Contexts, Texts, Intertexts

Estelle Haan

American Philosophical Society Press
Philadelphia

> Transactions of the
> American Philosophical Society
> Held at Philadelphia
> for Promoting Useful Knowledge
> Volume 112, Part 4

Copyright © 2023 by the American Philosophical Society for its Transactions series.

All rights reserved.

ISBN: 978-1-60618-130-0
Ebook ISBN: 978-1-60618-131-7
U.S. ISSN: 0065-9746

Library of Congress Control Number

2023933056

Front cover: Map of Naples, in Georg Braun and Frans Hogenberg, *Civitates Orbis Terrarum, Liber Primus* (Cologne: Gottfried von Kempen, 1582).

Cover design by Ellen B. Zanolle.

For Tony

CONTENTS

Acknowledgments ix
Abbreviations xi

Introduction   *Neapolim Perrexi*: Milton in Naples   1

Chapter 1   ***Assidua Auctorum Lectio*: Milton's Neapolitan Reading**   27

     1.1   Milton's Reading Practices in Italy   28
     1.2   Two Literary Gift Texts: Manso's *Pocula … Bina*   36

Chapter 2   **"Forms" of Beauty: Milton and the *Erocallia***   41

     2.1   Manso to Milton: *Forma* and *Decor*   46
     2.2   Milton to Manso: Vernal Youthfulness   55
     2.3   Milton Among the Erocallian Angels   59

Chapter 3   **"Poesie di Diversi": Milton, Manso, and the *Poesie Nomiche***   65

     3.1   The Phoenix and Poetic Self-Fashioning   68
     3.2   *Mansus* and the "Poesie di Diversi"   75
     3.2.1   Tasso, Marino, Milton   80
     3.2.2   Accademia degli Oziosi: *Mansus* and Pastoral *Otium*   85
     3.2.3   *Mansus Mansuetus*: Patterns of Wordplay   92
     3.2.4   *Modulantes … Cygni*: Literary Swans   97
     3.2.5   From Virgil to Chaucer to Spenser   104

Chapter 4   ***Non Tacita … Vita*: *Mansus*, Biography, and Miltonic Autobiography**   113

     4.1   Milton's *Vita di Giovanni Battista Manso*   114
     4.2   Manso, the Biographer   121
     4.3   Miltonic Autobiography and King Arthur   133
     4.4   Tasso and Milton: Two Deathbed Scenes   150

Chapter 5   ***Dialogus de Amicitia Scriptus*: Dialogue(s) of Friendship**   155

     5.1   *Amicitia, Benevolentia, Concordia*   160
     5.2   *Amicitia, Pietas, Fama*   165

	5.3 Manso: *Et Amicus et Pater*	168

Chapter 6   ***Dulciloquus ... Marinus*: Marino Re-Membered**   175

      6.1   *Angelus Ipse Fores*: Milton in St. Angelo a Foro   175
      6.2   *L'Adone* Re-Membered   184
      6.3   Marino and Two Italian Academies   194
      6.4   *Mansus* and Marinesque "Concettismo"   201

Appendix   *207*
Bibliography   *215*
Index Nominum et Locorum   *247*

ACKNOWLEDGMENTS

The present monograph could not have been realized without the generous help of librarians and archivists in Belfast, Cambridge, London, and Naples. I thank the Special Collections of The Queen's University of Belfast, and the Masters and Fellows of Christ's College, Cambridge, for facilitating limitless access to printed copies of Milton's writings and other printed materials pertinent to this study. Thanks are also due to Trinity College Library, Cambridge; the British Library, London; and the Biblioteca Nazionale, Naples.

I dedicate this work to my husband, Tony, whose computing, archival, and palaeographical skills are outweighed only by his gentleness, his cheer, and his love.

ABBREVIATIONS

Manuscripts

TM   Trinity College, Cambridge: MS R.3.4 (Milton's workbooks)

Libraries

ASBN	Museo dell' Archivio Storico Banco, Naples
ASMMS	Archivio Storico del Monte Manso di Scala, Naples
BAV	Biblioteca Apostolica Vaticana, Rome
BL	British Library, London
BNCF	Biblioteca Nazionale Centrale, Florence
BNN	Biblioteca Nazionale, Naples
BUG	Biblioteca Universitaria, Genoa

Reference Works/Anthologies

CIPI	*Carmina Illustrium Poetarum Italorum*, ed. G. G. Bottari, 11 vols. (Florence: Giovanni Gaetano Tartini and Sante Franchi, 1719–26).
DBI	*Dizionario Biografico degli Italiani*, 100 vols. (Rome: Istituto dell' Enciclopedia Italiana, 1960–2020).
Lewis and Short	*A Latin Dictionary*, eds. C. T. Lewis and Charles Short (Oxford: Clarendon Press, 1955).
NDB	*Neue Deutsche Biographie*, ed. Historische Kommission bei der Bayrischen Akademie der Wissenschaften (Berlin: Duncker und Humblot, 1953–).
ODNB	*Oxford Dictionary of National Biography*, 60 vols. (Oxford: Oxford University Press, 2004).
OLD	*Oxford Latin Dictionary*, ed. P. G. W. Clare (Oxford: Clarendon Press, 1968–82).
RE	*Paulys Realencyclopädie der Classischen Altertumwissenschaft*, eds. Georg Wissowa, Wilhelm Kroll, Karl Mittelhaus, and Konrat Ziegler, 85 vols. (Stuttgart: A. Druckenmüller, 1893–1978).

Journals

AJP	*American Journal of Philology*
AP	*Ancient Philosophy*
CC	*Comparative Criticism*
CJ	*Classical Journal*
CL	*Comparative Literature*
CLS	*Comparative Literature Studies*

CQ	*Classical Quarterly*
CW	*Classical World*
EHR	*English Historical Review*
G&R	*Greece and Rome*
HJ	*The Historical Journal*
HL	*Humanistica Lovaniensia: Journal of Neo-Latin Studies*
HTR	*Harvard Theological Review*
JEGP	*Journal of English and Germanic Philology*
JWCI	*Journal of the Warburg and Courtauld Institutes*
LI	*Lettere Italiane*
MLN	*Modern Language Notes*
MLQ	*Modern Language Quarterly*
MP	*Modern Philology*
MQ	*Milton Quarterly*
MS	*Milton Studies*
N&Q	*Notes and Queries*
PBA	*Proceedings of the British Academy*
PCPS	*Proceedings of the Cambridge Philological Society*
PMLA	*Publications of the Modern Language Association of America*
PR	*Philosophical Review*
RES	*Review of English Studies*
RQ	*Renaissance Quarterly*
RS	*Renaissance Studies*
SEL	*Studies in English Literature*
SP	*Studies in Philology*
SR	*Studies in the Renaissance*
SRev	*Sewanee Review*
SS	*Studi Secenteschi*
ST	*Studi Tassiani*
TAPhA	*Transactions of the American Philological Association*
TLS	*Times Literary Studies* (London)
UCPMP	*University of California Publications in Modern Philology*
UTQ	*University of Toronto Quarterly*

Introduction

Neapolim Perrexi:[1]
Milton in Naples

> Ma giunto, ch'egli fù poscia in Napoli il suo contentamento à molti doppi moltiplicò: percioche, egli rimase sommamente sodisfatto, e maravigliato insieme del sito, e dell'ampiezza di tutta la Città nel primo aspetto da lui riguardata, e della bellezza, e della Magnificenza di qualunque sua parte per se stessa considerata, & altrettanto appagato, e soprafatto dalle cortese, e da gli honori fattegli universalmente da ciascheduno.[2]

> But when he arrived later in Naples, his contentment was considerably multiplied: for he was extremely satisfied and simultaneously amazed by the site, and by the breadth of the whole city at his very first glance, and by its beauty, and by the magnificence of each of its regions individually considered, and he felt an equal sense of fulfillment in being overwhelmed by the courtesies and honors universally conferred upon him by each and every person.[3]

Such, according to Giovanni Battista Manso, was the spell cast by Naples and her environs upon Torquato Tasso during his sojourn in the city in 1588.[4] The picturesque seascape, the pleasant climate, the magnetism of the city's historical sites, and the hospitality with which he was greeted afforded the troubled poet appeasement, delight, and particular interest. With Manso as his guide, Tasso beheld the tombs of Virgil and Sannazaro; the grotto of Lucullus; the villa of Cicero; the

---

[1] John Milton, *Pro Populo Anglicano Defensio Secunda. Contra Infamem Libellum Anonymum cui Titulus, Regii Sanguinis Clamor ad Coelum Adversus Parricidas Anglicanos* (London: Thomas Newcomb, 1654), 85.

[2] Giovanni Battista Manso, *Vita di Torquato Tasso* (Venice: Evangelista Deuchino, 1621), 186. All subsequent references are, unless otherwise stated, to this edition.

[3] All translations are mine, unless otherwise stated.

[4] Cf. Manso's note, at *Vita di Torquato Tasso*, 186: "Tarquato va in Napoli la seconda volta an. 44" ("Torquato comes to Naples for the second time, in his 44th year").

waters of Cumae; the volcanic fires of Pozzuoli, Vesuvius, and its surroundings;[5] and much more.

Some five decades later Manso would prove host and guide to another poet, John Milton. David Masson presents an eloquent fantasy regarding Milton's potential reaction to a Neapolitan seascape similar to that admired by Tasso, a reaction he envisages as governed in part by a Miltonic alertness to Tassonian precedent:

> With none the less pleasure would Milton behold all this, because Tasso had beheld it before him, or because he had read Manso's description of it in the very pages in which it may be read still, or because the same Manso was with him to point out the separate beauties as he had pointed them out to Tasso fifty years before.[6]

The fact remains, however, that Milton preserves a frustrating silence about his Neapolitan sojourn and the sites that he doubtlessly beheld, whether as a consequence of Manso's hospitality or of his own volition. Thus, we have no direct record of his reactions to the city itself or to its picturesque surroundings. Something of what it had to offer him may be glimpsed by George Sandys's description just over two decades previously:

> Her throne is answerable to her dignity: placed under a smiling heaven, in a rich, and flourishing soile. Bounded on the South-east side with a bay of the Tyrrhen sea unacquainted with tempests; alongst which she stretcheth; and is backt by mountaines ennobled for their generous wines: whereof ascending a part, she enjoyeth the delicate prospects of Vesuvius, Surrentum, Caprae, Misenus, Prochita, and Aenaria. Her beauty is inferiour unto nether. The private buildings being gracefull, and the publike stately: adorned with statues, the worke of excellent workemen, and sundry preserved antiquities.[7]

Likewise, in contrast to his Florentine and Roman periods, evidence of Milton's participation in the cultural life of Naples is glaringly absent. Whereas his attendance at the Florentine Accademia degli Svogliati and the Accademia degli Apatisti is independently attested, with the minutes

---

[5] Manso, *Vita di Torquato Tasso*, 187.

[6] David Masson, *The Life of John Milton: Narrated in Connexion with the Political, Ecclesiastical, and Literary History of his Time*, 7 vols. (London: Macmillan, 1859–1894), I, 763.

[7] George Sandys, *A Relation of a Journey Begun in Anno Domini 1610* (London: William Barrett, 1615), 253–254.

of the former recording several performances of his Latin verse,[8] his involvement in Neapolitan academies, not least in the highly reputable Accademia degli Oziosi,[9] founded by none other than his Neapolitan host, Giovanni Battista Manso,[10] remains undocumented, despite the strong likelihood that he participated in its activities.[11] Whereas his dining at the Jesuit-run English College in Rome is attested by that

---

[8] The Svogliati minute book records Milton's performance of his Latin verse on at least three occasions. Most notable perhaps is the minute of 6/16 September 1638, which singles out "particolarmente" ("in particular") "il Giovanni Miltone Inglese" ("John Milton Englishman"), and makes a qualitative judgment about his performance: his reading of "una poesia Latina di versi esametri multo erudita" ("a very erudite Latin poem of hexameter verses") (Biblioteca Nazionale Centrale, Florence, MS Magliabecchiana Cl. IX, cod. 60, f. 48^r). See Estelle Haan, *From Academia to Amicitia: Milton's Latin Writings and the Italian Academies* (Philadelphia: American Philosophical Society, 1998), 19–20. Close scrutiny of that minute book reveals that this highlighting of uniqueness, nationality, and erudition in an individual performance is quite unparalleled. See Estelle Haan, *Both English and Latin: Bilingualism and Biculturalism in Milton's Neo-Latin Writings* (Philadelphia: American Philosophical Society, 2012), 97–98. Likewise, the minutes of 7/17 March and 14/24 March 1639 include Milton among those who read "alcuni nobili versi Latini" ("some noble Latin verses") and "diverse poesie Latine" ("various Latin poems") respectively, while his presence at a further meeting on 21/31 March is also attested (MS Magliabecchiana Cl. IX, cod. 60, ff. 52^r–52^v). See Haan, *From Academia to Amicitia*, 20–21. Evidence of Milton's attendance at the Apatisti, as first noted by Haan, *From Academia to Amicitia*, 36, is provided by a manuscript of Anton Francesco Gori (1691–1757) (Florence, Biblioteca Marucelliana MS A.36, ff. 11^r–142^v), usefully transcribed by Allessandro Lazzeri (see Allessandro Lazzeri, *Intellettuali e Consenso nella Toscana del Seicento: L'Accademia degli Apatisti* [Milan: A. Giuffrè, 1983], 57–121). At f. 53^r there occurs, under a list of the academy's membership for 1638, the name "Giovanni Milton inglese." Cf. Lazzeri, *Intellettuali*, 74.

[9] On the Accademia degli Oziosi, see, among others, Michele Maylender, *Storia delle Accademie d'Italia*, 5 vols. (Bologna: L. Capelli, 1926–1930), IV, 183–190; Vittor Comparato, "Società Civile e Società Letteraria nel Primo Seicento: L'Accademia degli Oziosi," *Quaderni Storici* 23 (1973): 359–388, and, in particular, Girolamo de Miranda, *Una Quiete Operosa: Forma e Pratiche dell'Accademia Napoletana degli Oziosi 1611–1645* (Naples: Fridericiana Editrice Universitaria, 2000). See also 8–9, 85–92.

[10] On Manso, see, among others, Angelo Borzelli, *Giovan Battista Manso Marchese di Villa* (Naples: Federico & Ardia, 1916); Michele Manfredi, *Gio. Battista Manso nella Vita e nelle Opere* (Naples: Jovene, 1919); Floriana C. Calitti, "Manso, Giovan Battista," *DBI* 69 (2007): 148–152; De Miranda, *Una Quiete Operosa*, 19–47; and, especially, Pietro Giulio Riga, *Giovan Battista Manso e La Cultura Letteraria a Napoli Nel Primo Seicento: Tasso, Marino, Gli Oziosi* (Bologna: Emil di Odoya, 2018).

[11] For further discussion, see 89–92.

institution's pilgrim book,[12] while his visit to the Vatican library, his attendance at a comedic opera, and his audience with Cardinal Francesco Barberini are evinced by *Epistola Familiaris* 9,[13] there are no equivalent documents describing any such interactions in Naples.

A Spanish province since 1502, and thus under viceregal rule,[14] Naples, as beheld by Milton, was a busy and bustling metropolis, or, in the words of Lorenza Gianfrancesco, "a labyrinth of streets and districts where different communities had found a home."[15] In the early seicento it had a population of some 250,000, making it one of the largest cities in the world.[16] By 1630 this had increased to 300,000. Its organization, while epitomizing the essentially bureaucratic, facilitated religious, secular, cultural, and intellectual diversity. This manifested itself in the emergence of a host of institutions, including monasteries, orphanages, hospitals, charity organizations, and academies, largely through the important powers of patronage.[17] As a major Mediterranean port it was very prosperous, affording merchants from all over the world the opportunity to set up businesses, and to interact with locals, a trend noticeably encapsulated by the ever expanding number of English merchants.[18] Topographically, this was reflected in the coexistence of the

---

[12] English College, Rome: Pilgrim Book: Entry for 20/30 October 1638. See Leo Miller, "Milton Dines at the Jesuit College: Reconstructing the Evening of October 30, 1638," *MQ* 13 (1979): 142–146; Edward Chaney, *The Grand Tour and the Great Rebellion: Richard Lassels and "The Voyage of Italy" in the Seventeenth Century* (Geneva: Slatkine, 1985), 245, 282–284; Estelle Haan, *John Milton's Roman Sojourns, 1638–1639: Neo-Latin Self-Fashioning* (Philadelphia: American Philosophical Society Press, 2020), 18–19.

[13] See *John Milton: Epistolarum Familiarium Liber Unus and Uncollected Letters*, ed. Estelle Haan, Supplementa Humanistica Lovaniensia XLIV (Leuven: Leuven University Press, 2019), 140–163; Haan, *John Milton's Roman Sojourns*, 139–173.

[14] See Paolo Mattia Doria, *Massime del Governo Spagnolo a Napoli*, ed. Vittorio Conti (Naples: Guida, 1973), 79–142.

[15] Lorenza Gianfrancesco, "From Propaganda to Science: Looking at the World of Academies in Early Seventeenth-Century Naples," *California Italian Studies* 3 (2012): 1–31, at 2.

[16] See, among others, Giuseppe Mormile, *Descrittione del Amenissimo Distretto della Città di Napoli* (Naples: Tarquinio Longo, 1617); Giulio Cesare Capaccio, *Neapolitanae Historiae ... Tomus Primus* (Naples: Io. Iacobus Carlinus, 1607); Carlo Celano, *Delle Notitie del Bello, dell'Antico, e del Curioso della Città di Napoli*, 10 vols. (Naples: Giacomo Raillard, 1692).

[17] See John A. Marino, *Becoming Neapolitan: Citizen Culture in Baroque Naples* (Baltimore: Johns Hopkins University Press, 2011), 119–120.

[18] See H. G. Koenigsberger, "English Merchants in Naples and Sicily in the Seventeenth Century," *EHR* 62 (1947): 304–326; Gigliola Pagano De Divitiis,

religious, the practical, the palatial, and the economic. Thus in 1617 Giuseppe Mormile could happily proclaim that "ogni Borgo sembra popolosa, & ornatissima città" ("every district resembles a populous and most ornate city").[19] Naples was also a city with a rich mythological past by virtue of its identification (by Strabo, among others) with the nymph Parthenope, one of the Sirens, who, having suffered καταποντισμός ("death by plunging into the sea"), was reputedly washed ashore, and given a monumental sepulcher (μνῆμα).[20] Or as Milton puts it:

> Credula quid liquidam Sirena, Neapoli, iactas,
>   Claraque Parthenopes fana Achelöiados,
> Litoreamque tua defunctam Naiada ripa
>   Corpora Chalcidico sacra dedisse rogo?
>   (*Ad Leonoram* 3.1–4)[21]

> Credulous Naples, why do you boast of your clear-voiced Siren, and of the famous shrine of Parthenope, daughter of Achelous, and that when she, a Naiad of the shore, died on your river bank, you committed her sacred body to a Chalcidian pyre?

It was Strabo's account, as Lorenzo Miletti observes, that presented "several of the features and themes that would become central to the construction of Naples' identity in later periods."[22] Pliny's assertion that *Neapolis ... ipsa, Parthenope a tumulo Sirenis appellata* ("Naples herself [was] named Parthenope after the tomb of the Siren")[23] was echoed in

---

English Merchants in Seventeenth-Century Italy, trans. Stephen Parkin (Cambridge: Cambridge University Press, 1990), 71–72.

[19] Mormile, *Descrittione*, 3.

[20] Strabo, 1.2.13; 5.4.7. Cf. Lycophron, 717–721; Virgil, *Georgics* 4.564; Ovid, *Metamorphoses* 14.101, 15.712.

[21] Cf. Milton, *A Maske*, 878–879: "And the songs of Sirens sweet,/By dead Parthenope's dear tomb." All quotations from Milton's shorter poems (Latin and English) are from *The Complete Works of John Milton: Volume III: The Shorter Poems*, eds. Barbara Kiefer Lewalski and Estelle Haan (Oxford: Oxford University Press, 2012; rev. 2014), hereinafter cited as Lewalski and Haan. I have modernized orthography and punctuation.

[22] Lorenzo Miletti, "Setting the Agenda: The Image of Classical Naples in Strabo's *Geography* and Other Ancient Literary Sources," in *Remembering Parthenope: The Reception of Classical Naples From Antiquity to the Present*, eds. Jessica Hughes and Claudio Buongiovanni (Oxford: Oxford University Press, 2015), 19–38, at 21.

[23] Pliny, *Naturalis Historia* 3.5.62.

1585 by Nicolaus Reusner, whose proclamation *Parthenope, Sive Neapolis. Parthenope, quae et Neapolis* ("Parthenope or Naples. Partheneope who is also Naples")[24] was corroborated by recourse to a whole host of classical and humanist writers, including Strabo, Virgil, Silius Italicus, Achilles Statius, Joseph Scaliger, Jacopo Sannazaro, Georgius Fabricius, and Giovanni Pontano, among others.[25] This emphasis on the city's rich mythological past was complemented by Flavio Biondo's essentially antiquarian tractate on its landscape (ca. 1453; pub. 1474),[26] by Lucio Giovanni Scoppa's scrupulous itemization of all the classical allusions to the ancient city of Partenope (1507),[27] by Leandro Alberti's comprehensive *Descrittione di Tutta Italia* (1550), and, not least, by Benedetto Di Falco's ever popular *Descrittione de I Luoghi Antichi di Napoli* (1549),[28] which served as a model for future guidebooks.[29] Such texts, in the words of John Marino, afforded "a constant reminder to the deeply ingrained Humanist tradition in Naples of their link to antiquity."[30] The fusion of classical mythology and precise

---

[24] See Nicolaus Reusner, *De Italia, Regione Europae Nobilissima Libri Duo* (Strasbourg: Bernardus Iobinus, 1585), 86. Cf. Natale Conti, *Mythologiae, Sive Explicationis Fabularum Libri Decem* (Lyon: Petrus Landrus, 1602), VII, 13: *nobilissimam Italiae civitatem Neapolim dictam fuisse Parthenopen de nomine unius Sirenum quae in iis locis mortua est* (746) ("Naples, Italy's most noble city was called 'Parthenope,' after the name of one of the Sirens, who died in those regions"); Sandys, *A Relation of a Journey*, 253: "But that it [sc. Naples] was first built by the inhabitants of Cuma is the most approved, and called Parthenope (a name most frequently given it by the Poets) of the Siren Parthenope: who was here intombed under a little hill not farre from the haven called the Mountaine; divinely honoured by the Neapolitans, and where oracles were said to be given: demolished by an earthquake."

[25] Reusner, *De Italia*, 87–100.

[26] Flavio Biondo, *Italia Illustrata* (Rome: Johannes Philippus de Lignamine, 1474).

[27] Lucio Giovanni Scoppa, *Parthenopei in Varios Authores Collectanea* (Naples: Sigismondo Mayr, 1507).

[28] Benedetto di Falco, *Descrittione de I Luoghi Antichi di Napoli e del Suo Amenissimo Distretto* (Naples: Francesco Sugganappo, 1549).

[29] See, among others, Harald Hendrix, "Topographies of Poetry: Mapping Early Modern Naples," in *New Approaches to Naples c. 1500–c. 1800: The Power of Place*, eds. Melissa Calaresu and Helen Hills (London: Routledge, 2016), 81–101; John A. Marino, "Constructing the Past of Early Modern Naples: Sources and Historiography," in *A Companion to Early Modern Naples*, ed. Tommaso Astarita (Leiden: Brill, 2013), 11–34.

[30] Marino, "Constructing the Past," 22.

urban topography,[31] perhaps most conspicuously evident in Enrico Bacco's *Il Regno di Napoli Diviso in Dodici Provincie* (1609),[32] lay at the heart of Naples's self-fashioning in print, and was mirrored in descriptions by such foreign visitors as Fynes Moryson, whose *Itinerary* was printed in London in 1617,[33] and Peter Heylyn, whose *Mikrokosmos* saw publication in Oxford in 1625.[34] It is reasonable to suppose that such works on Neapolitan topography and history had made their way into Milton's self-imposed reading list in advance of his Italian journey, a list that clearly included histories of other Italian cities, such as Venice.[35] This possibility is strengthened perhaps by William Poole's intriguing speculation that in the 1630s Milton may have availed himself of the resources of the private library of John Hales, housed in his chambers at Eton, among whose eclectic holdings was Philip Clüver's *Italia Antiqua* (1624).[36] In Clüver's innovative rewriting of Italian topography, sustained focus on the precise geographical locations of individual cities and their environs was complemented by their contextualization in an essentially global vision, and by their disentanglement from the past.[37]

But if Naples had a memorable past, so, too, did it possess a vibrant present. For artists it facilitated endless opportunities for commissions. It

---

[31] See Giovanni Muto, "Urban Structures and Population," in *A Companion to Early Modern Naples*, ed. Astarita, 35–61, at 36–37.

[32] Enrico Bacco, *Il Regno di Napoli Diviso in Dodici Provincie* (Naples: G. G. Carlino and C. Vitale, 1609).

[33] *An Itinerary Written by Fynes Moryson Gent. First in the Latine Tongue, and Then Translated by Him into English: Containing His Ten Yeeres Travell Through The Twelve Dominions of Germany, Bohmerland, Sweitzerland, Netherland, Denmarke, Poland, Italy, Turky, France, England, Scotland, and Ireland* (London: John Beale, 1617).

[34] Peter Heylyn, *Mikrokosmos. A Little Description of the Great World* (Oxford: John Lichfield and William Turner, 1625).

[35] On Milton's sustained reading program just prior to his Italian journey, see *Epistola Familiaris* 7 (dated 23 September 1637), in which he informs Charles Diodati that he has been studying Greek and Italian history, and requests that he send him a history of Venice (Bernardo Giustiniani's *De Origine Urbis Venetiarum Rebusque ab Ipsa Gestis Historia* [Venice, 1492]). See *John Milton: Epistolarum Familiarium Liber Unus and Uncollected Letters*, ed. Haan, 100–115, at 106–107, 114. See also William Poole, "'The Armes of Studious Retirement'? Milton's Scholarship, 1632–1641," in *Young Milton: The Emerging Author, 1620–1642*, ed. Edward Jones (Oxford: Oxford University Press, 2013), 21–47.

[36] Poole, "'The Armes of Studious Retirement'?" 33–35. See Philip Clüver, *Italia Antiqua* (Leiden: Elsevier, 1624), passim.

[37] See Giovanna Ceserani, *Italy's Lost Greece: Magna Graecia and the Making of Modern Archaeology* (Oxford: Oxford University Press, 2012), 39–40.

was here, for example, that Caravaggio had resided in 1606–1607, his art exerting a major influence upon such local painters as Giovanni Battista Caracciolo.[38] For local and traveling literati it could boast of countless academies,[39] including, among others, the Erranti,[40] the Incauti,[41] the Incolti,[42] the Infuriati,[43] the Solitari,[44] and, most notable, Manso's Oziosi, highly esteemed not only in Naples itself, but also by comparison with its sister academies elsewhere in Italy. These, like other Italian academies, established their own rules, and created an intellectual space and identity by devising a bespoke *impresa* (emblem), a visual encapsulation of their ethos, accompanied by a related motto. Attended by poets, dramatists, and leading clergy, they afforded their participants the opportunity to discourse on philosophical and literary topics, to recite their own compositions, and to engage in scholarly discussion and debate.[45]

---

[38] See Ann Sutherland Harris, *Seventeenth-Century Art and Architecture* (London: Laurence King Publishing, 2005), 134.

[39] Johannes Albert Fabricius lists (under Naples) the following academies: Addormentati, Ardenti, Arditi, Armeristi, Assetati, del Cimento, Colonna, Erranti, Incogniti, Incolti, Infuriati, Intronati, Investiganti, Laurenziana, Lunatici, Oscuri, Oziosi, Partenia, Pigri, Pontaniana, Ravvivati, Rinomati, Scatenati, Segreti, Sicuri, Sireni, Svegliati, Uniti, and Volanti. See Johannes Albert Fabricius, *Conspectus Thesauri Literarii Italiae* (Hamburg: Christ. Wilh. Brandt, 1730), 255–274. On Neapolitan academies in general, see, among others, Lorenzo Giustiniani, *Breve Contezza delle Accademie Istitute nel Regno di Napoli* (Naples: s.n., 1801); Carlo Minieri Riccio, "Cenno Storico delle Accademie Fiorite nella Città di Napoli," *Archivio Storico per le Provincie Napoletane* 3 (1878): 745–758; 4 (1879): 163–178, 379–394, 519–536; 5 (1880): 131–157, 349–373, 578–612.

[40] See Maylender, *Storia*, II, 312–313.

[41] See Maylender, *Storia*, III, 196.

[42] See Maylender, *Storia*, III, 209.

[43] See Maylender, *Storia*, III, 281–282.

[44] See Maylender, *Storia*, V, 207.

[45] On the Italian Academy, see, among others, Maylender, *Storia*, passim; E. W. Cochrane, *Tradition and Enlightenment in the Tuscan Academies 1690–1800* (Chicago: University of Chicago Press, 1961); Cesare Vasoli, "Le Accademie fra Cinquecento e Seicento e il Loro Ruolo nella Storia della Tradizione Enciclopedica," in *Università, Accademie e Società Scientifiche in Italia e in Germania dal Cinquecento al Settecento*, eds. Laetitia Boehm and Ezio Raimondi (Bologna: Il Mulino, 1980), 81–115; Lazzeri, *Intellettuali*; Arthur Field, *The Origins of the Platonic Academy of Florence* (Princeton, NJ: Princeton University Press, 1988); Jennifer Montagu, *An Index of Emblems of the Italian Academies* (London: Warburg Institute, 1988); James Hankins, "The Myth of the Platonic Academy of Florence," *RQ* 44 (1991): 429–475; Haan, *From Academia to Amicitia*, passim; De Miranda, *Una Quiete Operosa*, passim; Simone Testa, "Le Accademie Senesi e il Network

Socially, they served as an important intersection of intellectual, cultural, and religious life,[46] welcoming foreigners, and, in some cases, functioning as publishing houses in their own right.[47] As such, they constituted, in the words of Simone Testa, "networks" that were both "local" and "global."[48]

For most foreign travelers, Naples constituted the most southern point of the Italian journey, usually functioning as an extension to the Roman part of the itinerary, with the round trip from the capital city taking some fifteen days. Travelers were drawn by its natural beauty and by a particular magnetism that epitomized, in the words of Melissa Claresu and Helen Hills, "the power of place."[49] They typically resided for about five days, with the notable exception of Inigo Jones, who (in 1614) seems to have spent some two months in the city, "an unusually long time," as Edward Chaney points out,[50] and Jean-Jacques Bouchard, who spent some eight months there in 1632, during which time he became a member of the Oziosi, recording his impressions of the city, especially its religious and civic festivities, in a Diary that still remains one of the most important contemporary records of Spanish Naples.[51] In regard to sight-seeing, most visitors were drawn to the outskirts of the city (Pozzuoli, the Phlegraean Fields, Solfatara, the purported cave of the Sibyl, the Grotta di Posillipo, and Virgil's tomb) rather than to the city

---

Intellettuale della Prima Età Moderna in Italia (1525–1700): Un Progetto Online," *Bullettino Senese di Storia Patria* 117 (2010): 613–637; Simone Testa, *Italian Academies and Their Networks, 1525–1700: From Local to Global* (Basingstoke: Palgrave Macmillan, 2015), passim; Jane E. Everson, Denis V. Reidy and Lisa Sampson, eds., *The Italian Academies 1525–1700: Networks of Culture, Innovation and Dissent* (Cambridge: Legenda, 2016).

[46] See Gianfrancesco, "From Propaganda to Science," passim.

[47] See, for example, the list of volumes published under the impression of the Accademia degli Oziosi, at Maylender, *Storia*, IV, 188–190.

[48] See Testa, *Italian Academies and Their Networks*, passim.

[49] See Melissa Calaresu and Helen Hills, "Introduction: Between Exoticism and Marginalization: New Approaches to Naples," in *New Approaches to Naples*, eds. Calaresu and Hills, 1–8, especially 3: "The richness of early modern Naples is precisely its hinge-like character, positioned at the meeting place and exchange point of real and imagined spatial and political networks—between Madrid and the Hapsburg Empire, Rome, the Holy Land and the New World."

[50] See Edward Chaney, "Inigo Jones in Naples," in *English Architecture Public and Private: Essays for Kerry Downes*, eds. John Bold and Edward Chaney (London: Hambleton Press, 1993), 31–53, at 40.

[51] See Jean-Jacques Bouchard, *Journal II: Voyage dans Le Royaume de Naples; Voyage dans La Campagne de Rome* (Turin: Giappichelli, 1976), 178–227.

itself.[52] As Chaney remarks "[t]hough Naples was a far more prestigious resort than now, its 'environs' always rivalled the city itself for the travellers' attentions."[53] Interestingly, Posillipo and the tombs of Parthenope and Virgil are among the Neapolitan attractions itemized in the first Dialogue of Manso's *Erocallia* (1628). There Tasso, one of the dialogue's two speakers,[54] lauds "le delitiose pendici di Posilipo" ("the delightful slopes of Posillipo"), "la famosa sepoltura di Partenope" ("the famous burial-place of Parthenope"), and "'il glorioso sepolcro di Virgilio" ("the glorious tomb of Virgil").[55] The description won the praise of Jacopo Gaddi, who, upon his departure from Naples, had been gifted a copy of the work by its author.[56] That this may well have been something of an habitual gesture on Manso's part is suggested by the strong possibility that this work was one of two books (the other being Manso's *Poesie Nomiche* [1635])[57] presented by him to Milton, and subsequently allegorized as "twin cups" (*pocula ... bina*) in *Epitaphium Damonis* 181–183.[58]

---

[52] See Edward Chaney, "The Grand Tour and Beyond: British and American Travellers in Southern Italy, 1545–1960," in *Oxford, China and Italy: Writings in Honour of Sir Harold Acton on His Eightieth Birthday*, eds. Edward Chaney and Neil Ritchie (London: Thames and Hudson, 1985), 133–160.

[53] Chaney, *Evolution*, 117. For a useful discussion of visitors' reactions to the city, see Malcolm Letts, "Some Sixteenth-Century Travellers in Naples," *EHR* 33 (1918): 176–196.

[54] The second speaker is Cardinal Alfonso Gesualdo.

[55] Giovanni Battista Manso, *Erocallia Overo dell'Amore e della Bellezza Dialoghi XII* (Venice: Evangelista Deuchino, 1628), 2–3.

[56] Jacopo Gaddi, *De Scriptoribus Non Ecclesiasticis, Graecis, Latinis, Italicis Tomus Secundus* (Lyon: Jean Pierre Chancel, 1649), 121: *In exordio pr[imi] Dial[ogi] quem inscribit Gesualdum ab Alph[onso] Gesualdo Archiep[iscopo] Neapolis, & Card[inale] Decano Eloquenter describit, atque concelebrat litoralem oram urbemque Neapolis ... hoc opus à Marchione mihi donato ea ipsa qua Neapoli profectus sum hora* ("In the exordium of the first Dialogue which he inscribed 'Il Gesualdo' after Alfonso Gesualdo, Archbishop of Naples and Cardinal Deacon ... he eloquently describes and celebrates the shoreline and the city of Naples ... This work was gifted to me by the Marquis at the very same hour that I set out from Naples").

[57] Giovanni Battista Manso, *Poesie Nomiche* (Venice: Francesco Baba, 1635).

[58] See Michele de Filippis, "Milton and Manso: Cups or Books?" *PMLA* 51 (1936): 745–756. For fuller discussion, see 36–40, and Chapters 2 and 3.

It was probably in December 1638 that Milton left Rome for Naples.[59] The journey (in excess of one hundred miles) was in all likelihood broken up into several stages in order to facilitate overnight rest in villages or towns en route.[60] According to Milton's own testimony, he traveled in the company of "a certain Eremite friar" (*per Eremitam quendam*),[61] a company described by Campbell and Corns as "improbable."[62] Less improbable, however, was the role played by that friar in introducing Milton to Manso (*ad Ioannem Baptistam Mansum ... sum introductus*),[63] given the latter's previous links with, for example, the albeit heretical Dominican friar Tommaso Campanella,[64] his general association with Neapolitan Jesuits (under whose direction the young aristocrats of his own Collegio dei Nobili received instruction in the arts, intellectual culture, and martial practices),[65] and his joint attempt with Campanella in 1631 to found a seminary in Rome along similar lines.[66] It is impossible to ascertain the friar's identity, but, since contemplative hermits rarely traveled, he may have belonged to the order of Augustinian Hermits (also known as *Augustinian Friars/Friars Hermit*).[67] He was obviously well connected.

---

[59] See Gordon Campbell, *A Milton Chronology* (London: Macmillan, 1997), 63; Gordon Campbell and Thomas N. Corns, *John Milton: Life, Work, and Thought* (Oxford: Oxford University Press, 2008), 119. A December date for Milton's departure from Rome can be conjectured via reverse chronological calculation based upon his general statement in *Defensio Secunda* (concerning his first Roman sojourn) that he stayed in the city "for a period of about two months" (*ad bimestre fere spatium* [84]). This can then be traced back to his attested presence in Rome on 20 October 1638, when he dined in the English College. Barbara Lewalski, however, without any qualifying comment, posits "[l]ate in November, 1638 (probably)" as his departure date from Rome. See Barbara K. Lewalski, *The Life of John Milton: A Critical Biography* (Oxford: Blackwell, 2000), 96.

[60] See Masson, *Life*, I, 756.

[61] Milton, *Defensio Secunda*, 85.

[62] Campbell and Corns, *Life, Work, and Thought*, 119.

[63] Milton, *Defensio Secunda*, 85.

[64] See Jon R. Snyder, *Writing the Scene of Speaking: Theories of Dialogue in the Late Italian Renaissance* (Stanford CA: Stanford University Press, 1989), 186; Sean Cocco, *Watching Vesuvius: A History of Science and Culture in Early Modern Italy* (Chicago: University of Chicago Press, 2013), 53. On Campanella, see Luigi Firpo, "Campanella, Tommaso," *DBI* 17 (1974): 372–401, and sources cited therein.

[65] See Masson, *Life*, I, 760; Carolina Belli, "La Fondazione del Collegio dei Nobili di Napoli," in *Chiesa, Assistenza e Società nel Mezzogiorno Moderno*, ed. Carla Russo (Galatina: Congedo, 1994), 183–280.

[66] See Riga, *Giovan Battista Manso*, 25–26.

[67] See Campbell and Corns, *Life, Work, and Thought*, 119–120.

As Milton approached Naples he would have followed the typical route recommended by such travel-writers as Benedetto Di Falco[68] and Hieronymus Turler.[69] Thus, according to Turler, the traveler should journey from Posillipo via the famous tunnel known as "La Grotta di Virgilio," whose "width is such that two coaches laden with wares can conveniently pass through it at the same time" (*latitudinis tantae ut duo currus mercibus onusti una transire commode possint*).[70] The mountain itself, he continues, has been hollowed out with the greatest of industry to produce a tunnel with smooth and equal sides at each end, which are conjoined in an arched manner, its interior darkness illuminated only by the daylight afforded at its entrance.[71] That Milton was familiar with the tunnel is suggested by an allusion in his third Latin epigram in honor of the soprano Leonora Baroni, depicted therein as a second Parthenope, who has left Naples for Rome:

> Illa quidem vivitque, et amoena Tibridis unda
> Mutavit rauci murmura Pausilipi.
> (*Ad Leonoram* 3.5–6)

> She is, in fact, alive, and has exchanged the
> roarings of the raucous Posillipo for Tiber's
> pleasant waters.

Editors typically gloss *rauci murmura Pausilipi* (6) as a reference to either the traffic passing through,[72] or, less likely, to waves crashing at the foot of the mountain.[73] But the plural noun *murmura*, in combination with the adjective *raucus*, suggests vocal utterances, a reading reinforced by comparison with Milton's use of the phrase elsewhere in his Latin poetry.

---

[68] See Di Falco, *Descrittione de I Luoghi Antichi*, sig. Aiii^v–Cii^r.

[69] See Hieronymus Turler, *De Peregrinatione et Agro Neapolitano Libri II ... Omnibus Peregrinantibus Utiles ac Necessarii ac in Eorum Gratiam Nunc Primum Editi* (Strasbourg: Bernardus Iobinus, 1574), 91–94.

[70] Turler, *De Peregrinatione*, 91.

[71] Turler, *De Peregrinatione*, 91–92.

[72] See *The Latin Poems of John Milton*, ed. Walter MacKellar (New Haven, CT: Yale University Press, 1930), 249; *Milton: Complete Poems and Major Prose*, ed. Merrit Y. Hughes (New York: Odyssey, 1957), 131; Lewalski and Haan, 451.

[73] See *The Poems of John Milton*, ed. Thomas Keightley, 2 vols. (London: Chapman and Hall, 1859), II, 422; *John Milton: Poetical Works*, ed. David Masson, 3 vols. (London: Macmillan, 1874), III, 510. See also Douglas Bush, *A Variorum Commentary on the Poems of John Milton: Volume I: The Latin and Greek Poems* (New York: Columbia University Press, 1970), 151–152.

Thus, over a decade earlier, the undergraduate Milton had complained (to Charles Diodati) about Cambridge University:

> Stat quoque iuncosas Cami remeare paludes
> Atque iterum raucae murmur adire Scholae.
> (*Elegia* 1.89–90)

> It is resolved too that I am to return to the
> Cam's reedy marshes, and to incur once more
> the roaring of the raucous University.

Here *raucae murmur ... Scholae* (90) probably alludes to the vociferously raucous environment in which university disputations were delivered.[74] These were typically accompanied by hissing, shouting, and more, on the part of the student audience,[75] a clamor pejoratively depicted by Milton as frog-like croaking in a marshy landscape, emblematic of a sterile curriculum.[76] In light of this, the phrase in its second occurrence is most likely an allusion to the safe-guarding practice adopted by travelers of issuing warning shouts to oncoming traffic in the darkness of the Neapolitan tunnel. Thus, Turler proclaims:

> Unde moris est cum duo simul pluresve equis vel curribus eo in loco sibi invicem occurrunt, ut alla montagna vel alla marina clamitent, hoc est, *montem* vel *mare versus*, ut quisque illorum sciat in quam partem declinare debeat.[77]

---

[74] Cf. Bush, *Variorum*, I, 50: "the hoarse hum of a class immersed in logic." John K. Hale, *Milton's Cambridge Latin: Performing in the Genres, 1625–1632* (Tempe, AZ: Medieval and Renaissance Texts and Studies, 2005), 127, perceptively remarks: "he is going back to its [sc. Cambridge's] marshes and its 'raucae Scholae' (the disputations?)."

[75] Thus, in 1600, for example, Cambridge students had been warned to stop "standinge upon stalles, knockinge, hissinge and other immoderate behaviour." See Vincent Morgan and Christopher Brooke, *A History of the University of Cambridge II: 1546–1750* (Cambridge: Cambridge University Press, 2004), 129–130; Campbell and Corns, *Life, Work, and Thought*, 35.

[76] Cf., for example, Milton's *Prolusiones*, passim, and, for the disputational context in which such academic exercises were delivered, Hale, *Milton's Cambridge Latin*, 15–20.

[77] Turler, *De Peregrinatione*, 92. For the custom, see, among others, Letts, "Some Sixteenth-Century Travellers," 182; J. B. Trapp, *Essays on the Renaissance and the Classical Tradition* (Aldershot: Variorum, 1990), 6; Franco Strazzullo, *L'Antica Via del Marzano a Villanove* (Naples: Arte Tipografica, 1994), 40; Giovanni Capuano, *Viaggiatori Britannici a Napoli tra '500 e '600* (Salerno: Pietro Laveglia, 1994), 45; Salvatore Di Liello, *Il Paesaggio dei Campi Flegrei: Realtà e Metafora* (Naples: Electa Napoli, 2005), 68.

> Whence derives the custom that when two or more traveling by horseback or by coach meet simultaneously in the tunnel, they shout "alla montagna" or "alla marina," namely, "towards the mountain" or "towards the sea," so that each of them might know the direction in which he needs to swerve.

Or, in the words of Fynes Moryson:

> the carters or horsemen when they passe by the midst of the cave, use to give warning one to the other, crying vulgularly *Alla marina* (that is towards the sea) or *Alla Montagna* (that is towards the mountaine) according to the side on which they come.[78]

Turner relates that upon exiting the tunnel, Naples-bound (*dum ex hoc specu egrederis Neapolim versus*), one can see the tomb of Virgil (*sepulchrum Vergilii Maronis*).[79] This, according to John Evelyn, is:

> erected on a very steepe rock, in forme of a Small rotunda, or cupulated Columne; but almost over growne with bushes, & wild bay-trees: at this entrance is this Inscription
> Stanisi Cencovius
> 1589
> Qui cineres? Tumuli haec Vestigia, conditur olim,
> <Ille> hoc, qui cecinit Pascua, Rura, Duces
> Can. <Rec> MDLIII<I>.[80]

---

[78] Fynes Moryson, *Itinerary*, I, 113. That the custom endured well into the nineteenth century is attested by Antonio Bresciani, who expatiates upon the whole, contextualizing this din amid the mysterious darkness ("oscurità misteriose") that occasioned it. See Antonio Bresciani, "L'Ebreo di Verona: Racconto Storico dall'Anno 1846 all'Anno 1849," *Civiltà Cattolica* II (1851): 157–158. Cf. Lewis Engelbach, *Naples and the Campagna Felice. In a Series of Letters Addressed to a Friend in England in 1802* (London: R. Ackermann, 1815), 57: "We had not penetrated one-third of this dismal cavern, when the rattling of a cart, and a fellow's bawling out, *Alla marina*, frightened the horse to such a degree, that no whipping could make him stir an inch," glossed as "To avoid running against each other in the Grotta di Posilipo, it is customary to call out *Alla marina* (towards the sea); or, *Alla montagna* (towards the mountain)."

[79] Turler, *De Peregrinatione*, 92. For various and frequently conflicting discussions of the purported site(s) of Virgil's tomb, see, among others, J. B. Trapp, "The Grave of Virgil," *JWCI* 47 (1984): 1–31; Andrew Laird, "Dead Letters and Buried Meaning: Approaching the Tomb of Virgil," in *Tombs of the Ancient Poets: Between Literary Reception and Material Culture*, eds. Nora Goldschmidt and Barbara Graziosi (Oxford: Oxford University Press, 2018), 253–264; Irene Peirano Garrison, "The Tomb of Virgil Between Text, Memory, and Site," ibid., 265–280; Harald Hendrix, "Virgil's Tomb in Scholarly and Popular Culture," ibid., 281–298.

[80] See *The Diary of John Evelyn*, ed. E. S. De Beer, 6 vols. (Oxford: Clarendon Press, 1955), II, 337, where the description is dated ca. 8 February 1645. Among Evelyn's

Not far from here, Turler states, is located the tomb of Sannazaro, with its inscription, authored by Bembo.[81] Like other contemporary travel writers, Turler places a great deal of emphasis upon the alluring power of the graves and homes of distinguished Neapolitan writers, thereby inaugurating what Harald Hendrix has aptly described as "[t]he ritual of visiting places of memory."[82] In all of this it is worth emphasizing that for foreign visitors seicento Naples functioned a priori as a site of commemorating, of memorializing the ancient and modern dead. It is almost impossible to envisage Milton as having forgone the opportunity of visiting, whether in Manso's company or otherwise, the tomb of a classical poet,[83] upon whose verse and indeed triadic poetic progression (from *Eclogues* to *Georgics* to epic) he aligned his own poetic career.[84] And, given the fact that for the foreign traveler the viewing of Virgil's tomb was done in conjunction with that of Sannazaro, in what was

---

sources (for a full list, see ibid., 578–579) is John Raymond's *An Itinerary Contayning a Voyage, Made through Italy, in the Yeare 1646, and 1647* (London: Humphrey Moseley, 1648), 145–148, where, as noted by De Beer, ad loc., he erroneously writes (at 148) *Can. Rec* for *Can. Reg.* (i.e., "Canons Regular").

[81] Turler, *De Peregrinatione*, 93: *Non longe ab hoc sepulchro, quod Maroni destinatur, est sepulchrum Iacobi Sannazarii, cuius erudita opera exstant, huic sequentes versus inscripti sunt, quorum Bembus auctor esse perhibetur: Da sacro cineri flores, hic ille Maroni/Sincerus Musa proximus, ut tumulo* ("Not far from this tomb, which is designated that of Virgil, is the tomb of Jacopo Sannazaro, whose learned works are extant. Upon this are inscribed the following verses, of which Bembo is said to be the author: 'Render flowers onto his sacred ash. Here is that Sincere one, very close to Virgil in his Muse as in his tomb'"). Sannazaro was known by the Latin pseudonym *Actius Sincerus*.

[82] See Hendrix, "Topographies of Poetry," 98.

[83] Cf. Lois Potter, *A Preface to Milton* (rev. ed., London: Routledge, 1986), 13: "He could have visited 'Virgil's tomb', and places which figured in the *Aeneid*."

[84] Thus, the title page of Milton's *A Maske Presented at Ludlow Castle, 1634* (London: Humphrey Robinson, 1637) proclaims (in the words of Virgil's Corydon): *Eheu quid volui misero mihi! floribus austrum/Perditus* (*Eclogue* 2. 58–59) ("Alas, what have I brought upon my wretched self! Ruined, [I have unleashed] the South wind upon my flowers"). See Lewalski and Haan, cli. Likewise, the title page of the 1645 *Poems* enjoins its readers (in the words of Virgil's Thyrsis): *Baccare frontem/Cingite, ne vati noceat mala lingua futuro* (*Eclogue* 7. 27–28) ("Gird my brow with foxglove lest an evil tongue harms the future bard"). See Lewalski and Haan, 3. The speaker of Milton's *Epitaphium Damonis* is an essentially Virgilian Thyrsis. See Lewalski and Haan, xcv–xcvii, cxxviii–cxxix, 212–229, 488–500. See also Philip Hardie, "Milton's *Epitaphium Damonis* and the Virgilian Career," in *Pastoral Palimpsests: Essays in the Reception of Theocritus and Virgil*, ed. Michael Paschalis (Herakleion: Crete University Press, 2007), 79–100.

essentially a combined visit,[85] it does not seem unreasonable to suggest a Miltonic interest in the material commemoration of a writer on whose neo-Latin elegies he had previously drawn.[86] Once again, however, the absence of evidence makes it difficult to determine the truth of the matter.

However, other types of "evidence" concerning this much-neglected month or so (December 1638–January 1639) of Milton's life do exist. Foremost among these is Milton's 100-line hexameter poem *Mansus* (ca. Jan. 1639),[87] the focus of the present study. The poem's Headnote offers some details of Milton's reception by his Neapolitan host, informing us that "when the author was sojourning in Naples, he [Manso] attended him with the greatest of goodwill" (*Is auctorem Neapoli commorantem summa benevolentia prosecutus est*) "and conferred on him many kind services" (*multaque ei detulit humanitatis officia*).[88] What these acts of kindness were is impossible to determine with any level of specificity, but a guided tour of the city, introduction to men of learning (and, indeed, to recently printed Italian works), and the gift-giving of Manso's own published volumes rank at the top of the list of possibilities. *Defensio Secunda* furnishes some further information: that Manso acted as Milton's personal guide through the regions of the city and the viceroy's court (*qui et ipse me per urbis loca et Proregis aulam circumduxit*) and visited him on more than one occasion at his

---

[85] See Hendrix, "Topographies of Poetry," 99.

[86] In *Elegia Prima*, the carefree Milton imagines the intellectual benefits that Ovid might have enjoyed, had his fate in the environs of Tomis been no more severe than his own: *O utinam vates nunquam graviora tulisset/Ille Tomitano flebilis exul agro* (21–22) ("Oh, if only that bard and lamentable exile had never endured a more severe fate in the territory of Tomis"). The language closely echoes Sannazaro, *Elegia* 1.5.30: *ille, Tomitana quid iacet exul humo* ("he, who lies in exile in the territory of Tomis"). See *Iacobi Sannazarii Opera Omnia* (Lyons: Seb. Gryphius, 1536), 93–94. See also *CIPI* 8, 390–391. The verbal parallel was first noted by James Goode. See James Goode, "Milton and Sannazaro," *TLS* (13 August 1931): 621. Milton's sustained interest in Sannazaro would later manifest itself in his recourse to the "brief epic tradition" encapsulated by Sannazaro's *De Partu Virginis*, among others. See Olin H. Moore, "The Infernal Council," *MP* 16 (1918): 169–193; Stewart A. Baker, "Sannazaro and Milton's Brief Epic," *CL* 20 (1968): 116–132; Barbara K. Lewalski, *Milton's Brief Epic: The Genre, Meaning, and Art of Paradise Regained* (Providence, RI and London: Brown University Press and Methuen, 1966), 60–61; Silvia Giovanardi Byer, "Celestial Crusades and Wars in Heaven: The Biblical Epics of the Late 1500s" (PhD thesis, University of North Carolina, Chapel Hill, 2008).

[87] See *Poems of Mr. John Milton, Both English and Latin* (London; Humphrey Moseley, 1645), at *Poemata*, 72–76; Lewalski and Haan, 204–211, 481–488.

[88] *Poemata*, 72; Lewalski and Haan, 204–205.

lodgings (*et visendi gratia haud semel ipse ad hospitium venit*).[89] That repeated *ipse*, and the emphasis on the Italian humanist's desire to see him (*visendi gratia*) convey an element of Miltonic pride in the fact that he was the recipient of the personal attentions of such an illustrious man of his time. The inn (*hospitium*) in which Milton resided was certainly of a standard sufficiently high to host a distinguished marquis. Where it was located is impossible to determine, but we can conjecture that it was in a reputable area. And here an element of careful discernment would have been necessary, given the fact that many Neapolitan inns were far from satisfactory, their standards governed to a large extent by their location. Inns near the marketplace were, according to Fynes Moryson, "poore and base," the city as a whole "deserv[ing] no praise for faire Innes of good entertainement."[90] By contrast, inns near or in the prestigious Via Toledo, such as that in which Bouchard had lodged (in March 1632),[91] were both reputable and welcoming. Several were subsequently praised by name. These included the "Black Eagle"[92] and "The Three Kings," the last extolled in 1645 by John Evelyn for its good value and sumptuous food.[93] It was here, too, that Richard Symonds would stay in 1651, his accommodation and food (with wine at table) costing him five crowns for as many nights.[94]

As to procuring a guide for sight-seeing, Milton seems to have relied on Manso himself. Whereas John Evelyn and his friends "hired a Coach to carry us about the Towne,"[95] Milton, as noted previously, was conducted by Manso "through the regions of the city" (*per urbis loca*), a phrase that does not rule out the possibility of him being shown such extra mural sites as those witnessed by Tasso. Indeed, he could hardly have escaped the famous Phlegraean Fields and Solfatara with its

---

[89] Milton, *Defensio Secunda*, 85.

[90] Fynes Moryson, *Itinerary*, I, 112.

[91] See Dinko Fabris, *Music in Seventeenth-Century Naples: Francesco Provenzale (1624–1704)* (Aldershot: Ashgate, 2007), 1.

[92] See British Library, London: Harl. Misc. (v. 33), whose author advises: "When you come into this famous city, enquire for the Black Eagle; the host is a Dutchman (German), who will appoint one to go about and show you what is to be seen." See H. Maynard Smith, ed., *John Evelyn in Naples 1645* (Oxford: Blackwell, 1914), 2.

[93] See John Evelyn, *Diary*, ed. de Beer, II, 325: "31 [January 1645] About noone We enterd the Citty of Naples, allighting at the 3 Kings, a Place of treatement to excesse, as we found by our very plentifull fare all the tyme we were in Naples, where provisions are miraculously cheape, & we seldome sat downe to fewer than 18 or 20 dishes of the most exquisite meate & fruites, enjoying the Creature."

[94] Bodleian Library, Oxford: MS Rawl.D.121, 150.

[95] John Evelyn, *Diary*, ed. De Beer, II, 325.

bubbling springs of hot sulphur, located, as they were, en route to Manso's villa. It is a landscape that, as Marjorie Nicholson convincingly argued, may have exerted no slight influence on Milton's later depiction of hell in *Paradise Lost*.[96] Unremarked by scholars, morever, is Milton's potential recourse to an Italian sonnet, entitled "Solfanaria di Piazzuoli" by Manso himself:

> Nuda erma valle; a i cui taciti horrori
>   Accrescon tema ombre solinghe oscure,
>   Sulfuree rupi, acque bollenti impure,
>   Sanguigni fumi, e tenebrosi ardori.
>
> Voi, ch'in parte apprendeste i miei dolori
>   Da gli accesi sospiri, e l'aspre cure
>   Dal largo pianto, che disfar le dure
>   Selci potè co' suoi continui humori.[97]

> Naked, barren valley, whose silent horrors are accentuated by dark solitary shades, cliffs of sulphur, and impure boiling waters, bloody fumes, and gloomy heat.
>
> You, who have partly understood my pains from the burning sighs, and my harsh anxieties from the abundant lamentation, that with its continuous floods has the ability to undo the tough potency of flint.

Satan likewise addresses and internalizes the sulphuric setting, invoking:

> Regions of sorrow, doleful shades, where peace
> And rest can never dwell, hope never comes
> That comes to all; but torture without end
> Still urges, and a fiery deluge, fed
> With ever-burning sulphur unconsumed.
>   (*Paradise Lost* 1. 65–69)[98]

---

[96] Marjorie Nicolson, "Milton's Hell and the Phlegraean Fields," *UTQ* 7 (1938): 500–513.

[97] Manso, *Poesie Nomiche*, 36 (Sonnet XXXIV). On the sonnet's potentially Dantesque elements, see Riga, *Giovan Battista Manso*, 159.

[98] All quotations are from *John Milton: Paradise Lost*, ed. Alastair Fowler (London: Longman, 1998).

The fact that the sonnet was included in the *Poesie Nomiche*, potentially gifted by Manso to Milton, makes the possible link particularly interesting.

In the absence of independent evidence, however, it would be imprudent to attempt to map Milton's precise movements in Naples. The same can be said regarding his possible attendance at religious festivals in the city. As Dinko Fabris observes, "[t]he early seventeenth century saw a remarkable increase in collective devotion in Naples."[99] Among religious feast days that roughly coincided with Milton's sojourn were those of St. Niccolò da Bari (6 December), St. Lucia (13 December), the third feast of St. Gennaro (16 December), and the feast of St. Antonio Abate (17 January), the last also marking the commencement of Carnival season.[100] There is, however, one specific detail that seems to stand out: Milton's report that Manso "conducted him around" the Palazzo Reale of the Spanish viceroy (*me per ... Proregis aulam circumduxit*).[101] The viceroy in question was the distinguished Ramiro Felipe de Guzmán, Duke of Medina de las Torres.[102] Milton's Latin, as noted by Campbell and Corns, is somewhat "ambiguous," since "*circumduxit* seems to imply being 'led around' rather than being presented to the viceroy."[103] But even if that was the case, this guided tour would have been proudly afforded by a Marquis who had, in fact, been closely involved in the commissioning of the palace's frescoes in general,[104] and who had acted as consultant, and more, in relation to a specific series of militaristic frescoes, the iconographic program of Marcantonio Cavalieri. Indeed Cavalieri had made a point of seeking Manso's approval for the entire selection.[105] Likewise, it was Manso who had received a commission (on 29 March

---

[99] Fabris, *Music in Seventeenth-Century Naples*, 13.

[100] For discussion of the pomp and richness of Neapolitan religious festivals, see Fabris, *Music in Seventeenth-Century Naples*, 2–10.

[101] Milton, *Defensio Secunda*, 85.

[102] On Medina's viceroyalty, see Rosario Villari, *La Rivolta Antispagnola a Napoli: Le Origini (1585–1647)* (Bari: Laterza, 1967), chapters IV–VI; *Diccionario de Historia de España*, ed. Germán Bleiberg, 3 vols. (2nd ed. Madrid: Alianza, 1968–1969), II, 297–298; R. A. Stradling, "A Spanish Statesman of Appeasement: Medina De Las Torres and Spanish Policy, 1639–1670," *HJ* 19 (1976): 1–31.

[103] Campbell and Corns, *Life, Work, and Thought*, 120.

[104] See Vicenzo Pacelli, "Affreschi Storici in Palazzo Reale," in *Seicento Napoletano: Arte, Costume, e Ambiente*, ed. Roberto Pane (Milan: Edizioni di Comunità, 1984), 158–179.

[105] See Loredano Gazzara, "Giovanni Battista Manso, Promotore delle Arti e della Cultura," in *Manso, Lemos, Cervantes: Letteratura, Arti e Scienza nella Napoli del Primo Seicento*, ed. Roberto Mondola (Naples: Tullio Pironti, 2018), 39–67, at 57.

1629) from Giulio Cesare Fontana to supply historical source information (for the associated inscriptions) in relation to the movements of the third Duke of Alba, Fernando Álvarez de Toledo y Pimental (1507–1582),[106] a commission that he had indeed fulfilled.[107] Manso may well have made a point of highlighting and showcasing to his English guest these militaristic frescoes in whose creation he had played a key role. As for the possibility that Milton was granted a formal audience with the viceroy, the court records, now in the Archivo General de Simancas, have so far yielded no evidence. Certainly Ramiro was an erudite nobleman and bibliophile, as is attested by his extensive library, itself one of the most renowned in Naples and beyond.[108] He was also a Maecenas of his day, and dedicatee of several literary works, most recently the *El Macabeo Poema Heroico*, a Spanish imitation of Tasso's *Gerusalemme Liberata*, by the Portuguese Marrano, Miguel Silveyra, which had seen publication in Naples in 1638.[109] Although dismissed by George Ticknor as "written

---

[106] "Le pitture della stantia di Palazzo son hormai finite et mancha porci su le iscrittioni supplicando Vostra Signoria Illustre notar come si hanno da fare et ponerci l'anno, le istorie sono le seguenti. Quando sua Maestà inviò al ducha d'Alba per Vicario Generale in Italia; Quando entrò in Milano et soccorse Volpianio; Quando entrò in Napoli; La giornata di Civitella et lo di Ostia" ("The paintings pertaining to the Palace are finished and lacking in regard to their inscriptions. The request is that Your Distinguished Lordship should note the event and supply the year. The historical occasions are as follows: When his Majesty invited the Duke of Alba to be Vicar General in Italy; When he entered Milan and helped Volpianio; When he entered Naples; The day of Civitella and that of Ostia") (ASMMS, An/9, letter n5). See Pacelli, "Affreschi Storici in Palazzo Reale," 179 (Appendix VIII).

[107] The requested information was furnished by Manso in a Spanish letter of reply written either by Manso himself or by a member of his circle: "El Rey Don Filipe II Embia el Duque de Alva per su Virrey dette ...; El Duque de Alva entra en Milan y soccore a Vulpiano en Lombardia sitiado de Francesco ann. 1555; El Duque de Alba llega a Napoles ann. 1555; El Duque de Alva sitia a Hostia y al cabo de sangrientos assaltos la toma ann. 1556; El Duque de Alva socorre a Civitela y rompe los Franseses en Italia Nova ann. 1559" ("King Philip II invites the Duke of Alba as his Viceroy; The Duke of Alba enters Milan and helps Volpiano in Lombardy, besieged by the French in the year 1555; The Duke of Alba arrives in Naples in the year 1555; The Duke of Alba besieges Ostia, and, after bloody assaults, takes it in the year 1556; The Duke of Alba helps Civitella and breaks the French in modern Italy in the year 1559"). See Pacelli "Affreschi Storici in Palazzo Reale," 179 (Appendix IX).

[108] See Encarnación Sánchez García, "Il Viceré Medina de Las Torres a Napoli: Decoro del Lignaggio e Avanguardia Culturale," in *Palazzo Donn' Anna: Storia, Arte e Natura*, ed. Pietro Belli (Turin: Allemandi, 2017), 39–69, at 50. Ramiro's library was subsequently transferred to Spain (in 1649).

[109] Miguel Silveyra, *El Macabeo Poema Heroico* (Naples: Egidio Longo, 1638). Among other contemporary works dedicated to Ramiro were Andre Genuzio's novella *Del Re Dionisio*, Miguel Martinez de Toro's *Declaración de la Lei Única c.*

in the affected style of Góngora" and as "wanting in spirit, interest, and poetry throughout,"[110] this work, as Encarnación Sánchez García suggests, may have been made available to Milton by Manso, given the latter's personal and literary affiliations with Tasso,[111] this last point reiterated in *Mansus* itself.[112]

What can be stated with certainty is the fact that, architecturally speaking, the Palazzo Reale, as visited by Milton, exuded an unmistakable sense of Spanishness, a consequence of the imaginative thinking of its designer, Domenico Fontana. Among the building's Spanish influences, as Diana Carrió-Invernizzi points out, were the inclusion of a portico at ground level, the two-color effect created by the grey of the piperno and the red of the brickwork; the tripartite façade (which had been completed by 1616); the alignment of the royal chapel with the principal façade; the presence of two independent apartments; and the abandonment of two courtyards in favor of one, plus a larger central one, which had a garden open to the sea, after the design of Neapolitan cloisters. By 1620 its interior had been frescoed by Battistello Caracciolo, Giovanni Balducci, and Belisario Corezio.[113] And here, too, as Campbell and Corns parenthetically suggest, Milton may have tried

---

Si Quis Imperatori Maledixerit y Fren de Maldicientes, and Antonio Pérez Navarrete's *Politica de la Verdad y Alivio del Reyno de Nápoles*.

[110] See George Ticknor, *History of Spanish Literature*, 3 vols. (London: John Murray, 1849), II, 451: "[the] 'Macabeo' of Silveira, a Portuguese, who, after living long at the court of Spain, accompanied the head of the great house of the Guzmans when that nobleman was made viceroy of Naples, and published there, in 1638, this poem, to the composition of which he had given twenty-two years. The subject is the restoration of Jerusalem by Judas Maccabeus—the same which Tasso had at one time chosen for his own epic. But Silveira had not the genius of Tasso. He has, it is true, succeeded in filling twenty cantos with octave stanzas, as Tasso did; but there the resemblance stops. The 'Macabeo', besides being written in the affected style of Góngora, is wanting in spirit, interest, and poetry throughout."

[111] See Encarnación Sánchez García, "'Aplicossi a Render Immortal La Sua Memoria nel Regno': El Virrey Medina de las Torres en Nápoles (1636–1644)," in *La Nobleza y Los Reinos: Anatomía del Poder en La Monarquía de España (Siglos XVI–XVII)*, ed. Adolfo Carrasco Martínez (Madrid: Iberoamericana Vervuert, 2017), 361–394, at 379–380.

[112] See 114–121.

[113] See Diana Carrió-Invernizzi, "Royal and Viceregal Art Patronage in Naples (1500–1800)," in *A Companion to Early Modern Naples*, ed. Astarita, 383–404, at 392–393. See also Paolo Carla Verde, "L'Originario e Completo Progetto di Domenico Fontana per il Palazzo Reale di Napoli," *Quaderni dell' Istituto di Storia dell' Architettura* 42 (2003): 29–52; Paolo Carla Verde, "Domenico Fontana a Napoli (1592–1607): Le Opere per La Committenza Viceregale Spagnola," *Anuario del Departamento de Historia y Teoría del Arte* 18 (2006): 49–78.

out his spoken Spanish.[114] Certainly his knowledge of the language[115] is attested by Antonio Francini in his encomium of Milton prefixed to the 1645 *Poemata*.[116] Speculating as to where or with whom Milton may have spoken Spanish while in Italy, Campbell suggests that if Francini's ode postdates Milton's return from Naples, then "it could refer to contacts with the viceregal court, with which ... Manso was closely connected."[117]

In sharp contrast to the effusive *Mansus*, Milton's retrospective account of his Neapolitan sojourn in *Defensio Secunda* betrays a carefully crafted authorial self-fashioning as the essentially Protestant Englishman, forever defending the faith, and, in consequence, eliciting a purported apology from Manso:

> Discedenti serio excusavit se, tametsi multo plura detulisse mihi officia maxime cupiebat, non potuisse illa in urbe, propterea quod nolebam in religione esse tectior.[118]
>
> As I was leaving, he extended an earnest apology for failing to offer me greater services, stating that, although that was his foremost desire, he had been unable to do so in that city on account of the fact that I refused to be more guarded on the subject of religion.

---

[114] Campbell and Corns, *Life, Work, and Thought*, 120.

[115] The fact that Milton does not include Spanish among the languages that he acquired in childhood (see *Ad Patrem* 79–85, which mentions Greek, Latin, French, Italian, and Hebrew) may indicate a later, or, at least, a more gradual acquisition of that language.

[116] Antonio Francini, "Al Signor Gio. Miltoni Nobile Inglese," 59–60: "Ch' Ode oltr' all Anglia il suo più degno Idioma/Spagna, Francia, Toscana, e Grecia e Roma" ("For besides England: Spain, France, Tuscany, Greece, and Rome hear their most worthy language"). See *Poemata*, 8; Lewalski and Haan, 112–113. Further testimony is provided by Edward Phillips, who relates that Milton's daughters were required to read aloud "[t]he Hebrew (and I think the Syriac), the Greek, the Latin, the Italian, Spanish and French." See Edward Phillips, *The Life of Mr. John Milton*, in *The Early Lives of Milton*, ed. Helen Darbishire (London: Constable & Co. Ltd, 1932), 49–82, at 77. Likewise, Milton's daughter Deborah, as reported by John Ward, included Spanish among the languages that she read to her father (British Library, London: Add MS 4320, f. 232). For an excellent overview, see Gordon Campbell, "Milton's Spanish," *MQ* 30 (1996): 127–132, who, having examined such testimony alongside Milton's 1668 draft note on "The Verse" of *Paradise Lost*, and his possible association with three Spanish state papers, comes to the cautious conclusion that he "had a modest competence in the Spanish language, sufficient at least to translate from Spanish and hold his own in a conversation," even if "his command of Spanish literature was slight" (131).

[117] Campbell, "Milton's Spanish," 127.

[118] Milton, *Defensio Secunda*, 85.

Some tensions were probably inevitable. After all, Manso's devout Catholicism had manifested itself in print in his hagiography (1611) of Saint Patricia, which presented her miracles as historical fact.[119] And upon the eruption of Vesuvius in December 1631, it was he who had assumed a privileged position in a religious procession bearing the miraculous relics of San Gennaro, and had attributed the preservation of the city to the saint's intervention.[120] It is worth pointing out, too, that the academy of which he was the founder expressly forbade the discussion of subjects pertaining to theology or religion.[121] As Jon Snyder observes, "[a]ny hint of seditious talk among academicians would, at the very least, immediately have brought the wrath of the local authorities down on them."[122] We know from Milton's own testimony concerning his Florentine sojourns that he was hardly reticent about his religion, especially since Carlo Dati seems to have been more open-minded than his academic peers. That testimony seems indeed quite credible, voiced, as it is, in a private letter (*Epistola Familiaris* 10), postdating his Italian journey by almost a decade.[123] *Defensio Secunda*, however, is another

---

[119] Giovanni Battista Manso, *Vita, Virtù, e Miracoli Principali di S. Patricia Vergine* (Naples: Gio. Iacomo Carlino, 1611).

[120] In an extant letter Manso describes the miracle eloquently and in some detail: the procession bearing the saint's relics, his own role as privileged among the great crowd, the Cardinal removing the saint's blood from the tabernacle, raising the vessel to the erupting mountain, and making the sign of the cross, and the subsequent bowing of the cloud of fire, as if in veneration of the holy relics. See "Lettera del Signor Giov. Battista Manso, Marchese di Villa, in Materia del Vesuvio," *Archivio Storico per le Provincie Napoletane*, vol. 14, fasc. 3 and 4 (1889), 503–504, at 503. See also Cocco, *Watching Vesuvius*, 68; Estelle Haan, "'Coelum non Animum Muto'? Milton's Neo-Latin Poetry and Catholic Italy," in *Milton and Catholicism*, eds. Ronald Corthell and Thomas N. Corns (Notre Dame, IN: University of Notre Dame Press, 2017), 131–167, at 135.

[121] The statutes of the Oziosi are extant in the Biblioteca Nazionale, Naples, as "Regole dell'Accademia degli Oziosi": BNN, MS Brancacciana V.D.14, ff. 127^r–134^r. They were reprinted in Carlo Padiglione, *Le Legge dell'Accademia degli Oziosi in Napoli Ritrovate nella Biblioteca Brancacciana* (Naples: F. Giannini, 1878). See ibid., 19: "vietando che non si debba leggere alcuna materia di Tiologia, ò della Sacra Scrittura, delle quali per riverenza dobbiamo astenerci" ("forbidding the reading of any subject matter pertaining to Theology or to Holy Scripture, from which, out of reverence, we must abstain"). See also Haan, *From Academia to Amicitia*, 125.

[122] Jon R. Snyder, "Truth and Wonder in Naples circa 1640," in *Culture and Authority in the Baroque*, eds. Massimo Ciavolella and Patrick Coleman (Toronto: University of Toronto Press, 2005), 85–105, at 86.

[123] In the letter, dated 21 April 1647, Milton apologizes for the anti-papal content of his 1645 *Poemata* (obviously *In Quintum Novembris* and the epigrams on the Gunpowder Plot), which he is about to send Dati, and asks him to secure from his

case in point. In fact, Milton's aforementioned remarks about religious tensions between Manso and himself[124] should be read a priori in the context of such hyperbolic claims as his statement that he had heard from merchants in Naples of a so-called plot against him by the English Jesuits in Rome.[125] This, as Diane Benet has carefully argued, is probably no more than authorial recourse to the well-established "escape from Rome" genre, and the polemical stance facilitated by a literary topos.[126] Such

fellow academicians the open-mindedness that he himself used to show in response to Milton's freedom when discussing religious matters. See *John Milton: Epistolarum Familiarium Liber Unus and Uncollected Letters*, ed. Haan, 164–189, at 170–171, 182–184. In his letter of reply (1 November 1647), Dati picks up Milton's comment about freedom of expression, stating that he will indeed excuse, but not applaud, such sentiments even though uttered from the lips of a friend; in any case, they will not be an obstacle to his reception of the other poems, if Milton excuses his (Dati's) liberty of expression. See *The Works of John Milton*, eds. Frank A. Patterson et al., 18 vols. (New York: Columbia University Press, 1931–1940) (henceforth abbreviated to *CM*), XII, 310. Milton's letter and Dati's reply survive in holograph in the New York Public Library: John Milton Papers, 1647–1882: MSSCol 2011.

[124] Cf. Nicolas Heinsius's exaggeration in his letter of 1 March 1653 (to Isaac Vossius): *Imo invisus est Italis Anglus iste, inter quos multo vixit tempore, ob mores nimis severos, cum et de religione libenter disputaret, ac multa in Pontificem Romanum acerbe effutiret quavis occasione* ("Moreover that Englishman was disliked by the Italians, among whom he dwelt for a great deal of time, on account of his overly strict behavior, since he even disputed freely about religion, and blurted out many bitter statements against the Pontiff of Rome"). See Pieter Burman, ed., *Sylloges Epistolarum a Viris Illustribus Scriptarum*, 5 vols. (Leiden: Samuel Luchtmans, 1727), III, 667–671, at 669.

[125] *Defensio Secunda*, 85–86: *Romam autem reversurum, monebant Mercatores se didicisse per litteras parari mihi ab Iesuitis Anglis insidias, si Romam reverterem, eo quod de religione nimis libere locutus essem* ("As I was on the point of returning to Rome, the merchants warned me that they had learnt from their letters that, should I return to Rome, the English Jesuits were setting a plot for me, on account of the fact that I had spoken too liberally on the topic of religion"). Parker seems to take Milton's claim at face value, remarking: "His danger may not have been so great as he supposed, but there is no reason to doubt his sincerity or that of the merchants who warned him." See W. R. Parker, *Milton: A Biography*, 2 vols. (Oxford: Oxford University Press, 1968; revised ed., Gordon Campbell, 1996), II, 827.

[126] See Diana Treviño Benet, "The Escape From Rome: Milton's Second Defense and a Renaissance Genre," in *Milton in Italy: Contexts, Images, Contradictions*, ed. Mario A. Di Cesare (Binghamton, NY: Medieval and Renaissance Texts and Studies, 1991), 29–49. Benet convincingly shows that Milton's claim draws on the "Escape from Rome" narrative, exemplified by Anthony Munday, Edward Webbe, George Sandys, Fynes Moryson, and William Lithgow. See Anthony Munday, *The English Romayne Lyfe, 1582*, ed. G. B. Harrison (Edinburgh: Edinburgh University Press, 1966); *Edward Webbe, Chief Master Gunner, His Travailes. 1590*, ed. Edward Arber (London: Alex Murray & Son, 1869); George Sandys, *Travels, Containing an History of the … Turkish Empire* (London: W[illiam] Barrett, 1615); Fynes Moryson,

comments jar, too, with the good-humored religious tension governing both Manso's Latin distich in Milton's honor,[127] and *Mansus* itself. In short, the literary evidence, when viewed collectively, seems to suggest that, contrary to Milton's later comments, the relationship that he contracted with Manso approximated a friendship that was both filial and respectful, and one that transcended mere courtesy.[128] And it was quite unique in another sense. As a septuagenarian Manso stands out from among Milton's acquaintances in both Florence (Carlo Dati) and Rome (Giovanni Salzilli, Antonio Cherubini), all of whom were comparatively young. By 1639 Manso's literary career was already nearing its end. He would die in 1645, just two months after Milton's *Poemata* were entered into the Stationers Register.[129]

The present study seeks to map the literary import of Naples on Milton in the course of his one-month sojourn and beyond. As the first book devoted solely to *Mansus*, arguably the most accomplished of Milton's neo-Latin writings pertaining to his Italian period, it offers a series of fresh interpretations of the poem. It does so by situating it alongside Milton's seemingly voracious reading of contemporary Italian literature while abroad; by assessing the poem's academic, religious,

---

Itinerary (1617) (see note 33); William Lithgow, *The Totall Discourse of the Rare Adventures and Painefull Peregrinations of Long Nineteene Yeares Travayles from Scotland to the Most Famous Kingdomes in Europe, Asia and Affrica* (London: Nicholas Okes, 1632). An earlier example, namely, Thomas Wilson's *The Arte of Rhetorique, For The Use of All Suche as are Studious of Eloquence, Set Forthe in Englishe* (London: Ihon Kingston, 1560) (at sig. aiiii^v–Av^v), has recently been identified and discussed by Andrew Wallace. Wilson claimed that while in Rome he was charged with heresy and that his life was in mortal danger. See Andrew Wallace, *The Presence of Rome in Medieval and Early Modern Britain* (Cambridge: Cambridge University Press, 2020), 104–124. For a later example, see Sir Edward Herbert, *Autobiography* (composed in the 1640s), published in Strawberry Hill in 1764. See also Estelle Haan, "England, Neo-Latin, and the Continental Journey," in *Political Turmoil: Early Modern British Literature in Transition, 1623–1660*, ed. Stephen B. Dobranski (Cambridge: Cambridge University Press, 2019), 322–338.

[127] See *Poemata*, 4; Lewalski and Haan, 106–107, 415, and, for further discussion, 46–54.

[128] Cf. Milton, *Defensio Secunda*, 85: … *ad Ioannem Baptistam Mansum, Marchionem Villensem, virum nobilissimum atque gravissimum … sum introductus, eodemque usus, quamdiu illic fui, sane amicissimo* ("I was introduced … to Giovanni Battista Manso, Marquis of Villa, a most noble and influential man … For the duration of my time there I was treated by him in a most friendly manner").

[129] Thus, according to the Stationers Register, on 6 October 1645, "Master Mozeley. Entred … under the hands of Sr Nath. Brent and both the wardens a booke called Poems in English & Latyn, by Mr John Milton vj^d." See G. F. Briscoe, ed., *A Transcript of the Registers of the Worshipful Company of Stationers from 1640–1708*, 3 vols. (London: s.n. 1913–1914), I, 196.

topographical, and linguistic contexts; and by analyzing its classical, neo-Latin, Italian, and English intertexts. Read in these wider contexts, *Mansus* emerges as a polyvocal poem, a text about other texts, embracing not only its addressee's Latin encomium composed in Milton's honor, but also, and essentially, his published (and, possibly, unpublished) works: his *Vita di Torquato Tasso*, and, most notable, the *Erocallia* and the *Poesie Nomiche*. It is with these last two volumes that Milton's poem engages on many hitherto unnoticed levels.[130] It also draws on the writings of two Italian poets who benefitted from Manso's care and patronage, namely, Torquato Tasso and Giambattista Marino, alongside whose precedent Milton unabashedly aligns his Neapolitan experience. And he does so with a self-consciousness that is strikingly kaleidoscopic in essence. Like them, he is the recipient of Manso's hospitality and courtesy, but as the poem progresses, so too does his self-fashioning seem to vacillate between the two poets. At times *Mansus* is quasi-Tassonian in, for example, its appropriation of theories of friendship outlined in Tasso's dialogue on the subject ("Il Manso"),[131] its articulation of epic plans,[132] and its potential recasting of scenes from Manso's biography of the poet.[133] At others, it is quasi-Marinesque, in, for example, Milton's reinterpretation and self-appropriation of a cenotaph for Marino erected by Manso in his domestic chapel in Naples[134] or in the succinct critique of *L'Adone*, aptly contextualized in terms of reader response and the conceits of Marinism itself.[135] Such conceits, moreover, may be mirrored in the poem's Latinity.[136] Milton, in replying to Manso's tribute, to his hospitality, and indeed to his literary output, assumes a place of his own in a Neapolitan world, as he cleverly experiments with genre and with language(s), while simultaneously showcasing his reading of Italian literature while on Neapolitan soil.

---

[130] See Chapters 2 and 3.

[131] See Chapter 5.

[132] See 133–150.

[133] See 150–154.

[134] See 175–184.

[135] See 184–194.

[136] See 201–203.

Chapter 1

Assidua Auctorum Lectio:[1]
Milton's Neapolitan Reading

Milton may well have followed the traditional route to Naples, and enjoyed a tour of the city (and probably its outskirts) under Manso's expert guidance, but in other respects his Neapolitan sojourn seems to have been rather atypical of its day. Whereas for other travelers, the city's magnetism resided in its local sites or in the breathtaking vistas afforded by the Neapolitan seascape, for Milton, in all likelihood, it resided in its academic and literary treasures, as epitomized by humanists in general and by published volumes in particular. For in Naples he would have had the opportunity to immerse himself for a full month in academic culture, not least because his major contact happened to be the founder of, and leading figure in, a highly prestigious academy. He would also have benefitted from the accessibility of recently published Italian works. Again, in Manso, a distinguished poet and biographer, he would have found a perfect avenue and, indeed, exemplar. In this respect Milton's Neapolitan experience should be considered a fortiori in the context of the habitual reading practices that he adopted over the course of his Italian journey as a whole. We know, for example, from the testimony of Edward Phillips, that "curious and rare Books" were among items that Milton "pick'd up in his Travels," and arranged to be shipped home from Venice, as well as "a Chest or two of choice Musick-books of the best Masters flourishing about that time in Italy."[2] That the chests

---

[1] Carlo Dati, *Ioanni Miltoni Londiniensi*, at *Poemata*, 10; Lewalski and Haan, 114–115.

[2] Edward Phillips, *The Life of Mr. John Milton*, in *Early Lives*, ed. Darbishire, 59: "he arriv'd at Venice ... and Shipp'd up a Parcel of curious and rare Books which he had pick'd up in his Travels; particularly a Chest or two of choice Musick-books of the best Masters flourishing about that time in Italy, namely, Luca Marenzo [*sic*], Monte Verde, Horatio Vecchi, Cifa [*sic*], the Prince of Venosa, and several others." Cf. John Phillips, *The Life of Mr. John Milton*, in ibid., 17–34, at 21: "and then [he] proceeded to Venice, where hee shippd what books he had bought"; Anthony à Wood, *Fasti Oxonienses*, in ibid., 35–48, at 38: "after he had ship'd the books and other goods which he had bought in his travels"; John Toland, *The Life of John Milton*, in ibid.,

were more than one is worth noting, as is the fact that the books enclosed therein were relatively contemporary. William Poole is probably correct in his speculation that works read by Milton in Italy comprised not "huge folios," but "smaller format vernacular books, bought en route for the purpose."[3] But Milton also seems to have made a point of familiarizing himself with volumes, whether gifted to him or otherwise, authored by academicians and scholars, who showed him particular hospitality. It is highly likely, too, that he read and acquired works by other Italian writers with whom he crossed paths.

1.1 Milton's Reading Practices in Italy

That Milton was both an avid and a proactive reader of contemporary literature while on Italian soil is evinced in several ways. Thus, according to the testimony of the Florentine academician Antonio Francini, his "wish" was "to seek out for his treasure those whose memory, made eternal in learned pages, the world honors" ("La cui memoria onora/Il mondo fatta eterna in dotte carte,/Volesti ricercar per tuo tesoro").[4] Likewise, in the words of Carlo Dati, he was one for whom the constant reading of authors served as a traveling companion (*comite assidua auctorum lectione*).[5] And more than that. Milton's reading, his perennial traveling companion, so to speak, was proudly showcased by him to a wider audience in the Latin poetry and prose that he composed while in Italy. Occasionally this manifests itself explicitly through mention of, paraphrastic allusion to, or even quotation from, Italian works. More frequently, however, it rears its head implicitly through intertextual engagement with, and self-appropriation of, Italian authors and, at times, their linguistic methodologies, through ekphrasis, allegory, and the skillful manipulation of the Latin language. Central to his Italian self-fashioning then was Milton, the bibliophile; Milton, the scholarly

---

83–197, at 95: "he arrived in Venice. After spending one month here, and shipping off all the Books he collected in his Travels …"

[3] Poole, "'The Armes of Studious Retirement'?" 35, where he also lists among such possible purchases works whose imprimaturs Milton would either adapt or allude to in *Areopagitica*, when mocking the practice, on which see Leo Miller, "The Italian Imprimaturs in Milton's *Areopagitica*," *Papers of the Bibliographical Society of America* 65 (1971): 345–355.

[4] Antonio Francini, "Al Signor Gio. Miltoni Nobile Inglese," 51–53. See *Poemata*, 7; Lewalski and Haan, 110–113.

[5] Carlo Dati, *Ioanni Miltoni Londiniensi*, at *Poemata*, 10; Lewalski and Haan, 114–115.

participant in Italy's academic and cultural communities both past and present. Francini seems to capture the very essence of this in his cryptic, yet particularly insightful, acclamation: "you spoke with them [authors] in their works" ("parlasti con lor nell' opre loro").[6] It is thus worth pausing to reassess the essential truth of these comments and the implications that they might have for an interpretation of the poetic methodology of *Mansus*.

In the course of his travels through Florence, Rome, and Naples, Milton seems to have engaged in a sustained reading program that was probably akin to that which he had already undertaken in advance of his Italian journey.[7] In Florence, for example, that intellectual conversation with Italian volumes lauded by Francini had already emerged in Milton's relationship with the academician and Tuscan grammarian Benedetto Buonmattei.[8] This is evident from *Epistola Familiaris* 8, dated 10 September 1638,[9] thus written just a matter of months before Milton's Neapolitan period. Assuming a confident stance in relation to the perennial debate of the merits of the Tuscan tongue,[10] Milton had proudly demonstrated his alertness to the fact that his addressee was busily

---

[6] Francini, "Al Signor Gio. Miltoni Nobile Inglese," 54. See *Poemata*, 7; Lewalski and Haan, 112–113, 418.

[7] Milton's extensive reading of Italian literature just prior to his Italian journey is attested by some of his entries (tentatively datable to 1637 by the occurrence of the Greek *e* instead of the Italian *e* [on which see James Holly Hanford, "The Chronology of Milton's Private Studies," *PMLA* 36 [1921]: 251–314; Helen Darbishire, "The Chronology of Milton's Handwriting," *The Library* 14 [1934]: 229–235) in his *Commonplace Book*. These included Dante, *Divina Comedia* in Bernardino Daniello's commentary (Venice: Pietro da Fino, 1568) (see Milton, *Commonplace Book*, 12, in *The Complete Works of John Milton: Volume XI: Manuscript Writings*, ed. William Poole [Oxford: Oxford University Press, 2019], 117); Boccaccio, *Vita di Dante Alighieri* (Rome: Francesco Priscianese, 1544) (*Commonplace Book*, 182, ed. Poole, 211–212 [Milton's annotated copy is extant in the Bodleian Library, Oxford, as Arch. Af. 145, on which see William Poole, "John Milton and Giovanni Boccaccio's *Vita di Dante*," *MQ* 48 [2014]: 139–170]), and Ariosto, *Orlando Furioso* (precise edition undetermined) (*Commonplace Book*, 151, ed. Poole, 185).

[8] On Buonmattei, see A. M. Cinquemani, *Glad to Go for a Feast: Milton, Buonmattei, and the Florentine Accademici* (New York: Peter Lang, 1998), passim; Haan, *Bilingualism and Biculturalism*, 104–118; Michele Colombo, "Benedetto Buonmattei e La Questione della Lingua nel Primo Seicento," *Aevum* 77 (2003): 615–634.

[9] See *John Milton: Epistolarum Familiarium Liber Unus and Uncollected Letters*, ed. Haan, 116–139.

[10] Milton may well have obtained access to a copy of the *Delle Lodi della Lingua Toscana*, recited by Buonmattei in 1623 before the Accademia Fiorentina. See Haan, *Bilingualism and Biculturalism*, 113. Cf. Cinquemani, *Glad to Go for a Feast*, 13, who regards this as "a work that Milton might have seen."

engaged in the completion of the full-scale Tuscan grammar that would eventually see the light of day in 1643 as *Della Lingua Toscana ... Libri Due*.[11] And he had even offered two recommendations of his own. The first, made "with some temerity,"[12] was that Buonmattei "add a little something" (*paululum quiddam ... adicere*) for foreigners in regard to the correct pronunciation of Tuscan.[13] While acknowledging that the treatise was a "work-in-progress,"[14] Milton had drawn on earlier printed versions of the first part of the tract, which would have been accessible to him in either the first or second editions, published in Venice in 1623[15] and 1626, respectively.[16] Indeed, his recommendation may have been inspired by the technical and essentially provincial nature of the treatment of

---

[11] Benedetto Buonmattei, *Della Lingua Toscana ... Libri Due* (Florence: Zanobi Pignoni, 1643).

[12] Campbell and Corns, *Life, Work, and Thought*, 111.

[13] *Quo magis merito potes meminisse quid ego tanto opere abs te contendere soleam: uti iam incohatis, maiori etiam ex parte absolutis, velles, quanta maxima facilitate res ipsa tulerit, in nostram exterorum gratiam de recta linguae pronuntiatione adhuc paululum quiddam adicere* ("Hence may you all the more remember with good cause the challenge that I am in the habit of so earnestly setting you: that to those materials already begun and in greater part completed, and in accordance with the very extensive flexibility that the subject itself affords, you be willing to add, for the sake of us foreigners, still a little something concerning the correct pronunciation of the language") (*John Milton: Epistolarum Familiarium Liber Unus and Uncollected Letters*, ed. Haan, 126–127). Scholars have traditionally held the belief that Buonmattei disregarded Milton's request, given the seeming absence from the 1643 treatise of a specific section on pronunciation. For a correction of this misreading (itself the consequence of a misinterpretation of the phrase *paululum quiddam ... adicere*), see Haan, *Bilingualism and Biculturalism*, 108–111. There also exists the intriguing possibility that the manuscript of Buonmattei's *Trattato della Pronunzia* (BNCF, MS Magliabecchiana Cl. IV cod. 61), envisaged as book III of the *Della Lingua Toscana* (usefully edited by Piero Fiorelli as "Il 'Trattato della Pronunzia' di Benedetto Buommattei," *Studi Linguistici Italiani* 1 [1960]: 109–161 [to which edition subsequent page references refer]), is a late work partly inspired by Milton's recommendation, especially given Fiorelli's convincing arguments (at 110) for a date of 1644–1647 for that tract's composition. Indeed, now the discussion of the various meanings of *pronunzia* (118) is characterized by something rather new: a particular awareness that pronunciation should pertain to "ciascun popolo," and an associated acknowledgment of, and discernment between, the individual requirements of different nations in this regard (119, 120–128, 136–148). For further discussion, see Haan, *Bilingualism and Biculturalism*, 111–113.

[14] Lewalski, *Life*, 93.

[15] Benedetto Buonmattei, *Delle Cagioni della Lingua Toscana* (Venice: Alessandro Polo, 1623).

[16] Benedetto Buonmattei, *Introduzione alla Lingua Toscana* (Venice: Giovanni Salis, 1626).

pronunciation therein.[17] And ancient authorities were never far away: Milton's second recommendation was that Buonmattei incorporate a generically based list of exemplary Tuscan authors.[18] Although, as Cinquemani correctly observes, "[n]o document answering Milton's second request seems to exist,"[19] the recommendation itself, couched, in the language of Quintilian,[20] served as the climax of a leitmotif pervading a letter that consistently and honorifically equated its addressee with the ancient grammarian.[21] But it also did more than that by demonstrating Milton's scrutiny of contemporary Italian literature. In all of this, *Epistola Familiaris* 8, far from revealing, in the words of Cinquemani, "a rather cursory reading of Buonmattei's grammar," since "[p]erhaps, in 1638–39, Milton was preoccupied by travel,"[22] suggests the opposite: that during

---

[17] See Haan, *Bilingualism and Biculturalism*, 110–111.

[18] *Nec illa minus si in tanta scriptorum turba commonstrare separatim non gravabere quis post illos decantatos Florentinae linguae auctores poterit secundas haud iniuria sibi asserere: quis tragoedia insignis; quis in comoedia festivus et lepidus; quis scriptis epistolis aut dialogis argutus aut gravis; quis in historia nobilis. Ita et studioso potiorem quemque eligere volenti non erit difficile, et erit, quoties vagari latius libebit ubi pedem intrepide possit figere. Qua quidem in re inter antiquos Ciceronem et Fabium habebis quos imiteris; vestrorum autem hominum haud scio an unum* ("This next renown too will be no less: if you have no objection to pointing out individually who among such a throng of writers can justly claim for himself second place, next after those proclaimed authors of the Florentine tongue: who is illustrious in tragedy; who is witty and amusing in comedy; who is shrewd or authoritative in writing epistles or dialogues; who is noble in history: in this way it will not be difficult for the willing student to select the best of each kind, and, whenever it pleases him to range further afield, he will have ground on which he can plant his steps without fear. Indeed, in regard to this you will have among the ancients Cicero and Fabius to imitate; whether any of your own men—that I do not know") (*John Milton: Epistolarum Familiarium Liber Unus and Uncollected Letters*, ed. Haan, 128–129). Worthy of comparison is Milton's own generically-based list at *The Reason of Church-Government* (London: John Rothwell, 1641), 38–39: "whether that Epick form whereof the two poems of Homer, and those other two of Virgil and Tasso are a diffuse, and the book of Iob a brief model. ... Or whether those Dramatick constitutions, wherein Sophocles and Euripides raigne shall be found more doctrinal and exemplary to a Nation. ... Or if occasion shall lead to imitat those magnifick Odes and Hymns wherein Pindarus and Callimachus are in most things worthy."

[19] Cinquemani, *Glad to Go for a Feast*, 36. For this observation, see also Lewalski, *Life*, 93; Campbell and Corns, *Life, Work, and Thought*, 111.

[20] See Quintilian, *Institutiones Oratoriae* 10.1. 37ff, in which he offers a generically based, albeit highly subjective, overview of Greek and Roman writers. For further discussion, see Haan, *Bilingualism and Biculturalism*, 117–118.

[21] See Haan, *Bilingualism and Biculturalism*, 115–118.

[22] Cinquemani, *Glad to Go for a Feast*, 36.

his residency in Florence he had thoroughly familiarized himself with works penned by his addressee.

In the course of his first Roman sojourn, and thus again in advance of his arrival in Naples, Milton had composed *Ad Salsillum Poetam Romanum Aegrotantem*,[23] an accomplished set of scazons addressed to the poet and academician Giovanni Salzilli.[24] Reworking features from a Latin encomium, which Salzilli had presented in Milton's honor,[25] the poem moves far beyond its purported status as a get-well wish by its likely engagement with the recently published work of its Roman addressee. Although he was still relatively young,[26] Salzilli, it would seem, was already a prominent member of the Roman Accademia dei Fantastici.[27] Indeed, just one year prior to Milton's visit, he had seen the publication of fifteen Italian poems (11 sonnets, 3 canzoni, and 1 ottavo) in the *Poesie de' Signori Accademici Fantastici di Roma*.[28] As a relatively recent publication, this work would have been easily accessible to Milton (possibly even gifted to him by Salzilli, perhaps with the aforementioned encomium inscribed therein?).[29] *Ad Salsillum*, in short, had demonstrated its author's close reading of the Fantastici volume in general, and of Salzilli's poetry in particular,[30] evincing in the latter instance a Miltonic acknowledgment of the essentially Horatian quality of Salzilli's Italian verse.[31] His addressee was also a member,[32] and one of

---

[23] See *Poemata*, 70–72; Lewalski and Haan, 202–205, 478–481. That Milton composed *Ad Salsillum* in the course of his first visit to Rome is suggested by its positioning in the 1645 *Poemata* (where it precedes *Mansus*, which pertains to his Neapolitan sojourn), and by its description of Milton's arrival in Italy in language suggesting that it was a relatively recent event: *diebus hisce* (10) ("in these days").

[24] On Salzilli, see James A. Freeman, "Milton's Roman Connection: Giovanni Salzilli," *MS* 19 (1984): 87–104; Haan, *From Academia to Amicitia*, 81–98, and, especially, Haan, *John Milton's Roman Sojourns*, 29–97.

[25] Milton, *Poemata*, 4; Lewalski and Haan, 106–107, 415–416. See Haan, *From Academia to Amicitia*, 82–98; Haan, *John Milton's Roman Sojourns*, 47–59.

[26] Salzilli's relative youthfulness in 1638 is corroborated by newly uncovered evidence of the fact that he did not die until 1691. See Haan, *John Milton's Roman Sojourns*, 31–40.

[27] See Maylender, *Storia*, II, 348.

[28] *Poesie de' Signori Accademici Fantastici di Roma* (Rome: Grignano, 1637), 148–169.

[29] See Haan, *John Milton's Roman Sojourns*, 47.

[30] See Haan, *John Milton's Roman Sojourns*, 69–74.

[31] See Haan, *John Milton's Roman Sojourns*, 59–69.

[32] See Maylender, *Storia*, V, 379.

two Censors,[33] of the Roman Accademia degli Umoristi. All the more apt then was Milton's subtle incorporation and reworking of that academy's *impresa* (a cloud raining a shower upon the earth) and Lucretian motto (*redit agmine dulci*),[34] the associated context of salinity and distillation,[35] and perhaps the explication of the same (in 1611) by Girolamo Aleandro.[36] Once again, Milton's implicit self-fashioning was as an academician among Roman academicians, a meticulous reader and interpreter of contemporary Italian poetry and prose.

That this was also Milton's post-Neapolitan practice is corroborated by his return visit to Rome, and especially by *Epistola Familiaris* 9 (dated 30 March 1639).[37] Addressing Lucas Holstenius (Holste),[38] Milton would boast of being conducted by his addressee on a

---

[33] See Giacinta Gimma, *Elogi Accademici della Società degli Spensierati di Rossano* (Naples: Carlo Troise, 1703), 77–88, at 83. The other Censor was Giovanni Lotti (1604–1686), who was also a member of the Fantastici, and a future contributor (of an Italian poem, three Latin poems, and a further Latin distich) to the *Academia Tenuta da Fantastici a 12 di Maggio 1655. In Applauso della S[anti]tà di N[ostro] S[ignore] Alesandro VII* (Rome: Vitale Mascardi, 1655), at 69–70, 77–79, and 80.

[34] Lucretius, *De Rerum Natura* 6. 637.

[35] The Lucretian passage from which the motto derives describes the process of distillation, whereby the salinity of seawater is drawn up by the sun, by whose heat it is purified, before raining down again upon the earth. Salzilli may even have possessed his own personal *impresa* ("A Bird in her neast or hatching upon a Rock in the middle of ye Sea") and motto (*Salus in salo*), as observed by Richard Symonds during his Roman sojourn in 1649–1651, and described by him in his notebook (British Library, London: Egerton MS 1635, f. 49^r). For further discussion and possible links with *Ad Salsillum*, see Haan, *John Milton's Roman Sojourns*, 77–80.

[36] Girolamo Aleandro, *Sopra l'Impresa de gli Accademici Humoristi Discorso ... Detto nella Stessa Accademia* (Rome: Giacomo Mascardi, 1611). Cf. Giovanni Ferro, *Teatro d'Imprese*, 2 vols. (Venice: Giacomo Sarzina, 1623), II, 518–520, and, for later accounts, Athanasius Kircher, *Oedipi Aegyptiaci Tomus Secundus. Gymnasium sive Phrontisterion Hieroglyphicum in Duodecim Classes Distributum* (Rome: Vitale Mascardi, 1653), 9; Marcellino de Pise, *Moralis Encyclopaedia Id Est Scientiarum Omnium Chorus*, 4 vols. (Lyon: Laurentius Anisson, 1656), III, 323; Alessandro Sperelli, *Paradossi Morali* (Venice: Paolo Baglioni, 1666), II, 241. See Haan, *John Milton's Roman Sojourns*, 80–81.

[37] Milton's letter survives in the Vatican Library as Barb.lat. 2181, ff. 57^r–58^v. See Joseph McG. Bottkol, "The Holograph of Milton's Letter to Holstenius," *PMLA* 68 (1953): 617–627. For a modern edition, see *John Milton, Epistolarum Familiarium Liber Unus and Uncollected Letters*, ed. Haan, 140–163.

[38] On Lucas Holstenius, Librarian of the Barberini Library (1636), of Cardinal Francesco Barberini (1638), and subsequently of the Vatican Library (first custodian, 1641; second custodian, 1653), see Peter Fuchs, "Holste, Lukas," *NDB* 9 (1972): 548–550; Roberto Almagià, *L'Opera Geografica di Luca Holstenio*, Studi e Testi 102

guided tour of the treasures of the Vatican Library, treasures, described as a *conquisitissimam librorum suppellectilem* ("most select collection of books"). Here, too, he would delight in beholding ancient Greek manuscripts adorned by Holstenius's labors, some of which, still awaiting delivery to the printing press, he would compare to the souls in Virgil's underworld awaiting rebirth (citing almost verbatim Virgil, *Aeneid* 6. 679–680). He would also rejoice in being presented with a *duplici dono* ("a twofold gift") of one of Holstenius's printed works. The volume in question was in all likelihood Holstenius's *Porphyrii Philosophi Liber de Vita Pythagorae*, published in Rome in 1630.[39] Returning the gift, at least in a literary sense, Milton would couch his account of his Roman experiences in essentially Pythagorean language,[40] even incorporating, with a quasi pedantic scrupulosity, two Greek terms (ἀκρόαμα[41] and διδασκάλια),[42] whose etymology Holstenius had painstakingly explicated in his *Observationes ad Vitam Pythagorae a Porphyrio Scriptam* included in Part 2 of that work.[43] In complimenting learned scholars Milton habitually showcases his careful reading of those scholars' published output and of other Italian volumes.

(Vatican City: Biblioteca Apostolica Vaticana, 1942); F. J. Blom, "Lucas Holstenius (1596–1661) and England," in *Studies in Seventeenth-Century English Literature, History and Bibliography*, eds. G. A. M. Janssens and F. G. A. M. Aarts (Amsterdam: Rodopi, 1984), 25–39, and, especially, P. J. Rietbergen, *Power and Religion in Baroque Rome: Barberini Cultural Policies* (Leiden: Brill, 2006), 256–295.

[39] Leo Miller had proposed that the gifted volume in question was Holstenius's recently published *Demophili Democratis et Secundi, Veterum Philosophorum Sententiae Morales* (Rome: Mascardus, 1638), his Latin rendering of the axioms of the later Pythagoreans. See Leo Miller, "Milton and Holstenius Reconsidered: An Exercise in Scholarly Practice," in *Milton in Italy*, ed. Di Cesare, 573–587. For a counterargument, proposing as a more likely candidate Holstenius's *Porphyrii Philosophi Liber de Vita Pythagorae* (Rome: Typis Vaticanis, 1630), see Haan, *John Milton's Roman Sojourns*, 144–148.

[40] On the letter's Pythagorean language as read through a Virgilian lens (and especially by the reinvention of the *anabasis/katabasis* motifs in *Aeneid* 6) see Haan, *John Milton's Roman Sojourns*, 148–153.

[41] *cum ille* (sc. *Cardinalis Franciscus Barberinus*) *paucis post diebus* ἀκρόαμα *illud musicum magnificentia vere Romana publice exhiberet* ("when a few days later he [sc. Cardinal Francesco Barberini] presented to the public, and with truly Roman magnificence, that musical 'entertainment'").

[42] *pulchre tu quidem Angliae nostrae ex parte etiam tuae* διδασκάλια *persolvis* ("you are indeed handsomely repaying to our England (yours also in part) your debts of 'schooling'").

[43] Lucas Holstenius, *Observationes ad Vitam Pythagorae a Porphyrio Scriptam in Porphyrii Philosophi Liber de Vita Pythagorae*, [Part 2], 93–122, at 103–104. See Haan, *John Milton's Roman Sojourns*, 147–148.

Nowhere is this last point more evident than in *Mansus*. The poem's headnote alone, discussed later in this study,[44] alludes to two works by Tasso: his *Dialogo dell' Amicitia*, entitled "Il Manso," with which *Mansus* seems self-consciously to engage on a number of levels,[45] and the *Gerusalemme Conquistata*, from which Milton quotes, as it were, chapter and verse.[46] The poem proper, moreover, specifically alludes to Manso's *Vita di Torquato Tasso*,[47] a work which, as William Poole pertinently observes, "Milton probably also read,"[48] and episodes from which he imaginatively appropriates.[49] It also refers to Manso's *Vita di Giambattista Marino*, now lost, but extant in manuscript at the time of Milton's Neapolitan sojourn,[50] and, in all likelihood, shown to him by its author.[51]

---

[44] See 114–121, 155–159.

[45] See Chapter 5.

[46] See 114–117.

[47] *Mansus* 20–21.

[48] *The Complete Works of John Milton: Volume XI*, ed. Poole, 413. See also 124–128.

[49] See 150–154.

[50] *Mansus* 20–21. See 121–124.

[51] Among other volumes to which Milton may have been introduced by Manso was *Il Teatro delle Glorie della Signora Adriana Basile* (Venice; rpt Naples: s.n., 1628), a volume of encomiastic verse in honor of Adriana Basile, mother of the soprano Leonora Baroni, extolled by Milton in three Latin epigrams. The fact that this work was dedicated to Manso makes it a particularly strong candidate (see Domitio Bombarda's dedicatory letter "All' Illustriss[imo] Sig[nor] Mio, e Padrone sempre Colendiss[imo] Il Signor GIO[VANNI] BATTISTA MANSO MARCHESE DI VILLA," dated Venice, 1 April 1628, at *Il Teatro*, 3–14). In his second Latin epigram Milton's description of Leonora is very much as her mother's daughter, suggested not only by the fact that she is playing her mother's instrument (*Aurea maternae fila movere lyrae* [6] ["as you plucked the golden strings of your mother's lyre"]), but also perhaps by the juxtaposition of *maternae* and *fila*, thus facilitating a possible pun on *filum* ("string") and *filia* ("daughter"). Milton's phraseology, moreover, may echo a Latin poem by Giovanni Battista Russo at *Il Teatro*, 242: *Aurea seu citharae percurris fila, Basilis,/ ... Hinc trahis et fidibus mortalia corda canoris* ("Whether you pluck the golden strings of the lyre, Basile ... on this side you sway mortal hearts with your musical strings"). With Russo's *mortalia corda* (and the associated context in which the phrase occurs) cf. also Milton, *Ad Leonoram* 1.7–8: *facilisque docet mortalia corda/Sensim immortali assuescere posse sono* ("and readily teaches that mortal hearts can gradually become accustomed to an immortal sound"). For further discussion, see Haan, *John Milton's Roman Sojourns*, 123–137, especially 133–134. There, it is argued, Milton's otherwise unattested depiction of Parthenope as a "Naiad upon the shore" (<u>NAIADA Ripa</u> [*Ad Leonoram* 3.3 [emphasis mine]) may contain an anagrammatic pun on <u>ADRIANA</u> (emphasis mine), hence evoking perhaps the wordplay

1.2 Two Literary Gift Texts: Manso's *Pocula ... Bina*[52]

Most striking, perhaps, is the imaginative way in which *Mansus* seems to engage with two published volumes in particular: Manso's *Erocallia* (1628), and his *Poesie Nomiche* (1635), both of which were in all probability gifted to him, at some point during his Neapolitan sojourn, by the author himself. This is indicated by *Epitaphium Damonis*, composed in the wake of Milton's Italian journey. The fact that such gift-giving of his own works to his Neapolitan guests seems to have been Manso's habitual practice[53] further serves to reinforce the possibility. Having articulated his epic plans that, he states, he was reserving (*servabam* [180]) in the hope of sharing with the now deceased Charles Diodati,[54] Milton seems to signal two material texts that he was also keeping in reserve for his Anglo-Italian friend. He does so via an ekphrastic depiction of "two cups" (*pocula ... bina*), which, he claims, were presented to him by Manso:

> Haec tibi servabam lenta sub cortice lauri;
> Haec et plura simul, tum quae mihi pocula Mansus,
> Mansus, Chalcidicae non ultima gloria ripae,
> Bina dedit, mirum artis opus, mirandus et ipse,
> Et circum gemino caelaverat argumento.
> (*Epitaphium Damonis* 180–184).

> These things I was reserving for you beneath tough laurel-bark; these things, and more too, and also two cups which Manso gave me, Manso, not the least glory of the Chalcidian shore, a wonderful work of art, and wonderful in himself. He had engraved them all around with a twin subject.

He proceeds to describe their content in some detail. It suffices, at this juncture, to summarize the depicted scenes: in the center of one is the phoenix, unique, gloriously plumed in cerulean blue, gleaming with radiance as it looks round at the dawn rising from the sea's glassy waves (185–189).[55] On the other is a representation of Love, equipped with

---

on the name "Adriana" that peppers the volume (see *Il Teatro*, 31, 44, 59, 219, 224, and 240). See also 5.

[52] Milton, *Epitaphium Damonis* 181–183.

[53] As attested by Jacopo Gaddi, for which see 10.

[54] Charles Diodati died while Milton was abroad. He was buried in London on 27 August 1638. See Parish Register, St. Anne, Blackfriars, London.

[55] For further discussion, see 68–75.

quivers painted in cloud, armed with flashing weapons, torches, and arrows colored with bronze. But this is a Love who does not target trivial spirits or the ignoble hearts of ordinary people, but one who discharges his weapons upward through the spheres and inflames the sacred minds and forms of the gods (190–197).[56]

The ekphrastic description of cups in pastoral has a rich and varied tradition, ranging from Theocritus[57] and Virgil[58] to such Italian poets as Gangiorgio Trissino[59] and Luigi Alamanni,[60] both of whom had likewise employed the device in the context of a bucolic threnody. Milton's lines, however, have a more immediate import. Critical interpretations of the *pocula ... bina* are certainly not lacking. Keightley regarded them as affording Milton "an occasion ... for vying with Theocritus and Virgil."[61] Other editors believed that they were actual cups or goblets. For Masson, they constituted "an actual pair of cups or chased goblets."[62] According to Jerram, "[b]oth the singularity of the subjects chosen and the minuteness of each point in the picture render it almost impossible to suppose that we have here a mere invention of the poet, and not an actual thing described."[63] MacKellar glossed the lines as "the description of an actual pair of cups which Manso gave Milton," speculating that "[p]ossibly, since Manso was a man of literary taste, the passages from Theocritus and Virgil ... may have prompted the gift."[64] Crucially, Michele De Filippis, developing a suggestion first posited by John Black,[65] presented a convincing argument that the cups are equatable with Manso's dialogues on Platonic love in the *Erocallia* (1628) and his

---

[56] For further discussion, see 42–45.

[57] Theocritus, *Idyll* 1. 29–56.

[58] Virgil, *Eclogue* 3.36–48. As noted by MacKellar, "[t]here is nothing in Milton's description of the cups that is borrowed from Theocritus and Virgil." See *The Latin Poems of John Milton*, ed. MacKellar, 349.

[59] Giangiorgio Trissino, *Eclogue* (on the death of Cesare Trivulzio).

[60] Luigi Alamanni, *Eclogue* 1 (on the death of Cosimino Ruccelai).

[61] See *The Poems of John Milton*, ed. Keightley, II, 463–464.

[62] See Masson, *Life*, II, 92: "I have no doubt that the whole of this passage is a poetical description of the designs on an actual pair of cups or chased goblets which Milton had received as a keepsake from Manso at Naples, and had brought home with him ... Where are they now?"

[63] See C. S. Jerram, *The Lycidas and Epitaphium Damonis of Milton* (London: Longman, 1874), 122.

[64] See *The Latin Poems of John Milton*, ed. MacKellar, 349.

[65] John Black, *Life of Torquato Tasso with An Historical and Critical Account of His Writings*, 2 vols. (Edinburgh: John Murray, 1810), II, 467.

Italian rendering of Claudian's *Phoenix* in the *Poesie Nomiche* (1635).[66] Despite Condee's remark that "the question may be as insoluble as that of the two-handed engine,"[67] and Catherine Gimelli Martin's more recent misinterpretation of the *pocula ... bina* as "two Tassonian 'cups,' no doubt volumes of Tasso's works,"[68] De Filippis's argument is now universally accepted among Milton scholars.[69] Less frequently observed is a further corroboratory fact, namely, that elsewhere in *Epitaphium Damonis* pastoral objects (*fiscellae calathique et cerea vincla cicutae* [135] ["baskets, bowls, and pipes with waxen fastenings"]) are similarly employed in an allegorical sense to describe what are in all likelihood material texts presented as gifts (*munera* [134]) to Milton: the encomia (in Italian verse) by Antonio Francini, and (in Latin prose) by Carlo Dati, composed by the two Florentine academicians in Milton's honor, and subsequently prefixed (along with three other such tributes) to the 1645 *Poemata*.[70]

Milton certainly held Manso's gifts in high esteem. This is indicated by the language of wonderment used to describe and, indeed, to align the material object (*mirum artis opus* [183] ["a wonderful work of art"]) and its creator (*mirandus et ipse* [183] ["wonderful in himself"]). Such an alignment of the artist and his art, as Philip Hardie interestingly observes, "anticipates Milton's famous prescription for himself" in *Apology for Smectymnuus*:[71]

> And long it was not after, when I was confirm'd in this opinion,
> that he who would not be frustrate of his hope to write well

---

[66] See De Filippis, "Milton and Manso: Cups or Books?" cited at 10.

[67] See Ralph W. Condee, "The Structure of Milton's 'Epitaphium Damonis,'" *SP* 62 (1965): 577–594, at 592.

[68] Catherine Gimelli Martin, *Milton's Italy: Anglo-Italian Literature, Travel, and Religion in Seventeenth-Century England* (New York: Routledge, 2017), 70. Martin seems unaware of De Filippis's study (it is not cited in her bibliography).

[69] See Lewalski and Haan, 498. Cf. Philip Hardie, who regards the *pocula* as "two works by Manso: firstly the *Poesie Nomiche* ... and secondly, the *Erocallia*," adding in a note: "The crucial identification with Manso's works was made by De Filippis 1936." See Hardie, "Milton's *Epitaphium Damonis* and the Virgilian Career," 93.

[70] See *Poemata*, 5–10; Lewalski and Haan, 108–115. Contrast Masson, *Life*, II, 90, who interprets the phrase as "poetical names for little presents actually received from his Florentine friends." Cf. also *John Milton: Poetical Works*, ed. Masson, III, 541: "I do not doubt ... that Milton had actually received little gifts, or tokens of remembrance, from his Florentine friends, and that, to be in pastoral keeping, he names these '*fiscellae, calathique, et cerea vincla cicutae*.'"

[71] Philip Hardie, *Rumour and Renown: Representations of Fama in Western Literature* (Cambridge: Cambridge University Press, 2012), 567.

hereafter in laudable things, ought him selfe to bee a true Poem, that is, a composition, and patterne of the best and honourablest things.[72]

Manso is also extolled as "not the least glory of the Chalcidian shore" (*Mansus, Chalcidicae non ultima gloria ripae* [182]).[73] That the gifts were indeed the work of Manso himself is suggested by *caelaverat* (184),[74] implying the Neapolitan's agency. That they were, in a sense, a matching pair is suggested by *gemino ... argumento* (184).[75] The phrase may well reflect the fact that, in the words of Cedric Brown, "[t]he two scenes are paired in subject,"[76] but it may also signal a Miltonic acknowledgment of the works' shared structural and thematic progression from the earthly to the celestial, from corporeal love and beauty to their heavenly equivalents. That Milton, as he composed *Mansus*, was probably in possession of the two volumes, personally gifted to him (*mihi ... dedit* [*Ep. Dam.* 181–183]) by their author, is suggested by the fact that, as the Headnote to *Mansus* makes clear, it was only just shortly in advance of his departure from Naples, hence probably

---

[72] Milton, *An Apology Against a Pamphlet Call'd A Modest Confutation of the Animadversions Upon the Remonstrant Against Smectymnuus* (London: John Rothwell, 1642), 16.

[73] In light of such glowing praise and, especially, of the imaginative reconfiguration of Manso's book-gifts in the *Epitaphium Damonis*, Milton, as Cedric Brown suggests, may have subsequently sent the Neapolitan one of the separately printed copies of the poem (see Cedric C. Brown, *Friendship and Its Discourses in the Seventeenth Century* [Oxford: Oxford University Press, 2016], 86). That he did so to the Florentine Carlo Dati is attested by *Epistola Familiaris* 10 (21 April 1647), for which see *John Milton, Epistolarum Familiarium Liber Unus and Uncollected Letters*, ed. Haan, 170–171, 178–179. A seemingly unique copy of this previously unknown, anonymous, and undated printing, extant in the British Library as C57.d.48, was discovered by Leicester Bradner, and dated by him to "probably 1640." See Leicester Bradner, "Milton's *Epitaphium Damonis*," *TLS* (18 August 1932): 581. Harris Fletcher, however, upon examination of the poem's type and format, suggested as late a date as 1646 (see H. F. Fletcher, "The Seventeenth-Century Separate Printing of Milton's *Epitaphium Damonis*," *JEGP* 61 [1962]: 788–796). In reply to Fletcher, John Shawcross suggested either 1639 or 1640 on the grounds that the printer seems to be that of *A Maske* (1637) (see J. T. Shawcross, "The Date of the Separate Edition of Milton's *Epitaphium Damonis*," *SB* 18 [1965]: 262–265). The date of Milton's letter to Dati may lend support to Fletcher's 1646 dating. Parker, *Biography*, ed. Campbell, II, 822, states that "[t]here are almost certainly presentation copies of this anonymous work to be found in Italian libraries."

[74] As noted by Black, *Life of Torquato Tasso*, II, 467.

[75] Cf. Ovid, *Metamorphoses* 13.684: *longo caelaverat argumento*. As noted by Bush, *Variorum*, I, 319 "[t]he scenes on Ovid's cup (685–701) do not resemble Milton's."

[76] Brown, *Friendship and Its Discourses*, 82.

in the final days of his Neapolitan sojourn, that he "sent" that (completed) poem to Manso.[77] In all of this, the *Erocallia* and *Poesie Nomiche* certainly merit fresh scrutiny both in their own right, and in regard to their potential status as two among many intertexts with which Milton's poem seems to engage.

---

[77] Headnote to *Mansus*: *Ad hunc itaque hospes ille antequam ab ea urbe discederet, ut ne ingratum se ostenderet, hoc carmen misit* ("In consequence, that guest, before his departure from that city, sent him this poem in order that he might not appear ungrateful"). See *Poemata*, 72; Lewalski and Haan, 204–205.

Chapter 2

"Forms" of Beauty:
Milton and the *Erocallia*

Of the two volumes gifted to Milton by Manso, the first, in terms of their printing chronology, was the *Erocallia Overo dell' Amore e della Bellezza Dialoghi XII*, which had seen publication in Venice in 1628.[1] Injudiciously dismissed by De Filippis as "a pyramidal monument of tediousness,"[2] this albeit copious work (running to some 1,054 pages) offers a masterfully crafted and scrupulously documented exegesis of its subject. Carefully reworking and amplifying ideas previously articulated by Manso in his youthful *I Paradossi* (1608),[3] the whole is enhanced by the sheer extent of authorities cited therein, ranging from the biblical to the classical and the contemporary, and by the particular richness of its paratextual materials.[4] In this respect it preempts to some degree the exhaustive methodology of Manso's later voluminous, *Enciclopedia*, a

---

[1] See 10.

[2] De Filippis, "Milton and Manso," 753.

[3] Giovanni Battista Manso, *I Paradossi overo D'Amore Dialoghi* (Milan: Girolamo Bordoni, 1608). This edition of the work, according to a letter addressed to Manso (purportedly by Marino) and prefixed to the *Erocallia* (sig. a2^r–b2^v, at sig. a2^v–a3^r), was a pirated volume, based on a lost manuscript rediscovered at the bottom of a river. The validity of this claim was convincingly questioned by Thomas Denman in "Giovan Battista Manso and the Politics of Publishing *I Paradossi* (1608) and *Erocallia* (1628)," a paper delivered at the 60th Annual Meeting of the Renaissance Society of America in New York on 27–29 March 2014. On the relationship between the two works, see Riga, *Giovan Battista Manso*, 109–119.

[4] These include prefatory letters from Manso to King Philip IV of Spain (sig. *2^r–*8^r), and from Marino to Manso (sig. a2^r–b2^v), an "Argomento" of the work as a whole (sig. b3^r–b4^v), and individual "Argomenti" prefixed to each book, all probably composed by Marino himself. See Lorenzo Geri, "La Funzione del Paratesto negli *Erocallia* (1628) di Giovan Battista Manso," *Linguistica e Letteratura* 32 (2007): 61–77. It should be remarked, however, that Marino's authorship of the letter and of the "argomenti" cannot be validated for certain, given the poor state of the poet's health during his final days. See Thomas Denman, "A Gift Text of Hispano-Neapolitan Diplomacy: Giovan Battista Manso's *Erocallia* (1628)," *History of European Ideas* 42 (2016): 683–693, at 686.

work that failed to see publication during his lifetime.[5] Dedicated to King Philip IV of Spain, the *Erocallia* certainly epitomizes, in the words of Thomas Denman, "experimental diplomatic gift-giving"[6] between Italy and Spain. For its English recipient, too, the volume, one can imagine, constituted a gift of immense value, an Italian work, which, like the *Poesie Nomiche*, assumed a material pride of place alongside Latin encomiastic verse exchanged between a Neapolitan host and his guest.

As denoted by the title's Italianized coinage of the Greek noun ἔρος ("Love") and the adjective καλός ("beautiful"), Manso's twelve dialogues take as their subject love and beauty in their many forms. Divided into three "Quaderni," each of which comprises four subsections, they examine these concepts as manifested on a terrestrial and a celestial level.[7] The volume's first "Quaderno" is devoted entirely to love, which is scrutinized in regard to its precise definition (Dialogue I),[8] the reasons by which it is occasioned (Dialogue II),[9] its material causes (Dialogue III),[10] and its ultimate purpose (Dialogue IV).[11] Thus, as observed by one of the interlocutors of Dialogue I, none other than Tasso (here characterized by his forename "Torquato"), *love* can at times denote Cupid, the winged, blind god of classical mythology, son of Venus and Jupiter, most handsome, and traditionally "armato di facella, d'arco, e di faretra" ("armed with a torch, bow, and quiver").[12] But it can also possess resonances that are both Platonic and Pythagorean, encapsulating the

---

[5] This incomplete and still unpublished work is extant in the BNN as MS XIII. F.63. See Michele de Filippis, "G. B. Manso's *Enciclopedia*," *UCPMP* 20 (1937): 239–288; Carmela Lombardi, *Enciclopedia e Letturatura: Retorica, Politica e Critica della Letturatura in Una Enciclopedia del Primo Seicento* (Arezzo: Mediateca del Barocco, 1993).

[6] Denman, "A Gift Text of Hispano-Neapolitan Diplomacy," 684.

[7] With Manso's exploration of the ascending gradations of love and beauty, cf. Sonnets II–IV of his "Rime Amorose," at *Poesie Nomiche*, 4–6. These are entitled, respectively: "Amor Sensuale generato dalla Bellezza corporale della S.D.," "Amor Humano prodotto dalla bellezza dell'animo della S.D.," "Amor Divino destato dalla bellezza sopranaturale della S.D." See also 65.

[8] See "Dialogo Primo," entitled "Il Gesualdo, Overo della Cagion Formale dell'Amore: ove la sua perfetta diffinitione s'esamina," at *Erocallia*, 1–128.

[9] See "Dialogo Secondo," entitled "Il Loffredo, Overo della Cagion Facitrice dell'Amore," at *Erocallia*, 131–220.

[10] See "Dialogo Terzo," entitled "Il Capece, Overo della Cagion Materiale dell'Amore," at *Erocallia*, 225–338.

[11] See "Dialogo Quarto," entitled "Il Bisaccio, Overo della Cagion Finale dell'Amore," *Erocallia*, 343–400.

[12] *Erocallia*, 25.

aspiration of those in search of a heavenly ideal. For the Torquato of Dialogue IV, the most perfect, the most noble, and the most assured end of love is the unification of the soul with God, now reborn and forever immortalized in the human self.[13] It is the perfection of this celestial love, a perfection, which is itself derived from an alignment with the supernatural, that transcends natural forces.[14] In short, it constitutes "una imagine, un raggio, un'ombra di quell'eterno, e Celestiale, che colà sù riluce, & infiamma, e godesi perfettamente" ("an image, a ray, a shadow of that eternal and celestial [love], which shines forth, inflames, and perfectly rejoices").[15] The second "Quarderno" is devoted to beauty ("bellezza"), which is likewise analyzed as both an earthly attribute and a celestial aspiration. At times it signifies the essentially human and corporeal: "la bellezza corporale dell'huomo" ("the corporeal beauty of man").[16] At others, it has an import that is spiritual ("la bellezza spiritale dell'anima ragionevole" ["the spiritual beauty of the reasonable soul"]),[17] intellectual ("la bellezza intellettuale delle sustanze astratte" ["the intellectual beauty of abstract substances"]),[18] and ultimately divine ("la bellezza divina" ["divine beauty"]).[19] In all of this, "bellezza corporale" is set against beauty as an "immortal Idea," the viewing of which enables the beholder to be enraptured by a dazzling luminosity.[20] That these last

---

[13] *Erocallia*, 385: "Mà il più perfetto, il più nobile, e'l più certo fine d'Amore è'l partorire, che l'anima fà di se medesima in Dio à lui rinascendo, & in lui medesimo immortalandosi" ("But the most perfect, and the most assured end of Love is the act of birth, which the soul makes of itself into God by being reborn and by immortalizing itself in him").

[14] Thus, at *Erocallia*, 994, Torquato states: "Ma ... la perfettion dell'amor celestiale trascende di gran lunga le forze naturali della ragione ... l'humana ragione riceva dal celestial' Amore maggior perfettione nell'essere sopranaturale, e divino" ("But ... the perfection of celestial love far transcends the natural forces of reason ... human reason receives from celestial Love greater perfection in its supernatural and divine essence").

[15] *Erocallia*, 1022.

[16] See "Dialogo Quinto," entitled "Il Capua Primo, Overo della Bellezza Corporale dell'Huomo," at *Erocallia*, 407–578.

[17] See "Dialogo Sesto," entitled "Il Capua Secondo. Della bellezza spiritale dell' anima ragionevole," at *Erocallia*, 583–656.

[18] See "Dialogo Settimo," entitled "Il Capua Terzo. Della bellezza intelletuale delle sustanze astratte," at *Erocallia*, 661–709.

[19] See "Dialogo Ottavo," entitled "Il Capua Quarto. Della bellezza Divina," at *Erocallia*, 713–808.

[20] *Erocallia*, 388: "Hor costui ch'alla contemplatione di questa immortal Idea volgerà lo sguardo in un punto si ritroverà rapito da gli splendori d'ardentissime luci" ("He

sentiments would have held a particular resonance for the recipient of the gift is evinced by rapturous comments made by Milton in a letter to Charles Diodati, written just over one year prior to his departure for Italy:

> Nam de cetero quidem quid de me statuerit Deus nescio: illud certe: δεινόν μοι ἔρωτα, εἴπέρ τω ἄλλω, τοῦ καλοῦ ἐνέσταξε. Nec tanto Ceres labore, ut in fabulis est, Liberam fertur quaesivisse filiam quanto ego hanc τοῦ καλοῦ ἰδέαν, veluti pulcherrimam quandam imaginem, per omnes rerum formas et facies (πολλαὶ γὰρ μορφαὶ τῶν Δαιμονίων) dies noctesque indagare soleo, et quasi certis quibusdam vestigiis ducentem sector.[21]

> As indeed for what else God has planned for me, that I do not know, but this I do for sure: "He has instilled into me, if into anyone, a vehement love of the beautiful." Not with so much effort is Ceres, so the fable relates, said to have searched for her daughter Proserpina, as it is my custom day and night to search out this "idea of the beautiful," as a certain most splendid image, through all the shapes and forms of things ("for many are the shapes of things Divine"), and to pursue it as it leads me along as if on some clearly-defined tracks.

The volume's final "Quaderno" explores four paradoxes associated with the moral consequences of love and beauty: (i) that the least beautiful women merit the greatest love,[22] (ii) that most women should love men who love them least,[23] (iii) that the sole instrument of love is love itself,[24] (iv) that true love resides only in the dead.[25] Rounding off the collection is Manso's "Del Dialogo Trattato,"[26] a self-conscious interrogation of dialogistic methodology.

---

who turns his gaze to the contemplation of this immortal Idea will find himself in a single instant enraptured by the splendors of most ardent lights").

[21] Milton, *Epistola Familiaris* 7, dated 23 September 1637. See *John Milton: Epistolarum Familiarium and Uncollected Letters*, ed. Haan, 100–115, at 104–105.

[22] See "Paradosso Primo: Dialogo Nono," entitled "Il Belprato, Overo che si debbano amar più le men belle Donne," at *Erocallia*, 811–862.

[23] See "Paradosso Secondo: Dialogo Decimo," entitled "L'Orsino, Overo che le Donne debbono amar più, chi meno le ama," at *Erocallia*, 863–896.

[24] See "Paradosso Terzo: Dialogo XI," entitled, "Il Noia, Overo che l'Amor solo sia lo stormento dell'Amore," at *Erocallia*, 897–938.

[25] See "Paradosso Quarto: Dialogo XII," entitled "Lo Spinelli, Overo che non sia vero Amore, se non solamente ne' morti," at *Erocallia*, 939–1032.

[26] See "Del Dialogo Trattato del Marchese della Villa," at *Erocallia*, 1033–1064, for discussion of which, see 155–159.

Manso's crucial differentiation in the *Erocallia* between two types of love rears its head, quite literally, in the ekphrastic description at *Epitaphium Damonis* 190–197, lines which seem to evince a Miltonic acknowledgement of the work's structure and methodology:

> Parte alia polus omnipatens et magnus Olympus:
> Quis putet? Hic quoque Amor pictaeque in nube pharetrae,
> Arma corusca, faces, et spicula tincta pyropo;
> Nec tenues animas pectusque ignobile vulgi
> Hinc ferit, at circum flammantia lumina torquens,
> Semper in erectum spargit sua tela per orbes
> Impiger, et pronos nunquam collimat ad ictus;
> Hinc mentes ardere sacrae formaeque deorum.
> (*Epitaphium Damonis* 190–197)

> In another section is the boundless sky and great Olympus. Who would believe it? Here too is Love and his quivers painted in cloud, his flashing weapons, torches, and arrows colored with bronze. Nor is it trivial spirits or the ignoble hearts of ordinary people that he strikes from this position; instead, rotating his flaming eyes all about, he always discharges his weapons with energy in an upward direction through the spheres, never aiming his shots downwards. As a consequence, sacred minds and the forms of the gods are aflame.

Here Love is initially presented as Cupid, the mythological figure, equipped with his *pharetra* ("quiver" [191]) and customary weapons. But the focus of his aim moves beyond that of the terrestrial to embrace a celestial target. For this Love is a force motivated by an energy (*impiger* [196], itself a subtle nod perhaps to the Oziosi motto: *Non Pigra Quies*),[27] which enables him forever to shoot his arrows upwards (*in erectum* [195]) through the spheres (a point reinforced by *pronos nunquam ... ad ictus* [196] ["never aiming his shots downwards"]). His action has an import that is essentially divine: the kindling of the minds (*mentes* [197]) and the forms (*formae* [197]) of the gods themselves. These last two nouns may draw the attention of the discerning reader to Manso's Latin tribute composed in Milton's honor.

---

[27] See 85.

2.1   Manso to Milton: *Forma* and *Decor*

Ioannes Baptista Mansus,
Marchio Villensis Neapolitanus
ad Ioannem Miltonium Anglum

Ut *mens, forma*, decor, facies, mos, si pietas sic,
  Non Anglus verum hercle Angelus ipse fores.[28]

Giovanni Battista Manso,
Marquis of Villa, Neapolitan
to John Milton, Englishman

If your religion were as your *mind, beauty,* comeliness, appearance, character, you would be not an Angle, but, by Hercules, a very angel.

Thus proclaimed Manso in an encomium presented to his English guest during the course of his Neapolitan sojourn. Both the distich and *Mansus* itself merit fresh consideration in the precise context of the *Erocallia*. William Poole has offered the interesting speculation that Milton may have possessed a now lost *album amicorum*, in which his Italian acquaintances were invited to write their tributes.[29] It is equally possible that some of those encomia were inscribed upon volumes, either now lost or still undiscovered, that were presented to him by their authors. If Manso did indeed write his tribute in the gifted *Erocallia*, its terms of praise in general, and its choice of language in particular, would have possessed additional potency. The distich, irrespective of where it was actually inscribed, seems to have made a lasting impression upon its recipient. It would assume pride of place among the "written Encomiums"[30] prefixed to Milton's 1645 *Poemata*, placed, as it is, out of geographical and chronological order. Manso was, of course, the most distinguished of Milton's encomiasts, but his Latin tribute conveniently suited Milton's revisionist self-fashioning before an English audience in 1645 as an ardent Protestant while upon Italian soil.

---

[28] Milton, *Poemata*, 4; Lewalski and Haan, 106–107. Emphasis is mine.

[29] William Poole, *Milton and the Making of Paradise Lost* (Cambridge, MA: Harvard University Press, 2017), 46.

[30] The phrase is Milton's. See *The Reason of Church-Government*, 37: "But much latelier in the privat Academies of Italy … other things which I had shifted in scarsity of books and conveniences to patch up amongst them, were receiv'd with written Encomiums, which the Italian is not forward to bestow on men of this side the Alps."

Manso's epigram turns on its climactic pun (on Milton, the *Anglus*[31] and Milton, the potential *Angelus*), and its associated evocation of Bede's account of a joke made by Gregory the Great, upon seeing pagan young boys, who had been brought to Rome for sale:

> Rursus ergo interrogavit, quod esset vocabulum gentis illius. Responsum est quod Angli vocarentur. At ille: "Bene" inquit; "nam et angelicam habent faciem, et tales angelorum in caelis decet esse coheredes."[32]

---

[31] Milton's Englishness is likewise signaled by his other Italian encomiasts. In fact, in all but one of the titles of the five *testimonia* prefixed to the 1645 *Poemata*, he is addressed as either *Anglus* (*Ad Ioannem Miltonium Anglum* [Manso], *Ad Ioannem Miltonem Anglum* [Salzilli] [see *Poemata*, 4; Lewalski and Haan, 106–107]), "Inglese" ("Al Signor Gio. Miltoni Nobile Inglese" [Francini] [see *Poemata*, 5; Lewalski and Haan, 108–109]), or *Londiniensis* (*Ioanni Miltoni Londiniensi* [Dati] [see *Poemata*, 10; Lewalski and Haan, 114–115]). And even in the single instance where his Englishness is not highlighted in the actual title (David Codner, a.k.a. Matteo Selvaggio), *Anglia* herself becomes the focus of the distich proper (see *Poemata*, 4; Lewalski and Haan, 108–109, and, for the identification of Selvaggio as Codner, Chaney, *The Grand Tour and the Great Rebellion*, 244–251). This highlighting of national identity through the "gaze of international witnesses," as Paul Stevens puts it, seems to have left no slight an impression upon Milton. Thus, it was only during his return journey from Italy (on 10 June 1639), and in Camillo Cerdogni's *album amicorum* in Geneva, that he would initiate the practice of signing himself *Joannes Miltonius Anglus* (further discussed at 54). See Paul Stevens, "Archipelagic Criticism and Its Limits: Milton, Geoffrey of Monmouth, and the Matter of England," *The European Legacy* 17 (2012): 151–164, at 162. For useful assessments of Milton's sense of Englishness, see, among others, Thomas N. Corns, "Milton and the Limitations of Englishness," in *Early Modern Nationalism and Milton's England*, eds. David Loewenstein and Paul Stevens (Toronto: University of Toronto Press, 2008), 205–216; Paul Stevens, "Milton and National Identity," in *The Oxford Handbook of Milton*, eds. Nicholas McDowell and Nigel Smith (Oxford: Oxford University Press, 2009), 342–363.

[32] Bede, *Historia Ecclesiastica*, II.1. Text is that of *Bede's Ecclesiastical History*, eds. Bertram Colgrave and R. A. B. Mynors (Oxford: Clarendon Press, 1969), 132–134. Manso may have come across the joke in its original form in one of the editions of the *Historia Ecclesiastica* published in Strasbourg (1475), Antwerp (1550), and Paris (1587) (for his knowledge of Bede, cf. his citation of Bede's *Commentarius in Genesim*, at *I Paradossi*, 17: "*e Beda*, ferebatur *excellentia potestatis*," when discussing authorities for the agency of the spirit of love in the creation of the world). Alternatively, given Manso's hagiographical interests, attested by his *Vita, Virtù, e Miracoli Principali di S. Patricia Vergine* (1611), on which see 23, he may have encountered it in Gabriel Fiamma's virtually verbatim rendering in Italian in "La Vita di San Gregorio Magno Primo Papa di Questo Nome," in his *Le Vite de' Santi*, 4 vols. (Venice: Domenico Farri, 1602), II, Bk. 3, sig. 48^r–64^r, at sig. 49^r: "Tornò a domandare come si chiamavano que' popoli. Fù risposto Angli: che Latinamente si parlava allhora. Et Gregorio. Bene Angli, quasi Angeli, che hanno Angelici volti: &

And so he asked again what was the name of that people. The answer given was that they were called "Angles." But he said "Well are they so called, for they too possess an 'angelic' appearance and it is fitting that such are co-heirs of the angels in heaven."

Although this aspect of the distich has received the due attention of scholars,[33] in other respects the tribute as a whole has been noted largely for what it seemingly omits to mention: Milton's poetry. Thus, according to Parker, it is a "distich of qualified admiration,"[34] an opinion followed by Anthony Low.[35] Parker proceeds to observe that by comparison with the other four encomia composed by Milton's Italian acquaintances, it "alone makes no mention of verse," speculating that "Milton had perhaps not yet presented himself to the Neapolitan as a poet."[36] Likewise, Lewalski remarks: "Manso's epigram for Milton did not honor him as a poet."[37] In consequence, scholars have typically viewed *Mansus* as a Miltonic attempt to assert and to prove a poetic prowess hitherto

---

tali debbono essere i cittadini del Cielo" ("He returned to asking what those people were called. The response was: 'Angli,' as spoken in the Latin of that time. And Gregory said: 'Well are they termed "Angli" as though "Angeli," for they possess the countenances of Angels, and such must be the citizens of Heaven'"). Milton, citing Bede, would later summarize the episode in *The History of Britain* (London: James Allestry, 1670), 137–138: "it was answer'd by som who stood by, that they were Angli of the Province Deira, subjects to Alla King of Northumberland, and by Religion Pagans. Which last Gregory deploring, fram'd on a sudden this allusion to the three names he heard; that the Angli so like to Angels should be snatch't de ira, that is, from the wrath of God, to sing Haleluia." As noted by Poole, *The Complete Works of John Milton: Volume XI*, 136, Milton probably read Bede's *Historia Ecclesiastica* in *Rerum Britannicarum, id est Angliae, Scotiae, Vicinarumque Insularum ac Regionum Scriptores Vetustiores ac Praecipui* (Heidelberg: Commelinus, 1587), 147–280 (for the present passage, see ibid., 176), a collection that also includes texts of Geoffrey of Monmouth and Gildas (Milton accurately cites Gildas by page reference to this edition at *Commonplace Book*, 195 [ed. Poole, 255]). See also 138–139.

[33] See, among others, Anthony Low, "*Mansus*: In Its Context," *MS* 19 (1984): 105–126, at 106–109; Haan, *From Academia to Amicitia*, 130–136; Thomas Roebuck, "Milton and the Confessionalization of Antiquarianism," in *Young Milton*, ed. Jones, 48–71, at 50–52.

[34] Parker, *Milton: A Biography*, ed. Campbell, II, 827.

[35] Low, "*Mansus*: In Its Context," 106. At 108 he describes it as "a backhanded compliment."

[36] Parker, *Milton: A Biography*, ed. Campbell, II, 827.

[37] Lewalski, *Life*, 112.

unrecognized by the Neapolitan.[38] But this argument from a seeming silence can be countered, at least in part, by the fact that Manso explicitly praises Milton's *mens*, an umbrella term, whose meaning can embrace both "[t]he seat or organ of intellectual activities, the mind"[39] and "the instrument or seat of memory."[40] This last attribute won the praise of Milton's Florentine encomiasts. Thus Antonio Francini proclaimed: "Che s'opre degne di Poema o storia/Furon già, l'hai presenti alla memoria" ("For if ever deeds have been worthy of a poem or of history, you have them present in your memory").[41] Similarly, in Carlo Dati's eyes, Milton was one *cui in memoria totus orbis* ("in whose memory is the whole world").[42] That Milton performed his Latin poems from memory in the Italian academies is attested by his description of them as "some trifles which I had in memory" in *The Reason of Church-Government*.[43]

There is, however, another way in which Manso's distich does indeed stand apart from its sister tributes, namely, its sustained focus upon Milton's physical beauty.[44] Of course, this might be explained, at least in part, by the fact that Gregory's joke had been elicited by his acknowledgment of the handsome appearance of the newly arrived *pueri*:[45] their fair-skinned bodies (*candidi corporis*), their charming countenances (*venusti vultus*), and their beautiful hair (*capillorum ... forma egregia*).[46] Still, Manso's description of Miltonic beauty (*forma*,

---

[38] Thus Parker, *Milton: A Biography*, ed. Campbell, I, 175: "His lengthy (100 hexameters) and self-conscious *Mansus* was an effort, probably successful, to show the friend of Tasso and Marini [*sic*] that England, too, was productive of noble verse." Cf. Lewalski, *Life*, 112.

[39] See *OLD*, s.v. 1.

[40] See *OLD*, s.v. 4b.

[41] Antonio Francini, at *Poemata* 8; Lewalski and Haan, 112–113.

[42] Carlo Dati, at *Poemata*, 10; Lewalski and Haan, 114–115.

[43] Milton, *The Reason of Church-Government*, 37.

[44] The only other encomiast to mention physical beauty is Carlo Dati, who refers to Milton's *animi dotes corporisque* ("qualities of mind and of body") at *Poemata*, 10; Lewalski and Haan, 114–115.

[45] Andreas Lemke interestingly suggests that "Bede's use of the term *pueros* in the case of the Anglian boys may ... connote an inherent uncorrupt and naïve readiness to adopt the pure faith in God, untainted by doubt or false (unorthodox) interpretation." See Andreas Lemke, "Children and the Conversion of the Anglo-Saxons in Bede's *Historia Ecclesiastica Gentis Anglorum*," in *Childhood and Adolescence in Anglo-Saxon Literary Culture*, eds. Susan Irvine and Winfried Rudolf (Toronto: University of Toronto Press, 2018), 120–138, at 128.

[46] *Bede's Ecclesiastical History*, eds. Colgrave and Mynors, 132: *pueros venales positos candidi corporis ac venusti vultus, capillorum quoque forma egregia* ("There

decor, facies), when read in the specific context of the *Erocallia*, seems to encapsulate and indeed to epitomize that aforementioned "bellezza corporale dell'huomo" ("corporeal beauty of [a] man"), the subject of the volume's fifth Dialogue.[47] The choice of terminology, moreover, may draw upon Latin verses cited therein. Discussing the correlation between grace and beauty, Manso cites the opening lines of a Latin epigram by "one of our own who spoke in Latin" ("fra' nostrali che favellarono Latinamente"),[48] none other than Nicolò Franco. The poem in question is the first of a *centuria epigrammatum*, a collection of one hundred florid encomia composed by Franco in honor of Isabella of Capua, wife of Ferrante I Gonzaga. The work had seen publication in Naples in 1535 under the title *Hisabella*.[49] Introducing his citation of the first six verses of the ten-line poem,[50] Manso praises their author as one who "con maraviglioso artificio fè paragone frà la gratia, la bellezza, e la maestà donnesca in quei versi" ("with marvelous artifice made a comparison between grace, beauty, and womanly majesty in the following verses"):

> Bella Hisabella, magis cum te contemplor aperte,
> Te magis exornat gratia, *forma, decor*.[51]

> Beautiful Isabella, the more I openly contemplate you,
> the more do grace, *beauty, comeliness* adorn you.

That authorial artifice admired by Manso, and already evident in the opening wordplay on "bella" and "Hisabella," comes to the fore in the epigram's subsequent explication of the beauty that is both literally and linguistically inherent in its praised subject. It does so by expanding the nouns *gratia, forma,* and *decor* into qualities now presented on an

---

had been put up for sale boys possessed of fair-skinned bodies and charming countenances and also exceptionally beautiful hair"). Cf. Paulus Diaconus, *Sancti Gregorii Magni Vita*, in *Patrologia Latina Cursus Completus. Series Latina*, ed. J-P. Migne, 221 vols. (Paris: Garnier Frères, 1844–1864), LXXV, 42–60, at 50: *pueros venales positos lactei corporis ac venusti vultus, capillos quoque praecipui candoris habentes* ("There had been put up for sale boys possessed of milk-white bodies and charming countenances and also of hair of exceptional beauty"); Milton, *The History of Britain*, 137: "two comly youths were brought to Rome, whose fair and honest countenances ... ." For further discussion of this aspect, see Haan, *From Academia to Amicitia*, 132–133.

[47] *Erocallia*, 407–578.

[48] *Erocallia*, 537.

[49] Nicolò Franco, *Hisabella* (Naples: Giovanni Sultzbach and Mattia Cancer, 1535).

[50] For the full version of the epigram in question, see *Hisabella*, sig. A^r.

[51] *Erocallia*, 537. Emphasis is mine.

ascending scale in terms of their potency: *Gratia te gratam, formosam, forma, decoram/te decor ipse facit* ("attractiveness makes you attractive, beauty makes you beautiful, comeliness makes you comely").[52] Manso's encomium of Milton, it could be argued, linguistically echoes Franco's juxtaposition of *forma* and *decor*, while his addition of a further noun (*facies*) may punningly evoke the verb *facere* of the climactic *decor ipse facit*. His sequential nouns *decor, forma, facies*, moreover, may also rework *decor, forma, species*, the final three words of the last line of Franco's epigram (a line that Manso does not quote in the *Erocallia*).[53] It is worth remarking, too, that the identical six lines from Franco's poem are included by Francesco De Pietri in his summary (published in 1642) of topics discussed by Manso's Accademia degli Oziosi in the course of the previous thirty years. Once again, the context is that of an academic debate on the relative merits of beauty and of grace.[54] Having quoted the lines, De Pietri concludes: "Ove habbiamo la bellezza, la gratia, e'l decoro, il qual ne dinota la dignità, e la maestà della persona" ("Whence we regard beauty, grace, and comeliness as that which denotes the dignity and majesty of the person").[55]

The possible intertextual relationship between the two epigrams raises some interesting questions in regard to Manso's self-portraiture, and his view of his praised subject. Hitherto, and largely on account of his recourse to the *Anglus/Angelus* pun, Manso has been viewed as assuming the upper hand, adopting an essentially Catholic stance via a joke, which, although intrinsically good-humored, has been seen to occur solely at the expense of the so-called "pagan" Milton. Low comments: "Manso is analogous to Gregory, perhaps the greatest churchman since Peter himself,"[56] while Poole remarks: "Manso's testimonial ... turned on a slight dig at Milton's membership of a heretic church."[57] But even that

---

[52] *Erocallia*, 537–538.

[53] *Hisabella*, sig. Ai^r: *Tu non formosa es tandem, non ipsa decora,/Non speciosa, sed es forma, decor, species* (9–10) ("After all, you are not beautiful, not charming in yourself, but you constitute *beauty, comeliness, attractiveness*"). Emphasis is mine.

[54] See Francesco De Pietri, *I Problemi Accademici ... ove Le Più Famose Quistioni Proposte nell' Illustrissima Accademia de gli Otiosi di Napoli* (Naples: Francesco Savio, 1642), 89–91 ("Problema XXXII," entitled: "Qual sia maggiore, se la Bellezza, ò la Gratia" ["Which is greater: Beauty or Grace"]), at 89: "La Gratia è quella, che da Latini si dice *venustas, lepor, Gratia*, sicome Nicolò Franco nella sua Isabella" ("Grace is that which the Latins term *venustas, lepor, Gratia*, as does Nicolò Franco in his *Hisabella*").

[55] De Pietri, *I Problemi Accademici*, 89.

[56] Low, "*Mansus*: In Its Context," 107.

[57] Poole, *Milton and the Making of Paradise Lost*, 45.

viewpoint is undercut to some degree by Manso's clever, even quasi-heretical, interpolation of the interjectory *hercle* ("by Hercules"), an exclamatory invocation of a pagan god, ironically issuing from papal or quasi-papal lips. Campbell and Corns come closer to the potential truth in their observation that "[t]he reservation about the misplaced piety of the Protestant Milton is gracefully subverted by the reworking of the phrase attributed to Gregory the Great."[58] It is an argument that might equally be applied to the distich's possible engagement with Franco. Although the "artificio" of Franco's Latin epigram had won Manso's praise as "maraviglioso," its author's character and reputation were highly unorthodox. Having undertaken his early studies in Naples, Franco became embroiled in an anti-papal libel as a consequence of writing an infamous pamphlet attacking Pope Pietro Carafa. Arrested, imprisoned, interrogated, and tortured, he was sentenced to death, and executed by hanging on 11 March 1570 in Ponte Sant' Angelo in Rome.[59] Manso's decision to quote from and praise one of Franco's Latin epigrams in the *Erocallia* (and possibly to echo that citation in his encomium of Milton) may thus initially serve to surprise. But Franco, an ardent admirer of Tasso, in homage to whom he had published in 1539 his *Dialoghi Piacevolissimi*,[60] had academic interests akin to those of Manso, having authored a *Dialogo delle Bellezze*, published in Venice in 1542,[61] a work that Manso may well have consulted. In any case, Manso was a Neapolitan humanist whose prestigious status enabled him, in the words of Sean Cocco, to "skirt the edges of orthodoxy,"[62] a point reinforced by his aforementioned connections with the heretical Dominican friar Tommaso Campanella.[63] Read in this context, his tribute to Milton reveals its author as an encomiast whose self-fashioning is perhaps both papal and good-humouredly anti-papal, the latter appropriately mirroring

---

[58] Campbell and Corns, *Life, Work, and Thought*, 121.

[59] On Franco, see, among others, Carlo Simiani, *La Vita e Le Opere di Nicolò Franco* (Turin: L. Roux, 1894); Giuseppe De Michele, "Nicolò Franco. Biografia con Documenti Inediti," *Studi di Letteratura Italiana* 11 (1915): 61–154; Franco Pignatti, "Franco, Nicolo," *DBI* 50 (1998): 202–206; Franco Pignatti, "Nicolò Franco a Roma 1558–1570," *Archivio della Società Romana di Storia Patria* 121 (1998): 118–166; Eleonora Impieri, "Nicolo Franco, Prosatore e Poeta Tra Innovazione e Tradizione" (PhD thesis, University of Pisa, 2012).

[60] Nicolò Franco, *Dialoghi Piacevolissimi* (Venice: Altobello Salicato, 1539).

[61] Nicolò Franco, *Dialogo ... Dove Si Ragiona delle Bellezze* (Venice: Antonio Gardane, 1542).

[62] Cocco, *Watching Vesuvius*, 53.

[63] See 11.

the implication of the "heretic church"[64] of Protestantism (ironically described as *pietas*) to which his addressee belongs, and which denies him a place among Catholic angels. At the same time, it implicitly (yet interestingly) aligns Milton with the feminine, with a lady noted in her lifetime for her exceptional beauty (*forma*), a recurring leitmotif of Franco's *centuria*.[65] Perhaps Manso recognized in Milton something of that lingering beauty that had earned him the soubriquet "The Lady of Christ's College" during his Cambridge years,[66] a fact about which he had reminded his audience in *Prolusio* VI:

> A quibusdam, audivi nuper "Domina." At cur videor illis parum masculus? Ecquis Prisciani pudor? Itane propria quae maribus femineo generi tribuunt insulsi?[67]
>
> Recently I have been called "Lady" by some people. But why do I seem insufficiently masculine to them? Have they any respect for Priscian? Do these witless people attribute to the female sex what is properly masculine?

It was through this identity that Milton, according to Michael Lieb, "became known to others and as a result of which he was made to struggle with the whole notion of femininity such a designation implied."[68] One senses, however, that he took no small pride in an appellation that ultimately aligned him with Virgil, who, according to Donatus, was traditionally nicknamed *Parthenias* ("maidenish"/ "virginal").[69] As such, it contributed in no small degree to what Nicholas

---

[64] See Poole, *Milton and the Making of Paradise Lost*, 45.

[65] See, for example, *Hisabella*, sig. Bi^v: *Forma tua excelsa est* ("your beauty is lofty"); sig. Biii^r: *Forma oculis, et forma ore, et tibi forma capillis,/Fronte tibi forma, et pectore forma nitet* ("resplendent is the beauty in your eyes, beauty in your face, beauty in your hair, beauty in your brow, and beauty in your breast"); sig. Fi^v: *Forma tua in terris miracula talia monstrat* ("your beauty reveals such miracles upon earth"); sig. Kii^r: *Infinita tuae crescunt spectacula formae* ("the infinite spectacles of your beauty increase").

[66] See David V. Urban, "The Lady of Christ's College, Himself A 'Lady Wise and Pure': Parabolic Self-Reference in John Milton's *Sonnet* IX," *MS* 47 (2008): 1–23.

[67] Text is that of "Milton's Salting," in *Milton's Cambridge Latin*, ed. Hale, 239–293, at 282.

[68] Michael Lieb, *Milton and the Culture of Violence* (Ithaca, NY: Cornell University Press, 1994), 86.

[69] *Donatus auctus*, 22: *tam probum fuisse constat, ut Neapoli "Parthenias" vulgo appellaretur* ("it is agreed that he was so upright in that he was commonly known as 'Parthenias' in Naples"). Text and numbering follow *Vitae Vergilianae Antiquae*, eds.

McDowell has aptly described as Milton's "self-mythologizing as an English Virgil," a practice that "appears to have been not merely retrospective, but on-going at least from his time at Cambridge."[70] Indeed, that Virgilian soubriquet (with its etymological link to Parthenope herself) may even have surfaced during the course of Milton's Italian journey. This is suggested by the homeward-bound poet's implicit identification of his peregrinations through Catholic Italy with those of the Lady through Comus's forest when, on 10 June 1639, he signed Camillo Cerdogni's *album amicorum* in Geneva with the closing lines of *A Maske*:

> ... if Vertue feeble were,
> Heav'n it selfe would stoop to her. [71]

It resurfaces later in Milton's defense of his chastity while upon Italian soil[72] in a carefully worded rebuttal of Pierre Du Moulin's charges of sexual libertinism.[73] Chastity, after all, was absolutely central to Manso's definition of "bellezza spirituale,"[74] and, not least, to Milton's ultimate self-fashioning in *Mansus* as someone possessed of a *mens pura ... atque ignea virtus* (96) ("purity of heart ... and fiery virtue"), a passport to heaven itself.

Giorgio Brugnoli and Fabio Stok (Rome: Istituto Poligrafico e Zecca dello Stato, 1997). See Fabio Stok, "Why Was Virgil Called 'Parthenias'?" *Giornale Italiano di Filologia* 69 (2017): 157–170.

[70] See Nicholas McDowell, *Poet of Revolution: The Making of John Milton* (Princeton, NJ: Princeton University Press, 2020), 158.

[71] Milton, *A Maske*, 1022–1023. The signature continues: *Coelum non animo muto dum trans mare curro/Joannes Miltonius/Anglus*. The autograph book is now held in the Houghton Library in Harvard (MS Sumner 84). Cf. *The Life Records of John Milton*, ed. J. M. French, 5 vols. (New Brunswick, NJ: Rutgers University Press, 1949–1958), I, 419. See Haan, "'Coelum non Animum Muto'?" 132–133; McDowell, *Poet of Revolution*, 334–336.

[72] See Milton, *Defensio Secunda*, 87: *me his omnibus in locis, ubi tam multa licent, ab omni flagitio ac probro integrum atque intactum vixisse* ("In all these regions, where so much license exists, I lived unimpaired and untouched by every form of sin or reproach").

[73] See Peter Du Moulin, *Regii Sanguinis Clamor ad Coelum Adversus Parricidas Anglicanos* (The Hague: Adrian Vlacq, 1652), 10.

[74] See, for example, *Erocallia*, 609: "con l'Honestà, con la Vergogna, con la Castità ne temperi ne gli atti carnali, e ne liberi da' loro danni" ("with Honesty, with Shame, with Chastity one tempers carnal acts, and frees them from their detriments").

2.2   Milton to Manso: Vernal Youthfulness

Milton certainly knew how to repay a compliment, and more. In *Mansus* he offers his addressee a miniature encomium within an encomium, so to speak, one that, like Manso's Latin distich, lauds both physical and intellectual prowess:

> Hinc longaeva tibi lento sub flore senectus
> Vernat, et Aesonios lucratur vivida fusos,
> Nondum deciduos servans tibi frontis honores,
> Ingeniumque vigens, et adultum mentis acumen.
> (*Mansus* 74–77)

> Hence your lengthy old age is Spring-like beneath a lingering blossom, and, in its vigor, enjoys the profits of Aeson's spindles, preserving the glories of your brow not yet fallen, your intellect flourishing, and the sharpness of your mind mature.

Here it is Milton who seems to assume that pseudo-Gregorian stance, but now papal admiration of the pagan boys' *capillorum forma egregia* has been transformed into praise of Manso's own locks. Or perhaps not quite his own? The lines may jokingly allude to the Neapolitan's habit of wearing a wig to conceal his baldness. This he used to remove in a good-humored fashion and cast to the ground in the course of meetings of the Society of the Blessed Virgin, no less. Or, in the words of Giovanni Vittorio Rossi (pseud. Janus Nicius Erythraeus):

> Neque minus dicto audiens esse, si imperaretur caliendrum e capite, quo calvitiem occultabat, sibi eripere, et in terram abiicere; nam statim imperata faciebat; neque dubitabat, magno intuentium cum risu, caput pilis nudum ostendere.[75]

> No less attentive was he to the instruction to snatch from his head, and throw to the ground the wig with which he concealed his baldness, for he instantly did what he was instructed to do, and, amid the great laughter of eye-witnesses, had no hesitation in revealing his bald head.

---

[75] Ianus Nicius Erythraeus, *Pinacotheca Imaginum Illustrium, Doctrinae vel Ingenii Laude, Virorum*, 3 vols. (Cologne: Iodocus Kalcovius 1648), III, 58.

At least that has been the scholarly interpretation of the lines ever since Masson first drew attention to, and paraphrased, Rossi's testimony.[76] Thus Low remarks: "one may hardly doubt that the old man did a double-take when he read these words."[77] But even if Manso did detect a Miltonic jibe directed against his artificial crowning glory, so to speak, one senses that the erudite Neapolitan may also have discerned its potentially more subtle import. A closer reading of Milton's possible joke and of the context in which it occurs suggests hitherto unnoticed links with discussions of both nature and beauty in the *Erocallia* itself. The oxymoronic language (*longaeva ... senectus/Vernat ... vivida* [74–75]) serves to equate Manso's old age with vibrancy, and with an eternal youthfulness (via the mythological exemplum of Medea's rejuvenation of Aeson)[78] that gives the impression of a perpetual Spring (*vernat* [75]).[79] This impression is facilitated by the fact that Manso's blossoming flower (*flos* [74]) is slow to reach maturity (*lentus* [74]),[80] a Miltonic nod perhaps to the self-deprecatory pseudonym "Il Tardo," by which his

---

[76] See *John Milton: Poetical Works*, ed. Masson, III, 535: "and, as is the fashion in the club-meetings of the Blessed Virgin, in which he was ranked as one of the members (*ut mos est in sodalitiis B. Virginis, in quibus ille numerabatur*), he would good-humouredly bear to have his defects publicly exposed. If bid lick the ground with his mouth, or kiss the feet of his club-fellows, he would not refuse, or escape the authority of the master of the revels; nor was he less obedient if he were ordered to snatch from his head the periwig with which he concealed his baldness (*caliendrum e capite quo calvitiem occultabat*), but immediately did as he was ordered, and made no scruple about exhibiting, amid the great laughter of the beholders, his perfectly bald head (*neque dubitabat, magno intuentium cum risu, caput pilis nudum ostendere*)."

[77] Low, "*Mansus*: In Its Context," 119. By contrast, Stella Revard somewhat oddly regards Milton's line as a reference to "the many laurels of honor that the old man had had bestowed upon him." See Stella P. Revard, *Milton and the Tangles of Neaera's Hair: The Making of the 1645 Poems* (Columbia: University of Missouri Press, 1997), 216.

[78] For Medea's rejuvenation of Aeson (Jason's aged father) by filling his veins with a potion consisting of herbs, juices, and roots culled from a valley in Thessaly, see Ovid, *Metamorphoses* 7.251–293. For Milton's earlier recourse to the myth, cf. *Elegia* 2.7-8: *O dignus tamen Haemonio iuvenescere succo,/Dignus in Aesonios vivere posse dies* ("Oh how deserving you were of rejuvenation by means of an Haemonian potion, deserving of having the ability to live until the lifetime of Aeson").

[79] See *OLD*, s.v. *vernare*: "(of natural things) To carry on or undergo the process proper to spring." Cf. Ovid, *Metamorphoses* 7.284; Manilius, *Astronomica* 5.259; Seneca, *Hercules Oetaeus*, 454; Columella, *De Re Rustica*, 10.270, and, for its figurative use, Propertius, *Elegiae* 4.5.59.

[80] See *OLD*, s.v. 7b: "slow in reaching maturity."

addressee was known in the Oziosi.[81] In consequence, the honors of his brow (*frontis honores* [76])[82] (with a possible pun on *frons-frontis* ["brow"] and *frons-frondis* ["leaf"]), are not yet fallen (*Nondum deciduos* [76]).[83] Likewise, the description of his intellectual talents employs qualifiers (*vigens* [77] and *adultus* [77]) equally applicable to flourishing and ripening plants.[84]

This praise of the physical and intellectual qualities of one, whose self-referential inscription in his tribute to Milton was as a *Neapolitanus*, may assume additional significance when read in the context of Manso's description of Naples itself in the opening Dialogue of the *Erocallia*. There Torquato offers a glowing encomium of the city's location: its climate, the fecundity of its soil,[85] and, above all, the abundance of its perennially blooming plants and fruit, which, he states, create the impression of a forever enduring Springtime:

> Mà quel, ch'à me sommamente diletta, è l'abbondanza, la varietà, la delicatezza delle frutta, ove le rose, e' fiori in tutti i mesi dell'anno, fanno una sempre durevole Primavera; i pomi, che vecchi, e nuovi si colgono dallo stesso ramo, rendono perpetua State.[86]

> But what affords me the greatest delight is the abundance, the variety, the delicacy of the fruit, where the roses, and flowers in all the months of the year create a forever-lasting Spring; the apples, which old and new are taken from the same branch, make the State perpetual.

Part of the illusion of Spring's perpetuity resides in the coexistence on the same branch of the unripe and the ripe, of the young and the old, or, perhaps in the case of *Mansus*, of two Johns: *Ioannes*, the self-proclaimed *iuvenis peregrinus* (26) and Giovanni, the *fortunat*[*us*] *senex* (49), the *Diis dilect*[*us*] *senex* (70), both of whose names, whether in their

---

[81] See Filippo Gaetani, *La Schiava* (Naples: Tarq[uinio] Longo, 1613), 3–11, at 11, where Manso, in a dedicatory epistle to Pedro Fernández de Castro (dated 1 August 1613), describes himself as "il Tardo Principe." See also De Miranda, *Una Quieta Operosa*, 62; Gazzara, "Giovanni Battista Manso," 41.

[82] For the phrase, cf. Statius, *Silvae* 1.2.113; *Thebaid* 9.705.

[83] See *OLD*, s.v. 1: "Tending to fall or be dropped, cast, etc., falling." Cf. Pliny, *Naturalis Historia* 18.25.60: *folia decidua* ("falling leaves").

[84] See *OLD*, s.v. *vigeo*, 1 (c): "(of plants) to flourish, thrive." Cf. Lucretius, *De Rerum Natura* 2.361; Cicero, *Tusculanae Disputationes* 5.37. See also *OLD*, s.v. *adultus-a-um*, 1: "full-grown, mature, ripe (of plants, crops, etc.)." Cf. Horace, *Epode* 2.9; Seneca, *Hercules Furens*, 699; Statius, *Thebaid* 9. 410.

[85] *Erocallia*, 4–5.

[86] *Erocallia*, 5.

Latinized or Italian form, are, as it were, sprung from, and grow upon, the same etymological branch: "young" / *iuvenis* / "giovane" / Giovanni. More specific, the longevity of Manso's life, his slowly blooming flower, his locks/foliage not yet fallen from their source, and the vernal context seem to counter a lengthy discussion (in Dialogue IX) of the essential transience of earthly beauty: "la bellezza, il cui esser per punto come la vita d'un fior di Verno non è più che d'un giorno solo" ("beauty, the extent of whose existence, like the life of a flower in Springtime, is no more than a single day").[87] There the argument was reinforced by scholarly recourse to, and copious quotation from, classical authors. Thus, according to Theocritus (rendered into Latin verse), even the beautiful rose withers with time, as "its flower is swiftly worn away, while its sheen deteriorates with age" (*cito conteritur flos, et nitor ille senescit*). Such too is the fate of violets in Springtime. Likewise, white lilies (*candida ... lilia*), gracing the beautiful vallies, swiftly decay (*cito marcescunt*).[88] According to Ovid, beauty is a fragile bounty (*forma bonum fragile est*), an assertion corroborated by reference to the fact that violets and lilies do not bloom forever,[89] lines echoed by Nemesianus, and also quoted herein.[90] Similarly, Seneca can only lament the fact that lilies languish with their pale petals (*languescunt folio lilia pallido*), while roses wither away and fall from their stalk (*et gratae capiti deficiunt rosae*).[91] In this reading *Ioannes Baptista Mansus Neapolitanus* emerges as one whose physical being is perhaps both a microcosm of the beauty of Naples herself and a symbol of something more: His Spring-like longevity seems to belie the very arguments about the ephemeral nature of earthly beauty posited in the *Erocallia* itself.

---

[87] *Erocallia*, 850.

[88] Theocritus, *Idyll* 23. 28–32. See *Erocallia*, 850–851.

[89] Ovid, *Ars Amatoria* 2.113–118. See *Erocallia*, 852.

[90] Nemesianus, *Eclogue* 4. 21–24. See *Erocallia*, 852.

[91] Seneca, *Phaedra* 768–769. See *Erocallia*, 853.

2.3 Milton Among the Erocallian Angels

Other arguments from the *Erocallia* may serve to enhance Miltonic self-fashioning. In the closing lines of *Mansus* the speaker imagines his own apotheosis:

> Tum quoque, si qua fides, si praemia certa bonorum,
> Ipse ego caelicolum semotus in aethera divum,
> Quo labor et mens pura vehunt atque ignea virtus,
> Secreti haec aliqua mundi de parte videbo
> (Quantum fata sinunt), et tota mente serenum
> Ridens purpureo suffundar lumine vultus,
> Et simul aethereo plaudam mihi laetus Olympo.
> (*Mansus* 94–100)

> Then also, if faith exists anywhere, if the rewards for the righteous are assured, I myself, removed into the ethereal regions of the heaven-dwelling gods, whither toil, purity of heart, and fiery virtue conduct, will behold these things from some remote region of the universe (as far as the fates allow) and smiling with complete serenity of mind, my face will be suffused with blushing radiance, while at the same time I will joyfully applaud myself on heavenly Olympus.

This, the poem's climactic conclusion, has generally been regarded by scholars as a somewhat absurd and quite astonishing exhibition of Miltonic egotism. Thus Condee believes that "the incredible self-admiration Milton shows in the concluding lines" is one of the poem's "flaws," remarking that "[i]t would be difficult to defend [their] tone."[92] Poole, viewing the whole as a rather disconcerting act on Milton's part, states: "[w]e do not know what Manso made of this extraordinary egotism."[93] Likewise, McDowell comments: "it is ... a somewhat disconcerting poem in that it concludes with Milton imagining his own post-mortem existence after he has achieved the fame to which he aspires."[94] Crucially, these readings overlook the ironic self-mockery of *plaudam mihi* (100),[95] and its associated rewriting of the quasi-theatrical

---

[92] Ralph W. Condee, *Structure in Milton's Poetry: From the Foundation to the Pinnacles* (University Park: Pennsylvania State University Press, 1974), 99–100. See also idem, "*Mansus* and the Panegyric Tradition," *SR* (1968): 174–192, at 188–189.

[93] Poole, *Milton and The Making of Paradise Lost*, 47.

[94] McDowell, *Poet of Revolution*, 346.

[95] Milton had previously used the phrase in *Prolusio* VI to congratulate himself upon being more successful than Orpheus and Amphion. See John Milton, *Prolusio VI*, in

stance of Horace's foolish miser in *Satires* 1.1.66–67: *populus me sibilui, at mihi plaudo/ipse domi* ("the public hisses at me, but I applaud myself in my own home"), a stance which, in the words of Catherine Keane, "is guided by his self-interest and not by an interest in his own enlightenment."[96] The context, as Low aptly observes, "is such as to puncture and amusingly counterpoint [Milton's] surface solemnity."[97] But even in Low's view, the last line of *Mansus* is essentially "comic," an attempt "to amuse, and more specifically to tease the Catholic Manso."[98] One senses, however, that much more is at play here. Milton proffers a self-inscribed encomium that not only answers Manso's distich by echoing its terms, its tone, and at times its syntax, but also situates its speaker in, as it were, a celestial theater by evoking discussions of angelic beauty in Dialogue VII of the *Erocallia*.

That Milton is replying to Manso's tribute at this point is suggested by their shared emphasis upon *ipse*. But as *Angelus ipse fores* becomes *Ipse ego* (95), the imperfect subjunctive is transformed into a series of confidently articulated future tenses (*videbo* [97], *suffundar* [99], *plaudam* [100]), whereby a Mansonian prediction, albeit ironically voiced, is imagined as reaching its fulfillment. Similarly, Milton's physical and intellectual talents, as praised by his Neapolitan host, are reinterpreted in a novel context. Thus *mens* (Milton's intellectual talent as acknowledged by Manso) recurs, only to be qualified by the adjective *pura* (96), itself evocative of what David Urban has described as Milton's "preoccupation with chastity,"[99] now envisaged as a passport to Heaven. *Facies* (Milton's physical beauty) becomes his celestial *vultus* (99) suffused with radiance. Syntactically, too, *si pietas sic* (Manso's allusion to Milton's Protestantism) is mirrored in *si qua fides* (94), but not without jocular play perhaps on *fides* as simply "the quality of being worthy of

---

Ioannis Miltonii Angli Epistolarum Familiarium Liber Unus Quibus Accesserunt Eiusdem Iam Olim in Collegio Adolescentis Prolusiones Quaedam Oratoriae (London: Brabazon Aylmer, 1674), 113–124, at 116: *Atque hercle non possum ego nunc quin mihi blandiuscule plaudam qui vel Orpheo, vel Amphione multo sim meo iudicio fortunatior* ("Nor, by Hercules, can I refrain from applauding myself, rather flatteringly, on having, in my opinion, much better luck than Orpheus did, or Amphion"). Hale, *Milton's Cambridge Latin*, 253, aptly comments: "Milton outstrips Orpheus … because he has a fitter audience." See also Revard, *The Tangles of Neaera's Hair*, 223.

[96] Catherine Keane, *Figuring Genre in Roman Satire* (Oxford: Oxford University Press, 2006), 23.

[97] Low, "*Mansus*: In Its Context," 123.

[98] Low, "*Mansus*: In Its Context," 121, comparing the subversive last line of *Elegia Tertia*.

[99] Urban, "The Lady of Christ's College," 3.

belief,"[100] and, more formally, "Faith" in its postclassical sense as a specified religious system of belief.[101] This latter point is developed in the parenthetical *quantum fata sinunt* (98)[102] ("as far as the [pagan] fates allow"). The implication is that if Milton's purported "paganism," his Protestantism, his *fides*, or, in Manso's words, his *pietas*, permit, he could indeed become that Catholic *angelus* punningly foretold in the distich. After all, as Joad Raymond has observed:

> Protestants in Britain and elsewhere were interested in angels, and re-created angel doctrine in ways that responded to and fitted within their religious, political, and intellectual culture more broadly; their beliefs about angels were neither residual nor reactive.[103]

And Milton adds a further attribute: *ignea virtus* (96) ("fiery virtue"), one of those meritorious qualities for which membership of the heavenly host constitutes an assured reward (*praemia certa bonorum* [94]).

Read in the context of the *Erocallia* the Miltonic self, as envisaged here, is equatable with those, as described in Dialogue IV, whose earthly virtue is mirrored in their love of its celestial equivalent ("con amore della divina Virtù" ["with the love of divine Virtue"]), those in search of a union with a heavenly ideal, depicted as the reward ("premio") for their noble quest.[104] And more than that. Quasi-angelic in his blushing

---

[100] See *OLD*, s.v. 9. Cf. Ovid, *Metamorphoses* 9.371.

[101] See, for example, *Glossarium Mediae et Infimae Latinitatis*, eds. Charles de Fresne Du Cange, et al. (Niort: L. Favre, 1883–1887), s.v. *Fides: quae et Fides Catholica ... Ecclesia Catholica dicitur esse Domicilium fidei* ("Faith: which is also the Catholic Faith ... The Catholic Church is said to be the dwelling-place of Faith").

[102] Here, as observed by M.ª Teresa Muñoz García de Iturrospe, "Milton adopts the Latin term *fatum* ... before the English word 'Fate' means destiny as divine providence." See M.ª Teresa Muñoz García de Iturrospe, "Some Classical Patterns in John Milton's Latin Funerary Compositions," in *Estudios de Filología e Historia en Honor del Profesor Vitalino Valcárcel*, eds. Iñigo Ruiz Arzalluz, Alejandro Martínez Sobrino, M.ª Teresa Muñoz García de Iturrospe, Iñaki Ortigosa Egiraun, and Enara San Juan Manso, 2 vols. (Vitoria-Gasteiz: Universidad del País Vasco, 2014), II, 727–736, at 730. Milton's phrase likewise occurs at Vida, *De Arte Poetica* 3.192. Cf., more generally, Virgil, *Aeneid* 1.18; Ovid, *Metamorphoses* 5.534; Propertius, *Elegiae* 2.15.23; Tibullus, *Elegiae* 1.1.69, among others.

[103] Joad Raymond, *Milton's Angels: The Early-Modern Imagination* (Oxford: Oxford University Press, 2010), 13.

[104] See the paraphrase, at *Erocallia*, 375, of Pythagoras's inspiring promise "à coloro, che con amore della divina *Virtù* osservati gli havessero, in *premio* del lor bene operare il godimento dell' unione della stessa *Virtù* divina" ("to those who, in their observation of the love of divine *Virtue*, had, as a *reward* for their good work, enjoyment of union with the same divine *Virtue*"). Emphasis is mine.

radiance,[105] and bathed in a glowing luminosity, he possesses an attribute that, according to the *Erocallia*, was an essential hallmark of angels. Dialogue VII cites biblical authority in support of the belief that an angel is synonymous with a burning fire (*ignis urens*).[106] The angelic *facies* resembles that of the sun, and angelic feet are likened to a column of fire (*Facies eius erat ut Sol, et pedes eius tanquam columna ignis*).[107] It is in the seraphim, the highest rank, that the "angelic nature is chiefly resplendent" ("primieramente l'Angelica Natura risplende").[108] These angels are more bright and fiery than all the others. Likewise, according to Dionysius (the Areopagite), an angel is the image of God, the manifestation of a hidden light, a mirror, that is both pure and most splendid: *Angelus est imago Dei, manifestatio occulti luminis, speculum purum splendidissimum.*[109] The argument is reinforced by the testimonies of St. Augustine (*cum lux illa prima facta est, Angeli creati intelliguntur*: ["Angels are believed to have been created at the point when that first light was made]),[110] and, perhaps most strikingly, St. Thomas Aquinas:

> Angeli perficiuntur duplici lumine, lumine scilicet naturali, prout sunt intellectus quidam, et lumine gratuito perficiente ad actus hierarchicos, et utrumque lumen est unum in omnibus.[111]
>
> Angels are composed of a two-fold light, namely, a natural light, in accordance with certain powers of understanding, and a gratuitous light for the completion of hierarchical actions; and each light is singular in all respects.

---

[105] Cf. the description of Raphael at *Paradise Lost* 8.618–619 as an "angel with a smile that glowed/Celestial rosy red."

[106] *Erocallia*, 687–688, citing Psalm 104.4: *Qui facis Angelos tuos spiritus, et ministros tuos ignem urentem*" ("Who maketh his angels spirits; his ministers a flaming fire"). All biblical references, unless otherwise stated, are to the King James (authorized) version.

[107] *Erocallia*, 688. Cf. *Revelation* 10:1: "And I saw another mighty angel come down from heaven, clothed with a cloud: and a rainbow was upon his head, and his face was as it were the sun, and his feet as pillars of fire."

[108] *Erocallia*, 688. Cf. Tasso's praise of Manso himself ("Risplende il Manso" [*Gerusalemme Conquistata*, book 20, canto 142]) as cited by Milton in the Headnote to *Mansus*, for which, see 114.

[109] *Erocallia*, 688. Cf. Dionysius, *De Divinis Nominibus* 4: 22.

[110] *Erocallia*, 688. Cf. Augustine, *De Civitate Dei* 11: 19.

[111] *Erocallia*, 688. Cf. Thomas Aquinas, *Scriptum Super Sententiis*, II: 9.1.

Mansus, in short, concludes with a good-humored counterchallenge to the Mansonian charge of Milton's presumed inadmissibility to the angelic ranks. In an ironic self-appropriation of the Neapolitan's scholarly exegesis of angelic beauty and rank in the *Erocallia*,[112] the Protestant Milton *can* be an angel, even if he has to applaud himself (*plaudam mihi* [100]). This ultimate act of defiance is rendered all the more forceful in its intratextual echo of the angelic applause with which a Protestant bishop *was* indeed admitted into Heaven, at least as envisaged by Milton in his third Latin elegy:

> Agmina gemmatis *plaudunt* caelestia pennis;
> Pura triumphali personat aethra tuba.
> (*Elegia* 3.59–60).[113]

> The heavenly hosts *applaud* with jeweled wings; the pure ether resounds with a triumphal trumpet.

The bishop in question was none other than Lancelot Andrewes, acclaimed theologian, preacher, and translator of the King James Bible.

---

[112] It is worth noting in this regard Milton's evocation, in Ad *Leonoram* 1, of an essentially Catholic doctrine concerning angelology. The epigram's opening pronouncement: *Angelus unicuique suus (sic credite gentes)/Obtigit aethereis ales ab ordinibus* (1–2) ("A winged angel from the heavenly ranks [believe this you nations] has been allotted to each individual") echoes the Catholic tenet that guardian angels were allocated to *individuals*, as opposed to places or communities. See Raymond, *Milton's Angels*, 232. Not unlike the parenthetical *si pietas sic* (Manso's distich) or *si qua fides* (*Mansus* 94), this seeming acknowledgment of Catholic doctrine is couched in language of ambiguity: *sic credite gentes* (1) ("believe this, you nations"). Milton, rather than distancing himself from the belief, assumes a Catholic voice, whose articulation of a Catholic tenet is posited as a challenge to those of other religious persuasions, pejoratively depicted as *gentes* in perhaps the noun's postclassical meaning of "gentiles" or "heathens" (see, Lewis and Short, s.v. 2c: "In the ecc. fathers, *gentes*, like ἔθνος, opp. to Jews and Christians, pagan nations, heathens, gentiles." Cf. Lactantius, 2.13; Vulgate, Psalm 2.1, and Arnobius's eponymous *Adversus Gentes*). For further discussion, see Haan, *John Milton's Roman Sojourns*, 113–121. If the poem postdates Milton's Neapolitan sojourn (and the gifting to him of Manso's *Erocallia*), its embracing of Catholic angelology is perhaps all the more telling.

[113] Emphasis is mine. For *Elegia Tertia* (ca. September–December 1626), see *Poemata*, 16–19; Lewalski and Haan, cvi–cviii, 124–127, 428–430.

Chapter 3

"Poesie di Diversi": Milton, Manso, and the *Poesie Nomiche*

The second volume gifted by Manso to Milton was the *Poesie Nomiche*, a collection of the Neapolitan's Italian verse, which had seen publication in Venice in 1635.[1] Divided into "Rime Amorose,"[2] "Rime Sacre,"[3] and "Rime Morali,"[4] the tripartite organization of Manso's poetry seems to map an ascending trajectory from the shackles of earthly sinfulness to the ultimate liberation afforded by sanctity and moral redemption.[5] There follows "La Fenice," Manso's rendering of Claudian's *Phoenix* into ottava rima,[6] accompanied by a dedicatory letter to Giulio Caria,[7] a particularly apt gesture in that Caria had himself

---

[1] See 10.

[2] Printed with a separate title page ("Delle Rime del Marchese Di Villa Parte Prima. Che contiene l'Amorose"), the "Rime Amorose" (poems 1–115) comprise Part 1 of the volume (3–128). They consist of 95 sonnets, 13 madrigals, 2 sestine, and 5 canzoni. As noted by Riga, this section is the most remarkable, comprising, as it does, just over half of the entire work. See Riga, *Giovan Battista Manso*, 151.

[3] Printed with a separate title page ("Delle Rime del Marchese di Villa Parte Seconda. Che contiene le Sacre"), the "Rime Sacre" (poems 116–162) comprise Part 2 of the volume (131–180).

[4] Printed with a separate title page ("Delle Rime del Marchese di Villa Parte Terza. Che contiene le Morali"), the "Rime Morali" (poems 163–206) comprise Part 3 of the volume (183–241).

[5] See Riga, *Giovan Battista Manso*, 151. On the correlation between the volume's tripartite structure and the quasi-legalistic connotations of "Nomiche," see ibid., 148.

[6] *Poesie Nomiche*, 242–250. Cf. Tasso, *Il Mondo Creato*, V.1278–1591. See *La Fenice: Da Claudiano a Tasso*, ed. Bruno Basile (Rome: Carocci, 2004). See also Agnello Baldi, "La 'Fenice Rinascente' di Tommaso Gaudiosi e La Traduzione Letteraria nel Seicento Italiano," *SS* 18 (1977): 127–144.

[7] *Poesie Nomiche*, 251–252: "A Giulio Caria Il Marchese di Villa." Caria was a member of the Oziosi. See his sonnet in Maurizio Di Gregorio, *Rosario delle Stampe de' Tutti i Poeti, e Poetesse, Antichi, e Moderni, Cinquecento di Numero Tomo Ottavo, del Giardino de Tutte le Scienze* (Naples: G. G. Carlino, 1614), 132. Cf. De

translated Claudian's *De Raptu Proserpinae* into ottava rima.[8] Then, in a new section, marked by a new title page, and an address to the reader,[9] there occur 110 encomiastic "Poesie di Diversi a Gio: Battista Manso Marchese di Villa."[10] The "Tavola" (Index) is followed by Manso's explanatory notes (in Italian prose).[11]

In many respects the volume as a whole serves to showcase both the young and the old Manso, or, in Miltonic terms, the *iuvenis* and the *senex*, so to speak. Thus, as the printer's prefatory letter is careful to point out, most of the poetry contained therein was composed by the author "nel tempo della sua prima giovanezza" ("in the time of his early youth").[12] That sense of youthfulness is reinforced by the somewhat anachronistic portrait of Manso, the handsome, mustached young poet and warrior, alongside his family Coat of Arms (Di Scala),[13] and, not least, by several of the "Poesie di Diversi." Thus, in a sonnet, entitled "Predice la fama avvenire del Marchese di Villa ancor giovanetto" ("He foretells the future fame of the Marquis of Villa, still a young boy"), Angelo di Costanzo addresses the young Manso, whom he associates with the revivification of nature, its river banks, plains, and mountains, over which his poetry seems to exercise a spellbinding power.[14] Likewise,

---

Miranda, *Una Quiete Operosa*, 70. He contributed an encomium of Manso to the "Poesie di Diversi," at *Poesie Nomiche*, 270.

[8] Caria's version is praised herein by Manso, who, employing an analogy pertinent to this, his own rendering of a different Claudian poem, depicts the translator as a second sun, symbol of life and revivification, one possessed of the rays of clear judgment. Thus has he dragged Proserpina from the underworld to the serene heaven of the Italian language with no less amazement than that engendered by Claudian in Latin. See *Poesie Nomiche*, 251–252.

[9] *Poesie Nomiche*, 255–256: "A Lettori."

[10] *Poesie Nomiche*, 257–326.

[11] Separately paginated, these comprise: "Partimento del Canzoniere in Rime Amorose, Sacre, e Morali" (1–36), "Dichiaratione de gli Argomenti delle Rime Amorose" (37–65), notes to "Madrigali" (66–70), "Dichiaratione de gli Argomenti delle Rime Sacre" (71–85), and "Dichiarationi de gli Argomenti delle Rime Morali" (86–102).

[12] See "Lo Stampatore," at *Poesie Nomiche*, sig. a10^r.

[13] On the family Coat of Arms, see also 74.

[14] *Poesie Nomiche*, 257: "D'Italia, al suon de' tuoi soavi accenti/Fioriscono le rive, e i piani, e i monti,/Versan liquidi argenti i fiumi, e i fonti,/Stan cheti a udirti i più rabbiosi venti./E gli augelli, e le fere, e i pesci intenti/Sono a tuoi carmi sì famosi, e conti" ("At the sound of your sweet accents the streams and plains and mountains of Italy begin to bloom; clear silver rivers and springs pour forth their waters; the most furious winds are quiet in order to hear you. And the birds and wild beasts and fish are attentive to your songs so renowned and accomplished").

Giulio Cesare Caracciolo "praises the Marquis's first poetry" ("Loda le prime Poesie del Marchese").[15] On the other hand, the prefatory letter (by Alessandro Berardelli), dated as recently as 1 September 1635, heralds the present-day Manso as an author who has reached the height of his powers. Thus, on account of the "fama della sua universale, e profondo dottrina" ("fame of his universal and profound learning"), he is well known "in tutte l'Accademie d'Europa" ("in all the Academies of Europe"), and is "nominato nelle carte de' più pregiati Scrittori di questo secolo" ("named in the pages of the most esteemed Writers of this century").[16] Similarly, many of the "Poesie di Diversi" celebrate the more mature Manso, spanning, as they do, his full career right up until 1635, the date of publication. In short, the collection as a whole, both in terms of content and print culture, capably epitomizes that aforementioned Miltonic dictum: *longaeva tibi lento sub flore senectus/Vernat* (74–75).[17] That it won contemporary approval is attested by the opinion of the Oziosi academician Giuseppe Campanile:

> Delle sue Poesie Nomiche non discorro, ch'hebbero nome di Petrarchevoli, di Casesche, e poco dissuguali à quelle del Bembo.[18]
>
> I have no need to mention his *Poesie Nomiche*, which possess the rank of the poems of Petrarch, of Della Casa, and are not very unequal to those of Bembo.

By contrast, modern criticism is glaringly lacking, with the notable exception of Riga, whose various studies of the volume's genesis, contents, and its literary and Neapolitan contexts,[19] admirably demonstrate its status as "un modello di canzoniere morale,"[20] and as "one of the more complex and articulated poetic collections of seventeenth-century Naples."[21]

---

[15] *Poesie Nomiche*, 262.

[16] See Alessandro Berardelli to Pietro Michiele, in *Poesie Nomiche*, sig. a2^r–a5^v, at sig. a3^r.

[17] See 55–58.

[18] Giuseppe Campanile, *Prose Varie ... Divise in Funzioni Accademiche* (Naples: Luc' Antonio di Fusco, 1666), 166.

[19] See Riga, *Giovan Battista Manso*, 121–170.

[20] See Riga, *Giovan Battista Manso*, 144–161, at 144.

[21] See Pietro Giulio Riga, "Manso, Gli Oziosi e La Riflessione sulla Poesia Lirica Tra Paratesti ed Esegesi Accademica," in *Manso, Lemos, Cervantes*, ed. Mondola, 125–146, at 133.

3.1 The Phoenix and Poetic Self-Fashioning

In the center (*in medio* [185]) of this gifted book, according to Milton's ekphrastic description in *Epitaphium Damonis*, was a depiction of the following scene:

> In medio Rubri Maris unda et odoriferum ver,
> Litora longa Arabum et sudantes balsama silvae;
> Has inter Phoenix, divina avis, unica terris,
> Caeruleum fulgens diversicoloribus alis,
> Auroram vitreis surgentem respicit undis.
> (*Epitaphium Damonis* 185–189)[22]

> In the center are the waves of the Red Sea, and the sweetly smelling Spring, the distant shores of Arabia, and forests dripping balsam. Among these the phoenix, a divine bird, unique upon the earth, and gleaming bluish-green with multicolored wings, looks round at Aurora rising from the glassy waves.

The passage (together with its potential "sources") has certainly not lacked scholarly discussion. For the most part, however, this is both dated (pertaining largely to the 1930s), and all too indicative of an "anxiety of influence."[23] Thus Kathleen Hartwell argued in favor of Lactantius[24] (while not precluding Ovid,[25] Pliny,[26] and Claudian[27]) as Milton's source.[28] Rudolf Gottfried, on the other hand, proposed Tasso[29] as the

---

[22] Cf. the comparison of the angel Raphael to the phoenix at *Paradise Lost* 5.271–274: "to all the fowls he seems/A phoenix, gazed by all, as that sole bird/When to enshrine his relics in the sun's/Bright temple, to Aegyptian Thebes he flies," on which see Karen L. Edwards, "Raphael, Diodati," in *Of Paradise and Light: Essays on Henry Vaughan and John Milton in Honor of Alan Rudrum*, eds. Donald R. Dickson and Holly Faith Nelson (Newark: University of Delaware Press, 2004), 123–141.

[23] Harold Bloom, *The Anxiety of Influence: A Theory of Poetry* (Oxford: Oxford University Press, 1973).

[24] Lactantius, *De Ave Phoenice*.

[25] Ovid, *Metamorphoses* 15.391–407; *Amores* 2.6.54.

[26] Pliny, *Naturalis Historia* 10.2.3–5.

[27] Claudian, *Phoenix*.

[28] See Kathleen Hartwell, *Lactantius and Milton* (Cambridge, MA: Harvard University Press, 1929), 123–132.

[29] Tasso, *Il Mondo Creato* 5.1278–1591.

model.³⁰ In both instances the arguments for "influence" upon Milton are based, to a large degree, on the occurrence of several shared themes: the "uniqueness" of the phoenix (with both scholars even itemizing and comparing the respective number of occurrences of the adjective *unicus*/"unico"), its brilliant plumage, its awaiting the dawn, and the "cerulean" color of the bird's wings. The potential danger of such an approach is signaled, even if only implicitly, by a sense of unease characterizing their somewhat mangled conclusions. Thus, Hartwell remarks:

> There is no reason why fragmentary bits of Ovid, or Pliny, or of Claudian may not have drifted into Milton's consciousness and have left their mark on the poem, but there seems to be every reason to believe that the pattern of the whole passage is Lactantian.³¹

Gottfried concedes that "[t]he value of the word *unique* as proof of influence is questionable; but if it is accepted at all, it must be in the favour of Tasso rather than the Latin poet."³² While speculating that "after Milton had read Tasso ... non-Lactantian details coalesced in his mind,"³³ he does, however, demonstrate some intertextual alertness in his observation that "Tasso brings together from two different sources the same passages which appear to have been combined and diffused in Milton's consciousness before he wrote."³⁴ Michele de Filippis, however, rightly points out that the characteristics of Milton's description observed by both scholars are, in fact, features for which there are hundreds of other sources.³⁵ Added to this is the existence of no fewer than 128 passages on the phoenix in ancient literature, a point well demonstrated by Mary Fitzpatrick.³⁶

---

[30] See Rudolf Gottfried, "Milton, Lactantius, Claudian, and Tasso," *SP* 30 (1933): 497–503. On Tasso's rendering of Lactantius, see Bruno Basile, "Tasso Traduttore: La Versione Poetica del 'De Ave Phoenice' dello Pseudo-Lattanzio nel 'Mondo Creato,'" *LI* 31 (1979): 342–405.

[31] Hartwell, *Lactantius and Milton*, 132.

[32] Gottfried, "Milton, Lactantius, Claudian, and Tasso," 499.

[33] Ibid., 499.

[34] Ibid., 502.

[35] De Filippis, "Milton and Manso: Cups or Books," 746.

[36] Mary Cletus Fitzpatrick, "Lactanti De Ave Phoenice" (PhD thesis, University of Pennsylvania, 1933), 12–15. See also Kester Svendsen, *Milton and Science* (Cambridge, MA: Harvard University Press, 1956), 146–148.

De Filippis, developing his convincing interpretation of Milton's lines as a reference to Manso's "La Fenice" (in the *Poesie Nomiche*), tentatively added this work to the other potential "source" texts. The suggestion, dismissed rather too hastily by Bush,[37] is not without merit. Read in the context of the published volume, "La Fenice" is certainly describable as *in medio*, not only in that it is sandwiched between the *Poesie Nomiche* and the ensuing "Poesie di Diversi," but also in that it occupies what is virtually a central position as pages 242–250 of a volume totaling some 456 pages. Here Manso, contrary to his mock-modest self-description (in his dedicatory letter to Caria) as "a detractor from the phoenix's ancient immortality, a translator, who has stripped away that vivacity of spirit that Claudian afforded it,"[38] reveals himself as a talented translator. His version not only replicates in the target language the linguistic and etymological idiosyncrasies of the source text, but also employs, in quasi-Venutian terms, a "fluent strategy,"[39] marked by exuberant amplification (in no fewer than 26 ottave), extended description, and such linguistic embellishments as antonomasia, anaphora, and oxymoron.[40] As such, it fulfills most of the aforementioned criteria governing earlier arguments in favor of one "source" or another upon Milton. Thus the adjective "unique," though absent from Claudian's *Phoenix*,[41] is significantly present: "O mio nobile allievo unico, e caro" ("O my noble pupil, unique and rare"),[42] a concept developed in "Tu mio mirabil mostro eterno, e raro" ("You, my wonderful omen, eternal and rare").[43] Milton's *divina avis* (187) finds a parallel in Manso's rendering of Claudian's *par volucer superis* (11) as "A gran Divi simil" ("resembling the mighty gods").[44] Likewise, "cerulean," used to qualify the bird's resplendently multicolored plumage (*Caeruleum fulgens*

---

[37] Bush, *Variorum*, I, 320: "We may feel the same scepticism in regard to De Filippis' own suggestion, the Italian translation of Claudian in Manso's anthology, *Poesie Nomiche*."

[38] *Poesie Nomiche*, 251: "me, detrattore della sua antica immortalità; mentre in vece di tradurla ... io l'hò tradita, togliendole quella vivacità di spiriti, che Claudiano le diede."

[39] See Lawrence Venuti, *The Translator's Invisibility: A History of Translation* (London: Routledge, 1995), 58.

[40] See Baldi, "La Fenice Rinascente," 138–140.

[41] *Unicus* does, however, occur in Claudian's description of the phoenix in *De Consulatu Stilichonis* 2.414–420, at 417.

[42] *Poesie Nomiche*, 246.

[43] *Poesie Nomiche*, 246.

[44] *Poesie Nomiche*, 243.

diversicoloribus alis [188]), features in Manso's amplified transformation of Claudian's *antevolant Zephyros pinnae, quas caerulus ambit/Flore color sparsoque super ditescit in auro* (21–22) ("outspeeding the Zephyrs are its wings, colored by a flower-like cerulean blue and bespeckled with gold spots") into an image that is stunningly visual, even quasi-ekphrastic, in essence:

> Spirano gli occhi non più vista luce,
>   Di dolce foco il suo bel volto splende,
> D'un acceso vermiglio indi riluce,
>   La piuma, che superbo il capo rende.[45]

> His eyes exude a light no longer seen. His beautiful face shines with sweet fire. Of bright vermilion glows the plumage which endows his lofty head.

> De' piè le squamme poi minute, e spesse
>   E l'unghie, ostro Feniceo à lui colora,
> E sopra l'ali in bel lavor s'intesse
>   Ceruleo fior, che lasciv'ago infiora.[46]

> Phoenician purple colors the minute scales of his feet and his thick claws, and upon his wings in beautiful craftsmanship there is interwoven a cerulean flower, that the wanton needle embroiders with blossom.

Manso's emphasis upon the visual is matched by his amplification of the sensory. Thus, he develops the fragrance (*odor*) of the setting in which Claudian's phoenix is situated (59–60, 98) into "Odorato fasto" ("fragrant pomp");[47] "L'oderato sentier" ("the fragrant path");[48] "L'Indico odore" ("the fragrance of India"),[49] an interesting context in which to view Milton's choice of the adjective (*odoriferum* [185]) to describe the Spring (*ver* [185]). In all of this, however, it is both unwise and unnecessary to attempt to pin down a single "source." Rather Manso's "La Fenice" is more accurately describable as a rendering that seems to have served as a springboard for Milton's description, which, in turn, should be viewed a

---

[45] *Poesie Nomiche*, 243.

[46] *Poesie Nomiche*, 244. Cf. ibid., 245: "aurate piume" ("golden plumage").

[47] *Poesie Nomiche*, 246.

[48] *Poesie Nomiche*, 248.

[49] *Poesie Nomiche*, 249.

fortiori as a passage characterized by its rich intertextual engagement with both Latin and Italian versions of the bird at its center.

There remains, however, another context in which Milton's lines merit fresh scrutiny. His phoenix is depicted as looking round at Aurora, rising from the sea's glassy waves (*Auroram vitreis surgentem respicit undis* [189]). Although the bird's expectation of the dawn, as Hartwell and Gottfied observe, finds precedent in both Lactantius[50] and Tasso,[51] its occurrence in *Mansus* may afford both the phoenix and the object of its gaze a hitherto unnoticed allegorical import. As Cedric Brown remarks:

> [t]he attentive gaze in the single active verb *respicit* records a special ability of the bird: like the eagle (the symbol of Manso's Ozioso [sic] academy) it can look directly at the sun, here a sun rising.[52]

It is a perceptive observation that is worth reinforcing (Herodotus, after all, had likened the phoenix to the eagle),[53] and one that may also have a more contemporary import when examined alongside seicento discussions of the significance of the "Aquila" as the Oziosi's emblem. Francesco De Pietri, in the *Proemium* to his account of topics debated by the Oziosi, observes that the emblem of the eagle upon a hill, with its gaze fixed on the sun ("che riguarda il Sole"), functions as a "simbolo della Speculatione delle scienze" ("symbol of the speculation of knowledge"). In support of this interpretation, he quotes the remarks of the Italian ornithologist, Ulisse Aldrovandi:

> Aquila ad Solem conversa significat eum, qui nullum non contemnere laborem velit, et adversa quavis subire, dummodo ad gloriae, quae ex scientiarum cognitione procedit metam perveniat, Aquila enim mentis intentionem denotat, et sol scientiarum fons est, et origo.[54]

---

[50] Lactantius, *De Ave Phoenice* 35: *lutea cum primum surgens Aurora rubescit* ("as soon as saffron Dawn grows red upon her rising"). Cf. Hartwell, *Lactantius and Milton*, 131.

[51] Tasso, *Il Mondo Creato* 5.1361–1362: "Et al nascer del Sole indi conversa,/Del Sol già nato aspetta i raggi, e'l lume" ("And then it turns toward the birth of the Sun; it looks at the rays and the light of the already nascent Sun"). Text is that of Tasso, *Le Sette Giornate del Mondo Creato* (Viterbo: Girolamo Discepolo, 1607), 203. Cf. Gottfried, "Milton, Lactantius, Claudian, and Tasso," 500.

[52] Brown, *Friendship and Its Discourses*, 82.

[53] Herodotus, *Histories* 2.73.

[54] De Pietri, *Problemi Academici*, (Proemio), at sig. c2^v–c3^r. See also Ulisse Aldrovandi, *Ornithologiae Hoc Est De Avibus Historiae Libri XII* (Bologna:

> The Eagle turned toward the Sun signifies the individual who does not wish to despise work, or undertake any type of adversity, provided that he can attain the goal of glory, which proceeds from knowledge of the sciences. For the Eagle denotes the intention of one's mind, while the sun is the fount and source of knowledge.

This symbolism lies at the heart of authorial self-fashioning in both the *Poesie Nomiche* and the "Poesie di Diversi." In his dedicatory letter accompanying "La Fenice" Manso replaces the Oziosi eagle by the phoenix in his self-portrayal as that bird. Thus, he proclaims that, whereas Claudian's phoenix flew to the temple of Apollo in Cyrene, he (Manso) flies to the temple of Caria "à render le devote gratie al Sole, donatore della rinovellata sua vita" ("in order to render devoted thanks to the sun, bestower of the bird's renewed life"). Hoping that the rays of Caria's clear judgment ("raggi del vostro chiaro giuditio") will prove as efficacious as the sun's heat in restoring his work (and himself) from the detriments of old age ("de' danni della vecchiaia"),[55] he continues:

> Così vi priego, che traggiate anche dal Lethe dell'oblivione la più sua, che mia Fenice illustrandola colla luce delle vostre censure, e purgandola con le flamme delle vostre ammendationi.[56]

> So I beg you, that you also drag my Phoenix from the Lethe of the oblivion that is his by illuminating it with the light of your censure and purging it with the flames of your emendations.

The phoenix as poetic self underlies several of the "Poesie di Diversi," but now the sun, the fixed object of the bird's gaze, is Manso himself. Thus Anello Maria Palomba, in a sonnet, entitled "L'assimiglia al Sole" ("His Resemblance to the Sun"), heralds Manso as a "Sol de virtute" ("Sun of virtue"), whose beautiful rays enkindle the inspirational powers of the poet, likened to the "kindly Phoenix" ("Fenice ... alma"), "who gathers together a humble but ardent pyre" ("che rogo humili, ma ardente aduna").[57] For Giovanni Camillo Cacace, admission to Manso's Oziosi

---

Francesco de Franceschi, 1599), 74. Cf. Milton's emphasis on the roles played by *labor* and *mens* as a passport to heavenly apotheosis at *Mansus* 95–96: *Ipse ego caelicolum semotus in aethera divum,/Quo labor et mens pura vehunt atque ignea virtus* ("I myself, removed into the ethereal regions of the heaven-dwelling gods, whither *toil*, purity of heart, and fiery virtue conduct"). Emphasis is mine.

[55] *Poesie Nomiche*, 251.

[56] *Poesie Nomiche*, 252.

[57] *Poesie Nomiche*, 272. On the nurturing of the phoenix by the sun, cf. Claudian, *Phoenix* 14–15, and Manso's amplified version at *Poesie Nomiche*, 243. Cf. also

will enable him to become a "new Phoenix" ("nova Fenice").[58] Ferrante Rovitto's sonnet, entitled "Allude al motto dell'impresa dell'Accademia" ("He alludes to the motto of the Academy's *Impresa*"), addresses the Marquis directly, lauding "the rays of his ardent and bright virtue" ("i rai di tụa virtute ardente, e chiara"), whose ubiquitous radiance emulates the sun ("che per tutto fiammegia emula al Sole").[59] The equation was further facilitated by the fact that the coat of arms of Manso's ancestral family (di Scala) depicted a ladder reaching in an upward direction, one which, according to Ferdinando di Donno's sonnet, entitled "Sopra l'insegna della Scala" ("On the emblem of the ladder/'Scala'"), "affords an ascent from gloomy abysses to the great light of the Sun" ("onde s'ascende/Da cupi abissi al gran fanal del Sole").[60] Read in this context, Milton's ekphrastic phoenix, it could be argued, might likewise serve as an allegory of the poetic self, fixing a retrospective and respectful gaze upon Manso as a revivifying sun. Like the "Poesie di Diversi" (perhaps even etymologically embroidered into the Miltonic bird's variegated plumage (*diversicoloribus alis* [188]),[61] *Mansus* itself is hereby proferred to an addressee, who may indeed be punningly equated with the sun in the poem's earlier description of the dying wishes of Marino:

> Ille itidem moriens *tibi soli* debita vates
> Ossa *tibi soli* supremaque vota reliquit
> (*Mansus* 13–14)[62]
>
> Likewise, when he was dying, it was to
> you alone that that bard left his bones,

Claudian's description of the bird as greeting the sun (45), reworked by Manso as "Augel del Sole" ("Bird of the Sun"), at *Poesie Nomiche*, 243.

[58] *Poesie Nomiche*, 274.

[59] *Poesie Nomiche*, 288.

[60] *Poesie Nomiche*, 288.

[61] Emphasis is mine. With Milton's phraseology, cf. an epigram traditionally attributed to Virgil: *Marmoreusque tibi diversicoloribus alis/In morem picta stabit Amor pharetra* (9–10) ("and there will stand before you Cupid cast in marble, with multicolored wings, his quiver depicted according to custom"), for discussion of which, see *Anthologia Veterum Latinorum Epigrammatum et Poematum sive Catalecta Poetarum Latinorum in VI Libros Digesta*, ed. Pieter Burman (Amsterdam: Schouten, 1759–1763), I, 38–39. See also Edmund Spenser, *The Faerie Queene* 3.11.47: "On which there stood an Image all alone,/Of massy gold, which with his owne light shone;/And winges it had with sondry colours dight,/More sondry colours, then the proud Pavone/Beares in his boasted fan, or Iris bright,/When her discolourd bow she spreds through heven bright." Text is that of *The Faerie Queene*, ed. A. C. Hamilton (Oxford: Routledge, 2013). The colored plumage described is that of Cupid.

[62] Emphasis is mine.

> as was their due; to you alone, his final
> wishes.

The repetition of *tibi soli* is not only quasi-hymnic in essence, but also, and especially, enhanced by possible wordplay on *solus* ["alone"] and *sol* ["sun"]),[63] whereby Manso is, as it were, both the unique recipient of the final offerings of a dying poet/phoenix, and a sun-god to whom they are honorifically rendered.[64]

3.2 *Mansus* and the "Poesie di Diversi"

While "La Fenice" occupies a central position in the *Poesie Nomiche*, it also possesses a structural function that is symbolically transitional: from Manso's Italian verse to the ensuing section, comprising the "Poesie di Diversi" in his honor. These encomia are presented not as a mere appendix to the collection, but as a miniature volume in its own right (even if pagination is sequential upon the preceding content), one that is, moreover, proudly showcased by a separate title page and a new letter to the reader.[65] That letter signals the merits of the ensuing pieces, emphasizing chronology as the determining factor of their ordering,[66] and taking pains to remark that no textual alterations have been made "in regard to the excellence of the compositions or to the dignity of those who composed them" ("à rispetto dell'eccellenza delle compositioni, nè

---

[63] Worthy of comparison is the wordplay on "sole" ("sun")/"solo" ("alone")/"sole" ("is accustomed to") in the sonnets of Ferrante Rovitto, Ferdinando di Donno, and Francesco Falese at *Poesie Nomiche*, 288–289.

[64] For Milton's later reworking of the *solus/sol* pun on a macaronic level, cf. Raphael as "A phoenix ... that *sole* bird ... / ... in the *sun's*/Bright temple ...," at *Paradise Lost* 5. 272–274, quoted in n22. Cf. also Satan's parodic invocation of the sun at *Paradise Lost* 4.32–37: "O thou that ... /Lookst from thy *sole* dominion ... / ... / to thee I call,/ ... and add thy name,/O *Sun*, to tell thee how I hate thy beams." Emphasis is mine.

[65] Manso's showcasing of the "Poesie di Diversi" at this point in the volume may have been influence by the *Della Lira del Cavalier Marino Parte Terza* (Venice: Giovanni Battista Ciotti, 1616), which likewise concludes in a section (with a new title page [307], letter to the reader [308], and with sequential pagination [309–370]) entitled "Poesie di Diversi. Al Cavalier Marino."

[66] *Poesie Nomiche*, 255: "secondo l'ordine de' tempi, ch'à lui furono da gli Autori stessi mandate" ("in accordance with the chronological order in which they were submitted by the Authors themselves"). On chronology as the governing factor, cf. the letter to the reader prefacing the "Poesie di Diversi al Cavalier Marino" (on which see previous note) at *Della Lira*, 308: "non si è osservato altro ordine, che quello del tempo" ("no other order was observed than chronological").

della dignità di coloro, che le composero").[67] There follow 110 encomia (106 sonnets[68] and 4 canzone).[69] Among the contributors are such esteemed authors as Tasso, Marino, Angelo Di Costanzo, Ascanio Pignatello, and Giulio Cesare Caracciolo. In short, the whole is an elaborate exercise in self-promotion,[70] advertising the height of Manso's contemporary reputation, while simultaneously revealing the extent of his networking with learned poets and academicians. It is this last section of the volume that is of particular relevance to *Mansus*.

Milton's Italian experience, as noted earlier, reveals him as a poet who readily responded to contemporary literary vogues.[71] Among these the encomiastic seems to have exerted a particular magnetism. For example, his three Latin epigrams addressed to Leonora Baroni,[72] pertaining to either or both of his Roman sojourns, assume a place alongside a volume of *Applausi* that was currently being planned in the soprano's honor (it would eventually see publication in 1639).[73] Indeed, some of the poems eventually included therein were probably circulating in manuscript in Rome, perhaps receiving their trial performance in the city's foremost academies, at a time when news of the planned volume was undoubtedly in the air.[74] Milton's third Latin epigram interestingly describes Leonora as *Romulidum studiis ornata secundis* (7) ("adorned by the favorable enthusiasm of the sons of Romulus"). This acknowledgment may extend beyond the responses of members of a Roman audience actually listening to her performance to embrace an essentially literary

---

[67] *Poesie Nomiche*, 255.

[68] See *Poesie Nomiche*, 257–311. One contribution, at 286–287 (by Estonne Stordito), actually comprises 4 sonnets, which are designated as "Corone."

[69] See *Poesie Nomiche*, 312–315 (Antonio Bruni); 316–321 (Gabriel Zinani); 322–324 (Torquato Accetto); 324–326 (Teofilo Gallicini).

[70] Several of the "Poesie di Diversi" and other encomia of Manso, with corrections in Manso's hand, are extant in the BNN as MS XIII. C. 82. See Pietro Giulio Riga, "Alcune Note sulle Tendenze Letterarie nell' Accademia degli Oziosi di Napoli," in *Le Virtuose Adunanze. La Cultura Accademica tra XVI e XVIII Secolo*, eds. Clizia Gurreri and Ilaria Bianchi (Avellino: Edizioni Sinestesie, 2014), 159–171, at 168.

[71] See 29–34.

[72] See *Ad Leonoram Romae Canentem*, and two further epigrams *Ad Eandem* at *Poemata*, 42–43; Lewalski and Haan, 160–163, 448–451.

[73] *Applausi Poetici alle Glorie della Signora Leonora Baroni*, ed. Francesco Ronconi (Bracciano: Giovanni Battista Cavario, 1639).

[74] For discussion of Milton's three epigrams in the context of the *Applausi*, see Haan, *From Academia to Amicitia*, 105–117; Haan, *John Milton's Roman Sojourns*, 112–137.

reaction, the latter reading rendered possible by the twofold meaning of *studium* as "enthusiasm" and "intellectual activity."[75]

In the case of *Mansus*, a not dissimilar Neapolitan encomiastic vogue is signaled, but much more explicitly so. This is evinced by the Headnote's description of Manso as *apud Italos clarus* ("famous among/[in the writings of?][76] the Italians"), and, especially, by the poem's opening lines. Of particular note here is the inclusion of the adverb *quoque* (*Haec quoque, Manse, tuae meditantur carmina laudi/Pierides* [1–2] ["These verses *too*, Manse, do the Pierians compose in your praise"]),[77] and the description of Manso as one who is "very well known to the choir of Phoebus" (*tibi, Manse, choro notissime Phoebi* [2]), by which god he, like Gallus and Maecenas, has been honored (3–4). The language reworks a detail from the song of Silenus in Virgil's sixth *Eclogue*, in which the "choir of Phoebus" is described as rising in honor of Gallus: *utque viro Phoebi chorus adsurrexerit omnis* ("and how the whole choir of Phoebus rose up before the man" [*Eclogue* 6.66]).[78] That Gallus (like Manso) was both a soldier and a poet[79] makes the analogy particularly pertinent. But the phrase assumes additional significance, given its explicit association with Manso in the "Poesie di Diversi." Thus, Don Vincenzo Toraldo, proclaiming the rebirth of ancient poetry in Manso's very pen, depicts the Pierides ("le figlie di Pierio") as subdued and vanquished ("e dome, e vinte"), as they weave for him garlands of victory. "It is in our age," he continues, "that Phoebus has renewed the glories of his extinct Choir" ("Sì che ne l'età nostra in voi rinova/Le glorie Febo del suo Choro estinte").[80] Likewise, according to Scipione Sambiasi, Manso wins the admiration of "Febo frà i chori Aonii" ("Phoebus among the Aonian choirs").[81] In Milton's appropriation the

---

[75] See *OLD*, s.v. 2: "enthusiasm, eagerness (for)"; s.v. 7: "intellectual activity, esp. of a literary kind, or an instance of it, study."

[76] See *OLD*, s.v. *apud*: 6: "[i]n the writings of, 'in' (a writer); in (a book)."

[77] Emphasis is mine.

[78] All quotations are from *Vergil: Eclogues*, ed. Robert Coleman (Cambridge: Cambridge University Press, 1977).

[79] On Virgil's representation of Gallus, see, among others, R. B. Rutherford, "Virgil's Poetic Ambitions in *Eclogue* 6," *G&R* 36 (1989): 42–50; A. J. Woodman, "The Position of Gallus in *Eclogue* 6," *CQ* 47 (1997): 593–597; Francis Cairns, *Sextus Propertius: The Augustan Elegist* (Cambridge: Cambridge University Press, 2006), 120–122; Aaron M. Seider, "Genre, Gallus, and Goats: Expanding the Limits of Pastoral in *Eclogues* 6 and 10," *Vergilius* 62 (2016): 3–23.

[80] *Poesie Nomiche*, 262. For further discussion of possible links between the two poems, see Haan, *From Academia to Amicitia*, 140.

[81] *Poesie Nomiche*, 280.

choir is similarly demythologized in its transformation into that of contemporary poets. The transformation may well have been facilitated by Jean Luis De La Cerda's gloss on the Virgilian phrase as: *Chorus Phoebi, videlicet, Musae, Nymphae, Poetae* ("the Choir of Phoebus, evidently, Muses, Nymphs, *Poets*").[82] It is alongside these Italian encomia that Milton juxtaposes *Mansus*. With linguistic self-consciousness, hinting perhaps at his code-selection of Latin,[83] as opposed to Italian, he adds a parenthetical allusion to *Camoena* (*si nostrae tantum valet aura Camoenae* (5) ("if the breath of our Camena has power so great"). *Camoena*, one of the Muses (as identified with Roman water deities), occurs elsewhere in Milton's Latin poetry to signal the choice of Latin as linguistic medium. Thus, in *Elegia Sexta*, he had asked Charles Diodati: *At tua quid nostram prolectat Musa camoenam?* (3) ("But why does your Muse entice my Camena?"). Here, as Bush suggests, the juxtaposition of *Musa* and *Camoena* seems to signal a

---

[82] Jean Luis De La Cerda, *P. Virgili Maronis Bucolica et Georgica Argumentis, Explicationibus, et Notis Illustrata* (Cologne: Bernhard Wolter, 1628), 122. Emphasis is mine. On Milton's recourse to De La Cerda's edition of the Virgilian corpus, see Craig Kallendorf, "Epic and Tragedy—Virgil, La Cerda, Milton," in *Syntagmatia: Essays on Neo-Latin Literature in Honour of Monique Mund-Dopchie and Gilbert Tourney*, eds. Dirk Sacré and Jan Papy (Leuven: Leuven University Press, 2009), 579–593; Haan, *Bilingualism and Biculturalism*, 172–174, 193, 196.

[83] Latin encomia of Manso are comparatively rare. See the two poems, by Christopher Martinius and Antonio Biaguazzoni, prefixed to Manso's *I Paradossi*, at sig. B4^r–B4^v. Martinius's poem ([*inc.*] *Insequeris bellum: penetralia pandis amoris* ["You pursue war: you reveal the innermost qualities of love"]) contrasts Manso's military achievements with his insights into love (the theme of the volume in question), teasing out the oxymoronic coexistence of *amor* and *bellum*. Biaguazzoni's encomium ([*inc.*] *Fortia te Scyticos iaculantem tela per hostes* ["as you hurl brave weapons in the midst of your Scythian enemies"]) depicts Manso as a fierce warrior beheld by Venus. Adjudging him as surpassing Mars himself, the goddess wishes that he had felt the flames of love and fantasizes about the military vengeance he could have wrought on her behalf. For later examples, see Giuseppe Battista, *Epigrammatum Centuria Prima* (Venice: Baba, 1659), 23: *De Ioanne Baptista Manso Otiosorum Academiae Principe*: *Emicuit Caesar, gens est mirata Quirini,/In bello dexter, dexter in eloquio./Parthenope stupeat Mansum, qui sustulit unus/Barbariem calamo, barbariem gladio* ("On Giovanni Battista Manso, Principal of the Accademia degli Oziosi: Caesar has darted forth [to the amazement of the nation of Quirinus], skillful in war, skillful in eloquence. Let Parthenope be amazed by Manso, who has single-handedly stood up to barbarity with his pen, to barbarity with his sword"). See also the same author's epitaph of Manso appended to *Centuria Tertia* of that work, especially its opening wordplay: *Ioanni Baptistae Manso,/Temporis dente non manso,/Sed totum mansuro per aevum* ("To Giovanni Battista Manso, who has not been bitten by the tooth of Time, but is destined to endure through every generation"). Here Battista plays on Manso's name (in *manso* [past participle of *mandere*: "to bite"] and in *mansuro* [future participle of *manere* ["to remain"/"endure"]).

contrast between Diodati's probable use of Greek (in the lost letter to which the elegy replies) with Milton's use of Latin in this instance.[84] In this reading, *si ... tantum valet* (*Mansus* 5) assumes additional potency: if my Latin poem proves to be as efficacious as its Italian sister tributes. And if so, then Manso will sit among the ivies and laurels of victory: *Victrices hederas inter laurosque sedebis* (6).[85] In short, he will be decked with accoutrements befitting such Latin poets as Horace.[86]

Mansus can also take its place alongside Italian laurels, so to speak, the "Poesie di Diversi," with which it shares a range of themes. Some of these parallels, which I have discussed elsewhere,[87] are probably best viewed collectively as a somewhat predictable and even inevitable reflection of contemporary responses to Manso's well-established reputation: the acknowledgment of the Marquis's fame in both literature and warfare;[88] his equation with the paragon of patrons, Maecenas;[89] his

---

[84] Bush, *Variorum* I, 115. See also Lewalski and Haan, 439.

[85] The line is a virtually verbatim echo of *Ad Patrem* 102, for discussion of which, see 168–171.

[86] Cf. Horace, *Odes* 1.1.29–32.

[87] See Haan, *From Academia to Amicitia*, 137–148.

[88] See Headnote to *Mansus*: *vir ingenii laude, tum litterarum studio, nec non et bellica virtute apud Italos clarus in primis est* ("a man more famous than any other among the Italians, not only for the reputation of his genius and his pursuit of literary studies, but also for his bravery in war"). Cf. Antonio Biaguazzone, "Loda la mano impiegata nell'armi, e nello scriver d'Amore" ("He praises the hand which is employed in arms and in writing about love") (*Poesie Nomiche*, 266); idem, "Loda l'imprese dell' armi, e i dialoghi dell' Amore" ("He praises his exploits in arms and his dialogues on love") (266); Giovanni Soranzo, "Passagio dall'Imprese militari allo scriver d'Amore" ("The transition from military enterprises to writing about love") (271); Scipione Sambiasi, "Glorioso colla spada, e colla penna" ("Glorious with the sword and with the pen") (280). Similarly, Anello Sarriano, in a sonnet entitled "Dà morte con la spada, e vita con la penna" ("He deals death with the sword, and life with the pen"), addresses him as "MANSO, che sai trattar forte, e canoro/Ne la guerra il valor, in pace il canto" ("MANSO, who knows how to use brave valor in war, and harmonious song in peace") (301). See also Scipione Errico, "Loda l'attioni nella guerra, e lo studio nelle scienze" ("He praises his exploits in war and his study in the sciences") (302); Gio. Battista Comentati, "Lodato nella guerra, e nella pace" ("He is praised in war and in peace") (304); Andrea Vittorelli, "Loda nella militia, e nella dottrina" ("Praise in warfare and in learning") (310); Vincenzo Petrone, "Paragona le lodi nel guerreggiare, e nello scrivere" ("He compares his praise in warfare and in writing") (310). See Haan, *From Academia to Amicitia*, 137–139.

[89] *Mansus* 3–4: *Quandoquidem ille* [sc. *Phoebus*] *alium haud aequo est dignatus honore/Post Galli cineres et Mecaenatis Etrusci* ("inasmuch as he [Apollo] has deemed no one else worthy of equal distinction since the death of Gallus and Etruscan Maecenas"). Estonne Stordito salutes Manso as a "novo Mecena, e glorioso" ("a

explicit association with triumphal laurel wreaths of poetry and victory;[90] his links with Jupiter and Apollo.[91] But in other instances points of contact seem to suggest something more.

3.2.1 Tasso, Marino, Milton

From the opening lines of *Mansus*, Milton seems to take almost quite literally as his point of departure an Italian sonnet, entitled "Il loda nelle lodi del Tasso, e del Marino" ("Praise inherent in the praises of Tasso and Marino") by the dramatist and poet Angelita Scaramuccia:[92]

---

modern and glorious Maecenas") (*Poesie Nomiche*, 286), and, again, as a "Maecenas whose name will never have an end" ("Mecenate, il cui nome unqua haurà fine") (287).

[90] *Mansus* 5–6: *Tu quoque, si nostrae tantum valet aura Camoenae,/Victrices hederas inter laurosque sedebis* ("You too, if the breath of our Camena has power so great, will sit among the ivies and laurels of victory"). Giulio Cesare Caracciolo, at *Poesie Nomiche*, 262, depicts Manso as girt with "allori di sacra fronde" ("laurels of sacred foliage"); Giambattista Marino, at 268, envisages Manso's brow as "Di verde trionfal cinto" ("encircled with triumphal verdure"). According to Giacomo Colonna, at 272, Phoebus is preparing supreme glories for Manso's deserving locks in the form of an adornment of gold and of laurel ("Fregi d'oro, e d'allor, glorie supreme/Prepari Febo al tuo ben degno crine"). Likewise, in the words of Donato Antonio Cito, at 284, "Febo al tuo crine'l suo bel Lauro cede" ("Phoebus yields to your hair his beautiful Laurel").

[91] *Mansus* 70–71: *te Iuppiter aequus oportet/Nascentem, et miti lustrarit lumine Phoebus* ("Jupiter must have favored you at birth, and Phoebus must have looked upon you with kindly glance"), for discussion of which, see also 95–96. Giovanni Ambrosio Biffi, at *Poesie Nomiche*, 267, compares Manso to Jupiter, Apollo and Mars ("Il pareggia à Giove, Apollo, & à Marte"). Thus, Manso's valor renders him a second Jupiter, flashing with lightning ("Un folgorante Giove il tuo valore/Ti rende"). Antonio Gallerati, at 267, compares him to Apollo in terms of warfare and song ("Il paragona ad Apollo nell'arme, e nel canto"). Cf. idem at *Poesie Nomiche*, 268: "Honorato da Apollo, e da Marte" ("Honored by Apollo and by Mars").

[92] Angelita Scaramuccia (born in Montecassiano some time between 1580 and 1590, and with 4 February 1638 as the *terminus post quem* for his death) was quite a prolific dramatist in his day. Among his published works are several comedies, including *Gli Amor Concordi* (Macerata: Pietro Salvioni, 1618), *La Schiava di Cipro* (Macerata: Pietro Salvioni, 1624), *Il Garbuglio* (Macerata: Pietro Salvioni, 1624), *La Damigella* (Rome: Pietro Salvioni 1631), *La Vagante di Egitto* (Rome: Pietro Salvioni, 1631), and *Il Belisario* (Rome: Lodovico Grignano, 1635). He also authored *Discorso Historico ... sopra l'Origine, e Rovina di Ricinia, e dell' Edificatione, ed Avenimenti di Monte Cassiano* (Loreto: Paolo and Giovanni Battista Serafini, 1638). See Pietro Giulio Riga, "Scaramuccia, Angelita," *DBI* 91 (2018): 320–322. See ibid. for confusion among scholars about his gender, arising from his self-appellation

> Gloria di Pindo, honor del secol nostro,
>   Pregio di Febo e Marte, al cui gentile
>   Eccelso nome io riverente humile,
>   MANSO, inchino'l pensier, sacro l'inchiostro.
> Cedano à voi l'alte corone, e l'ostro,   5
>   Voi, cui la fama oltre a l'estrema Thile
>   Porta raccolta in sen d'heroico stile
>   Di saver, di valor mirabil mostro.
> Voi protettor de l'alta, che Buglione
>   Tromba cantò con celebrato grido,   10
>   Voi del plettro dolcissimo d'Adone.
> Di me peregrin tratto à questo lido
>   Per sì, di veder voi, nobil cagione,
>   Gradite il cor divoto, il voler fido.[93]

> Glory of Mount Pindus, honor of our age, merit of Phoebus and Mars, to your noble, sublime name, MANSO, I reverently and humbly incline my thought, and consecrate my ink. Let lofty garlands and purple yield to you, you whose fame a collection (of poems) carries within its heroic style beyond furthermost Thule—a wonderful prodigy of your wisdom and valor. You were the patron of the lofty trumpet which sang of Bouillon with its renowned blare; you were the patron of the very sweet plectrum of *L'Adone*. Accept the devoted heart and loyal desire of myself, a foreigner, brought to this shore for the noble reason of seeing you.

Here Manso, hailed as the glory of Mount Pindus, and worthy of lofty garlands ("l'alte corone" [5]) and of purple, is celebrated as the patron ("protettor" [9]) of: (a) Tasso, unnamed, but signaled implicitly by reference to Godfrey of Bouillon ("Buglione" [9]) in *Gerusalemme Liberata* (1581);[94] (b) Marino, again unnamed, but signaled by the periphrastic "very sweet plectrum of Adonis" ("plettro dolcissimo

---

"Angelita." His self-descriptions in his work (including the present poem) clearly signal his identity as male.

[93] *Poesie Nomiche*, 300.

[94] Tasso, *Gerusalemme Liberata* (Parma: Erasmo Viotti, 1581). The epic nature of the work is highlighted in Scaramuccia's "alta …/Tromba" (9–10), evocative of the *tuba*, the classical symbol of martial epic (cf., for example, Statius, *Thebaid* 7.628–631; 11.49–56; Martial, *Epigrams* 8.3.22, 10.64.4, 11.3.8), on which see Alessandro Barchiesi, "Masculinity in the 90's: The Education of Achilles in Statius and Quintilian," in *Roman and Greek Imperial Epic*, ed. Michael Paschalis (Herakleion: Crete University Press, 2005), 47–75, at 65–66.

d'Adone" [11]), an allusion to *L'Adone* (1623),[95] Marino's poetic rendering of the myth of Venus and Adonis. Then the sonneteer introduces himself as a foreigner ("me peregrin" [12]), brought to this shore ("tratto à questo lido" [12]) for a very noble purpose, that of seeing Manso himself.[96]

The structural and thematic progression of the sonnet from wreaths of victory to the renown secured by Manso's patronage of Tasso and Marino (with indirect allusion to a poem by each) to the speaker as a foreigner reaching Italian shores is quite strikingly mirrored and amplified in *Mansus*. Thus, as noted earlier, Manso will sit among the ivies and laurels of victory (6). There follows a reference to: (a) Tasso, now explicitly named (*Te pridem magno felix concordia Tasso/Iunxit* [7–8] ["In the past a happy bond of friendship joined you to the mighty Tasso"]) and, by implication, his *Gerusalemme Conquistata* (1593), in whose eternal pages the Italian poet has inscribed Manso's name (*et aeternis inscripsit nomina chartis* [8]), an inscription quoted directly in the poem's Headnote;[97] (b) Marino, again explicitly named (*dulciloquum ... Marinum* [9] ["sweetly-speaking Marino"]), and described as an *alumnus* (10) ("foster-child"), who enjoyed Manso's patronage "as he proclaimed in verbose song the Assyrian love-affairs of the gods" (*Dum canit Assyrios divum prolixus amores* [11]), an implicit allusion to *L'Adone*, via Venus's appellation "Assyrian."[98] Milton's direct naming of the two Italian poets may well be related to the continued emphasis in *Mansus* on the importance of inscribed *nomina*, a point to which this discussion will return.[99] Like "dolcissimo" (11), Milton's *dulciloquus* (9) signals the "sweetness" of Marino's language, but his addition of the

---

[95] Marino, *L'Adone* (Paris: Oliviero di Varano, 1623).

[96] *Poesie Nomiche*, 300. See Haan, *From Academia to Amicitia*, 142–143. Scaramuzzia also extols Manso in his comedy *La Vagante di Egitto*, III.2. Here, the servant Contrulla, boasting of his Neapolitan identity, lists among examples of Neapolitan poets Sannazaro, Tasso, Marino and '[l]o Marchise Manso ca vive mò, chiù bravo de tutti li nominati" ("the Marquis Manso who is alive today, more brave than all the aforementioned"). See Scaramuccia, *La Vagante di Egitto*, 64.

[97] *Mansus*, Headnote: *erat enim Tassi amicissimus; ab quo etiam inter Campaniae principes celebratur in illo poemate cui titulus Gerusalemme Conquistita, lib. 20:* "Fra cavalier magnanimi e cortesi/Risplende il Manso" ("for he was a very good friend of Tasso, by whom he is also celebrated among the princes of Campania in that poem which is entitled *The Conquest of Jerusalem*, book 20: 'Among great-hearted and courteous knights Manso is resplendent ...'"). The reference is to *Gerusalemme Conquistita* 20.142. See *Poemata*, 72; Lewalski and Haan, 204–205, 482.

[98] Cf. Milton, *A Maske*, 1002: "Sadly sits th'Assyrian Queen."

[99] See 84–85.

potentially pejorative adjective *prolixus* (11) not only highlights *L'Adone*'s length (over 5,000 octavos) and verbosity, but, as argued later in this study, evokes perhaps the two extremes of the Marinesque style as perceived by the poem's earliest readers, and as scrutinized in what amounted to print warfare.[100] Like Scaramuccia, Milton proceeds to introduce himself as a foreigner, a *peregrinus* (26), but his self-fashioning is subtly different. For this *peregrinus* is qualified by the adjective *iuvenis* (26) ("young"),[101] whereby John (*Ioannes*) punningly mirrors Giovanni ("giovane"/ "young") Battista Manso, while simultaneously contrasting with the twice addressed *senex* of the poem.[102] Scaramuccia's self-description as one who has been "tratto à questo lido" (12) is perhaps hinted at in Milton's comparable use of the perfect participle in *Missus Hyperboreo ... ab axe* (26) ("sent from the Hyperborean sky"). Likewise, the reference to what constituted in effect Scramuccia's intra-Italian travels (between Montecassanio and Rome)[103] is mirrored, at least at first glance, in *Italas ... per urbes* (29). Now, however, human agency is conflated with the divine in the form of the Miltonic Muse, poorly nourished in a cold northern climate, but self-consciously audacious, even rash, in a flight (*volitare* [29])[104] that is evocative of Ennius's self-penned epitaph: *volito vivus per ora virum*,[105] ("I fly victorious on the lips of men"), its associated bird-imagery,[106] its appropriation by Virgil,[107] and,

---

[100] See 184–194.

[101] With Milton's phraseology, cf. Baptista Mantuanus, *De Sancto Rocho*, 11–13, in *Fastorum Libri Duodecim* (Cologne: Maternus Cholinus, 1561), 206: *Iam iuvenis studio impulsus Romana videndi/Limina, et ossa patrum cryptis abscondita sacris/Est aggressus iter Latias peregrinus ad oras* ("Already the *young foreigner*, driven by an eagerness to see the thresholds of Rome, and the bones of his fathers buried in sacred crypts, undertook a journey to the shores of Latium"). Emphasis is mine.

[102] *Mansus* 49: *Fortunate senex*; 70: *Diis dilecte senex*, discussed at 57–58 and 87–88.

[103] See Riga, "Scaramuccia, Angelita."

[104] For Milton's implementation of the metaphor of flight to describe his Italian journey, cf. *Ad Salsillum* 10–14: *Diebus hisce qui suum linquens nidum/Polique tractum ... / ... / ... /Venit feraces Itali soli ad glebas* ("who in recent days has left his own nest and region of the sky ... and has come to the fertile clods of Italian soil").

[105] See Ennius, *Varia* 17–18 V². Cf. Cicero, *Tusculanae Disputationes* 1.34, 1.117.

[106] Michael Putnam views the Ennian image as denoting a bird "flying before the faces of men." See Michael C. J. Putnam, *Virgil's Poem of the Earth: Studies in the Georgics* (Princeton, NJ: Princeton University Press, 1979), 166.

[107] Virgil, *Georgics* 3.8–9: *temptanda via est, qua me quoque possim/tollere humo victorque virum volitare per ora* ("I must attempt a way whereby I too can elevate myself above the ground, and 'fly victorious on the lips of men.'") All quotations

perhaps, a Miltonic quest for poetic immortality.[108] At the same time, this imaginative reworking of a poem by *Angelita* Scaramuccia (emphasis mine) is particularly apt, a coded response perhaps by another, this time Miltonic, "little Angel" to Manso's punning distich?[109] More generally, the concept announced in the Italian sonnet's title: that praise of Manso coexists with, and is intrinsically linked to, the praises bestowed upon him by Tasso and Marino is later developed in *Mansus* (49–53) into the prediction of a Mansonian fame by association. Central to that fame are the perennial powers afforded Manso by the inscription of his "name" in literary works.[110] Tasso, in Milton's words, has "inscribed [Manso's] name in his eternal pages" (*et aeternis inscripsit nomina chartis* [8]). He has done so by explicit mention of him in the *Gerusalemme Conquistata*, and also, and especially, by the honorific title of his Dialogue on Friendship (*Il Manso*),[111] a point likewise made in the Headnote to *Mansus*.[112] Winning the praises of Tasso was no mean feat, as Milton's lines imply. Indeed, Ascanio Pignatello, in an encomium entitled "Il ringratia d'haverlo lodato a Torquato Tasso," proclaims the felicity of the contemporary age in witnessing Tasso's elevation of Manso's name.[113] Marino, too, had secured Manso's fame in print in his effusive "Lettera all' Autore" (dated 16 March 1625) prefixed to Manso's *Erocallia*.[114] And both poets had, as it were, written their own names into Manso's

---

from Virgil, unless otherwise stated, are from *P. Vergili Maronis Opera*, ed. F. A. Hirtzel (Oxford: Clarendon Press, 1942).

[108] For Milton's use of flight imagery to describe his artistic aspirations, cf. his announcement to Charles Diodati in *Epistola Familiaris* 7 (dated 23 September 1637): Πτεροφυῶ et volare meditor, sed tenellis admodum adhuc pennis evehit se noster Pegasus: humile sapiamus ("'I am growing wings' and I am practising flight, but as yet our Pegasus is raising himself up on very delicate wings: let my wisdom be grounded in humility"). See *John Milton, Epistolarum Familiarium Liber Unus and Uncollected Letters*, ed. Haan, 101, 104–105, 111. For a later example, see *Paradise Lost* 7.3–4: "above the Olympian hill I soar,/Above the flight of Pegasean wing."

[109] See 46.

[110] According to Angelo di Costanzo, at *Poesie Nomiche*, 257, Manso's name ("i'l tuo nome") has no fear of time or death.

[111] For further discussion, see Chapter 5.

[112] *Mansus*, Headnote: *Ad quem Torquati Tassi dialogus exstat de Amicitia scriptus* ("There is extant a dialogue on Friendship, which Torquato Tasso addressed to him").

[113] *Poesie Nomiche*, 261: "Felice è questa età, che sorger visto/Sì chiaro hà'l nome vostro" ("Blessed is this age which has seen the elevation of your name so luminous").

[114] See *Erocallia*, sig. a2^r–b2^v ("Lettera del Cavalier Gio. Battista Marino all' Autore"). See also 41.

eternal pages by contributing encomiastic sonnets to the "Poesie di Diversi." No fewer than six sonnets by Tasso seem to be afforded pride of place therein, assuming their position as nos. 2–7 of the 110 poems.[115] The first of these interestingly proclaims the inscribed Manso: thus "the gods have written your name not only in one thousand pages, but in beautiful metal or in stone" ("E'l nome vostro in bel metallo, o in pietra/Scriver si dee, non solo in mille carte" [5–6]).[116] Then just eight pages later there occur three sonnets by Marino.[117] Read in this context, *Mansus* itself serves as a Miltonic act of inscription, an encomiastic gesture that is thus both Tassonian and Marinesque.[118]

3.2.2 Accademia degli Oziosi: *Mansus* and Pastoral *Otium*

A recurring leitmotif of the "Poesie di Diversi" is the unique nature of the *otium* that Manso's academy eponymously afforded its members. In short, the name "Oziosi" and the academy's *impresa* (the aforementioned eagle sitting on a hill with its gaze firmly fixed upon the sun),[119] and associated motto (*Non Pigra Quies*),[120] signified, in the words of their esteemed inventor, Francesco De Pietri, "non già dell' otio scioperato, ò neghittosa, ma del letterario, e virtuoso" ("a leisure that is not idle or negligent, but one that pertains to literature and to virtue.")[121] It is not entirely surprising, therefore, that Giovanni Camillo Cacace's sonnet,

---

[115] *Poesie Nomiche*, 257–260.

[116] *Poesie Nomiche* 257. The sonnet is entitled "Loda 'l valor mostrato nelle guerre" ("He praises his valor demonstrated in warfare"). Likewise, at 279, Ottavio Sbarra describes Manso as "celebrato in mille Eroiche carte" ("celebrated in a thousand heroic pages").

[117] *Poesie Nomiche*, 268–269.

[118] In *Mansus* the immortalizing powers of inscribing are also presented as reciprocated in Manso's role as biographer of both poets (18–23), and in Milton's implicit quest for his own biographer (85). For further discussion, see Chapter 4.

[119] See 72–73.

[120] See Maylender, *Storia*, IV, 183.

[121] Francesco De Pietri, *I Problemi Accademici*, sig. C2^v (*Proemio*). To elucidate the essentially active nature of this *otium*, De Pietri invokes Cicero's reference to Scipio's potentially cryptic remark that "he was never less 'at leisure' than when he was 'at leisure'" (*numquam se minus otiosum esse quam cum otiosus ... esset*) (Cicero, *De Officiis* 3.1). For the suggestion that this academic contrast between intellectual activity and slothful inertia was remembered much later by the poet of *Paradise Lost* (especially in the depiction of the fallen angels in Book 1), see Anna K. Nardo, "Academic Interludes in *Paradise Lost*," *MS* 27 (1991): 209–241, at 217–219.

entitled "Desidera esser seco nell' Accademia" ("He longs to be with him in the Academy"), dismisses, in a series of four negatives, the traditional features of pastoral *otium*: a comfortably couched dwelling, the cool shade of a tree, the earth enveloped by flowers, the sweet murmur of a river, only to substitute in their place the haunts of Hebe, Athena, the Muses, a divine Cupid playing his sacred lyre, and the Castalian spring. It is here that "Manso happily enjoys a leisure that is not slothful" ("MANSO, gode non PIGRO OTIO felice"), and it is here that the speaker envisages himself assuming a place of his own.[122] The seemingly antipastoral likewise lies at the heart of Girolamo Stella's implementation of essentially civic language in his sonnet addressed "All'Accademia delli Otiosi fondata dal Marchese" ("To the Oziosi Academy founded by the Marquis"), an academy herein described as a wise senate ("saggio senato"), and a theater of valor (Teatro di valor"), the door to which is none other than Manso himself ("cui MANSO è porta").[123] Other contributors, however, do attempt to reconcile the bellicose and the pastoral. Thus, for Tomaso Ciamboli, the Oziosi does indeed afford the poet an essential refuge from hostile warfare:

> Però fuggendo a te da le crud' armi
>   Di tai nemici anch'io, dal volgo fuori
>   In sì nobil magion tento ritrarmi.
> Ove l'Otio spargendo ampi sudori
>   Sù i bei campi di gloria al suon de' carmi,
>   Miete palme, e trofei di mille honori.[124]

> Yet I too, by fleeing to you from cruel battle and from such enemies, try to retire from the populace outside into so noble a dwelling, where leisure, by lavishing toil in abundance upon the beautiful fields of glory to the sound of music, wins palms and trophies of a thousand honors.

In a series of striking oxymorons, *otium* itself is presented as facilitating academic toils very different from those effected in war, whose battlefields are hereby transformed into the beautiful fields ("bei campi") of a *locus amoenus*. It is here, amid the sound of bucolic music, as opposed to the sound of war, that the speaker can win metaphorical "palms." Francesco Vivo describes the leisurely repose of the Oziosi

---

[122] *Poesie Nomiche*, 274.

[123] *Poesie Nomiche*, 298.

[124] *Poesie Nomiche*, 281.

Eagle in its lazy nest, while simultaneously contrasting it with Manso's military activity, only to equate himself with that bird by addressing Manso as his sun.[125] Valeriano Seca Vescovo d'Alife, proclaiming "Il loda nell' Otio dell'Academia") ("Praise inherent in the Leisure of the Academy"), situates Manso's military achievements alongside his "otio" by appropriating traditional aspects of the *locus amoenus* on a metaphorical level. Thus the Academy's glorious stillness ("vostra quiete gloriosa") is likened to that possessed by the earth, which, though motionless, is forever productive, her womb fertile with grass and abounding in flowers.[126] Likewise, Donato Facciuti, hymning the "leisure" afforded by the Academy amid the toils of war and studies ("Otio dell'Accademia frà le fatiche della guerra, e degli studi"), salutes Manso as an invincible warrior and an accomplished writer, winner of the heroic laurels of war and poetry. In short, he is both a modern Achilles and a modern Homer.[127] And for Francesco Mega, who "Chiede esser ammesso nell'Accademia" ("Asks to be admitted to the Academy"), Manso's "otio," significantly qualified as wise ("saggio"), constitutes a force that possesses a particular magnetism, the whole resulting in a collective musicianship that vanquishes the harmony of the heavens.[128]

In *Mansus*, by contrast, the traditional aspects of *otium* are strikingly reinstated. This is evinced by the poem's inherent pastoralism, its various and varying representations of the *locus amoenus*, and, especially, by its rich intertextual engagement with Virgil's *Eclogues*. By addressing Manso as *Fortunate senex* (49) and *Diis dilecte senex* (70), Milton implicitly equates the Neapolitan with the Tityrus of Virgil's first *Eclogue*, while his own implicit self-fashioning is as that poem's Meliboeus, who twice apostrophizes Tityrus as *fortunate senex* (46, 51). Its first occurrence signals Meliboeus's acknowledgment of the seemingly perennial security afforded Tityrus by his pastoral landscape: *Fortunate senex, ergo tua rura manebunt/et tibi magna satis* (46–47) ("Blessed old man! So these lands will remain yours, and large enough for you"). The accolade in itself is not enough. Rather, by following it with the telling adverb *ergo*, Meliboeus proffers, in the words of Gregson Davis, "a *subjective inference* regarding Tityrus' *eudaimonia*."[129] Milton

---

[125] *Poesie Nomiche*, 295.

[126] *Poesie Nomiche*, 275.

[127] *Poesie Nomiche*, 301.

[128] *Poesie Nomiche*, 300.

[129] Gregson Davis, *Parthenope: The Interplay of Ideas in Vergilian Bucolic* (Leiden: Brill, 2012), 29. On *eudaimonia*, the Aristotelian concept of ideal happiness or well-being, see, among others, John L. Ackrill, "Aristotle on Eudaimonia," *PBA* 60 (1974):

echoes the sequence by proclaiming *Fortunate senex, ergo ...* (49), only to transform a subjective forecast of perennial agrarian security, even if dismally tainted by stone and marshland,[130] into something much more lofty: a prediction of the eternal fame afforded Manso by his connections with two famous poets: Tasso and Marino (49–53). The second occurrence of *fortunate senex* in Virgil's poem is also a second prediction. Having forecast that Tityrus's flocks will be impervious to disease, Meliboeus presents an idealized vision of the pastoral landscape, its streams, cool shade, the sleep-inducing humming of bees, and birdsong, which, he predicts, his addressee will be blessed to enjoy.[131] This "full-blown fantasy of total felicity"[132] embraces the characteristic ingredients of the pastoral *locus amoenus*.[133] In short, the repeated *fortunate senex*, as Robert Coleman aptly notes, "introduces a wistful transformation of the humble realities of Tityrus' land into an idyllic landscape,"[134] one which, in the words of Davis "prominently frames a picture of a future irreversible bliss that, at bottom, reflects [Meliboeus'] own subliminal fantasies of perfect *eudaimonia*."[135] Significantly, in *Mansus*, the reiteration of the *fortunate senex* motif substitutes different qualifiers: *Diis dilecte senex* (70) ("Old man, beloved of the gods"), whereby a Meliboean prediction of future happiness is replaced by a Miltonic inference of past divine blessings, which must have been bestowed upon Manso at the time of his birth (*te .../Nascentem* [70–71]).[136] Again the whole is linked to the Neapolitan's association with

---

339–359; Brendan Cook, *Pursuing Eudaimonia: Re-Appropriating the Greek Philosophical Foundations of the Christian Apophatic Tradition* (Newcastle upon Tyne: Cambridge Scholars Publishing, 2013); Øyvind Rabbås, "*Eudaimonia*, Human Nature, and Normativity: Reflections on Aristotle's Project in *Nicomachean Ethics* Book I," in *The Quest for the Good Life: Ancient Philosophers on Happiness*, eds. Øyvind Rabbås, Eyjólfur K. Emilsson, Hallvard Fossheim, and Miira Tuominen (Oxford: Oxford University Press, 2015), 88–112.

[130] Virgil, *Eclogue* 1.47–48: *quamvis lapis omnia nudus/limosoque palus obducat pascua iunco* ("even though bare rock and marshland with its muddy reeds obstruct all the pastures").

[131] Virgil, *Eclogue* 1.51–58.

[132] Davis, *Parthenope*, 29.

[133] For the characteristic features of the *locus amoenus*, see Ernst Robert Curtius, *European Literature and the Latin Middle Ages* (London: Routledge, 1953), 195, quoted at 91.

[134] *Vergil: Eclogues*, ed. Coleman, 83.

[135] Davis, *Parthenope*, 29.

[136] Cf. Fra Giulio Carrafa's sonnet at *Poesie Nomiche*, 261, which depicts Manso as impervious to the perils of life, and likens him to a boat sailing safely, unimpaired by

mighty poets. Thus, Jupiter must have been favorable to him at his birth, and Apollo and Mercury must have looked upon him with kindly glance (70–72). The equation of Manso with Tityrus and of Milton with Meliboeus operates on a syntactical level also. *Mansus* seems, at first glance, to mirror the contrasting *tu* and *nos*, which serve to emphasize the antithesis in Virgil's opening lines between the respective situations of Tityrus and Meliboeus: *Tityre, tu* (1) recline in the shade; *Nos* (3) are fleeing our homeland; *nos* (4) are fleeing our homeland; *tu, Tityre* (4) recline in the shade. These, as Davis pertinently observes, are placed "in metrically salient positions in the hexameter as well as in a doubly chiastic arrangement involving the name, Tityrus (*tu—nos—nos—tu*; and *Tityre, tu—tu Tityre*)."[137] Milton, however, while retaining the Virgilian chiasmus, extends it over the course of some 52 lines. Significantly, too, he transforms the whole into a series of shared parallels (as opposed to contrasts) between addressee and speaker, and between the literary landscapes of Italy and England. These are designated by the adverbs *quoque*, qualifying the *tu* (Manso), and *etiam*, qualifying the *nos* (Milton): *Tu quoque* (5) will sit amidst laurels, etc.; *Nos etiam* (30) have heard swans singing on the Thames; *Nos etiam* (38) worship Apollo; *Tu quoque* (52) will be applauded by posterity.

The potential association of Manso's Oziosi with pastoral *otium* and its associated *locus amoenus* rears its head later in the description of Apollo's retreat to the cave of Chiron:[138]

> Tantum ubi clamosos placuit vitare bubulcos
> Nobile mansueti cessit *Chironis in antrum*,[139]

---

the song of the Sirens, and weathering the storms of everyday life. This is rendered possible because "*Havesti al nascer tuo benigna stella,/*Che placido si rende'l mar, e'l lido,/E per dritto sentier t'adduce al porto*" ("*You were born under an auspicious star, which renders the sea and coastline so calm, and leads you to the harbor by a direct route*"). Emphasis is mine.

[137] Davis, *Parthenope*, 18.

[138] Apollo's visit to Chiron's cave was viewed by John Carey as a Miltonic invention. See *The Poems of John Milton*, eds. John Carey and Alastair Fowler (London: Longman, 1968), 263. Bruce Braswell, by contrast, drew attention to general precedent in both Ovid and Pindar. See Bruce Braswell, "Apollo at Chiron's Cave: A Note on Milton's 'Mansus,' 59–60," *Arethusa* 3 (1970): 197–203. Douglas Bush sought a path midway. See Bush, *Variorum*, I, 276: "Milton may have had some authority for Apollo's visiting Chiron's cave during his year of servitude, or he may have invented the item on the strength of Chiron's being the tutor of Aesculapius and Achilles."

[139] With the line-ending *Chironis in antrum*, cf. Ovid, *Metamorphoses* 2.630; Valerius Flaccus, *Argonautica* 1.407, and, for a neo-Latin parallel, Poliziano, *Praefatio* to *Manto* (*Sylvae* I) (describing the withdrawal of the Argonauts to Chiron's cave):

> Irriguos inter saltus frondosaque tecta,
> Peneium prope rivum. Ibi saepe sub ilice nigra
> Ad citharae strepitum blanda prece victus amici
> Exilii duros lenibat voce labores.
> (*Mansus* 59–64)

> But when he wished to avoid the clamorous herdsmen, he withdrew into the famous cave of the gentle Chiron, amid the well-watered pastures and leafy dwellings beside the river Peneus. It was there, beneath a dark oak tree, that he would be overcome by the winsome entreaties of his friend and would often alleviate exile's cruel hardships by singing in accompaniment to the resounding lyre.

That the lines may serve as an allegory of the Accademia degli Oziosi and of performances therein by its members (including perhaps those by Milton himself?) is suggested by the likely wordplay on Manso's name via the adjective *mansuetus* (60),[140] whereby the Neapolitan is implicitly equated with the centaur Chiron, whose cave (*antrum* [60]/Oziosi) provides a retreat for Apollo/academicians/Milton.[141] By association, a foremost mythological tutor[142] is hereby recast as a seicento "Principe"

Chironis ad antrum (5). Text is that of Angelo Ambrogini Poliziano, *Prose Volgari Inedite e Poesie Latine e Greche Edite e Inedite*, ed. Isidore del Lungo (Hildesheim: Georg Olms, 1976). For further discussion, see Estelle Haan, "John Milton Among the Neo-Latinists: Three Notes on *Mansus*," *N&Q* 44 (1997): 172–176, at 174–175; Haan, *From Academia to Amicitia*, 149–164.

[140] For similar punning on *Mansus/mansuetus*, cf. Jacopo Gaddi, *De Scriptoribus Non Ecclesiasticis Tomus Secundus*, 120: *Mansus mansuetus et modestus* ("Manso, tame and modest"), and, for general wordplay (in Latin) on his name, Giuseppe Battista's epitaph, quoted in n83.

[141] The Apollo/Milton analogy may indeed be prefigured at *Mansus* 24–25: *Ergo ego te Clius et magni nomine Phoebi,/Manse pater, iubeo longum salvere per aevum* ("And so, father Manso, I wish you, in the name of Clio and of mighty Phoebus, a long and healthy life"). My point was anticipated by Revard, *Milton and the Tangles of Neaera's Hair*, 219: "Clearly, Milton thinks of Apollo's visit to Chiron in the vale of Tempe as parallel to his own visit to evergreen springtime Naples, the garden of Italy, and to Manso's villa."

[142] Chiron was the celebrated tutor of Achilles and Asclepius. Cf., among others, Homer, *Iliad* 11.830–831; Ovid, *Ars Amatoria* 1.11, 1.17, *Fasti* 5.379–414; Poliziano, *Praefatio* to *Manto*, 1–30. Discussing this last passage, Dustin Mengelkoch aptly draws attention to Poliziano's "emphasis on the tutorial nature of the setting, Chiron's cave" and the associated "remoteness in which Chiron fosters Achilles' education." See Dustin Mengelkoch, "Statian *Recusatio*: Angelo Poliziano and John Dryden," in *Brill's Companion to Statius*, eds. W. J. Dominik, C. E. Newlands, and K. Gervais

governing, and indeed hosting, a very different type of educational "academia." The quasi-pedagogical setting is further enhanced by the adjective *nobile* (60) describing the *antrum* in question—a punning allusion perhaps to the Collegio dei Nobili, founded by Manso,[143] now reconfigured as a *locus amoenus* that affords its esteemed membership the benefits of pastoral *otium*. Or, in the words of Ernst Robert Curtius:

> a beautiful, shaded natural site. Its minimum ingredients comprise a tree (or several trees), a meadow, and a spring or brook. Birdsong and flowers may be added. The most elaborate examples also add a breeze.[144]

Milton's setting includes pastures (61), woodland (61), a stream (62), the shade of an oak tree (62), seclusion (59–60), and the performance of "music"/ "poetry" (64, 69) before a charmed audience. In this reading the god's ensuing ability to captivate his audience by his music/poetry (*carmen* [69]) is perhaps a Miltonic self-encomium that is daringly eulogistic, for the performance in question evokes a quasi-Orphic response: thus river banks and boulders move from their foundations, cliffs nod, trees rush down their slopes, and even lynxes grow tame (65–69).[145] The allegorical potential of the whole is reinforced by Milton's parallel methodology at *Epitaphium Damonis* (125–138), a pastoral that postdates *Mansus* by just one year. There, Milton as Thyrsis states that he will never tire of the memory of Tuscan shepherds (125–128), and mentions by name the Florentine academicians Carlo Dati and Antonio Francini (*Quin et nostra suas docuerunt nomina fagos/Et Datis et Francinus* [136–137] ["why, Dati and Francini have taught their own beech trees my name"). The personified *Charis* and *Lepos* (127) resemble the types of names (anagrammatic or otherwise) assumed by Italian academicians and may contain veiled references to unidentified Florentines. The lines also allegorize academic performance in general and Milton's in particular, as a pastoral contest,[146] while the encomiastic tributes bestowed upon him are reconceived as pastoral gifts: baskets,

---

(Leiden: Brill, 2015), 562–578, at 569. Milton had compared his own tutor, Thomas Young, to Chiron at *Elegia Quarta* 27–28.

[143] See 11.

[144] Curtius, *European Literature and the Latin Middle Ages*, 195.

[145] See also 195–201.

[146] Milton, *Epitaphium Damonis* 132: *Et potui Lycidae certantem audire Menalcam* ("And I was able to listen to Menalcas competing with Lycidas"); 133: *Ipse etiam tentare ausus sum* ("I even dared to offer my own attempts").

bowls and pipes with waxen fastenings (134–135).[147] The allegory would be elucidated by Milton himself in a letter to Carlo Dati. Here he expresses the hope that the poem (a copy of which he has sent to the Florentine)[148] might serve as a token of his regard for Dati and his fellow academicians "especially in those few little verses which were incorporated in emblematic fashion" (*vel illis paucis versiculis emblematis ad morem inclusis*).[149] Perhaps the *versiculi* that constitute *Mansus* 59–69 serve a similar purpose.

3.2.3 *Mansus Mansuetus*: Patterns of Wordplay

Mansuetus ... Chiron (60) is indeed prefigured in the poem's earlier depiction of Marino as Manso's *alumnus* (10). The language is closely evocative of Ovid's account, in *Fasti* 5, of the care that Chiron bestowed upon the youthful Asclepius.[150] The application of the adjective *mansuetus* to a centaur, while initially serving to surprise, finds a fitting place alongside Ovid's suppression of Chiron's hybrid nature, and associated highlighting of his potential humanity.[151] Thus he is described as a *iustus senex* (5.384), who, through the power of music, has the ability to impose some form of restraint upon the warlike "hands" (*manus*) of Achilles, destined to kill Hector in brutal combat, but now "detained in the strains of the lyre."[152] The whole is marked by wordplay on *manus*

---

[147] See also 38.

[148] See 39.

[149] See *Epistola Familiaris* 10 (dated 21 April 1647) in *John Milton: Epistolarum Familiarium Liber Unus and Uncollected Letters*, ed. Haan, 164–189, at 170–171, 180.

[150] *Mansus* 9–10: *Mox tibi dulciloquum non inscia Musa Marinum/Tradidit: ille tuum dici se gaudet alumnum* ("Next, the Muse, not without knowledge, entrusted to you the sweetly-speaking Marino; he rejoiced in being called your foster-child"). Cf. Ovid, *Metamorphoses* 2.633–634: *semifer interea divinae stirpis alumno/laetus erat mixtoque oneri gaudebat honore* ("meanwhile the centaur was rejoicing in his foster-child of heavenly stock, glad at the combined sense of responsibility and honor").

[151] See Ian Brookes, "The Death of Chiron: Ovid, *Fasti* 5.379–414," *CQ* 44 (1994): 444–450.

[152] See Ovid, *Fasti* 5. 385–386: *ille manus olim missuras Hectora leto/creditur in lyricis detinuisse modis* ("he is believed to have detained in the strains of the lyre the hands destined at some point to send Hector to his death"). Cf. Statius, *Silvae* 2. 1.88–89, 5.3.193–194.

and χείρ ("hand"), the Greek origin of the name Chiron,[153] an origin that is perhaps punningly encapsulated in *mansuetus* (past participle of *mansuescere* [from *manus* ("hand") + *suescere* "to accustom"]).[154] Milton's potential equation of Manso with Chiron thus elicits a variety of etymological signifiers.

The *Mansus/mansuetus* wordplay is anticipated earlier in the poem in two possible anagrammatic puns: on *Manse* (1, 2) and *manes* (15), and on *mansuetae* and *Manse tuae* (1). These merit consideration alongside anagrammatic play on Manso's name (and the Oziosi itself) in the "Poesie di Diversi." Precedent can be found in Girolamo Genuino's hugely popular *Metamorphoses Nominum, sive Metatheses Litterarum, sive Anagrammata in Quinque Libros Divisa*, first published in Naples in 1633, and then in Rome (1635 [Mascardi]; 1640 [Andreas Phaeus]). There the anagrams are frequently developed in associated explicatory Latin epigrams, which self-consciously signal the contrast between the syntactically incorporated verses (printed in a Roman font) and their expansion (printed in italics). Thus Genuino presents no fewer than four epigrams on Manso (three of which he develops in Latin verse),[155] a further four on the Academia degli Oziosi and its motto,[156] and others on such Oziosi members as Marino,[157] De Pietri (to whom are addressed three anagrams and associated epigrams,[158] and to which De Pietri replied in an anagram and poem of his own, likewise included herein),[159] Geronimo Fontanella,[160] Onofrio d'Andrea,[161] and Simone Sparano.[162]

Wordplay on Manso's name (and on its possible etymological and phonological affinities) features prominently in the "Poesie di Diversi." Indeed, several encomiasts pun on "Manso" and "mano" ("hand"). Thus,

---

[153] Brookes, "The Death of Chiron," 445–449. See also Barbara Weiden Boyd, "Arms and the Man: Wordplay and the Catasterism of Chiron in Ovid *Fasti* 5," *AJP* 122 (2001): 67–80.

[154] For the possible pun, see Ovid, *Epistulae ex Ponto* 4.5.28: *ad vos mansuetas porriget ille manus* ("he will stretch out his gentle hands before you").

[155] See Girolamo Genuino, *Metamorphoses Nominum, sive Metatheses Litterarum, sive Anagrammata in Quinque Libros Divisa* (Rome: Mascardi, 1635), 57, 58, 60, 77.

[156] *Metamorphoses Nominum*, 39, 42.

[157] *Metamorphoses Nominum*, 53.

[158] *Metamorphoses Nominum*, 55, 58, 63.

[159] *Metamorphoses Nominum*, 115.

[160] *Metamorphoses Nominum*, 59.

[161] *Metamorphoses Nominum*, 60.

[162] *Metamorphoses Nominum*, 60.

Tasso proclaims "hai verso me possente, e larga mano" ("towards me you have shown a mighty and generous hand").[163] At times wordplay becomes the poem's central conceit, as in the case of Gennaro Grossi's sonnet extolling "Lodi espresse nel nome" ("Praises expressed in his name"). This punningly points out the virtues of Manso's "sovereign hand" inherent in his very name:

> La MAN SOvrana, onde'l Monarca Hispano
>   Debellò più d'un campo, e più d'un mostro,
>   Voli' hai, Signor, da ogni tenzon lontano
>   Solitaria à trattar penna, ed inchiostro.[164]

> Sir, you wished that that sovereign hand, with the help of which the Spanish Monarch won more than one battlefield and overcame more than one monster, far from every strain, should use the pen and ink in solitude.

The same device is used by Margherita Sarrocchi:

> Già mira in te risorti il secol nostro
>   Gli antichi honori, e'l tuo gran nome addita
>   Di Virtù MAN SOvrana altero mostro.[165]

> Already our age admires the ancient honors which have been revived in you, and your mighty name indicates your sovereign hand as a proud demonstration of your valor.

At times his "mano" is seen to mirror and epitomize the virtues of Manso's mind ("mente"), as in Andrea Santamaria's encomium, entitled "Paragona la mente, e la mano"[166] ("He makes a Comparison between the mind and the hand"). At others, it is celebrated as the epitome of various forms of bellicose activity:[167] fulminating in war,[168] even associated with

---

[163] *Poesie Nomiche*, 259.

[164] *Poesie Nomiche*, 277.

[165] *Poesie Nomiche*, 303.

[166] *Poesie Nomiche*, 285.

[167] Giulio Caracciolo, at *Poesie Nomiche*, 282; Cecco Loffredo, at *Poesie Nomiche*, 296.

[168] Tomaso Pipini, at *Poesie Nomiche*, 293.

cruelty,[169] and audacity.[170] At others, it is the agent of scholarship itself. Thus Antonio Biaguazzone, in a piece entitled "Loda la mano impiegeta nell' armi, e nello scriver d'Amore" ("He praises the hand which is employed in arms and in writing about Love"), regards Manso's wise and warlike "mano" as wielding not a pen, but arrows ("non ... penna, ma strale"),[171] while Giovanni Battista Composti extols "this pen in your hand" ("questa penna in man").[172] Other contributors play on Manso and the metaphorical "manto" or "mantle," gloriously donned or displayed by nature in response to his poetry. Thus, according to Luigi Carrafa, the sun is the proud possessor of a "mantle" of more beautiful rays,[173] while, for Girolamo Stella, the "mantle" of the Summer blossoms in response to Manso's poetry.[174] Other encomiasts pun on Manso and Mantua.[175]

Manso's forenames, not least "Battista" (*Baptista*) and his formal title ("Marchese di Villa"), also provide rich material for etymological play. Thus does Gennaro Grossi, in the aforementioned sonnet, extol his Neapolitan friend:

> Tu de la terra sei Febo secondo,
>   Ch'al Veglio alato, e rio l'invide prove
>   a*BATTI STA*nche, e lui sommergi al fondo.
> Di tue glorie il gran *MAR, CHE SE*mpre nove
>   Piaggie, e Reggie circonda, adduce al Mondo
>   Te *DI VILLA*, e Cittade, hor Pane, hor Giove.[176]

> You are the earth's second Phoebus, you who have again proved the envy of the winged old man, as you overthrow him in his weariness and submerge him in the depths.
>   The great sea of your glories, which always encircles new shores and palaces, reveals you to the universe—you who are

---

[169] Hettore Pignatelli, at *Poesie Nomiche*, 290.

[170] Tomaso Pipini, at *Poesie Nomiche*, 293; Fulvio Andrantonelli, at *Poesie Nomiche*, 299.

[171] *Poesie Nomiche*, 266.

[172] *Poesie Nomiche*, 292. Cf. Anello Sartiano, at *Poesie Nomiche*, 301.

[173] *Poesie Nomiche*, 273.

[174] *Poesie Nomiche*, 298.

[175] Giovanni Pietro Bacchetta, at *Poesie Nomiche*, 275; Scipione Errico, at *Poesie Nomiche*, 302.

[176] *Poesie Nomiche*, 277.

> now Pan of the villa and now Jupiter of the
> city.

A not dissimilar pun may be veiled in Milton's account of the divine blessings with which, he presumes, Manso must have been graced:

> te Iuppiter aequus oportet
> Nascentem, et miti lustrarit lumine Phoebus
> Atlantisque nepos.
> (*Mansus* 70–72)
>
> Jupiter must have favored you at birth, and
> Phoebus and the grandson of Atlas must
> have looked upon you with kindly glance.

The verb *lustrare* (71), occurring here in the sense of "To cast one's eyes over,"[177] possesses the primary meaning of "To purify ceremonially."[178] As such, it is associated with the Roman ritualistic practice of *lustratio* ("purification"),[179] a term that was appropriated in its Christian sense to mean *baptism*,[180] and one that Milton would later use (in *De Doctrina Christiana*) to describe the baptism of Christ by John the Baptist.[181] In this reading, another "John the Baptist" (*Ioannes Baptista Mansus*,[182] is, perhaps, the recipient, rather than the bestower, of a poetical baptism, conferred by a trinity of pagan deities.

---

[177] See *OLD*, s.v. 5.

[178] See *OLD*, s.v.1.

[179] See W. W. Fowler, *Lustratio*, in *Anthropology and the Classics: Six Lectures Delivered before the University of Oxford*, ed. R. R. Marrett (Oxford: Clarendon Press, 1908), 169–191; Friedrich Boehm, *Lustratio*, *RE* 13 (1927): 2029–2039.

[180] See Russ Leo, "Milton's Aristotelian Experiments: Tragedy, *Lustratio*, and 'Secret Refreshings' in *Samson Agonistes* (1671)," *MS* 52 (2011): 221–252, at 248–249.

[181] Milton, *De Doctrina Christiana*, Book I, Chapter 28: *Qua ratione baptismus Ioannis, quatenus aut non omnino aut non statim spiritum conferebat, initiatio quaedam sive lustratio ad doctrinam evangelii recipiendam promulgata (ex antiquo ritu Hebraeorum, quo omnes proselytae baptizabantur) potius quam absoluta foederis obsignatio, videtur fuisse: spiritus enim solus obsignat, I Cor. 12.13*. ("For which reason, the baptism enacted by John, inasmuch as it conferred the spirit either not entirely or not immediately, seems to have been promulgated as a certain type of initiation or purification for the reception of the gospel's teaching (in accordance with the ancient rite of the Hebrews, whereby all proselytes were baptized), rather than as an absolute sealing of the covenant: for it is the spirit alone that seals. I *Cor*. 12.13"). Text is that of *The Complete Works of John Milton: Volume VIII: De Doctrina Christiana*, eds. John K. Hale and J. Donald Cullington, 2 vols. (Oxford: Oxford University Press, 2012), II, 744. Translation is mine.

[182] Emphasis is mine.

3.2.4 *Modulantes ... Cygni*: Literary Swans

By far the most prevalent motif employed in the "Poesi di Diversi" is that of the poet and his fellow academicians as literary swans. Crucially, these pertain to both the present (in the form of Oziosi members and Manso himself) and the past (in the form of Virgil and Sannazaro). Giovanni Camillo Cacace, aspiring to membership of the academy, envisages himself as a swan singing in their company:

> O se frà quelle in sorte esser mi lice:
> Potrò cantar anch'io Cigno sù l'onde.[183]
>
> O, if I can have the good fortune to be
> among such men, I too will be able to sing
> as a Swan upon the waves.

Scipione Mocia's sonnet, entitled "Nella fondation dell'Academia degli Otiosi" ("On the foundation of the Accademia degli Oziosi"), describes its members as "Sacro di nobil Cigni ... stuol canoro" ("A sacred, tuneful flock of noble Swans").[184] Likewise, they constitute, for Annibale Caracciolo, "Novi Cigni formar sacri concenti" ("modern Swans [who] create sacred music");[185] for Ferrante Rovitto, "Schiera di Cigni al canto unica, e rara" ("a flock of Swans that is unique and rare in song"),[186] and, for Hettore della Marra, "i più sublimi Cigni" ("more sublime Swans").[187] The motif finds its most perfect embodiment in Manso himself, the perennial "Cigno," variously described as "sacro" ("sacred"),[188] "candido" ("white"),[189] "immortale" ("immortal"),[190] and "canoro" ("tuneful").[191] As such, he is also the heir to an important tradition of Neapolitan swan/poets. Thus, Giovanni Pietro Bacchetta, in a sonnet entitled "Il Paragona al Marone, & al Sannazaro" ("A Comparison to

---

[183] *Poesie Nomiche*, 274.

[184] *Poesie Nomiche*, 276.

[185] *Poesie Nomiche*, 277.

[186] *Poesie Nomiche*, 288.

[187] *Poesie Nomiche*, 293.

[188] Francesco Mega, at *Poesie Nomiche*, 300; Giacomo Arcamone, at *Poesie Nomiche*, 308.

[189] Girolamo Stella, at *Poesie Nomiche*, 298.

[190] Scipione Errico, at *Poesie Nomiche*, 302.

[191] Lelio Mazzucci, at *Poesie Nomiche*, 304; Onofrio d'Andrea, at *Poesie Nomiche*, 306; Giacomo Arcamone, at *Poesie Nomiche*, 308.

Virgil and to Sannazaro"), depicts Manso and his fellow Oziosi as "concordi Cigni" ("tuneful Swans"), located in the environs of Vesuvius, where the sea washes the lovely shore that preserves the ashes of "duo Cigni" ("two Swans") in particular, namely, Virgil and Sannazaro.[192]

The prevalence of the poet/swan analogy in the "Poesie di Diversi" invites a fresh reading of its occurrence in *Mansus*. With an emphatically articulated *Nos etiam* (30), Milton reveals that he too can boast of literary swans, both present and past. He does so in what is arguably one of the poem's most imaginative and intertextually rich appropriations:

> Nos etiam in nostro modulantes flumine cygnos
> Credimus obscuras noctis sensisse per umbras,
> Qua Thamesis late puris argenteus urnis
> Oceani glaucos perfundit gurgite crines;
> Quin et in has quondam pervenit Tityrus oras.
> (*Mansus* 30–34)

> We, too, believe that we have heard swans singing in our river amid night's dark shadows, where the silver Thames with pure urns soaks her green locks in Ocean's wide waters. Indeed, even Tityrus once reached these shores.

The Neapolitan "Sebeto" is replaced by the Thames, whose swans symbolize the literary heritage of England in general, and of London in particular, to which Milton lays claim. That claim is reinforced by the occurrence of the motif in the vernacular verse of early modern England.[193] Thus, William Vallans's *A Tale of Two Swanns* (1590) focuses on the birds' cruising of the river Lee, only to proclaim:

> these two so fruitfull shall become,
> That all the Swannes, yea, the verie Thames
> Shall be replenisht with their princely race.[194]

Edmund Spenser's *The Ruines of Time* (1591), set "beside the shore/Of silver streaming Thamesis" (1–2), envisages Philip Sidney as a "snowie Swan" (590), singing "the prophecie/Of his owne death in dolefull

---

[192] *Poesie Nomiche*, 275.

[193] See Stewart Mottram, *Ruin and Reformation in Spenser, Shakespeare, and Marvell* (Oxford: Oxford University Press, 2019), 54–70.

[194] William Vallans, *A Tale of Two Swanns. Wherein Is Comprehended the Original and Increase of The River Lee* (London: Roger Ward, 1590), sig. A3^v.

Elegie" (594–595).[195] And in Spenser's *Prothalamion* (1596), again set "Along the shoare of silver streaming Themmes" (11), the speaker beholds "two Swannes of goodly hewe,/Come softly swimming downe along the Lee" (37–38). The analogy is at the heart of Ben Jonson's prefatory poem to Hugh Holland's *Pancharis* (1603):

> Who saith our Times nor have, nor can
>   Produce us a blacke Swan?
> Behold, where one doth swim;
>   Whose Note, and Hue,
> Besides the other Swannes admiring him,
>   Betray it true:
>   A gentler Bird, then this,
> Did never dint the breast of Tamisis (1–8)[196]

and his associated depiction of the author cruising the rivers of Britain and beyond in fulfillment of Apollo's injunction: "Nor let one River boast/Thy tunes alone;/But prove the Aire, and saile from Coast to Coast" (35–37).[197] The motif likewise underlies Michael Drayton's topographical swansong, *Poly-Olbion* (1612),[198] and, perhaps most famously, Jonson's salutation of Shakespeare, prefixed to the First Folio (1623):

> Sweet Swan of Avon! what a sight it were
>   To see thee in our waters yet appeare,
> And make those flights upon the bankes of Thames,
>   That so did take Eliza, and our James! (71–74)[199]

But it was in the neo-Latin poetry of the sixteenth-century British antiquarian John Leland that the poet/swan analogy manifested itself most notably.[200] Thus, according to Leland's *Synchrisis Cygnorum et*

---

[195] All quotations are from *The Yale Edition of the Shorter Poems of Edmund Spenser*, eds. William A. Oram, Einar Bjorvand, Ronald Bond, Thomas H. Cain, Alexander Dunlop, and Richard Schell (New Haven, CT: Yale University Press, 1989).

[196] Hugh Holland, *Pancharis* (London, V[alentine] S[immes], 1603), sig. a7^v. Line-numbering is mine.

[197] Ibid., sig. a8^r.

[198] Michael Drayton, *Poly-Olbion* (London: Humphrey Lownes, 1612).

[199] Ben Jonson, "To The Memory of My Beloved, The Author Mr. William Shakespeare," in *Mr. William Shakespeares Comedies, Histories, & Tragedies* (London: Isaac Iaggard and Edward Blount, 1623), sig. a4^r–a4^v, at sig. a4^v. Line-numbering is mine.

[200] For my preliminary thoughts on this topic, see Haan, "John Milton Among the Neo-Latinists," 173–174; Haan, *From Academia to Amicitia*, 166–167.

Poetarum, published in 1589, the swan is white in body, the poet is white in heart (*Candidus est toto concentor corpore cygnus,/Pectora sunt vatis candidiora nive* [3–4]); the swan loves icy rivers, the poet loves his own spring (*Laetus olor gelidis fluviis gaudere videtur,/Gaudet illimi fonte poeta suo* [5–6]); both sing a song in Springtime (7–10), and both seek the cool shade in the heat of Summer (11–14). In short: *Quis neget albenteis cygnos nunc atque poetas/convenisse suis undique nominibus?* (15–16) ("Now who would deny that snow-white swans and poets resemble each other in all respects?").[201] Leland's much lengthier poem, *Cygnea Cantio* (1545), situates the swan/poet allegory in the specific context of the Thames.[202] Pertaining to the tradition of chorographic writing, whereby landscape serves both to embed and to embody history,[203] the poem carefully maps the swan's Thames-side itinerary downstream from Oxford to Greenwich. It is an itinerary that affords its author the opportunity to showcase his antiquarian knowledge. James Carley's observation that "Leland, more than any of his contemporaries, knew every detail of the river and its history"[204] is evinced by the author's claim in the Dedicatory Letter prefixed to the work:

> Huius ego aliquando, vel ab ipsis fontibus, ripas, sinus, anfractus, divortia, maeandros, denique et mediamnes insulas omnes curiosissime collustravi, et memoriae commendavi.[205]

---

[201] John Leland, *Synchrisis Cygnorum et Poetarum*, in *Principum ac Illustrium Aliquot et Eruditorum in Anglia Virorum, Encomia, Trophaea, Genethliaca et Epithalamia a Ioanne Lelando Antiquario Conscripta* (London: Thomas Orwin, 1589), 1–2. Line-numbering is mine.

[202] John Leland, Κύκνειον Ἇσμα. *Cygnea Cantio* (London: Reyner Wolfe, 1545). For discussion of Leland's poem in particular and of the author in general, see the series of articles and chapters by James P. Carley: "John Leland's 'Cygnea Cantio': A Neglected Tudor River Poem," *HL* 32 (1983): 225–241; "John Leland," in *The Spenser Encyclopedia*, eds. A. C. Hamilton, Donald Cheney, David A. Richardson, and William W. Barker (Toronto: University of Toronto Press, 1990), 433; "The Manuscript Remains of John Leland, 'The King's Antiquary,'" *Text: Transactions for the Society for Textual Scholarship* 2 (1985): 111–120, and "Leland, John (*c.* 1503–1552), Poet and Antiquary," *ODNB* (Oxford: Oxford University Press, 2004), http//www.oxforddnb.com.

[203] On chorographic poetry, see Andrew McRae, "Early Modern Chorographies," in *The Oxford Handbooks Online* (Oxford: Oxford University Press, 2015), https://www.oxfordhandbooks.com/view/10.1093/oxfordhb/9780199935338.001.001/oxfordhb-9780199935338-e-102; Andrew Hadfield, "Chorography, Map-Mindedness, Poetics of Place," in *A Companion to Renaissance Poetry*, ed. Catherine Bates (Oxford: Wiley Blackwell, 2018), 485–497.

[204] Carley, "John Leland's 'Cygnea Cantio,'" 229.

[205] Leland, *Cygnea Cantio*, sig. Aiii^r.

> At some time I have with the greatest of care surveyed and committed to memory all the banks, curves, byways, diversions, meanderings and islands from the very source of this river.

That the letter is addressed to King Henry VIII is particularly pertinent, given the fact that the swan, as Cathy Shrank observes, was synonymous with royalty.[206] The poem proper (running to 700 hendecasyllabic verses) itemizes individual towns and locations, identifying them by the Celtic placenames by which they were known during the Roman or Saxon periods.[207] The process of identification is explicitly self-conscious, as is attested by the work's copious paratextual materials, and, especially, by its extensive commentary, which traces the history of more than 100 named sites and associated personages back to their earliest recorded history. The whole dovetails into what is, in effect, an extravagant 300-line encomium of Henry, and a concluding song of farewell, in which the swan, not unlike the speaker of *Mansus*,[208] envisages its death and subsequent departure from the riverbanks, culminating in it securing an abode in the heavens, and a final request that it be remembered by posterity.[209]

Bird imagery lies at the heart of Milton's self-portraiture as an English traveler abroad. In *Ad Salsillum*, for example, he is the *alumnus ille Londini Milto* (9) ("Milton, that foster-child of London"), who, having left behind his native nest (*qui suum linquens nidum* [10])[210] and

---

[206] Cathy Shrank, *Writing the Nation in Reformation England, 1530–1580* (Oxford: Oxford University Press, 2004), 97.

[207] See, for example, *Hydropolis*, at Leland, *Cygnea Cantio*, line 64 (sig. Bii^r); *Pontes* (line 75 [sig. Bii^v]), and *Trenovantum* (line 201 [sig. Ci^r]) (line-numbering is mine), and their respective explication (as Dorchester [sig. I.ii^r], Reading [sig. Mii^v–Miii^r], and London [sig. Niv^r]), in the work's copious *Elenchus antiquorum nominum* ("Index of ancient names").

[208] See *Mansus*, 94–100, quoted and discussed at 59–63.

[209] John Leland, *Cygnea Cantio*, 691–696 (sig. Eii^v–Eiii^r): *Iam longum Viridis sinus valeto./Te praeconia: te manent coronae./Me coelum petit arduum canentem./At Cygni interea tui memento./Nutritor Tamesis valeto chare,/Et Cygnis facilis faveto nostris* ("Now farewell forever, Greenwich. For you there await lauds and garlands. The heights of Heaven are seeking me as I sing, but in the meantime remember your Swan. Farewell, Thames, my beloved nourisher, and readily show favor upon our Swans"). Cf. ibid., 391–394 (sig. Civ^v): *Certe non moriar, petam sed astra/Coelites habiturus inter ipsos/Sedem conspicuo polo micantem:/Phoebus noster ubi coruscat almus* ("Assuredly, I shall not die. Rather, I will seek out the stars, destined as I am to assume an abode gleaming in glorious Heaven, among the heaven-dwellers themselves, where our fostering Phoebus shines resplendently").

[210] On the imagery of a bird leaving its nest and its possible evocation of an individual *impresa* and motto (possibly Salzilli's) that used to grace the Roman Accademia degli

the inclement weather of England (11–13), is newly arrived upon Italy's fertile soil: *venit feraces Itali soli ad glebas* (14).[211] That sense of nurturing afforded by England, itself implied by the noun *alumnus*, etymologically related to the verb *alo-alere* ("to nourish"), is, however, countered in *Mansus*, for now the Miltonic *Musa* (27) is described as *gelida vix enutrita sub Arcto* (28) ("poorly nourished beneath the icy Bear").[212] Nonetheless, she has ventured in her rashness to fly through the cities of Italy (*Imprudens Italas ausa est volitare per urbes* [29]). *Imprudens* and the Muse's associated audacity may be a veiled reference to the works that Milton composed in the course of his Italian sojourn.[213] Alternatively, it may hint at the frequently articulated caveats about the potential dangers that Catholic Italy posed to the Protestant traveler.[214] That tradition found its most eloquent voice in Roger Ascham,[215] and it was one to which Milton would purportedly subscribe in *Defensio Secunda*.[216] But this Miltonic *Musa*/swan[217] is *imprudens* in other ways too, and especially by comparison with the eponymous bird of Leland's poem.

Umoristi, of which Salzilli was a member, see 33. For possible links with one of Salzilli's Italian sonnets, see Haan, *John Milton's Roman Sojourns*, 72–74.

[211] The bird analogy finds precedent in *Epistola Familiaris* 7, for which see 84. Indeed, the context for Milton's incipient flight in that instance (the letter is dated 23 September 1637) may well be his combined anticipation of his imminent travels abroad, and a heightened sense of excitement and self-belief, originating perhaps from his writing (and re-drafting) of *Lycidas* (dated November 1637 in TM).

[212] See Z. S. Fink, "Milton and the Theory of Climatic Influence," *MLQ* 2 (1941): 67–80.

[213] Cf. *John Milton: Poetical Works*, ed. Masson, III, 532: "Perhaps an allusion to the things he had written in Italy."

[214] For discussion of early modern attitudes to continental travel, see, among others, Sara Warneke, *Images of the Educational Traveller in Early Modern England* (Leiden: Brill, 1995); Edward Chaney, *The Grand Tour*; Edward Chaney, *The Evolution of the Grand Tour: Anglo-Italian Cultural Relations since the Renaissance* (London: Frank Cass, 1998).

[215] According to Ascham, Italy was a second Circe, whose "inchantmentes" were to be avoided by the vulnerable Protestant English traveler. Otherwise, he would return "worse transformed," an "Englishman Italianated," who, having lost his religious and national identity, would transport to his homeland "Papistrie or worse." See Roger Ascham, *The Scholemaster* (London: John Daye, 1570), sig. 24^v–26^v. See also Haan, "England, Neo-Latin, and the Continental Journey," 322–324.

[216] See 23–25.

[217] Leland also suggests a correlation between Muse and swan. Cf. Carley, "John Leland's 'Cygnea Cantio,'" 228: "sometimes the swan seems to represent the Muse in a more general sense."

At the outset it should be remarked that Milton's possible self-alignment with Leland is not entirely surprising, given the existence of what Philip Schwyzer has acutely described as "a curious and potentially instructive resemblance in the lives and deeds"[218] of both poets, not least, the fact that they were both born in the first decade of their respective centuries, and were educated at St Paul's School, London, and Christ's College, Cambridge. Particularly noteworthy, however, is Milton's imaginative re-reading of Oziosi swans through a Lelandian lens, whereby they are both Anglicized and located within an essentially British chorographic tradition that seems, nonetheless, eager to reach outward and beyond geographical and literary liminalities. Leland's swan boasts that it has fended off hunger (*dum ... famem repello* [11]) amid the bywaters of the Thames by feeding upon tender plants (*depastis teneris ... herbis* [12]) and fish (*pisciculis* [13]), nourishment described as *cibo suavi* (13) ("sweet food"). It is only in the course of such replenishment that the bird is overcome by the desire to migrate further afield in order to study the green banks of the Isis with keen eyes (*intentis oculis* [18]) and fresh scrutiny (*novaque cura* [18]) as far as the river's convergence with the salt waters of the inflowing sea (*quousque salsas/undas imbiberent maris refusi* [19–20]). By contrast, the Miltonic *Musa* (27), despite, or perhaps because of, her lack of nourishment (*vix enutrita* [28]) in her native land, has set her topographical sights not, as in Leland, upon Thames-side towns, but upon the cities of Italy herself (*Italas ... per urbes* [29]).[219] Milton's initial stance then is perhaps as a swan who has transported the chorographic tradition to Italian shores. Significantly, however, it is one that casts a retrospective glance via a clever tour de force. Milton immediately reinstates his Englishness by revisiting his homeland, at least poetically speaking, in that proud proclamation (30–34) that he, too, has heard swans singing, and, this time the location is indeed his native river, the Thames. It is alongside the company of Thames-side swans in general, and perhaps of Leland in particular, that

---

[218] See Philip Schwyzer, "John Leland and His Heirs: The Topography of England," in *The Oxford Handbook of Tudor Literature, 1485–1603*, eds. Mike Pincombe and Cathy Shrank (Oxford: Oxford University Press, 2009), 238–253, at 239.

[219] The arrival in Italy of the Miltonic *Musa*, as described here, seems to both echo and ultimately to reverse the geographical direction of the Muse's itinerary in Leland's *Commigratio Bonarum Literarum in Britanniam* (see *Principum ac Illustrium*, 3). There, repudiating the rumor that the *Camoenae* have never crossed the Alpine snows to Britain, despite the fact that the polished Muse, having abandoned Athens, took up her abode in Italy (*venit ad Italicos Musa polita lares* [4]), the speaker announces that the Muses have in fact leapt across those snows (*Musas transiliisse nives* [6]), and made their way to Britain.

Milton too can assume his own chorographic place. It is also worth pointing out that in *Epitaphium Damonis*, composed in the wake of his Italian journey, and itself indebted to chorographic literature,[220] Milton offers, in the words of Thomas Roebuck, a "contextualization of his own life and writings within the many rivers and waters of Britain."[221] The poem, as Su Fang Ng remarks, "reorients the poet from the outwardly looking perspective of foreign travel to an inward turn to Britishness."[222] The whole is reinforced, moreover, by the fact that, as Roebuck observes, several of the rivers across which Milton envisages his reputation echoing (the *Abra*/Humber [176], the *Tamara* [178], and, not least, the Thames: *Thamesis meus ante omnes* [177]), "designate important boundary points in ancient Britain."[223]

3.2.5 From Virgil to Chaucer to Spenser

In *Mansus*, however, one important boundary point is crossed in several ways. Noteworthy in this regard is the poem's careful situating of the aforementioned swans, not in the main body of the Thames itself, but at a key point (*qua* [32]) where the river converges with the English Channel, hyperbolically described as the *Oceani ... gurges* (33) ("the waters of the Ocean"). It is a location that significantly affords them (and their song) access to a geographical space that extends far beyond local waterways. Milton himself, after all, has already left the Thames behind, having made his way to Italian shores. And for this he can cite an important poetical predecessor: *Quin et in has quondam pervenit Tityrus oras* (34) ("Indeed, even Tityrus once reached these shores"). In all likelihood, the allusion is to Chaucer,[224] who visited Italy on two occasions (1372–1373 and

---

[220] See Roebuck, "Milton and the Confessionalization of Antiquarianism," 50.

[221] Ibid., 50.

[222] Su Fang Ng, "Milton, Buchanan, and King Arthur," *RES* 70 (2019): 659–680, at 674.

[223] Roebuck, "Milton and the Confessionalization of Antiquarianism," 50.

[224] Indeed, John Hale's translation dares to make the purported identification explicit in his rendering of the line as "Our Chaucer came before me to this land." See *John Milton: Latin Writings: A Selection*, ed. and trans. John K. Hale (Assen: Van Gorcum and Tempe, AZ: Medieval and Renaissance Texts and Studies, 1998), 107. Here, however, he appends a caveat: "But the line may mean instead that Italian pastoral poetry, personified in Virgil's Tityrus, had reached England and was honoured there (David K. Money's suggestion)" (ibid., 107). Money's interpretation, surprisingly regarded by Campbell and Corns (*Life, Work, and Thought*, 411), as "the more likely" in view of "[t]he context, which speaks of the Thames," is, in fact, undercut by several linguistic and contextual details: (i) the use of the demonstrative pronoun *has* (34) to

1378).[225] It was by the appellation "Tityrus" that Chaucer was denoted by Spenser on no fewer than three occasions in *The Shepheardes Calender* (*Februarie* 92, *June* 81, and *December* 4). That form of identification, described by Patrick Chaney as "Spenser's most peculiar and memorable presentation,"[226] is further reinforced by the work's paratextual materials,[227] and by E.K.'s glosses to Spenserian terms and literary contexts for which there is Chaucerian precedent. Noteworthy too is the

---

describe the shores (*oras* [34]) in question: surely "these shores" mean the shores upon which Milton, Manso, and the poem are located (cf. *Haec ... carmina* [1] to describe *Mansus* itself), i.e., the shores of Italy (not England)?; (ii) the occurrence of the adverb *quondam* (34), which suggests a unique instance in the past rather than a continuous literary tradition (Italian pastoral), whose importation to England was far from instantaneous; (iii) the associated context of the potential transcendence of liminality. Hence the confluence of the Thames with the "Ocean," itself negating the idea that Britain is somehow divided from the rest of the world, is mirrored by the precedent of a poet/swan (Chaucer), who did indeed leave that river and, as it were, swam the whole way to Italy. Milton's boastful description of Tityrus's arrival via the verb *pervenit* (34) (in the sense perhaps of "[w. emphasis on success of journey] To get through [to], penetrate [to]" [*OLD*, s.v. 2]), may look back to Nemesianus, *Eclogue* 2, in which Alcon, vying for the attentions of a beloved, and in lines likewise characterized by the language of self-defense, includes among his boasts the instance that Tityrus (Virgil) made his way (*pervenit*) to Rome: *nec sumus indocti calamis: cantamus avena,/qua divi cecinere prius, qua dulce locutus/Tityrus e silvis dominam pervenit in urbem* (*Eclogue* 2. 82–84) ("Nor am I unskilled in the reed-pipe. I sing on a flute, upon which gods have previously sung, upon which Tityrus sweetly sang, before leaving the woodlands, and making his way to the imperial city"). For the identification of Nemesianus's Tityrus as Virgil in this particular instance, see *The Eclogues of Calpurnius and Nemesianus*, ed. Charles Haines Keene (Hildesheim: Georg Olms, 1969), 177; *Nemésien, Oeuvres*, ed. Pierre Volpilhac (Paris: Les Belles Lettres, 1975), 68; *Hirtengedichte Aus Spätrömischer und Karolingischer Zeit: Marcus Aurelius Olympius Nemesianus, Severus Sanctus Endelechius, Modoinus, Hirtengedicht Aus Dem Codex Gaddianus*, ed. Dietmar Korzeniewski (Darmstadt: Wissenschaftliche Buchgesellschaft, 1976), 121; *The Eclogues of Nemesian and the Einsiedeln Manuscript*, ed. J. B. Pearce (San Antonio, Texas: Scylax Press, 1992), 55.

[225] Chaucer, during his first visit in 1372–1373, spent about three months in Italy. As esquire of the King's chamber, he had been sent with a trading mission to Genoa. He was accompanied by two Genoese of high rank—Giovanni del Mare and Jacopo Provano. The purpose of his second visit to Italy in 1378 was to deliver the king's greetings to Bernabo Visconti, lord of Milan. Milton's visit of course lacks such an official purpose.

[226] See Patrick Cheney, "'Novells of His Devise': Chaucerian and Virgilian Career Paths in Spenser's *Februarie* Eclogue," in *European Literary Careers: The Author from Antiquity to the Renaissance*, eds. Patrick Cheney and Frederick A. de Armas (Toronto: University of Toronto Press, 2002), 231–267, at 233.

[227] Chaney, "'Novells of His Devise,'" 233, points out that the dedicatory Epistle's opening sentence, commencing "Uncouthe unkiste, Sayde the old famous Poete Chaucer ...," paraphrases Chaucer, *Troilus*, I.809: "Unknowe unkist."

fact that the appellation is both mentioned and explicated by Thomas Speght in his *Life of Chaucer*, prefixed to his 1602 edition of Chaucer's works (which edition Milton is known to have used):[228]

> Master Spenser in his first Eclogue of his Shepheards Kalender, calleth him Titirus, the god of Shepheards, comparing him to the worthinesse of the Romane Titirus Virgil.[229]

Speght makes explicit the implications of Spenser's use of the name Tityrus, recognizing its associated presentation of Chaucer as a second Virgil. After all, the Tityrus/Virgil equation is a tradition that, in the words of Stephen Guy-Bray, "is almost as old as the poems themselves,"[230] and one that has a long and much debated critical history.[231]

---

[228] That Milton read Chaucer in Speght's 1602 edition is evinced by cross-references in his note-taking (in his *Commonplace Book*) from "The Merchant's Tale," "The Wife of Bath's Tale," "The Man of Physick," and the translation from *The Romance of the Rose*. See *The Complete Works of John Milton: Volume XI*, ed. Poole, 74, 392.

[229] "The Life of Our Learned English Poet, Geffrey Chaucer," in *The Workes of Our Ancient and Learned English Poet, Geffrey Chaucer, Newly Printed*, ed. Thomas Speght (London: Adam Islip, 1602), sig. bii^r–ciii^v, at sig. ciii^v.

[230] Stephen Guy-Bray, "How to Turn Prose into Literature: The Case of Thomas Nashe," in *Early Modern Prose Fiction: The Cultural Poetics of Reading*, ed. Naomi Conn Liebler (New York: Routledge, 2007), 33–45, at 34.

[231] Some scholars have argued that the Tityrus of Virgil, *Eclogue* 1, was, in effect the poet's own pseudonym. Thus, for example, Paul Alpers cites verbal parallels between the description of Tityrus in *Eclogue* 1.2: *silvestrem tenui Musam meditaris avena* ("you compose a woodland muse upon a delicate reed") and Virgil's poetic self-fashioning at *Eclogue* 6.8: *agrestem tenui meditabor harundine Musam* ("I will compose a rustic muse upon a delicate reed"). See Paul J. Alpers, *The Singer of The Eclogues: A Study of Virgilian Pastoral* (Berkeley: University of California Press, 1979), 109. Contrast, however, *The Pastoral Poems: The Text of the Eclogues*, trans. E. V. Rieu (Baltimore: Penguin, 1967), 124: "I do not believe that he [sc. Virgil] wished us to take either Tityrus or Meliboeus for himself. He is their creator." It is certainly true that the name Tityrus, as Heather Williams points out, was used by Propertius (*Elegiae* 2.34.72) and Ovid (*Amores* 1.15.25; *Epistulae ex Ponto* 4.16.33) to signify Virgil himself or his *Eclogues* more generally. See *The Eclogues and Cynegetica of Nemesianus*, ed. Heather J. Williams (Leiden: Brill, 1986), 7–8. It was also used by Martial (*Epigrams* 8.55.8) and Sidonius Apollinaris (*Epistulae* 8.9.5 uu. 12 and 56) to refer specifically to the *Eclogues*. See *The Eclogues and Cynegetica of Nemesianus*, ed. Williams, 7. Of particular interest is the occurrence of the identification in the works of Virgil's pastoral successors, Calpurnius Siculus and Nemesianus, and, especially, in the context of poetic self-praise. In Calpurnius, *Eclogue* 4, for example, Corydon boasts of his ownership of a reed-pipe upon which Virgil/Tityrus first played: *Tityrus hanc* [sc. *fistulam*] *habuit, cecinit qui primus in istis/montibus Hyblaea modulabile carmen avena* (4.62–63) ("Tityrus once owned

Closer examination of the occurrence of the appellation Tityrus in *Mansus*, glossed by Bush as "Milton's earliest reference to Spenser's *Shepheardes Calender*,"[232] suggests hitherto unnoticed points of contact between the two poems. It is worth remarking, for example, that the Tityrus/Chaucer correlation in *Februarie* occurs in the course of a dialogue between a young and an old shepherd.[233] Like the speaker of *Mansus*, a *iuvenis* (26), who is the self-professed product of an icy northern climate (26–28) and symbol of a nation that "endures wintry Bootes for long nights" (*Brumalem patitur longa sub nocte Boöten* [37]), the youthful Cuddie complains of a cold climate: "Winter's rage" (1); "bitter blasts" (2); "The kene cold blowes" (3); "My ragged rontes all shiver and shake" (5),[234] all of which run contrary to his "springing youngth" (52), the possible pun adeptly matching season to burgeoning youthfulness. In response, Thenot, who prefers the winter, relates "a tale of truth,/Which I cond of Tityrus in my youth,/Keeping his sheepe on the hils of Kent" (91–93). Central to that tale, and its quasi-Aesopian fable of the Oak and the Briar, is the potential conflict between, yet the essential coexistence of, vernal youthfulness and decaying old age. After all, as Steven Marx observes, "[o]ld age is a version of pastoral, complementary and yet opposed to the pastoral of youth."[235] Thus the Briar's self-proclaimed beauty and articulated contempt for the Oak's unsightly decay are undercut by its need of physical proximity to that tree ("Hard by his

---

this [pipe], who among these hills of yours was the first to sing his tuneful lay on the Hyblaean pipe"). In response, Meliboeus, in recognition of his pastoral peer's self-acclaimed sense of poetic *aemulatio*, proffers a sobering observation: *magna petis, Corydon, si Tityrus esse laboras./ille fuit vates sacer et qui posset avena/praesonuisse chelyn, blandae cui saepe canenti/allusere ferae, cui substitit advena quercus* (64–67) ("You strive for mighty things, Corydon, if you endeavor to be Tityrus. He was a bard inspired and one who could outplay the lyre with the reed-pipe. While he sang, wild beasts often frolicked, and the oak approached and halted"). Corydon can only retort: *est—fateor, Meliboee,— deus* (70) ("He is, I admit, a poet divine"). Nemesianus, drawing upon Calpurnius, develops, in *Eclogue* 2, the Virgil/Tityrus identification, and in language upon which Milton, as argued in n224, seems to draw.

[232] Bush, *Variorum*, I, 273.

[233] On old age in pastoral, see, among others, A.W. Skarstrom, "'Fortunate Senex': The Old Man, A Study of the Figure, His Function and His Setting" (PhD thesis, Yale University, 1971); Harry Berger Jr., "The Aging Boy: Paradise and Parricide in Spenser's *Shepheards Calender*," in *Poetic Traditions of the English Renaissance*, eds. Maynard Mack and George de Forest Lord (New Haven, CT: Yale University Press, 1982), 25–46, and, especially, Steven Marx, "'Fortunate Senex': The Pastoral of Old Age," *SEL* 25 (1985): 21–44.

[234] Cf. the Argument to the poem: "For as in this time of yeare, so then in our bodies, there is a dry and withering cold."

[235] Marx, "'Fortunate Senex,'" 22.

side" 115]), whose shade affords crucial protection,[236] and by its subsequent withering by winter's cold (225–236) when the Oak is felled by a Husbandman. *Mansus*, it could be argued, seems to pick up several such motifs, only to reverse them in a young man's defense of old age. Thus, Cuddie's disparaging address "Ah foolish old man" (51) is transformed into the laudatory *Fortunate senex* (49). Likewise, his dismissal of his elder's intellectual prowess ("I deeme, thy braine emperished bee" [53]) is both countered and inverted by Miltonic praise of Manso's *Ingeniumque vigens, et adultum mentis acumen* (77) ("flourishing intellect and mature sharpness of mind"), its terminology aptly epitomizing "acutezza"/*acumen* and "ingegno"/*ingenium* as defined by the *Vocabulario degli Accademici della Crusca* (1612):

> ACUTEZZA astratto d'acuto, in senso metaforico. Sottigliezza d'ingegno. Lat. *acumen.*[237]
>
> ACUMEN. Abstract acuity, in a metaphorical sense. Subtlety of ingenuity. Lat. *Acumen.*
>
> INGEGNO. Acutezza d'inventare, e ghiribizzare, che che sia, senza maestro, o avvertitore. Lat. *Ingenium.*[238]
>
> INGEGNO. Acumen to invent and devise anything without master or informant. Lat. *Ingenium.*

Most striking, perhaps, is Milton's potential refutation of the Briar's criticism of the Oak's tottering head, withered foliage, and consequential "baldness":

---

[236] See D. M. Rosenberg, *Oaten Reeds and Trumpets: Pastoral and Epic in Virgil, Spenser, and Milton* (Lewisburg, PA: Bucknell University Press, 1981), 64: "Tityrus-Chaucer, represented by the Oak, bestows upon the younger shepherd-poet, Spenser, who is a wise briar, an ample shelter of wisdom and poetic tradition. The new poet, for all his innovative talents, expresses his dependence on, and reverence for, the great Oak of English poetry."

[237] *Vocabulario degli Accademici della Crusca* (Venice: Giovanni Alberti, 1612), 17.

[238] *Vocabulario degli Accademici della Crusca*, 444. Cf. Simona Morando, "Passions as Limits and Resources in 17th Century Italian Literature: Giambattista Marino's *Adone* (1623)," in *The Human and its Limits: Explorations in Science, Literature and the Visual Arts*, eds. Margareth Hagen, Randi Koppen, and Margery Vibe Skagen (Oslo: Scandinavian Academic Press, 2012), 255–270, at 257: "*Ingegno* is that intellectual capability which appeals to imagination and invention, hence to the senses, to bypass the limits of rationality and, in a strong expectation of wonder, achieve the creativity of thought and art. The passions of the soul solicit the *ingegno* and promote the creation of art and literature."

> Through rusty elde, that hath rotted thee:
> Or sicker thy head veray tottie is,
> So on thy corbe shoulder it leanes amisse.
> Now thy selfe hath lost both lopp and topp,
> Als my budding braunch thou wouldest cropp
> (54–58)

> His toppe was bald, and wasted with wormes,
> His honor decayed, his braunches sere
> (113–114)

> And oft his hoarie locks downe doth cast,
> Where with my fresh flowretts bene defast
> (181–182)

Such disparaging comments are forcefully reversed in Milton's praise of Manso's old age, and the associated metaphor of vernal blossoming (*Hinc longaeva tibi lento sub flore senectus/Vernat* [74–75] ["Hence your lengthy old age is Springlike beneath a lingering blossom"]), whereby the Spenserian "honor decayed" (114) is recast as the "honors" of a Neapolitan *frons* (as both "brow" and, punningly, "leaf") that are not yet "deciduous" (*Nondum deciduos servans tibi frontis honores* [76] ["preserving the glories of your brow not yet fallen"]),[239] as if in fulfillment of the Spring-loving Cuddie's hypothetical vision: "But were thy yeares greene, as now bene myne" (59). In short, *Mansus* seeks to resolve the dichotomy of youth and old age by reconciling two potentially conflicting polarities. This it achieves by lauding Manso in language evocative of youthfulness, and by Milton's later self-imagining as a virtual *senex*, who "has measured out the span of life" (*permensus tempora vitae* [85]) and is "in the fullness of years" (*Annorumque satur* [86]). The scenario is somewhat reminiscent of the speaker of *Il Penseroso*, who, in the words of Marx, "idealizes his aged future ... by envisioning his attainment of 'old experience' as another such sylvan sage":[240]

> And may at last my weary age
> Find out the peacefull hermitage,
> The Hairy Gown and Mossy Cell,
> Where I may sit and rightly spell,
> Of every Star that Heav'n doth shew,
> And every Herb that sips the dew;
> Till old experience do attain
> To somthing like Prophetic strain.
> These pleasures Melancholy give,

---

[239] See 55–58.

[240] Marx, "'Fortunate Senex,'" 41.

And I with thee will choose to live.
(*Il Penseroso* 167–176)

The concluding lines of *Mansus* take this one stage further in their daring representation of the imagined death and apotheosis of the Miltonic self (94–100).[241] It is here, moreover, that the whole seems to come full circle. According to Onofrio d'Andrea, Manso differs from the swan in one important respect. His musicianship and his poetic talents confer upon him immortality, in contrast to the swan, whose most beautiful singing is closely aligned to death itself.[242] The import of the dying swan's song certainly featured among subjects discussed by the Oziosi during Manso's lifetime. Francesco De Pietri, summarizing an academic debate on the most efficacious means of avoiding the fear of death ("Qual sia il più efficace mezzo per non temer la Morte"), cites Aristotle's comment that the dying swan sings in conscious awareness that it is awaiting the repose afforded by death.[243] To this remark are further adduced the authorities of Ovid and Cicero. Thus Ovid proclaims: *carmina iam moriens canit exequialia Cygnus* ("the swan while already dying sings its funereal song"),[244] while Cicero comments that it is not without reason that swans are attributed to Apollo, since it is from him that they seem to possess divination, foreseeing the good that is attendant upon death, and thus dying as they sing, and doing so with pleasure.[245] According to Giuseppe Battista, the Oziosi had debated "Why the Swan,

---

[241] See 59–63.

[242] *Poesie Nomiche*, 305.

[243] De Pietri, *I Problemi Accademici*, 224–229 ("Problema" LXXXII), at 225. Cf. Aristotle, *History of Animals*, 615b (denied by Pliny at *Naturalis Historia* 10.64). For further examples of the swan's song, see Aeschylus, *Agamemnon* 1444–1445; Ovid, *Tristia* 5.1.11–14. See also W. Geoffrey Arnott, "Swan Songs," *G&R* 24 (1977): 149–153; Frederick Ahl, "Amber, Avalon, and Apollo's Singing Swan," *AJP* 103 (1982): 373–411; Carole Elizabeth Newlands, *Playing with Time: Ovid and the Fasti* (Ithaca, NY: Cornell University Press, 1995), 184.

[244] De Pietri, *I Problemi Accademici*, 225. Cf. Ovid, *Metamorphoses* 14.430, in which the mournful dirge of Canens for the transformed Picus is compared to a dying swan's lament. On Ovid's implementation of swan imagery, see Sophia Papaioannou, *Epic Succession and Dissension: Ovid, Metamorphoses 13.623–14.582, and the Reinvention of the Aeneid* (Berlin: Walter de Gruyter, 2005), 149–156.

[245] De Pietri, *I Problemi Accademici*, 225. Cf. Cicero, *Tusculanae Disputationes* 1.1.73. See also *Homeric Hymn to Apollo* (no. 21), in which swans are depicted as accompanying with their encomiastic song Apollo, who responds by playing his lyre. As noted by Papaioannou, *Epic Succession and Dissension*, 153: "The poet of the *Hymn* employs the same word (λιγυρός)—a term later to become a technical word for lyric poetry—for both the swan song and Apollo's music."

though close to death, still sings" ("Perchè canti il Cigno vicino a morte").[246] Likewise, they had discussed the various reasons why Horace had called swans *purpurei* ("Perchè Orazio chiamasse i Cigni purpurei").[247] Part of their argument resided in their interpretation of the adjective *purpureus* as "resplendent" (and hence evoking the radiance ["splendore"] emanating from the swans' whiteness), in support of which meaning they cited the precedent of Catullus (*purpureaque ... luce* [64. 275]),[248] and Virgil (*lumen ... purpureum* [Aeneid 1.590–591; 6.640–641]).[249] By the end of *Mansus*, it is Milton, the *iuvenis peregrinus*, one of England's tuneful swans, who is endowed with his own *purpureum ... lumen* (99), as, in an envisaged apotheosis, he proclaims his transcendence of death itself.

---

[246] See Giuseppe Battista, *Le Giornate Accademiche* (Venice: Combi & La Noù, 1673), III, 170. At III, 171, Battista interestingly cites a comment of Georg Braun about swans on the Thames singing with great cheer upon the approach of ships: "Giorgio Braun dice, che in Inghilterra nel mare a Londra più vicino le schiere de'Cigni cantano festivamente sul venir delle Navi" ("Georg Braun says that in England, in the sea closer to London, flocks of swans sing cheerfully upon the approach of ships"). Cf. Georg Braun and Frans Hogenberg, *Civitates Orbis Terrarum* (Cologne: Bertram Bochholtz, 1599), I, s.v. *Londinum*: *Olores autem agminatim, laeto occursu, & festivis cantibus subeuntes classes excipiunt* ("Swans in their flocks happily go to meet approaching fleets and receive them with cheerful song"). Braun is, in fact, quoting verbatim a remark made by Paolo Giovio in *Regionum et Insularum atque Locorum Descriptiones: videlicet Britanniae, Scotiae, Hyberniae, Orchadum, item Moscoviae et Larii Lacus* (Basel: Petrus Perna, 1578), 12.

[247] Battista, *Le Giornate Accademiche*, III, 182. Cf. Horace, *Odes* 4.1.10: *purpureis ales oloribus*. See Henk Schoonhoven, "Purple Swans and Purple Snow (Hor. C.IV 1, 10 and *Eleg. in Maec*. 62)," *Mnemosyne* 31 (1978): 200–203.

[248] Catullus 64. 275: *purpureaque procul nantes* (s.c. *undae*) *a luce refulgent* ("and floating afar they (the waves) reflect a brightness from the resplendent light").

[249] Virgil, *Aeneid* 1. 590–591: *lumenque iuventae/purpureum* ("the resplendent radiance of youth"); *Aeneid* 6.640–641: *et lumine vestit/purpureo* ("and clothes with resplendent light"). Cf. Battista, *Le Giornate Accademiche*, 185.

Chapter 4

Non Tacita ... Vita: *Mansus*, Biography, and Miltonic Autobiography

Death can also be transcended by the immortalizing power of biography. In this respect *Mansus* both incorporates and juxtaposes several "brief lives," as it were: of Manso, of two of his biographical subjects (Tasso and Marino), and, ultimately, of Milton himself. Here the Headnote to the poem functions as an important biographical and autobiographical signifier. It is worth remarking that headnotes, as employed in the 1645 *Poemata*, can serve a variety of purposes. Some advertise authorial age, showcasing by implication Milton's youthful talent;[1] others omit age;[2] others focus upon the location of the addressee.[3] Some are multifunctional, as in the case of *Ad Salsillum Poetam Romanum Aegrotantem. Scazontes*, signaling poetic vocation, nationality, circumstance, and, self-referentially, meter. In *Epitaphium Damonis*, by contrast, the headnote is entirely replaced by an *Argumentum*.[4] Read in this context, the Headnote to *Mansus* seems strikingly atypical.

---

[1] In the *Elegiarum Liber*, for example, five of the seven elegies bear the heading *Elegia*, followed by the Latinized number of that elegy, then the formula *Anno aetatis*, coupled with an umbrella numeral, such as 17 (to indicate, for example, the year between Milton's seventeenth and eighteenth birthdays). By contrast, the two Latin elegies to Charles Diodati lack this feature, bearing instead the respective headings *Elegia Prima ad Carolum Diodatum* and *Elegia Sexta. Ad Carolum Diodatum Ruri Commorantem*. The practice of dating by age recurs in several of the poems included in the *Sylvarum Liber*. See, for example, *In Quintum Novembris, Anno aetatis 17*. In the case of the two threnodies of Cambridge worthies, however, title and age are reversed as *Anno aetatis 16. In Obitum Procancellarii Medici* and *Anno aetatis 17. In Obitum Praesulis Eliensis*, a reversal possibly governed by a wish to avoid any ambiguity that might arise between the stated authorial age and the date of the death lamented.

[2] This is true of *Naturam Non Pati Senium, De Idea Platonica*, and the more mature pieces: *Ad Patrem, Ad Salsillum, Mansus*, and *Epitaphium Damonis*.

[3] Thus, *Elegia Sexta. Ad Carolum Diodatum Ruri Commorantem*, and the three epigrams to Leonora Baroni: *Ad Leonoram Romae Canentem*.

[4] This offers a summary of the lifelong *amicitia* between Thyrsis and Damon, Thyrsis's wanderings abroad, his receiving the news of Damon's death, his

4.1 Milton's *Vita di Giovanni Battista Manso*

Ioannes Baptista Mansus Marchio Villensis, vir ingenii laude, tum litterarum studio, nec non et bellica virtute apud Italos clarus in primis est. Ad quem Torquati Tassi dialogus exstat de Amicitia scriptus; erat enim Tassi amicissimus; ab quo etiam inter Campaniae principes celebratur in illo poemate cui titulus *Gerusalemme Conquistata*, lib. 20:

> "Fra cavalier magnanimi e cortesi
> Risplende il Manso ... "

Is auctorem Neapoli commorantem summa benevolentia prosecutus est, multaque ei detulit humanitatis officia. Ad hunc itaque hospes ille antequam ab ea urbe discederet, ut ne ingratum se ostenderet, hoc carmen misit.

Giovanni Battista Manso, Marquis of Villa, is a man more famous than any other among the Italians, not only for the reputation of his genius and his pursuit of literary studies, but also for his bravery in war. There is extant a dialogue on Friendship, which Torquato Tasso addressed to him; for he was a very good friend of Tasso, by whom he is also celebrated among the princes of Campania in that poem which is entitled *The Conquest of Jerusalem*, book 20:

> "Among great-hearted and courteous knights
> Manso is resplendent ..."

When the author was sojourning in Naples, he attended him with the greatest of goodwill, and conferred on him many kind services. In consequence, that guest, before his departure from that city, sent him this poem in order that he might not appear ungrateful.

Here, in fact, the reader is presented with a miniature biography of Manso, summarizing his contemporary reputation among Italians for his intellectual and military prowess, his role as addressee of Tasso's

---

subsequent grief. Then in a pastoral decoding we are told that Damon signals Charles Diodati, descended through his father's family from the Tuscan city of Lucca, but in other respects English, a young man outstanding in terms of intellect, learning, and other most illustrious virtues. Here the methodology of Milton's *Argumentum* anticipates his explication of the allegory of *Epitaphium Damonis* 125–138 to Carlo Dati in *Epistola Familiaris* 10, discussed at 91–92. It may also emulate medieval explications of Virgil's pastoral allegory (by, for example, Fulgentius and Silvestris). For a parallel in neo-Latin pastoral, cf. Petrarch's meticulous explication of the allegorical content of his *Bucolicum Carmen* in a Latin letter to his brother (*Epistolae Familiares* 10. 4 [ca. 1346]). For this, and for further points of contact between the two poems, see Estelle Haan, "Pastoral," in *A Guide to Neo-Latin Literature*, ed. Victoria Moul (Cambridge: Cambridge University Press, 2017), 163–179, at 167–170.

Dialogo dell' Amicitia, his close friendship with the Italian poet, and his honorific inclusion by name in the *Gerusalemme Conquistata*. Here, too, the Headnote assumes a uniquely bilingual character, as Milton, turning from Latin to Italian, quotes from the Tassonian poem the relevant chapter and verse, so to speak. A fresh examination of the whole serves to reveal its biographical, literary, and potentially autobiographical import.

The year 1619 saw the publication in Naples of Francesco De Pietri's *Compendio della Vita di Torquato Tasso Scritta da Gio. Battista Manso*.[5] This synopsis of the basic content of Manso's forthcoming work (which would eventually appear in 1621), produced with Manso's approval,[6] was aimed at satisfying, at least for the time being, the curiosity of an eager public. Importantly, however, as Riga aptly notes, it also served to celebrate Manso himself.[7] In his dedicatory letter to Galeazzo Franco Pinello, third Duke of Cerenza,[8] De Pietri describes Manso's imminent *Vita* as an "opera di molto pregio" ("a work of great value") not only by virtue of its subject matter, but also because it is the product of the "Principe della nostra Academia" ("Principal of our Academy"), namely, Manso's Accademia degli Oziosi.[9] In essence then De Pietri avails of the opportunity to present the literary Manso and Tasso side by side, and does so in eulogistic terms. Initially he draws upon Manso's self-description in the *Vita*:

> & essendo egli allo'ncontro così stretto amico del Tasso, come i suoi versi, e le prose in molti luoghi, e spetialmente la Gerusalemme, e'l Dialogo dell' Amicitia, ch'egli intitolò il Manso, fecino fede.[10]

---

[5] Francesco De Pietri, *Compendio della Vita di Torquato Tasso Scritta da Gio. Battista Manso* (Naples: Gio. Domenico Roncagliolo, 1619). For a modern edition, see Bruno Basile, "La Più Antica Biografia del Tasso," *Italianistica: Rivista di Letteratura Italiana* 24 (1995): 525–539.

[6] See Basile, "La Più Antica Biografia," 525. De Pietri, at *Compendio*, 7, takes pains to point out that, while abridging the copious manuscript at hand, he has consulted the authority of Manso to confirm the truth of any statements, and has taken particular care to follow Manso's original wording insofar as is possible.

[7] See Riga, *Giovan Battista Manso*, 68.

[8] See Carlo De Lellis, *Discorsi delle Famiglie Nobili del Regno di Napoli*, 3 vols. (Naples: G. F. Paci, 1663), II, 153–154, 165.

[9] De Pietri, *Compendio*, 3.

[10] Manso, *Vita di Torquato Tasso*, 4.

and since he was such a close friend of Tasso, as his poetry and prose testify in many passages, and especially *The Jerusalem*, and *The Dialogue on Friendship*, which he entitled "Manso."

Crucially, however, he introduces that section with a miniature biography of his own:

> Giovan Battista Manso Cavalier, e Baron Napolitano assai conosciuto per lo suo valore, non meno nell'armi, che nelle lettere; & altrettanto stretto amico del Tasso (come i suoi versi, e le prose in molti luoghi, e specialmente nella Gerusalemme, e nel Dialogo dell' amicitia, ch'egli intitolò il Manso, ne rendono testimonianza).[11]

> Giovan Battista Manso, Count and Neapolitan Baron, well known for his worth no less in arms than in letters; and an equally close friend of Tasso (as his poetry, and prose bear witness, and especially in *The Jerusalem*, and in *The Dialogue on Friendship*, which he entitled "Manso").

It is to this encomiastic synopsis of Manso's life, and the Tassonian works itemized therein, that Milton's equivalent biographical "compendium," so to speak, bears a striking, though hitherto unnoticed, resemblance. Milton, however, reverses the order, as outlined in the accounts by both Manso and De Pietri, by giving precedence to the *Dialogo dell' Amicitia*, and by transferring the titular signifier to the *Gerusalemme*. In so doing, he foregrounds the role of *amicitia* in the present poem, whereby "Il Manso" shines forth as both dialogue[12] and person. And more than that. Moving beyond De Pietri's and Manso's simple paraphrase, he showcases his reading of the epic in question[13] by citing the actual book number, and quoting the relevant verses: *Gerusalemme Conquistata*, Bk 20, Canto 142: "Fra cavalier magnanimi e cortesi/Risplende il Manso" ("Among great-hearted and courteous knights/Manso is resplendent").[14] Here, in fact, Milton truncates the second half of the second verse, which reads in its complete form: "Risplende il Manso; e doni, e raggi ei versa" ("Manso is resplendent,

---

[11] De Pietri, *Compendio*, 6.

[12] On the role of dialogue in *Mansus*, see Chapter 5.

[13] Cf. Poole, *Milton and the Making of Paradise Lost*, 311–312: "Milton cites the lines ... under the form *Gerusalemme Conquistata*, which he must therefore have been reading."

[14] See *Di Gerusalemme Conquistata del Sig. Torquato Tasso Libri XXIIII* (Rome: Guglielmo Facciotti, 1593), 240.

and pours forth both gifts and radiance"). In so doing, he intensifies the dramatic force of "risplende."

The Tassonian quotation merits consideration in its original context, and, more broadly, in relation to the circumstances in which Tasso, according to Manso's *Vita*, composed the work in question. The *Gerusalemme Conquistata*, we learn, was the product of Tasso's literary activity upon his return to Naples in the autumn of 1592, in the course of which sojourn the poet rediscovered peace of mind, and the welcome opportunity to apply himself to his studies.[15] Here he devoted his energies to "sua maggior poema" ("his major poem"), and "in picciolissimo tempo quasi compiè la riformagione della sua Gerusalemme, ch'egli chiamò Conquistata") ("in a very short time, virtually completed the revision of his *Gerusalemme*, which he named the *Conquistata*").[16] Central to Tasso's literary productivity was the delight that he derived from the beauty of his Neapolitan surroundings, not least, Manso's villa, located "on the most delightful sea-shore" ("nella dilettevolissima piaggia del mare"), enhanced by its "elevated" ("elevato") site, and "encompassed by the most beautiful gardens" ("di bellissimi giardini circuito").[17] Here, too, we are told, both Manso and his mother, no less, encouraged the poet to write *Il Mondo Creato*.[18] For the Tasso of Manso's *Vita* then, it was a combination of the Neapolitan landscape and the support of Manso's

---

[15] Manso, *Vita di Torquato Tasso*, 205.

[16] *Vita di Torquato Tasso*, 205. Cf. 208: "godendo egli tranquillità nella menti, e salute nel corpo insieme ... ripigliò incontanente con grandissimo ardore, & allegrezza i suoi più severi, e faticosi studi; onde quivi diede compimento alla Gerusalem Conquistata" ("enjoying tranquility of mind and physical good health as well ... he was insatiable in resuming with great ardor and joy his more serious and laborious studies; whereupon he completed the composition of the *Gerusalemme Conquistata*").

[17] *Vita di Torquato Tasso*, 208: "Dimorava all'hora il Manso nella dilettevolissima piaggia del mare in un bel casamento alquanto sopra gli altri elevato, & attorno di bellissimi giardini circuito, i quali dalla vegnente Primavera di nuove frondi, e di variati fiori tutti rivestiti, con la verdura, e col soave odore di quelli, e molto più con la purità dell'aria per sì fatto modo Torquato dalla sua invecchiata melinconia ricrearono, che trà per questo, e per la libertà, ch'egli si prendeva in quella casa, che non pure d'un singolar' amico, mà sua propria stimava" ("Manso lived at that time upon the most delightful sea-shore in a beautiful building, somewhat elevated above the others, and encompassed by the most beautiful gardens, which, upon the approach of Spring, were all clothed once more with new leaves and varied flowers, whose verdure and sweet scent, and, much more, the purity of the air served to revive Tasso from his age-old melancholy, on this account and on account of the freedom which he derived in that house—an opinion not only of a singular friend, but also his own").

[18] *Vita di Torquato Tasso*, 209.

family home that served as an important catalyst for the revivification of his epic plans.

That familial network of support (and Tasso's implicit gratitude for such) rears its head in *Gerusalemme Conquistata* 20, a book regarded by Claudio Gigante as the most interesting of the four new books by which the original *Gerusalemme Liberata* was extended and substantially revised.[19] Here Tasso reworks and redefines Goffredo's dream in *Gerusalemme Liberata* 14.1–9,[20] peppering the whole with biblical paraphrase and classical allusion, not least to Cicero's *Somnium Scipionis*.[21] At the same time, in a series of what Gigante aptly terms "ottave encomiastiche,"[22] he extols contemporary or near-contemporary noble families (including those of d'Este, de Medici, della Rovere, and Gonzaga), now presented as thronging Paradise itself. Of particular note is the presence of distinguished Neapolitans who had afforded Tasso support and patronage.[23] And it is among these that Manso assumes a place of his own. Or perhaps not quite of his own. Closer inspection of his aforementioned inclusion by name (Canto 142) reveals that it is preceded by two further encomia (Cantos 141–142) of the nobility of Manso's familial ties. In this regard, Tasso clearly revised plans initially articulated in a letter to Manso (dated 24 July 1592). There he had conveyed his intention to name in his poem courtiers pertaining to two families in particular: Loffredo (by way, so he states, of a compliment to

---

[19] See Claudio Gigante, *"Vincer Pariemi Più se Stessa Antica": La "Gerusalemme Conquistata" nel Mondo Poetico di Torquato Tasso* (Naples: Bibliopolis, 1996), 115. Among other perceptive studies of this much neglected poem are C. P. Brand, "Stylistic Trends in the *Gerusalemme Conquistata*," in *Italian Studies Presented to E. R. Vincent on his Retirement from the Chair of Italian at Cambridge*, eds. C. P. Brand, Kenelm Foster, and Uberto Limentani (Cambridge: W. Heffer, 1962), 136–153; Walter Stephens, "Reading Tasso Reading Vergil Reading Homer: An Archaeology of Andromache," *CLS* 32 (1995): 296–319; Matteo Residori, *L'Idea del Poema: Studio sulla Gerusalemme Conquistata di Torquato Tasso* (Pisa: Scuola Normale Superiore, 2004); Bryan Brazeau, "Who Wants to Live Forever? Overcoming Poetic Immortality in Torquato Tasso's *Gerusalemme Conquistata*," *MLN* 129 (2014): 42–61.

[20] On Goffredo's dream in *Gerusalemme Liberata*, see Giovanna Scianatico, *"L'Idea del Perfetto Principe": Utopia e Storia nella Scrittura del Torquato Tasso* (Naples: Edizioni Scientifiche Italiane, 1998), 29–63; idem, *L'Arme Pietose. Studio sulla Gerusalemme Liberata* (Venice: Marsilio, 1990), 193–225.

[21] For an excellent overview of Goffredo's dream in *Gerusalemme Conquistata* in relation to its generic origins, and its debt to biblical and classical literature, see Gigante, *"Vincer Pariemi Più se Stessa Antica,"* 115–141.

[22] Gigante, *"Vincer Pariemi Più se Stessa Antica,"* 141.

[23] See Gigante, *"Vincer Pariemi Più se Stessa Antica,"* 141–144.

Manso's mother [whom Tasso erroneously believed to be Vittoria Loffredo, but who was, more accurately, Vittoria Pugliese]),[24] and Bel Prato (by way of a compliment to Manso's wife, Costanza Belprato),[25] only to continue:

> De la sua non ho fatta menzione, giudicando c'a la sua propria virtù ed al suo proprio merito si convengano lodi maggiori de la sua propria persona.[26]
>
> I have not made any mention of yourself, judging that in regard to your own virtue and your own merit greater praises coexist in your very self.

That Tasso clearly changed his mind (although his autograph manuscript of the poem does not mention Manso by name)[27] is attested by the published work. This augments his original conception as outlined here to include, in fact, all three: (1) Loffredo ("il gran Loffredo" [Bk 20, Canto

---

[24] That Manso's mother was Vittoria Pugliese is attested by many sources. See, for example, Lorenzo Giustiniani, "Lettera al ch. Signor D. Luigi Targioni intorno alla Vita, ed alle Opere di Gio. Battista Manso Napoletano Marchese di Villa," *Giornale Letterario di Napoli per Servire di Continuazione all'Analisi Ragionata de' Libri Nuovi* 60 (1796): 3–34, at 5–6: "La madre chiamossi *Vittoria Pogliese*, e non già *Loffredo*, come dice l'erudito *Serassi*" ("His mother was called Vittoria Pogliese, not Loffredo, as the learned Serassi states") (see Pierantonio Serassi, *La Vita del Tasso* [Rome: Pagliarini, 1785], 421, 477n5); Carmine Modestino, *Della Dimora di Torquato Tasso in Napoli negli Anni 1588, 1592, 1594* (Naples: Vaglio, 1859), 4; Riga, *Giovan Battista Manso*, 14. Manso movingly describes his mother as a "matrona non pure di gran valore, e di santissimi costumi, mà oltre a ciò di maravigliosa ingegno dotata" ("a woman endowed not only with great valor and the most revered forms of behavior, but also, moreover, with marvelous genius"). See Manso, *Vita di Torquato Tasso*, 209.

[25] *Le Lettere di Torquato Tasso*, ed. Cesare Guasti, 5 vols. (Florence: Felice Le Monnier, 1853–1855), V, 111: "Per la servitù la quale ho con Vostra Signoria, ho voluto nominar due cavalieri principali del mio poema de la famiglia de' Loffredi per la signora sua madre, e de'Belprati per la signora sua consorte" ("In regard to my indebtedness to Your Lordship I wanted to name two principal courtiers in my poem of the family of Loffredi [with respect to your mother] and of Belprato [with respect to your wife])." Manso had married Costanza Belprato in 1586. See Riga, *Giovan Battista Manso*, 15–16.

[26] *Le Lettere di Torquato Tasso*, ed. Guasti, V, 111.

[27] For this discrepancy between the autograph manuscript (extant in the BNN as MS Vind. lat.72) and the published work, see Gigante, *"Vincer Pariemi Più se Stessa Antica,"* 150; Torquato Tasso, *Gerusalemme Conquistata: Ms. Vind.Lat.72 della Biblioteca Nazionale di Napoli*, ed. Claudio Gigante (Alessandria: Edizioni dell'Orso, 2010), ad loc. See, in general, Anthony Oldcorn, *The Textual Problems of Tasso's "Gerusalemme Conquistata"* (Ravenna: Longo, 1976).

141]); (2) Costanza Belprato, daughter of Bernardino, second Count of Anversa,[28] hereby alluded to implicitly in "'l Conte … d'Anversa" (Bk 20, Canto 142); (3) Manso (Bk 20, Canto 142). Thus does the Marquis assume a climactic position, presented not only as a courtier resplendent in a masculine world of "great-hearted knights," but also as the son and husband of noble females.

Those "cavalier magnanimi," alongside whom Tasso affords Manso pride of place, are mirrored perhaps in the *magnanimi heroes*, the knights of Arthur's Round Table, who, as we learn from *Mansus* (82–83), feature in the plans of another epicist, Milton himself. And the Headnote seems to hint at Milton's self-alignment with the Italian epic poet. The sentence immediately following the Tassonian verses proclaims: *Is auctorem Neapoli commorantem summa benevolentia prosecutus est, multaque ei detulit humanitatis officia* ("When the author was sojourning in Naples, he attended him with the greatest of goodwill, and conferred on him many kind services"). At first glance, and given the preceding quotation from the *Gerusalemme Conquistata*, the noun *auctor* could, syntactically speaking, easily refer to Tasso himself, who, after all, was the recipient of many acts of kindness by Manso, by whom he was hosted on several occasions,[29] most notably, perhaps, during that Neapolitan sojourn in the autumn of 1592. In reality, of course, *auctor* refers to Milton, author of the present poem, and the hospitality likewise afforded him by Manso. One senses, however, that the Latin phraseology is a subtle, yet skillfully double-edged signifier of Milton's Tassonian self-fashioning in the poem itself. In all of this, the Headnote to *Mansus*, while ostensibly lauding its subject, serves to subsume an Englishman into the biographical and academic worlds of seicento Naples. Both here

---

[28] See Riga, *Giovan Battista Manso*, 15–16.

[29] See, for example, Manso, *Vita di Torquato Tasso*, 195: "prese opportunità d'irsene con Gio. Battista Manso, nella sua città di Bisaccio" ("he took the opportunity to reside with Gio. Battista Manso, in his city of Bisaccio"). Cf. *John Milton: Poetical Works*, ed. Masson, II, 368–369: "Tasso … had been led, in his wanderings over Italy, to Manso's door at Naples (1588). Manso, then in his twenty-eighth year, while Tasso was in his forty-fifth, had received the illustrious unfortunate, had kept him in his splendid villa at Naples and in his country-house at Bisaccio, had tended him in his fits of gloom, and soothed him in those moments when the frenzy was at its strongest, and the air around him was full of visions and voices, and he would call on Manso to look and listen. Thus had grown up a friendship which lasted with Tasso's life. Twice again he had been Manso's guest; it was in Manso's house, in one of these visits, that he completed his *Gerusalemme Conquistata*, in one of the books of which he introduces Manso's name." See Martina Riccio, "Torquato Tasso nel Castello di Bisaccia. L'Amicizia con Giovan Battista Manso," *Riscontri* 1 (2018): 73–81.

and in the poem proper Milton advertises to an audience of *accademici* the breadth of his reading of near contemporary Italian literature, as he takes his place quite literally alongside Italian poets befriended and nurtured by Manso. In short, history seems to be repeating itself.

4.2 Manso, the Biographer

If the Headnote offers a Miltonic/De Pietrian "brief life" of Manso, the poem itself both acknowledges and celebrates its addressee's own biographical talents:

> Nec satis hoc visum est in utrumque, et nec pia cessant
> Officia in tumulo; cupis integros rapere Orco,
> Qua potes, atque avidas Parcarum eludere leges:
> Amborum genus et varia sub sorte peractam
> Describis vitam moresque et dona Minervae,
> Aemulus illius Mycalen qui natus ad altam
> Rettulit Aeolii vitam facundus Homeri.
> (*Mansus* 17–23)

> But it did not seem to you that this was enough for them both [sc. Tasso and Marino], nor did your dutiful services cease at the grave: you longed to snatch them unharmed from Orcus, as far as you were able, and to cheat the greedy laws of the Fates: you record in writing the ancestry of both, and their lives lived under varying fortunes, their characters, and their gifts for Minerva, rivaling that man born near lofty Mycale, who eloquently related the life of Aeolian Homer.

That the lives of his two subjects were not without some turmoil is suggested by the phrase: *varia sub sorte peractam/Describis vitam* (20–21). Although the adjective *varius* might simply signify "different in each case,"[30] thereby drawing a contrast between the respective lots of Tasso and Marino, its more likely meaning is in the sense "(of fortunes, circumstances, or sim.) changeable, fluctuating, inconstant, etc."[31] As such, it seems to signal a Miltonic alertness to the vicissitudes of fortune that each of the two poets endured in the course of his individual life. Marino, after all, had suffered imprisonment on no fewer than three

---

[30] *OLD*, s.v. *varius*: 3.

[31] *OLD*, s.v. *varius*: 5. Cf. Plautus, *Truculentus* 219; Cicero, *Pro Cluentio* 58; Tacitus, *Historiae* 3.80.

occasions (in 1598, 1600, and 1611), while his literary career had been blemished (on 11 June 1624) by the fact that his *L'Adone* was placed by Urban VIII in the Index of prohibited books. On the other hand, that poem achieved huge success, and a wealth of supporters,[32] while Marino himself was highly esteemed by the academies of Italy, elected as "principe" of both the Roman Umoristi (in 1623) and the Neapolitan Oziosi (in 1624),[33] with the Neapolitan Infuriati strenuously vying, albeit unsuccessfully, to appoint him to their ranks.[34] These elevations were hailed in florid orations, and his performances were lauded by many. His role as principal of the Oziosi was, however, short-lived, as he died less than one year later (on 26 March 1625).

Such vicissitudes were doubtlessly described in detail by Manso in that (now lost) *Vita di Giambattista Marino*[35] to which Milton refers.

---

[32] For further discussion of the reception of *L'Adone*, see 184–201.

[33] See James V. Mirollo, *The Poet of the Marvelous: Giambattista Marino* (New York: Columbia University Press, 1963), 89–90.

[34] So great was the emulation among the Infuriati that it led to Marino being threatened with assassination. See Mirollo, *The Poet of the Marvelous*, 89.

[35] See Lorenzo Crasso, *Elogii d'Huomini Letterati*, 2 vols. (Venice: Combi & La Noù, 1666), I, 310–311: "Ne scrisse pur nondimeno la vita [sc. di Marino], la quale è rimasta manoscritta" ("Nonetheless, he wrote the life [sc. of Marino], which has remained in manuscript"). The *Vita di Giambattista Marino* was included by Manso in his will among works that should see posthumous publication. See the transcription of Manso's will in Manfredi, *Gio. Battista Manso*, 251–260, at 259: "Item voglio che, seguita mia morte, si debbano stampare tutte le opere da me composte, che in quel tempo si troveranno in stato da potersi pubblicare ed imprimere ... Vite di tre poeti napoletani, T. Tasso, G.B. Marini, e Giac. Sannazaro" ("Likewise, it is my wish that, after my death, all the works composed by me should be published and printed .... The Lives of three Neapolitan poets: T. Tasso, G. B. Marino, and Iac. Sannazaro"). Manso's "Testamento" survives in two copies, one in the Archivio di Stato di Napoli, the other in the Archivio Storico di Monte Manso, Naples. See Manfredi, *Gio. Battista Manso*, 251; See also Denman, "A Gift Text of Hispano-Neapolitan Diplomacy," 685. The existence of the *Vita di Giambattista Marino* among Manso's manuscripts is attested by Francesco Daniele in his nineteenth-century *Vita* of Francesco De' Pietri. Daniele proceeds to claim that it was through his own efforts that the same manuscript was transported to the Reale Biblioteca Borbonica, now the Biblioteca Nazionale Vittorio Emanuele III in Naples. See Francesco Daniele, *La Vita di Francesco de' Pietri Giureconsulto e Storico Napoletano* (Naples: Simoniana, 1803), xxi. Subsequent attempts to find the manuscript there have proved ineffectual. See Carlo Antonio De Rosa, *Ritratti Poetici di Alcuni Uomini Antichi e Moderni del Regno di Napoli* (Naples: Cartiera del Fibreno, 1834), 133, who paraphrases Daniele's remarks, only to conclude: "ma per quante ricerche da noi si sieno adoperte, non ci è riuscito ivi rinvenirla" ("but no matter how much research I have undertaken, I have been unable to find it there"). In short, the manuscript is now regarded as lost, a huge detriment to scholarship. Cf. Riga, *Giovan Battista Manso*, 65.

Indeed, it is not unreasonable to suppose, as Riga does, that it had been Manso's intention to complete a life of Marino on a scale comparable to that of his *Vita di Torquato Tasso*,[36] motivated perhaps by a desire to correct what he saw as the inaccurate public image of the poet. The work (and perhaps even the manuscript) in question is almost certainly alluded to by Manso's contemporary and fellow biographer of the poet, Giovan Francesco Loredano,[37] in his note "A' chi legge" in his own *Vita del Cavalier Marino* (1633), when mentioning biographies of the poet that are forthcoming in Rome and in Naples.[38] That it was a long-term project is suggested by an undated letter from Loredano to Manso, in which he contrasts his own biography, which he claims to be the product of a few hours, with Manso's, which he predicts will be the more perfect and favored. Still, he takes pleasure in the fact that his *Vita* will appear first in print.[39] Crucially, for the present purposes, Manso's *Vita di Giambattista Marino* was extant in manuscript at the time of Milton's visit, and in all likelihood was shown by the Neapolitan to his English guest. If so, it was doubtlessly met with a Miltonic pleasure similar to that voiced in *Epistola Familiaris* 9, when in the course of a guided tour of the Vatican Library he was shown by Lucas Holstenius "Greek authors in manuscript enhanced by [Holstenius's] painstaking labors."[40] Perhaps it also assumes

---

[36] Riga, *Giovan Battista Manso*, 65.

[37] On Loredano, principal of the Venetian Accademia degli Incogniti, friend and correspondent of Manso, see Clizia Carminati, "Loredan, Giovan Francesco," *DBI* 65 (2005): 761–770; Riga, *Giovan Battista Manso*, 39–40, 65–66, 186–187.

[38] Giovan Francesco Loredano, *Vita del Cavalier Marino* (Venice: Giacomo Sarzina, 1633), sig. a3^r–a3^v: "Hora, ch'io intendo questa stessa uscire in Roma, e in Napoli da alcune celebri penne" ("I hear that the same is coming out in Rome and in Naples from some famous pens"). In all likelihood the reference is to (a) the biography by Giacomo Filippo Camola: *Breve Racconto della Vita del Sig. Cavalier Marino Descritta dal Sig. Giacomo Filippo Camola, Academico Humorista, detto L'Infecondo* (Rome: Mascardi, 1633), and (b) Manso's own *Vita* of Marino. See also Riga, *Giovan Battista Manso*, 65–66; 186–187. A biography by Francesco Chiaro, had already seen publication in Naples, having been appended to Marino's *La Strage degli Innocenti* (Naples: Ottavio Beltrano, 1632).

[39] Giovan Francesco Loredano, *Lettere*, 2 vols. (Bologna: Gioseffo Longhi, 1674), I, 54: "La vita del Marino fù un' aborto di poche hore: quella di V.S. sarà un parto, tanto più perfetto, quanto più favorito dal tempo. Godo però d'esser stato il primo à darla alla luce, onde non le sarò inferiore in tutte le cose" ("The Life of Marino was an abortion, lasting a few hours: that produced by Your Lordship will be a birth the more perfect, the more it is favored by time. However, I take pleasure in being the first to deliver, whereby I will not be inferior to you in all respects").

[40] See Milton, *Epistola Familaris* 9, in *John Milton: Epistolarum Familiarium Liber Unus and Uncollected Letters*, ed. Haan, 140–163, at 146–147: *et permultos insuper manuscriptos auctores Graecos tuis lucubrationibus exornatos adspicere licuit* ('I

a forever undetectable place of its own among the multiple intertexts with which *Mansus* engages.

By contrast, Manso's *Vita di Torquato Tasso*, as noted previously, had seen publication in Venice in 1621.[41] It had also been reprinted by the same publisher in 1625, with a second edition appearing in Rome in 1634.[42] This highly romanticized and frequently anecdotal[43] biography certainly signaled the highs and lows (or in Miltonic terms the *varia ... sors* [20]) of Tasso's life. The work was hugely influential in its day,[44] especially in promulgating the story of the poet's insanity as a consequence of his love for Leonora d'Este.[45] Using the testimony of Tasso's own letters, Manso interrogates the nature and symptoms of the poet's "malinconia,"[46] his "delirio,"[47] his "malia,"[48] and the associated "apparitione,"[49] while also revealing his own first-hand observation of such obsessive delusions, frenzy, and paranoia. He devotes a lengthy section to Tasso's final days, and his untimely death just a few days prior to his laureate crowning on the Campidoglio in Rome.[50] Milton's

---

was permitted to look over ... a great number of Greek authors in manuscript enhanced by your painstaking labors"). For further discussion, see Haan, *John Milton's Roman Sojourns*, 148–153.

[41] On the publication of Manso's *Vita*, see "Nota al Testo," in *Manso, Vita di Torquato Tasso*, ed. Bruno Basile (Rome: Salerno Editrice, 1995), 303–318.

[42] *Vita di Torquato Tasso Scritta da Gio. Battista Manso Marchese Della Villa* (Rome: Francesco Cavalli, 1634).

[43] See Michele de Filippis, "Anecdotes in Manso's 'Vita di Tasso' and Their Sources," *UCPMP* 18 (1936): 443–502.

[44] See Stefano Prandi, "Sulla 'Vita di Torquato Tasso' di Giambattista Manso," *LI* 47 (1995): 623–628; Riga, *Giovan Battista Manso*, 67–93.

[45] The connection between Tasso's madness and Leonora had been popularized even in England from an early date. See John Eliot, *Ortho-Epia Gallica. Eliots Fruits for the French* (London: John Wolfe, 1593), 30: "This Youth fell mad for the love of an Italian lasse, descended of a great house, when I was in Italie." Similarly, Scipio Gentili seems to accept it as a fact in the hendecasyllabic verses prefixed to his Latin translation of the *Gerusalemme Liberata*. See *Scipii Gentilis Solymeidos Libri Duo Priores de Torquati Tassi Italicis Expressi* (London: John Wolfe, 1584). Nonetheless, it was largely through Manso's *Vita* that the story was most widely known. See C. P. Brand, *Torquato Tasso: A Study of the Poet and of his Contribution to English Literature* (Cambridge: Cambridge University Press, 1965), 207–209.

[46] Manso, *Vita di Torquato Tasso*, 126–128.

[47] *Vita di Torquato Tasso*, 128–131.

[48] *Vita di Torquato Tasso*, 134–136.

[49] *Vita di Torquato Tasso*, 136–145.

[50] *Vita di Torquato Tasso*, 221–233. For further discussion, see 150–154.

probable knowledge of the *Vita*, and of its account of Tasso's insanity in particular, is suggested by *Ad Leonoram* 2, composed in all likelihood during the course of his second Roman visit (January/February 1639), and thus significantly postdating his Neapolitan sojourn. There he alludes to Tasso's madness in consequence of his love for "another Leonora": *Altera Torquatum cepit Leonora poetam* (1) ("Another Leonora captivated the poet Torquato"). The phrase assumes additional force when read alongside Manso's account of "Tre Leonore una delle quali fù l'amata di Tor[quato]" ("Three Leonoras, of one of whom Tor[quato] was enamored"):[51] (1) Leonora d'Este,[52] (2) Contessa San Vitale,[53] (3) a damigella of Leonora d'Este,[54] each of whom, as Riga argues, may represent spiritual, sensual, and profane love, respectively.[55] Milton dwells on the ultimately fatal nature of Tasso's insanity: *Cuius ab insano cessit amore furens* (2) ("who became mad and died on account of his insane love for her"), imagining one of its symptoms by reference to Pentheus, king of Thebes: *Quamvis Dircaeo torsisset lumina Pentheo/ Saevior* (7–8) ("Even if he had rolled his eyes more fiercely than Dircaean Pentheus"),[56] himself the tormented Euripidean subject of multiple hallucinations (not least, seeing two suns in the sky).[57]

Milton's succinct summary in *Mansus* of Manso's biographical methodology signals the Neapolitan's emphasis on his subjects' *genus* (20), *vitam* (21), *mores* (21), and *dona Minervae* (21). The ordering of nouns serves to map the structural progression certainly of the *Vita di Torquato Tasso*, and, most likely, that of the now lost *Vita di Giambattista Marino*. Here the former can serve as a useful case study.

---

[51] *Vita di Torquato Tasso*, 50. Manso designates the respective Leonoras as "Prima" (51), "Seconda" (57), and "Terza" (59).

[52] *Vita di Torquato Tasso*, 51–57.

[53] *Vita di Torquato Tasso*, 57–59.

[54] *Vita di Torquato Tasso*, 59–62.

[55] Riga, *Giovan Battista Manso*, 81–82, argues that Leonora d'Este denotes spiritual involvement devoid of any physical or erotic implications, Contessa San Vitale encompasses sensual impulses, while the third Leonora symbolizes profane love and its associated carnal pleasures.

[56] Cf. Euripides, *Bacchae*, passim; Ovid, *Metamorphoses* 3.577–578: *adspicit hunc Pentheus oculis, quos ira tremendos/fecerat* ("Pentheus looks upon him with eyes, which his anger had rendered terrifying").

[57] See Euripides, *Bacchae* 918. Pentheus's eventual *sparagmos* at the hands of his mother and the Bacchantes (see Euripides, *Bacchae* 1114–1136; Ovid, *Metamorphoses* 3.701–733) is mirrored perhaps in Milton's epigram in the phonological and tonal dismemberment of *Torquatus* (1) in <u>torsisset</u> (7), whereby Tasso is both literally and linguistically enveloped by the symptoms of his insanity.

From the opening pages Tasso's life is contextualized alongside the essential nobility of his family ancestry (*genus*).[58] Thus, we are told, his mother (Porzia de Rossi) was descended from the most illustrious line of the Avoli, and "from branches of the most famous families in Italy" ("da' rami delle più famose famiglie dell'Italia"),[59] and his father, Bernardo, "was from the Tassi, one of the most respectable families of Bergamo" ("fù de' Tassi una delle più riguardevoli famiglie di Bergamo").[60] There follows the *vita* proper, after which Manso presents a lengthy overview of Tasso's "costumi" or, in Milton's words, his *mores* (21). The Latin noun implies "[h]abitual conduct (of an individual or group), character, disposition, ways,"[61] and also denotes "a person's character as a standard of conduct."[62] It is a discerning observation on Milton's part. In fact, Manso both exaggerates and idealizes Tassonian "costumi" to the extent that his account, as Riga has observed, assumes the tone of a pedagogical tract, its terminology not far removed from that of the statutes of the Oziosi itself.[63] And it does so very self-consciously. Manso prefaces this section by proclaiming his intention:

> aggiungere un breve raccontamento prima delle fattezze, e della statura del suo corpo, appresso delle qualità dell' animo, e de' costumi, & alla fine dell'eccellenza dello 'ngegno.[64]

> to add a brief account firstly of the features, and the stature of his body, followed by the qualities of his soul and of his customs, and, finally, of the excellence of his genius.

What follows is far from "breve." Instead, over the course of no fewer than fifty pages Manso carefully itemizes each Tassonian *mos*, as it were, by explicitly naming and signaling it in a marginal note. In short, we are presented with a whole litany of Tassonian traits, including obedience, truthfulness, friendship, affability, kindness, generosity, magnanimity, bravery, confidence, perseverance, temperance, modesty, silence, humility, self-deprecation, gentleness, clemency, honesty, sense of

---

[58] Manso, *Vita di Torquato Tasso*, 5–11.

[59] *Vita di Torquato Tasso*, 5–6. See also, and especially, 7–11.

[60] *Vita di Torquato Tasso*, 6; see also 7.

[61] *OLD*, s.v. *mos*: 5.

[62] *OLD*, s.v. *mos*: 5d.

[63] See Riga's excellent discussion at *Giovan Battista Manso*, 83–87.

[64] *Vita di Torquato Tasso*, 236.

shame, abstinence, prudence, maturity, sense of forethought, loyalty, and genius.[65]

Manso has also, according to Milton, described the *dona Minervae* (21) of his biographical subjects. The phrase at first sight may seem surprisingly pejorative in that it was twice used by Virgil to describe the Trojan Horse, no less.[66] Hitherto glossed by editors as a Miltonic acknowledgment of the "intellectual gifts" of the two Italian poets,[67] the phrase, when read in its original context, possesses an essentially material import. Here, as in Virgil, *Minervae* is an objective genitive, signaling gifts/offerings made to or for Minerva.[68] After all, as Clyde Murley pertinently remarks, "the horse was not represented or regarded as a gift to the Trojans from their enemies."[69] Rather, *donum*, as Donatus observed, signifies an offering to gods, as opposed to *munus*, which denotes a gift to men.[70] Likewise, Isidore of Seville proclaims: *dona proprie divina dicuntur, munera hominum* ("*dona* are pertinently described as pertaining to gods; *munera* as pertaining to men").[71] In this reading the *dona* in question likewise constitute material constructs, the *literary products* of both Tasso and Marino offered, like the Trojan

---

[65] *Vita di Torquato Tasso*, 236–285: "Fattezze" (236–238), "Habilità, e Gratia" (238–239), "Costumi, e Giustitia" (239), "Obbedienza" (240), "Osservanza" (240–242), "Veracità" (242), "Amicitia" (243), "Affabilità" (244), "Benedicenza" (244), "Liberalità" (245–248), "Magnanimità" (248–250), "Fortezza" (250), "Valore" (250), "Confidanza" (251), "Patienza" (251–252), "Costanza" (252–253), "Perseveranza" (253–255), "Temperanza" (255), "Modestia" (256), "Silentio" (256–257), "Humiltà" (258), "Dispregio di se" (258–259), "Mansuetudine" (259–261), "Clemenza" (261–262), "Honestà" (262–263), "Vergogna" (263–264), "Continenza" (264–265), "Astinenza" (265–267), "Prudenza" (267–269), "Simulatione" (269), "Maturità" (269–270), "Accorgimento" (270), "Providenza" (270–271), "Ordine" (271–272), "Fede" (272–277), "Speranza" (277–279), "Carità" (279–283), "Ingegno" (283–285).

[66] Virgil, *Aeneid* 2.189. Cf. *Aeneid* 2.31.

[67] See Bush, *Variorum*, I, 272.

[68] See *P. Vergili Maronis Aeneidos Liber Secundus*, ed. R. G. Austin (Oxford: Clarendon Press, 1964), 41 and 92.

[69] See Clyde Murley, "'Et Dona Ferentis,'" *CJ* 22 (1927): 658–662, at 659.

[70] Donatus (on Terence, *Eunuchus* V.9.27): *sed donum, praemium Diis datur: munus, praemium hominibus*. Text is that of *P. Terentii Afri Comoediae Sex cum Interpretatione Donati et Calphurnii et Commentario Perpetuo*, ed. Arn. Henr. Westerhoven (The Hague: Isaac van der Kloot, 1732), 565. Murley, "'Et Dona Ferentis,'" 660, notes that *donum* is used ten times in the *Aeneid* of gifts of men to men, seven times of gifts of gods to men, and twenty-one times of offerings of men to gods.

[71] Isidore, *Etymologies*, VI, 26. See, *Patrologia Latina*, ed. Migne, LXXXII (1850), 254. Cf. Murley, "'Et Dona Ferentis,'" 660.

Horse, and now in a metaphorical sense, as gifts to the goddess of wisdom.

Certainly, Manso was far from reticent in both "describing" and itemizing Tasso's literary *dona*, in a section that, as in Milton, follows the account of the *mores* of the Italian poet. Emphasizing the "inventione" of Tasso's "ingegno," he begins by drawing attention to the generic versatility of his literary output:

> Egli scrisse in tutte le maniere, e di verso, e di prosa. ... Scriss' egli in tutte, e tre i generi della Poesia, e ciò sono l'Epica, la Drammatica, e la Melica.[72]
>
> He wrote in all styles, both in verse, and in prose. ... He wrote in all three genres of Poetry, and these are Epic, Dramatic, and Lyric.

This is followed by a brief overview and a critical synopsis of each Tassonian work in turn, named herein as *Gerusalemme*,[73] *Rinaldo*,[74] *Sette Giorni*,[75] *Aminta*,[76] *Torismondo*,[77] *Poemetti*,[78] *Sonetti*,[79] *Canzoni*,[80] and *Madrigali*.[81]

In all of this, Manso is presented by Milton as a rival of Herodotus, the purported biographer of Homer (22–23). The βίος/Life in question, now regarded by modern scholarship as pseudo-Herodotean,[82] had seen publication (and unambiguously so, under the name of Herodotus) in the *editio princeps* of *Homeri Opera*, printed in Florence in 1488,[83] and

---

[72] Manso, *Vita di Torquato Tasso*, 286.

[73] *Vita di Torquato Tasso*, 286–287.

[74] *Vita di Torquato Tasso*, 287.

[75] *Vita di Torquato Tasso*, 287–288.

[76] *Vita di Torquato Tasso*, 288.

[77] *Vita di Torquato Tasso*, 288–289.

[78] *Vita di Torquato Tasso*, 289.

[79] *Vita di Torquato Tasso*, 289.

[80] *Vita di Torquato Tasso*, 289–290.

[81] *Vita di Torquato Tasso*, 290–291.

[82] See N. Bryant Kirkland, "Herodotus and Pseudo-Herodotus in the *Vita Herodotea*," *TAPhA* 148 (2018): 299–329.

[83] *Homeri Opera*, ed. Demetrius Chalcondylas (Florence: Bernardo and Nero Nerli, 1488), sig. Aiii^r–Aix^r. See, in particular, the opening claim at sig. Aiii^r: Ἡρόδοτος Ἁλικαρνασσεὺς περὶ Ὁμήρου γενέσιος καὶ ἡλικίης καὶ βιοτῆς τάδε ἱστόρηκε, ζητήσας ἐπεξελθεῖν ἐς τὸ ἀτρεκέστατον ("Herodotus of Halicarnassus has recorded the

likewise in the 1504 Aldine edition.[84] That Milton was familiar with the work is suggested by his description of the biographer as *facundus* (23) ("able to express oneself fluently, eloquent").[85] He would later borrow from it the term "Melesigenes" (used therein to describe Homer)[86] in *Paradise Regained* 4. 259: "Blind *Melesigenes* thence *Homer* call'd."[87] Stella Revard, noting that "[t]he pseudo-Herodotean life of Homer is both a biography and a travel book," offers the interesting speculation that in *Mansus* "Milton, the much-traveled young English poet, was perhaps also suggesting his own connection with the epic poet Homer."[88] Perhaps, indeed, but he is also paving the way for his own quasi-Herodotean self-portraiture later in the poem:

> Nos etiam colimus Phoebum, nos munera Phoebo
> Flaventes spicas et lutea mala canistris
> Halantemque crocum (perhibet nisi vana vetustas)
> Misimus, et lectas Druidum de gente choreas.
> (Gens Druides antiqua sacris operata deorum
> Heroum laudes imitandaque gesta canebant.)
> Hinc quoties festo cingunt altaria cantu

---

following history of Homer's origins, time, and life, and has aimed to achieve the greatest accuracy"). Cf. Bernardo Nerli's dedicatory letter to Piero de Medici, at ibid., sig. Ai^r: *Ad haec non solum Homeri opera quaecunque reperiuntur quaeque eius feruntur imprimenda curavi, verum etiam his adieci Herodotum, Plutarchum, atque Dionem, qui et poetae vitam litteris diligentissime mandaverunt* ("I have not only seen to the publication of these works that are found to be by Homer, and those which are said to be by him, but I have also added to these Herodotus, Plutarch, and Dio, who also most diligently entrusted to literature the life of the poet").

[84] *Homeri Opera* (Venice: Aldus Manutius, 1504), I, sig. 1i^v–22^v.

[85] See *OLD*, s.v. *facundus*.

[86] *Homeri Opera*, ed. Demetrius Chalcondylas, sig. Aiiii^r: χρόνου δὲ προϊόντος, ἐξελθοῦσα ἡ Κρηθηῒς μετ' ἄλλων γυναικῶν πρὸς ἑορτήν τινα ἐπὶ τὸν ποταμὸν τὸν καλούμενον Μέλητα, ἤδη ἐπίτοκος οὖσα, τίκτει τὸν Ὅμηρον, οὐ τυφλὸν ἀλλὰ δεδορκότα· καὶ τίθεται ὄνομα τῶι παιδίωι Μελησιγένεα, ἀπὸ τοῦ ποταμοῦ τὴν ἐπωνυμίαν λαβοῦσα ("When some time had elapsed, as Cretheis was proceeding with other women to a festival at the river called Meles, and was now ready to give birth, she bore Homer, who was not blind, but could see. And she named the child 'Melesigenes,' taking the name from the river").

[87] Text is that of *The Complete Works of John Milton: Volume II: The 1671 Poems: Paradise Regain'd and Samson Agonistes*, ed. Laura Lunger Knoppers (Oxford: Oxford University Press, 2008). For very useful discussions, see Gordon Campbell, "Milton and the Lives of the Ancients," *JWCI* 47 (1984): 234–238, and Stella P. Revard, "Across the Alps—An English Poet Addresses an Italian in Latin: John Milton in Naples," in *Travel and Translation in the Early Modern Period*, ed. Carmine G. Di Biase (Amsterdam: Rodopi, 2006), 53–64.

[88] Revard, "Across the Alps," 55–56.

> Delo in herbosa Graiae de more puellae
> Carminibus laetis memorant Corineïda Loxo
> Fatidicamque Upin, cum flavicoma Hecaërge,
> Nuda Caledonio variatas pectora fuco.
> (*Mansus* 38–48)

> We, too, worship Phoebus; to Phoebus we have sent gifts of golden ears of corn, rosy apples in baskets, the fragrant crocus (unless the proclamations of ancient lore be in vain), and choirs chosen from the Druid race. (The Druids, an ancient race, well versed in the rituals of the gods, used to sing the praises of heroes, and their exploits worthy of imitation.) Hence as often as Greek girls in grassy Delos encircle the altars in festive song according to custom, they commemorate in joyful song Loxo, daughter of Corineus, and prophetic Upis, together with Hecaerge of the golden tresses, their bare breasts colorfully painted with Caledonian woad.

Making a case for the worshipping of Apollo in Britain,[89] Milton describes the practice of the ancient Britons, in whose company he proudly situates himself (*Nos etiam* [38]). The phrase echoes his earlier acknowledgment (30) of the literary merit of British, and more specifically, Thames-side swans/poets.[90] In what follows, he claims that the Britons delivered gifts of corn, apples, and flowers to Apollo, thereby mirroring the practice of the three Hyperborean nymphs: Loxo, Upis, and Hecaerge. The lines draw upon Herodotus's account, in book 4 of his *Histories*, of the geographical trajectory by which offerings eventually made their way from the Hyperborean north to Delos.[91] Here we read that, according to Delian testimony, sacred offerings wrapped in straw were brought from the Hyperboreans to Scythia, where, after passing from nation to nation, they first made their way to Delos in the charge of

---

[89] On the worship of Apollo by ancient Britons, see John Selden, "Notes upon Drayton's Polyolbion," in *Opera Omnia*, ed. David Wilkins, 3 vols. (London: John Walthoe, 1726), III, 1785–1786.

[90] See 98–111.

[91] Herodotus, *Histories* 4: 33–35. See, among others, William Sale, "The Hyperborean Maidens on Delos," *HTR* 54 (1961): 75–89; Barbara Kowlazig, *Singing for the Gods: Performances of Myth and Ritual in Archaic and Classical Greece* (Oxford: Oxford University Press, 2007), 118–123; Véronique Chankowski, *Athènes et Délos à L'Époque Classique: Recherches sur L'Administration du Sanctuaire d'Apollon Délien* (Paris: De Boccard, 2008), 106–108.

two maidens, named Hyperoche and Laodice, in the protective company of five men. It was only upon the failure of their messengers to return that the Hyperboreans began the practice of wrapping the offerings in straw and taking them to their borders. Upon the death in Delos of the two Hyperborean maidens, boys and girls cut their hair as a sign of mourning: the girls, before their marriage, cutting off a tress and laying it, wrapped around a spindle, on the tomb; the boys entwining locks of their hair around a green stalk, likewise placed on the tomb. At this point Herodotus inserts an alternative tradition: that before the time of Hyperoche and Laodice, two other maidens, named Arge and Opis, came from the Hyperboreans to Delos by the same route. He also differentiates between the respective recipients of the offerings: Ilithia (goddess of childbirth), to whom Hyperoche and Laodice bore thanks-giving offerings, and Apollo and Artemis, to whom Arge and Opis presented their gifts. These latter two maidens are in consequence honored in a different way. Thus, the women of Delos collect gifts for them, naming them in a hymn composed in their honor by Olen of Lycia.[92] From Delos, too, we are told, the islanders and Ionians learned to sing hymns in their praise. Furthermore, ashes from thigh bones burnt upon the altar are scattered on their burial place.[93]

It is upon this second tradition and its hymnic ritual of commemoration that Milton draws. But whereas Herodotus mentions just two maidens, Arge and Opis, Milton adds a third: Loxo.[94] This detail he derives from Callimachus's version of the tradition in *Hymn* 4 (to Delos),[95] from which he also probably borrows the name Hecaerge (292).[96] Callimachus itemizes gifts of "cornstalks and holy sheaves of

---

[92] Pausanias, *Description of Greece* 5.7.8, mentions Olen of Lycia as the author of a hymn to the Hyperborean maiden Achaeia, and relates that Melanopos of Kyne composed an ode to Opis and Hecaerge.

[93] All references are to *Herodotus: The Histories*, trans. A. D. Godley, 4 vols. (Cambridge MA: Harvard University Press, 1920–1925).

[94] All three are likewise named as Loxo, Opis, and Hecaerge by Nonnus at *Dionysiaca* 5.480 and 48.330.

[95] See Callimachus, *Hymn* 4. 283–299.

[96] Precedent for the pairing of Haecerge and Opis in Latin poetry is provided by Claudian, *De Consulatu Stilichonis* 3.253–256: *iungunt se geminae metuenda feris Hecaërge/et soror, optatum numen venantibus, Opis/progenitae Scythia: divas nemorumque potentes/fecit Hyperboreis Delos praelata pruinis* ("To these are joined the twin sisters Hecaerge, who inspires terror among beasts, and Opis, a deity beloved of hunters, Scythian maids, whose preference for Delos over the frosts of the north made them goddesses and queens of the woods"). This is a particularly apt subtext, given Manso's attested knowledge of Claudian's poetry, on which see 65–72.

ear-corn" (283), refers to the three maidens as "daughters of Boreas" (293), and describes a custom whereby girls of Delos, upon the sounding of the marriage-hymn, bring offerings of their hair to the maidens,[97] while boys offer to young men the first harvest of down upon their cheeks (296–299). As hinted at in *Nos etiam* (38), Milton includes himself, at least figuratively speaking, in that long line of ancient early Britons who brought (and continue to bring) "golden ears of corn" (*flaventes spicas* [39]) as offerings to Apollo. And more than that. The passage as a whole suggests a self-alignment of the essentially male young foreigner sent from the Hyperborean skies (*missus Hyperboreo iuvenis peregrinus ab axe* [26])[98] with the three Hyperborean females, now imaginatively recast as British Druidesses. Milton embellishes the whole with telling details of his own that, in the words of Revard "even more closely connect [the maidens] to Britain."[99] Thus Upis is endowed with prophetic powers (*fatidicam* [47]), and, by association, is aligned with the aforementioned Druids; Hecaerge has golden hair (*flavicoma* [47]), just like the ancient Britons.[100] Most notable, Loxo is reconfigured as the daughter of Corineus (*Corineïda* [46]), one of the founders of Britain,[101] a statement otherwise unattested,[102] and thus probably Milton's invention. All three, moreover, are stained with woad, an essentially British custom.[103] As in both Herodotus and Callimachus, they are commemorated in festive song proclaimed upon grassy Delos by Greek girls, whose ritualistic act of "encircling" (*cingunt* [44]) the altars may subtly rework the description (in the first Herodotean tradition) of female locks of hair as twisted (εἰλίξασαι) around spindles, or those of boys as entwined (εἰλίξαντες) around a green stalk, as they ritualistically place the aforementioned items

---

[97] Likewise, Pausanias, *Description of Greece* 1.43.4, relates that the daughters of the Delians cut their hair in honor of Hecaerge and Opis.

[98] See 83.

[99] Revard, "Across the Alps," 57.

[100] Cf. Lucan, *De Bello Civili* 3.78: *flavis ... Britannis*; John Leland, *Cygnea Cantio* 470: *flavicomos ... Britannos*.

[101] Corineus came to Britain with the Trojan Brutus. He won Cornwall in return for his defeat of the giant Gogmagon. See Geoffrey of Monmouth, *Historia* 1.12

[102] Geoffrey of Monmouth, by contrast, names Corineus's daughter as Gwendolen. See *Historia* 2.4: *Duxit itaque Locrinus filiam Corinei Guendoloenam nomine* ("And so Locrinus married Corineus' daughter, named Gwendolen"). This disparity is also noted by William Poole. See *The Complete Works of John Milton: Volume XI*, ed. Poole, 313.

[103] According to Caesar, *De Bello Gallico* 5.14, *omnes vero se Britanni vitro inficiunt, quod caeruleum efficit colorem* ("all Britons, in fact, dye themselves with woad, which produces a dark blue color"). Cf. Pliny, *Naturalis Historia* 22.2.2.

upon the tomb (of Hyperoche and Laodice).[104] In short, the conflation of Herodotus and Callimachus in *Mansus* demonstrates the efficacy of the poem's earlier invocation of both Clio and Apollo (*Clius et magni nomine Phoebi* [24]), hitherto regarded by scholars as a compliment to *Manso's* biographical and poetical talents,[105] but perhaps also a proleptic signifier of the integration of historiography and poetry that lie at the heart of *Milton's* methodology.

4.3 Miltonic Autobiography and King Arthur

Just as Milton writes himself both intertextually and intratextually into "history" and its poetic reconfiguration, so too does he assume an implicit place alongside those British Druids, who "used to sing the praises of heroes, and their exploits worthy of imitation" (*Heroum laudes imitandaque gesta canebant* [43]).[106] He does so by proclaiming his own epic aspirations, the composition of an *Arthuriad*, into which description he also inscribes himself and his associated sense of Britishness:

> Si quando indigenas revocabo in carmina reges
> Arturumque etiam sub terris bella moventem,
> Aut dicam invictae sociali foedere mensae
> Magnanimos heroas, et (o modo spiritus adsit!)
> Frangam Saxonicas Britonum sub Marte phalanges.
> (*Mansus* 80–84)

---

[104] Herodotus, *Histories* 4: 34.

[105] See, for example, *Milton: Complete Shorter Poems*, ed. John Carey (London: Longman, 1997), 264: "Phoebus is invoked because Manso has befriended poets, Clio because he has written accounts of their lives."

[106] With the phraseology, cf. Milton, *Ad Patrem* 46; Vida, *De Arte Poetica* 1.544, on which see 171–172. On the association of Druids with poetry, cf. Milton, *Lycidas* 53: "Where your old Bards, the famous Druids lie." See also Caesar, *De Bello Gallico* 6.14, where, however, the medium of verse, as Richard Terry observes, was undertaken "for practical, mnemonic reasons ... Caesar offers no suggestion that the Druids wrote verses as an end in itself." See Richard Terry, *Poetry and the Making of the English Literary Past 1660–1781* (Oxford: Oxford University Press, 2001), 126. Cf. Diodorus Siculus 5.31.2–5; Lucan, *De Bello Civili* 1.450–456, 3.399–428. Cf. also Michael Drayton's implicit linking of "bards" and Druids at *Poly-Olbion*, 2: "Yee sacred Bards, that to your Harps melodious strings/Sung th'ancient Heroës deeds (the monument of Kings)/And in your dreadfull verse ingrav'd the prophecies,/ ... / ... as those Druids taught, which kept the British rites,/And dwelt in darksome Groves, there counsailing with sprites." See, in general, T. D. Kendrick, *The Druids: A Study in Keltic Prehistory* (London: Methuen, 1927); A. L. Owen, *The Famous Druids: A Survey of Three Centuries of English Literature on the Druids* (Oxford: Clarendon Press, 1962); Stuart Piggott, *The Druids* (London: Thames and Hudson, 1968).

> If ever I summon back into verse our native kings,
> and Arthur instigating wars even under the ground;
> or if I tell of great-souled heroes of a table rendered
> invincible by the bond of fellowship, and (if only
> the breath of inspiration be present!) I shatter the
> Saxon phalanxes in a British war.

Milton's announcement serves as both an apt justification of, and a confident response to, the articulated viewpoint of his Italian encomiasts, by whom he was consistently lauded a fortiori as an epic poet. Thus, according to Giovanni Salzilli of Rome, the Thames (a metonym for the London-born Milton) can claim a victory over the Homeric Meles, the Virgilian Mincius, and the Tassonian Sebeto.[107] Likewise, for Matteo Selvaggio (David Codner),[108] England boasts of Milton as one who proves a match for Greece's Homer and Rome's Virgil.[109] In the eyes of the Florentine academicians Antonio Francini and Carlo Dati, it is Milton himself who epitomizes the epic hero. Thus is he ranked by Francini among "heroes," regarded by Italians as "superhuman," as an "artisan almost divine," motivated by a quest for an engagement with heroism itself.[110] Likewise, for Dati, he is a "modern Ulysses" (*novus Ulysses*), whose ubiquitous peregrinations are both literal and literary.[111] John Newman poses a pertinent question:

> What had Milton done in 1639, what was he showing to fellow poets and to the world of letters in general that could possibly justify this kind of praise? Is something lost or suppressed—something in Italian?[112]

The answer probably resides in Milton's self-presentation while upon Italian soil as, in the words of William Poole, "an epic poet, even though he was one as yet without an epic poem."[113] Clearly, however, he was in possession of epic plans. That these were still at an early stage at the time of the composition of *Mansus* is suggested by the hypothetical *Si quando*

---

[107] See *Poemata*, 4; Lewalski and Haan, 106–107. See also Haan, *John Milton's Roman Sojourns*, 47–53.

[108] See 47.

[109] See *Poemata*, 4; Lewalski and Haan, 108–109.

[110] See *Poemata*, 5–7; Lewalski and Haan, 108–111.

[111] See *Poemata*, 10; Lewalski and Haan, 114–115.

[112] J. K. Newman, "Milton and the Pastoral Mode: The *Epitaphium Damonis*," *Illinois Classical Studies* 15 (1990): 379–397, at 387.

[113] Poole, *Milton and the Making of Paradise Lost*, 46.

(80), and, especially, by that alternative *Aut dicam* (82). This Miltonic sense of deliberation merits comparison perhaps with that "chois" of epic subject (as described later in *The Reason of Church-Government*) offered by Tasso "to a Prince of Italy," a gesture self-consciously mirrored, on that occasion, in Milton's hypothetical "inclination to present the like offer in our own ancient stories."[114] Of course, the choice would ultimately be Milton's, but particularly noteworthy in *Mansus* is the unapologetic candor with which he offers to another "Prince of Italy," so to speak, alternating sketches of his incipient epic plans. All the more striking, too, in that this was a literary project, whose details (as we learn from *Epitaphium Damonis*) he was keeping closely guarded (*Haec tibi servabam* [180]), and whose disclosure was intended for the ears of his very close friend Charles Diodati. Even in that instance, however, the announcement of both the project and its reception (*Ep. Dam.* 162–178) is interestingly juxtaposed with Manso's own literary output in the form of those "twin cups" (*pocula ... bina* [*Ep. Dam.* 181–183]), two works by Manso himself.[115] These too, gifted by their author to Milton, were in turn to be shown (possibly gifted?) by Milton to his Anglo-Italian friend.

That his envisaged epic and Manso were closely connected in Milton's mind need not entirely surprise. The Neapolitan was, after all, *Tassi amicissimus*, and had secured a place of his own in Tassonian

---

[114] Milton, *The Reason of Church-Government*, 38: "And lastly what King or Knight before the conquest might be chosen in whom to lay the pattern of a Christian Heroe. And as Tasso gave to a Prince of Italy his chois whether he would command him to write of Godfreys expedition against the infidels, or Belisarius against the Gothes, or Charlemain against the Lombards ... it haply would be no rashnesse from an equal diligence and inclination to present the like offer in our own ancient stories." This passage is described as "astonishing" by Gordon Teskey, by whom it is also regarded as indicative of "the fracturing consequences of the theory of the heroic poem" as evinced by Italian epic theorists. See Gordon Teskey, *Delirious Milton: The Fate of the Poet in Modernity* (Cambridge, MA: Harvard University Press, 2006), 137. Tasso had announced the offer in an undated letter to Count Ferrante Tassone. See *Delle Lettere Familiari del Sig. Torquato Tasso*, 2 vols. (Bergamo: Comino Ventura, 1588), II, sig. 42^v: "per soddisfar il Signor Principe, gli dò l'elettione di tutti questi soggetti ... Espedition di Goffredo, et de gli altri Principi contra Infedeli, & ritorno. ... Espedition di Bellesario contra Gothi. ... Espedition di Carlo [il Magno] contra Longobardi" ("in order to satisfy the Prince, I give him the choice of all these subjects ... The Expedition of Godfrey and of other Princes against the Infidels, and their return. ... The Expedition of Belisarius against the Goths. .... The Expedition of Charlemagne against the Lombards"). The "Prince of Italy" to whom Tasso made the offer (of actually five possible epic subjects) was Francesco Maria II della Rovere, Duke of Urbino. He is misidentified as "Duke Alfonso II of Ferrara" in *Complete Prose Works of John Milton*, eds. D. M. Wolfe et al., 8 vols. (New Haven, CT: Yale University Press, 1953–1982), I: 814.

[115] See 36–40.

epic.[116] But he was also a very firm believer in the hierarchy of genres (whereby epic assumed the highest place),[117] and in the prerequisite of careful epic planning. Describing Tasso's original decision to compose the *Gerusalemme Liberata*, Manso had taken pains to itemize the stages by which the Italian poet came to organize his initial thoughts:

> Quivi determinò egli di comporre'l suo divino poema della Gerusalemme, e primieramente rinvenne la favola, e dispose le parti sue, e scelse le persone, che doveva introducervi, e dirizzò tutto il filo dell'opera à lodare, le grandezze di casa da Este.[118]
>
> He first came upon the story, arranged its sections, selected the characters whom he was to introduce, and directed the whole thread of the work as a means of praising the greatness of the house of d'Este.

The finished work he had extolled as "la forma del Poema heroico non prima conosciuta, o al meno non ricevuta nella nostra lingua" ("a form of heroic poetry not previously known or at least not received in our language").[119] Still, even when epic plans were realized, the published result did not always win universal favor. Indeed, contemporary criticism of *Gerusalemme Liberata*, succinctly summarized by Manso as "varie oppositioni, che furono contro la sua *Gerusalemme* fatte, e publicate" ("various oppositions which were leveled and published against his *Jerusalem*"),[120] had led Tasso to publish in 1585 a tractate in its defense,[121] and had ultimately contributed to his full-scale revision of the whole in *Gerusalemme Conquistata*. The result was, in the words of Bryan Brazeau, "an authorized and 'reformed' version of the poem," one

---

[116] See Headnote to *Mansus* at 114.

[117] This is attested by Manso's miniature tractate on poetry, included in his incomplete *Enciclopedia* (extant in the BNN as MS XIII F. 63) at ff. 188^v–189^r. Here, seeking to demonstrate the superiority and excellence ("eccellenza") of epic poetry, he regards this genre as more challenging than that of dramatic and lyric poetry in that it requires from the poet deeper intelligence ("più profonda intelligenza"). He also emphasizes its stylistic grandeur ("la grandezza") and its encyclopedic breadth, which, in his view, render it more enjoyable than tragedy, comedy, pastoral and other lesser and more constrictive genres, such as the hymn, the ode, the epigram, the sonnet, or the canzone. See Riga, *Giovan Battista Manso*, 108–109.

[118] Manso, *Vita di Torquato Tasso*, 39.

[119] *Vita di Torquato Tasso*, 287.

[120] *Vita di Torquato Tasso*, 69.

[121] Tasso, *Apologia in Difesa della Sua Gierusalemme Liberata* (Mantua: Francesco Osana, 1585).

marked by its stricter conformity to counter-reformation orthodoxy and its closer alignment to neo-Aristotelian epic theory.[122]

It is not unreasonable to suppose that epic (Tassonian and otherwise) would have featured among literary discussions between Milton and his Neapolitan host.[123] Thomas Roebuck offers an insightful reading of the claim to ancient British history in *Mansus* as an implicit response on Milton's part to debates that he had held with Manso on the historical priority of the Catholic Church in England. This latter, he argues, is suggested by Manso's recourse to the *Anglus/Angelus* pun in his epigram, itself "invok[ing] Bede's role as a polemical weapon in Counter-Reformation debates."[124] Nicholas McDowell takes the argument one stage further by claiming that the epigram suggests "Manso's awareness that Milton was considering writing an epic about British history."[125] If Milton needed authoritative support for the validity of his ruminations, he would have found it in Tasso's *Discorsi dell' Arte Poetica* (1587), a work that, just five years later, he would recommend for teaching "what the laws are of a true Epic poem."[126] Discussing the most appropriate historical era from which an epic subject should be drawn, Tasso signals the benefits of "tempi nè molto moderni, nè molto remoti" ("times that are neither very modern nor very remote"). Highlighting the poetic license that they can afford ("nè della licenza di fingere ci privano" ["they do not deprive us of the license to invent"]), he proceeds to cite "i

---

[122] See Brazeau, "Who Wants to Live Forever?" 43–44.

[123] In *The Reason of Church-Government* Milton presents his poetic ambitions as having been greatly enhanced by his Italian journey, not least by conversations with Italian literati. Speaking of his favorable reception in the Italian academies and of the "written Encomiums" bestowed upon him, he continues: "I began thus farre to assent both to them and divers of my friends here at home, ... that ... I might perhaps leave something so written to aftertimes, as they should not willingly let it die." See Milton, *The Reason of Church-Government*, 37. My point is likewise made, but naively argued, by John Black in Appendix xxxv, entitled "On the probability that the conversation of Manso, and the example of Tasso, inspired Milton with the design of writing an epic poem." See Black, *Life of Torquato Tasso* II, 459–476, especially 460 (commenting on this passage): "That it was the conversation, and encouragement of Manso, which first directed Milton to the pursuit of the epic palm, seems probable from this."

[124] See Roebuck, "Milton and the Confessionalization of Antiquarianism," 51.

[125] McDowell, *Poet of Revolution*, 346.

[126] Milton, *Of Education* (London: s.n. 1644), 6: "that sublime art which in Aristotles poetics, in Horace, and the Italian commentaries of Castelvetro, Tasso, Mazzoni, and others, teaches what the laws are of a true Epic poem." For an excellent overview of the potential influence of Italian critical theory upon Milton's deliberations regarding his choice of epic subject, see Teskey, *Delirious Milton*, 133–147.

tempi di Carlo Magno, e d'Artù" ("the times of Charlemagne and of Arthur") as a perfect example.[127] These latter times had certainly appealed to the young Milton:

> Next, (for heare me out now Readers) that I may tell ye whether my younger feet wander'd; I betook me among those lofty Fables and Romances, which recount in solemne canto's the deeds of Knighthood founded by our victorious Kings; & from hence had in renowne over all Christendome. There I read it in the oath of every Knight, that he should defend to the expence of his best blood, or of his life, if it so befell him, the honour and chastity of Virgin or Matron.[128]

Indeed, the chivalric Arthur could even be appropriated to serve a jocular purpose, as in Milton's good-humored comparison (in *Prolusio* VI [1628]) of the purported courage of his Cambridge fellow students to the storming of the castle of fire by *validissimi illi Regis Arthuri pugiles* ("those most valiant champions of King Arthur").[129]

As for the historical Arthur, the *locus classicus*, so to speak, was Geoffrey of Monmouth's *Historia Regum Britanniae*, a hugely influential work in itself,[130] and one that was certainly well known to Milton.[131]

---

[127] Tasso, *Discorsi ... dell'Arte Poetica; et in Particolare del Poema Heroico* (Venice: Giulo Vassalini, 1587), sig. 5ᵛ. See also Ettore Allodoli, *Giovanni Milton e l'Italia* (Prato: Vestri & Spighi, 1907), 25–26.

[128] Milton, *An Apology for Smectymnuus*, 16–17.

[129] Milton, *Prolusio* VI, at *Prolusiones*, 127: *nec validissimi illi Regis Arthuri pugiles, igniti et flammigantis Castelli incantamenta vicerunt facilius, et dissiparunt* ("nor did those most valiant champions of King Arthur more easily overpower and scatter the enchantments of the blazing castle of fire").

[130] On the huge success of Geoffrey's *Historia*, especially in England and northern France, see *Geoffrey of Monmouth: The History of the Kings of Britain*, ed. Michael D. Reeve, trans. Neil Wright (Woodbridge, Suffolk: The Boydell Press, 2007), vii, which notes the listing of no fewer than 217 manuscripts.

[131] This is evinced by, inter alia, Milton's *Commonplace Book*. See Milton, *Commonplace Book*, 14, in *The Complete Works of John Milton: Volume XI*, ed. Poole, 121: *in fabulis nostris notatur Sodomitici peccati rex Mempricius* ("in our myths King Mempricius is noted for the sin of Sodomy"). Cf. Geoffrey of Monmouth, *Historia Regum Britanniae*, 2: ch. 6, in *Rerum Britannicarum ... Scriptores*, 1–92, at 11: *sese Sodomitanae libidini dedidit, non naturalem Venerem naturali voluptati praeferens* ("he gave himself up to the lusts of Sodomon, preferring unnatural Sex to natural pleasure"). As noted by Poole, 121, the fact that Milton's comment is in Latin suggests a direct reference to Geoffrey. Paul Stevens draws attention to Milton's description here of Geoffrey's stories as *fabulis nostris*, remarking: "When Milton first read Geoffrey, there is no sense that he is reading the history of any people but his own—Geoffrey's stories are 'our legends.'" See Stevens, "Archipelagic Criticism

Geoffrey's unabashed account of Arthur's historicity was denounced and refuted by the Italian humanist Polydore Vergil[132] in his *Anglica Historia* (published in three different versions in 1534, 1546, and 1555).[133] The rejection of the historical Arthur by Polydore, itself, in the words of Paul Stevens, "greeted as a national insult,"[134] led John Leland to publish in 1544 his *Assertio Inclytissimi Arturii Regis Britanniae*, a neo-Latin defense of the Arthurian legend, specifically directed against Polydore's attack.[135] Central to the strengths of Leland's argument was the antiquarian's rich synthesis of archival documentation with a meticulous analysis of material remains, oral traditions, etymologies, and place-names.[136] The work's popularity was greatly enhanced by the appearance

---

and Its Limits," 158. Several details of Milton's *Arthuriad*, as described in *Mansus*, and, more extensively in *Epitaphium Damonis*, find precedent in Geoffrey's *Historia*: Arthur as leader of the British resistance to Germanic invaders (*Mansus* 84; *Historia* 9.1ff.); the roles played by Brennus and Belinus (*Ep. Dam.* 164; *Historia* 3.1–10); the story of Uther Pendragon falling in love with Igerne, wife of Gorlois, his gaining access to her (through the magical powers of Merlin) in the form of her husband, and his subsequent fathering of Arthur (*Ep. Dam.* 166–168; *Historia* 8.19). One legendary tradition promulgated by Geoffrey was the purported Trojan origins of a Britain founded by Brutus, grandson of Aeneas. At *Epitaphium Damonis* 162–163, Milton couches his articulated plans for an *Arthuriad* in essentially Trojan terms by way of a reference to Dardanus, one of Troy's mythical founders: *Ipse ego Dardanias Rutupina per aequora puppes/Dicam* ("I will proclaim Dardanian ships over the Rutupian seas"). Cf. his equation of the city of London with Troy/Dardanus at *Elegia* 1.73: *Tuque urbs Dardaniis Londinum structa colonis* ("And you, London, a city built by Dardanian settlers"), and his description of the English people as *Teucrigenas populos* ("Trojan-born peoples") in *In Quintum Novembris* 2.

[132] On Polydore Vergil, see, among others, Denys Hay, *Polydore Vergil, Renaissance Historian and Man of Letters* (Oxford: Clarendon Press, 1952); Richard Koebner, "'The Imperial Crown of This Realm': Henry VIII, Constantine the Great, and Polydore Vergil," *Bulletin of the Institute of Historical Research* 26 (1953): 29–52.

[133] Milton, in his *Commonplace Book*, mentions Peter Martyr's citation of Polydore Vergil. See Milton, *Commonplace Book*, 185, in *The Complete Works of John Milton: Volume XI*, ed. Poole, 232: [*Petrus Martyr*] ... *citatque authorem Polydorum nostros homines aliquando suos reges compulisse ad rationem reddendam pecuniae male administratae* ("[Peter Martyr] ... cites the authority of Polydore that our people have sometimes compelled their own kings to give a reason for the poor administration of funds"). Cf. Peter Martyr Vermigli, *In Librum Iudicum ... Commentarii* (Zurich: Christophorus Froschoverus, 1565), sig. 60^v.

[134] Stevens, "Archipelagic Criticism and Its Limits," 156.

[135] John Leland, *Assertio Inclytissimi Arturii Regis Britanniae* (London: Reyner Wolfe, 1544).

[136] See James P. Carley, "Polydore Vergil and John Leland on King Arthur: The Battle of the Books," *Interpretations* 15 (1984): 86–100.

in 1582 of an English translation by Richard Robinson.[137] And the debate continued to rage, culminating perhaps in the *Historiae Britanniae* (1597–ca. 1607) of Richard White of Basingstoke. White's defense of the mythical history of Britain, running to some 1,000 pages, was, in the words of Alan MacColl, an "attempt to reclaim 'the British history' for the Catholic tradition."[138]

It is against this highly polemical backdrop that Milton's Arthurian interests in general, and his 1639 plans for an *Arthuriad* in particular, can fruitfully be examined. Helen Cooper, in a pioneering article, made the pertinent observation that "recent scholarship generally has elided Milton's interest in Arthurian history almost into invisibility."[139] She compensated for this shortcoming by carefully mapping Milton's evolving attitudes toward Arthur from his youthful fascination to his eventual disillusionment with, and distrust of, Arthur's credibility in general (as articulated most famously in *The History of Britain*),[140] and of Geoffrey of Monmouth's account in particular.[141] Perhaps most notable, however, was her demonstration of the liberating potential afforded Milton by the medieval romance tradition, with its "absence of any claim to historicity,"[142] and her elucidation of Miltonic methodology as evinced by the readiness with which he continuously supplemented Geoffrey's version by recourse to a rich variety of other sources. Several illuminating studies followed. Paul Stevens made an excellent case for the influence of Geoffrey's representation of ancient Britons and liberty upon the young Milton's poetic ambitions and sense of national identity.[143] Su Fang Ng, in turn, eloquently argued that Milton's thoughts about Arthur were profoundly shaped by George Buchanan.[144] There is, of course, always

---

[137] Richard Robinson, trans., *A Learned and True Assertion of the Original, Life, Actes, and Death of the Most Noble, Valiant, and Renoumed Prince Arthure, King of Great Brittaine ... Collected and Written of Late Yeares in Lattin, by the Learned English Antiquarie of Worthy Memory John Leyland* (London: John Wolfe, 1582).

[138] See Alan MacColl, "Richard White and the Legendary History of Britain," *HL* 51 (2002): 245–257, at 245.

[139] Helen Cooper, "Milton's King Arthur," *RES* 65 (2014): 252–265, at 252.

[140] See Milton, *The History of Britain*, 119: "Arthur ... more renown'd in Songs and Romances, then in true Stories"; 122–126, esp. 122–123: "But who Arthur was, and whether ever any such reign'd in Britain, hath bin doubted heertofore, and may again with good reason."

[141] See Milton, *The History of Britain*, 123–126.

[142] Cooper, "Milton's King Arthur," 257.

[143] Stevens, "Archipelagic Criticism and Its Limits," passim.

[144] Ng, "Milton, Buchanan, and King Arthur."

the danger that the benefits of scholarly hindsight can render a disservice to the Miltonic moment that was 1639. The fact that Milton eventually abandoned Arthur as epic subject does not, and should not, undermine the seeming conviction with which he articulated his incipient plans for an *Arthuriad* in *Mansus* (and not long afterward in *Epitaphium Damonis*). Although, as Nicholas McDowell points out,"[i]t is unlikely that Milton had ever given much historical credit to the legends of the 'British Troy' and King Arthur,"[145] *Mansus* and *Epitaphium Damonis* suggest that he was seriously contemplating the imaginative poetic possibilities that such legends might afford. That "history" could indeed be modified and supplemented[146] was, after all, a license granted the epic poet by none other than Tasso himself:

> e tutti i successi, che si fatti trovarà, cioè che meglio in un'altro modo potessero essere avvenuti sensa rispetto alcuno di vero ò di Historia, à sua voglia muti e rimuti, e riduca gli accidenti delle cose à quel modo ch'egli giudica migliore, co'l vero alterato il tutto finto accompagnando.[147]

> and all such events that he finds, namely, those that could, in other respects, have occurred without any regard for truth or history, he may alter at will, and change again, and he may rearrange the accidents of circumstances in the manner that he considers best, combining complete fiction with doctored truth.

Whether Milton had actually put pen to paper is impossible to determine. Perhaps, as Masson suggests, such a grandiloquent statement as *nescio quid mihi grande sonabat/Fistula* (*Ep. Dam.* 155–156) ("my pipe was sounding some lofty tune") indicates his initial attempts at actual composition.[148] Arthur does not feature among Milton's literary plans as

---

[145] McDowell, *Poet of Revolution*, 364.

[146] For discussion of this hugely debated subject, see, among others, Daniel Javitch, "The Disparagement of Chivalric Romance for its Lack of Historicity in Sixteenth-Century Italian Poetics," in *Romance and History: Imagining Time From the Medieval to the Early Modern Period*, ed. Jon Whitman (Cambridge: Cambridge University Press, 2015), 187–199; Karen Sullivan, *The Danger of Romance: Truth, Fantasy, and Arthurian Fictions* (Chicago: The University of Chicago Press, 2018).

[147] Tasso, *Discorsi dell'Arte Poetica*, sig. 10^r.

[148] See Masson, *Life*, II, 96: "He had actually made a beginning in the new direction! Only a beginning, however." Su Fang Ng suggests that *ipse ego* (*Ep. Dam.* 162) "revises the self-naming of the Pseudo-Virgilian four-line *incipit* to the *Aeneid*: *Ille ego, qui quondam* ...", and argues that Milton's emphatic *ipse* "stresses his independence from the Latin tradition." See Ng, "Milton, Buchanan, and King Arthur," 673.

preserved in the Trinity Manuscript, although there is much evidence therein of his interest in, and reading of, British history. Even here, though, his notes pertain to a projected drama, as opposed to an epic.[149] Of course, it is not impossible that he kept a separate notebook for epic, which has since been lost. Irrespective of the form in which they took, Milton's initial plans for the *Arthuriad* described in 1639 surely constituted something more than what Putnam Jones regarded (almost a century ago) as "a nebulous dream."[150] On the contrary, they may well have involved his close scrutiny and careful calibration of a heatedly debated subject, and of the truth or otherwise governing such contradictory explications of the Arthurian legend, not least the claims to the historical veracity of the king at their center.

Read in the light of this debate and, in particular, of Leland's defense of Arthur's authenticity, the verses from *Mansus* seem to signal a Miltonic alertness to both the patriotic and the skeptical interpretations of Arthur, and, not least, to the creative possibilities of epic itself. Line 81 (*Arturumque etiam sub terris bella moventem*) has traditionally been interpreted by Milton scholars as an otherwise unattested reference to Arthur waging war in the underworld, itself an "intriguing idea," as Gordon Teskey observes.[151] Thus MacKellar states: "I have not found Milton's authority for representing King Arthur as moving wars beneath the earth."[152] Several possible sources have been proposed. John Carey cites the Welsh *Spoils of Annwfn* (Book of Taliesin, poem 30), in which Arthur and his men raid a fortress representing the Celtic Hades,[153] an improbable source, given that text's obscurity.[154] Less unlikely is Helen Cooper's suggestion that Milton may be evoking the legend of Arthur's purported survival in a cave beneath Mount Etna.[155] But although that

---

[149] Trinity College Library, Cambridge University, MS R.3.4, ff. 35–41.

[150] See P. F. Jones, "Milton and the Epic Subject from British History," *PMLA* 42 (1927): 901–909, at 902.

[151] Gordon Teskey, *Spenserian Moments* (Cambridge, MA: Harvard University Press, 2019), 114.

[152] *The Latin Poems of John Milton*, ed. MacKellar, 331.

[153] *Milton: Complete Shorter Poems*, ed. Carey (1st ed., 1968), 264.

[154] As noted by Cooper, "Milton's King Arthur," 254. For a useful contextual overview, see Patrick Sims-Wallace, "The Early Welsh Arthurian Poems," in *The Arthur of the Welsh: The Arthurian Legend in Medieval Welsh Literature*, eds. Rachel Bromwich, A. O. H. Jarman, and Brynley F. Roberts (Cardiff: University of Wales Press, 1991), 33–71, at 54–55.

[155] Cooper, "Milton's King Arthur," 254, who traces the first record of the legend back to the early thirteenth-century *Otia Imperialia* of Gervase of Tilbury. See

legend was well known in Italy, thus making it an attractive candidate,[156] the Arthur of Etna, as Cooper concedes, was regarded as recovering from his wounds rather than instigating warfare. Perhaps the most plausible interpretation of the line remains that offered by Tillyard, who speculated that "Milton meant to reiterate the legend that Arthur was re-embodied in the house of Tudor."[157] According to this tradition, Arthur himself was envisaged as having been reborn.[158] Appended to Leland's *Assertio* is a Latin poem, entitled *Arturius Redivivus*,[159] in which the hope that Arthur will be revivified (*revicturum .../Arturum* [2–3]) serves as a form of consolation to Britons who mourn his death. That hope is seen as realized in the very present (*tempus adest* [4]), not least in the Tudor clan whereby, in fulfillment of the prophecies of old, an essentially bellicose Arthur, now reborn, advances victoriously into the breezes (*Victor prodit redivivus in auras* [4]), his agency ensuring that the "palm of Mars" (*Martia ... palma* [7]) makes its way once more to the Britons. The whole is evocative of the souls of Virgil's underworld destined to proceed to the upper light (*inclusas animas superumque ad lumen ituras* [*Aeneid* 6.680]),[160] and, more specific, of the pageant of Rome's future heroes (still awaiting birth into the upper air) afforded by Anchises to Aeneas in *Aeneid* 6. 756–892.

But if Milton's line signals his contemplated reconfiguration of the Arthurian legend in imaginative ways, so too might it be double-edged in its import, hinting perhaps at that literary "warfare" about Arthur's authenticity that had ensued in consequence of Polydore's controversial

---

Gervase of Tilbury, *Otia Imperialia: Recreation for an Emperor*, ed. and trans. S. E. Banks and J. W. Binns (Oxford: Clarendon Press, 2002), 334–337.

[156] Cooper, "Milton's King Arthur," 254, suggests that Milton may have heard of the tradition in Italy, if he had not come across it before, and continues "the Italian location would make the allusion in a poem written for Manso especially appropriate."

[157] E. M. W. Tillyard, *The Miltonic Setting Past and Present* (Cambridge: Cambridge University Press, 1938), 190.

[158] See David A. Summers, "Re-Fashioning Arthur in the Tudor Era," *Exemplaria* 9 (1997): 371–392; David Starkey, "King Henry and King Arthur," in *Arthurian Literature XVI*, eds. James P. Carley and Felicity Riddy (Cambridge: Brewer, 1998), 171–196.

[159] Leland, *Assertio Inclytissimi Arturii Regis Britanniae*, f. 37^v.

[160] Milton, as discussed at 34, would quote this line (almost verbatim) just a few months later in *Epistola Familiaris* 9 (dated 30 March 1639) in an allegorical depiction of Lucas Holstenius's edited Greek manuscripts awaiting their emergence into print form. See Milton, *Epistola Familaris* 9, in *John Milton: Epistolarum Familiarium Liber Unus and Uncollected Letters*, ed. Haan, 140–163, at 146–147; Haan, *John Milton's Roman Sojourns*, 148–153.

refutation of Geoffrey's account. Leland describes it as such in the Dedicatory Epistle prefixed to his aforementioned work: *grave ... bellum a Polydoro Galfredi manibus indictum* ("the serious war declared by Polydore upon the ghost of Geoffrey of Monmouth"), only to continue: *durum me Hercule et impium cum manibus decertare* ("by Hercules, it is a cruel and impious act to engage in battle with a ghost").[161] In this reading, and by a Miltonic reversal of agency, Arthur, even when buried beneath the ground (*etiam sub terris* [81]),[162] continues to instigate on earth a posthumous (literary) warfare (*bella moventem* [81]).[163]

Integral to Milton's projected reconfiguration of Arthur and his Court is the sense of camaraderie afforded by the Round Table, described herein as "the great-souled heroes of a table rendered invincible by the bond of fellowship" (*invictae sociali foedere mensae/Magnanimos heroas* [82–83]). The detail does not occur in Geoffrey of Monmouth, a point stressed by Cooper,[164] who suggests that Milton may have derived it from John Harding's "romance-influenced" *Chronicle* (1543),[165] a work that he is known to have read.[166] It should be noted, however, that Milton moves beyond Harding's "table rounde," and the worth and valor of its "knightes honourable," depicted therein as agents of "actes marciable," and "the worthieste of every realme."[167] He does so by placing particular emphasis

---

[161] Ibid., sig. Ai^v–Aii^r.

[162] See *OLD*, s.v. *sub*: 1b: "under the surface of (earth, water, etc.)" Cf. Plautus, *Aulularia* 628: *qui sub terra erepsisti*; Horace, *Epistles* 1.6.24: *quicquid sub terra est*. According to Leland, *fuit ... rex Arturius sepultus valde profunde* ("King Arthur was buried very deep") in the earth for fear that his remains would be vandalized by the Saxons. Thus, his tombstone was dug some seven feet beneath the ground (*quasi pedum septem sub terra*), while his tomb was located a further nine feet deeper (*novem pedum inferius*) (*Assertio*, f. 27^r).

[163] See *OLD*, s.v. *movere*: 17 b: "to stir up (strife, hostilities): esp. *bellum* or *arma* [*mov*]*ere*." Cf., for example, Sallust, *Catilina* 30.2; Virgil, *Georgics* 1.509.

[164] Cooper, "Milton's King Arthur," 253.

[165] Cooper, "Milton's King Arthur," 253.

[166] See Milton, *Commonplace Book*, 242, in *The Complete Works of John Milton: Volume XI*, ed. Poole, 283: "The office of Knighthood Harding sets out in Arturs round table to use thire bodies to defend where law would not redresse. Cronicle in Arture." Cf. *The Chronicle of Jhon Harding* (London: Richard Grafton, 1543), sig. lxiiii^r (chapter lxxii) (incorrectly cited by Poole as "lxiii^r, in chapter lxii"): "The table rounde, of knightes honourable ... // ... their rule was wronges to oppresse/With their bodies, where lawe might not redresse." Poole dates Milton's entry to "early 1640s; probably early 1641," based on his dropping of the "idle final e" from 1640 onward, for which practice and dating, see J. T. Shawcross, "One Aspect of Milton's Spelling: Idle Final 'E'," *PMLA* 78 (1963): 501–510, at 510.

[167] Harding, *Chronicle*, sig. lxiiii^r.

upon the essential fellowship by which its members were bound (with *foedus* [82] suggesting perhaps the sworn Oath by which they were united), and the epic heroism (*Magnanimos heroas* [83]) at the core of their existence. Although Cooper is correct in her observation that "in the seventeenth century as now, ... one does not have any specific source for knowing that the Round Table is part of the Arthurian scheme of things,"[168] it is worth pointing out that Leland had devoted a full chapter of his *Assertio* precisely to the *Orbicularis Arturii Mensa*.[169] Here he was careful to signal the quasi-heroic criteria required for its elite membership:

> Non haec patebat omnibus nobilibus, sed illis tantum,
>   Lucida quos ardens evexit ad aethera virtus,
>   Virtus sola virens nullis moritura diebus.[170]

> This was not accessible to all men of nobility, but only to those whom resplendently ardent virtue has elevated to the ether, flourishing virtue which alone is destined never to die.

The passage reworks the Sibyl's account, in *Aeneid* 6, of the heroism and exceptional virtue that function as a prerequisite for an escape from the underworld to the upper air:

> pauci, quos aequus amavit
> Iuppiter aut ardens *evexit ad aethera virtus*,[171]
> dis geniti potuere.
>   (*Aeneid* 6. 129–131)[172]

> A few whom Jupiter in his justice has loved,
> or whom ardent virtue *has elevated to the*

---

[168] Cooper, "Milton's King Arthur," 253.

[169] See Leland, *Assertio*, ff. 10^r–10^v. See also Martin Biddle, *King Arthur's Round Table: An Archaeological Investigation* (Woodbridge: The Boydell Press, 2000), 483–484.

[170] Leland, *Assertio*, f. 10^r.

[171] Cf. Statius, *Thebaid* 2.571–572: *fulmineus Dorylas, quem regibus ardens/aequabat virtus*.

[172] Emphasis is mine. Jean Luis De la Cerda explicates the lines as: *neque satis fuit esse heroes, sed etiam ut a Iove amarentur, et ut ipsi virtute praestarent* ("it was not enough that they were heroes but also that they were loved by Jupiter, and that they themselves excelled in virtue"). See *P. Virgilii Maronis Priores Sex Libri Aeneidos Argumentis, Explicationibus, Notis Illustrati*, ed. Jean Luis De La Cerda, (Lyon: Horatius Cardon, 1612), 631.

> *heavens*, being begotten of the gods, have had
> the ability to do so.

The Round Table, in Leland's view, constituted in effect a bond of fellowship (*societas*) that is still held in memory and replicated in more recent practice:

> Quid? Quod nec memoria, nec societas Orbicularis chori recentioribus saeculis ex animis nobilium excidit.[173]

> What then? Neither the memory nor the fellowship of the Round Table has, in more recent centuries, left the minds of noble men.

Then there is, as Walter Savage Landor would later describe it, Milton's "glorious verse": *Frangam Saxonicas Britonum sub Marte phalanges* (84).[174] The language is, quite literally, striking in its harsh consonantal violence. It is a violence whose forcefulness serves to surprise in, as Tillyard puts it, "the crash of *frangam* after the hushed parenthesis of *O modo spiritus adsit*,"[175] and in the jangling assonance of *frangam*/*phalanges*. It would certainly have resonated with Manso, who, as the Headnote puts it, was *bellica virtute apud Italos clarus in primis* ("more famous than any other among the Italians for his bravery in war"), and one whose military prowess had been saluted in the *Poesie di Diversi*,[176] and not without a realistic acknowledgment of the violence of war. Thus, it is "amid the blood and horror of Mars" ("fra'l sangue, e'l Martiale horrore")[177] that he secures his spoils, armed, as he is, with a death-dealing sword ("Dà morte con la spada")[178] as he "terrifies the enemy in the battle-field" ("L'hoste nel campo atteri").[179] There, too, as if in a re-appropriation of that Tassonian term of praise "risplende," whereby Manso was presented as "resplendent" among fellow courtiers, one contributor proclaims: "Mal discerno Signor, qual più risplende/Per

---

[173] Leland, *Assertio*, f. 10ᵛ.

[174] Walter Savage Landor, *Imaginary Conversations*, "Southey and Landor, Second Conversation," in *The Works of Walter Savage Landor*, 2 vols. (London: Edward Moxon, 1846), II: 154–174, at 173.

[175] E. M. W. Tillyard, *Milton* (London: Chatto & Windus, 1930), 91.

[176] See 79–80.

[177] Antonio Biaguazzone, at *Poesie Nomiche*, 266.

[178] Anello Sarriano, at *Poesie Nomiche*, 301.

[179] Vincenzo Petrone, at *Poesie Nomiche*, 310.

tè, se'l saggio Apollo, o'l fiero Marte" ("Sir, I fail to discern who is more resplendent in you: wise Apollo or fierce Mars").[180]

In *Mansus* the perpetrator of such violence is not Arthur, nor even those *Pugiles Arturio Familiares* ("Personal Champions of Arthur"), to whom Leland had devoted a full chapter,[181] but Milton himself.[182] And his agency is unmistakably revealed in that first-person future (*Frangam* [84]), as if in a resounding *assertio* of his own. Bush's speculation as to whether *frangam Saxonicas* might "embody a sort of pun"[183] is perhaps validated by Isidore of Seville's implicit derivation of the name "Saxon" from the Latin noun *saxum* ("rock"): *Saxonum genus ... unde et appellatum quod sit durum et validissimum genus*[184] ("the Saxon race ... named thus for the reason that it is a harsh and extremely tough race"). That this was a tradition that persisted is attested by the *Gesta Ottonis*, a hexameter chronicle of the deeds of the Holy Roman Emperor, Otto I, by Roswitha of Gandersheim (*fl.* 935–973):[185]

> Postquam rex regum, qui solus regnat in aevum
> Per se cunctorum transmutans tempora regum
> Iussit Francorum transferri nobile regnum
> Ad claram gentem Saxonum nomen habentem
> A saxo per duritiam mentis bene firmam.[186]

---

[180] Gio. Battista Comentati, at *Poesie Nomiche*, 304.

[181] See *Assertio*, ff. 6ʳ–9ᵛ. With Leland's phraseology, cf. the *Arthuri pugiles* of Milton, *Prolusio* VI, discussed at 138.

[182] Here my reading moves beyond John Hale's observation that "simple British (Celtic) patriotism ... leads [Milton] to envisage *joining* Arthur in the Saxon-smashing" (emphasis mine). See John K. Hale, *Milton's Languages: The Impact of Multilingualism on Style* (Cambridge: Cambridge University Press, 1997), 57. I argue that Milton envisages *himself* as a second Arthur. See Ng, "Milton, Buchanan, and King Arthur," 672: "he imagines himself into Arthur's place. Rather than Arthur, it is Milton who shatters Saxon phalanxes with his very breath."

[183] Bush, *Variorum*, I: 280, who cites in support of his suggestion Virgil, *Georgics* 1.267: *frangite saxo*; *Aeneid* 1.179: *frangere saxo*.

[184] Isidore, *Etymologiae* IX.2.100.

[185] On Roswitha of Gandersheim, a tenth-century Benedictine nun, author of plays, hagiographies, and historical epic poetry, see, among others, Phyllis R. Brown, Linda A. McMillin, and Katharina M. Wilson, eds., *Hrotsvit of Gandersheim: Contexts, Identities, Affinities, and Performances* (Toronto: University of Toronto Press, 2004); Phyllis R. Brown and Stephen L. Wailes, eds., *A Companion to Hrotsvit of Gandersheim (fl. 960)* (Leiden: Brill, 2013). Her literary output was discovered by Conradus Celtis, and published in 1501, on which see next note.

[186] Roswitha of Gandersheim, *Gesta Ottonis* 1–5. Text is that of *Opera Hrosvitae Illustris Virginis et Monialis Germanae Gente Saxonica Ortae Nuper a Conrado*

> After the king of kings, who alone reigns for eternity, changing the times of kings from one to the other, ordered that the noble kingdom of the Franks be transferred to the famous Saxon people, who derive their name from rock on account of their steadfast hardiness of mind.

Likewise, in the mid-thirteenth-century *Gesta Regum Britanniae* (a rendering of Geoffrey of Monmouth into 5,000 Latin hexameters) attributed to the Breton monk William of Rennes, the poet issues a stark warning to Mordred:

> tibi foedera nulla
> sint cum Saxonibus. Nam rem cum nomine ducunt:
> Saxones a saxis, quibus hii sunt asperiores
> Austerique magis.[187]

> Do not form any treaty with the Saxons. For the Saxons derive their nature, together with their name, from stones, than which they are more rough and more unyielding.

Milton's potential pun on "Saxon" and *saxum* would find a fitting place in a poem responding to a distich that played on "Angle" and "angel." Perhaps indeed his envisaged act of smashing the Saxons (who, as Stevens remarks, were consistently configured by Geoffrey as "the Britons' negative other, their antithesis ... outsiders, latecomers, pagans")[188] is a hyperbolic crushing of that so-called "pagan" self, jokingly hinted at by Manso therein. And he will do so with the force of a pen implicitly equated with the sword itself, as if in a self-appropriation of contemporary praises bestowed upon his addressee's twofold literary

---

Celte Inventa (Nuremburg: Sodalitas Celtica, 1501). Line numbering is mine. Jay Lees finds in these lines "a clear echo" of the pun on *Petrus* (Peter) and *petra* (rock) in Jesus's proclamation at Matthew: 16:18: "Thou art Peter, and upon this rock I will build my church," noting, too, that the verse "was used by the papacy to support its claim to primacy in the church." See Jay T. Lees, "Hrotsvit of Gandersheim and the Problem of Royal Succession in the East Frankish Kingdom," in *Hrotsvit of Gandersheim*, eds. Brown, McMillin, and Wilson, 13–28, at 17.

[187] *Gesta Regum Britannie* 9.201–204. Text is that of *The Historia Regum Britannie of Geoffrey of Monmouth V: Gesta Regum Britannie*, ed. and trans. Neil Wright (Cambridge: D. S. Brewer, 1991). At lix, Wright suggests that since Isidore does not explicitly derive the name "Saxon" from *saxum*, the poet's etymology may be "drawn from another source or from common received wisdom rather than directly from Isidore's *Etymologiae*."

[188] Stevens, "Archipelagic Criticism and Its Limits," 155.

and militaristic talents.[189] In a self-consciously ironic recasting of that quasi-Orphic ability attributed earlier in the poem to Apollo's song: *barathro nec fixa sub imo/Saxa stetere loco* (65–66) ("nor did *rocks*, lodged in the lowest ravine, remain in their place"),[190] Milton inscribes himself into his envisaged *Arthuriad* as a future epicist who will in quasi-Arthurian, indeed quasi-Lycidean, terms "shatter"[191] or "break apart" (*frangam*) the *saxa* (rocks) that constitute the *Saxonicas ... phalanges* (Saxon phalanxes).[192] The Miltonic act of "breaking" is mirrored in the phonological dismemberment of the adjective *Saxonicus*, qualifying the phalanxes in question. And the whole may come full circle in a possible echo and inversion of Tasso's punning description of militaristic resistance[193] in the *Gerusalemme Conquistata*:

> Tutti facean di lor folta *falange*,
> Qual Roma hauria lodata, e Pella, e *Sparta*;
> Ch'impeto alcun non la perturba, ò *frange*,
> O si fermi in battaglia, ò si diparta:
> E s'avien, che si volga, e loco cange,
> Non si vede però confusa, ò *sparta*.
> Così appressava alhor Germania, e Francia,
> Scudo à scudo, elmo ad elmo, e lancia à lancia.
> (*Gerusalemme Conquistata*, 18.15)[194]

---

[189] See 79.

[190] Emphasis is mine.

[191] Cf. *Lycidas* 3–5: "I com to pluck your Berries harsh and crude,/And with forc'd fingers rude,/Shatter your leaves before the mellowing year."

[192] The phalanx, a squared ordering of infantry drawn up in close rank formation, was regarded in the seventeenth century as the ideal battle formation. On Milton's alertness to its benefits, see *The Reason of Church-Government*, 25: "every parochiall Consistory is a right homogeneous and constituting part being in it selfe as it were a little Synod, and towards a generall assembly moving upon her own basis in an even and firme progression, as those smaller squares in battell unite in one great cube, the main phalanx, an embleme of truth and stedfastnesse." Cf. *Paradise Lost* 1. 549–550 (of Satan's legions): "anon they move/In perfect phalanx"; 4. 977–980 (of the encounter between Gabriel's troops and Satan): "the angelic squadron bright/Turned fiery red, sharpening in mooned horns/Their phalanx, and began to hem him round/With ported spears"; 6.398–400: "Far otherwise the inviolable saints/In cubic phalanx firm advanced entire,/Invulnerable, impenetrably armed." See James Holly Hanford, "Milton and the Art of War," *SP* 18 (1921): 232–266, at 249–256; Barbara M. Fisher, *Noble Numbers, Subtle Words: The Art of Mathematics in the Science of Storytelling* (London: Associated University Presses, 1997), 63–64.

[193] On Tasso's enhancement of military detail in the battle scenes of his revised poem, see Gigante, *"Vincer Pariemi Più se Stessa Antica,"* 99–113.

[194] See *Di Gerusalemme Conquistata del ... Tasso*, 196. Emphasis is mine.

> They all form a thick *phalanx*, which would have won the praise of Rome and Macedonia and *Sparta*, one which no attack can disturb or *break*, whether detained in battle or departing. And even when it turns and changes position, it does not seem confused or *dispersed*. Thus did it approach Germany and France, shield to shield, helmet to helmet, and spear to spear.[195]

Here the enemy *cannot* break ("non ... fr<u>ange</u>") the sturdy formation of the phalanx ("fal<u>ange</u>"), its integrity upheld not only by assonance, but also by its description as "non ... sparta," a punning recasting (yet etymological preservation) of "Sparta" herself. Milton threatens the very opposite in his predicted shattering of lines (and words) that are both military and poetic.

4.4 Tasso and Milton: Two Deathbed Scenes

In *Mansus* biography and autobiography ultimately coalesce in what may well be a Miltonic rewriting of a particular episode from Manso's *Vita*: the climactic deathbed scene of Tasso himself. Earlier in the poem Milton had made a prediction that continues to puzzle readers: *Dicetur tum sponte tuos habitasse penates/Cynthius* (54–55) ("Then it will be said that Cynthius has dwelt of his own accord in your [i.e. Manso's] home"). Low describes the lines as "by far the most complex and subtle thus far in their use of classical allusion,"[196] while Bush proffers his own interpretation: "Milton is saying that Apollo (i.e. poetry) voluntarily dwelt in Manso's house."[197] Although Cynthius is indeed a name for Apollo (derived from Mount Cynthus, the god's birthplace), its occurrence here, in combination with the contracted perfect infinitive *hab<u>itasse</u>* (emphasis mine), may punningly allude to Tasso's strong bond of friendship with Cardinal <u>Cinzio</u> (emphasis mine) Passeri Aldobrandini.[198] If so, it is a pun that finds an interesting Tassonian precedent. In a canzone, prefixed to the *Gerusalemme Conquistata*, Tasso

---

[195] Emphasis is mine.

[196] Low, "*Mansus*: In Its Context," 114.

[197] Bush, *Variorum*, 1, 276.

[198] With this possible wordplay, cf. *Mansus/mansuetus* (60) and the potential anagram *Manse tuae/mansuetae* (1).

offers his hearty congratulations to Cinzio, the epic's dedicatee,[199] by proclaiming:

> Et hor, ch'in sè l'alberga,
> L'alta Roma dico io, non *Cintho*, ò Delo;
> Mille virtù, cosparte
> In lui, rimira; e le consacra in carte.[200]

> And she who in herself is his host, I mean not *Cynthus* or Delos, but lofty Rome, admires the thousand virtues besprinkled upon him, and consecrates them in her pages.

The friendship between the two men is particularly evident in Manso's account of Tasso's final days. Thus we read that the poet, having been invited by Cardinal Cinzio to Rome for the purpose of his laureate coronation ("la corona dell' alloro") at the Campidoglio, arrived in the city in November 1595, only to learn that the ceremony would have to be postponed because of inclement weather and the Cardinal's illness.[201] Then just five months later (April 1596) Tasso, himself now seriously ill, decided to spend his final days in the Monastery of San Onofrio:

> deliberò d'andarsene a viver quelli ultimi giorni (ch'egli, ò per la gravezza dell'indispositione, ò per altra congettura, che se n'havesse, stimava dovere esser pochissimi) sù nel Monasterio di Santo Honofrio.[202]

> he decided to go and live those last days (which he, either because of the severity of his indisposition or because of some other conjecture which he possessed, estimated must be very few) up in the Monastery of San Onofrio.

Thus did the Monastery become Tasso's final dwelling-place, his *penates* (54), so to speak. It is here that he died in the very month nominated for the rescheduled laureate ceremony, and it is the Monastery's Church that

---

[199] See Angelo Ingegneri's dedicatory letter "All' Illustrissimo et Reverendissimo Signore, Il Signor Cinthio Aldobrandini, Card. Di S. Giorgio, Padrone, et Benefattore," at *Di Gerusalemme Conquistata del ... Tasso*, sig. *2^r-*3^v.

[200] Tasso, "Per La Promotione al Cardinalato dell' Illustrissimo et Reverendissimo Signore, Il Signor Cinthio Aldobrandini," at *Di Gerusalemme Conquistata del ... Tasso*, sig. *4^r-*6^r, at sig. *4^v. Emphasis is mine.

[201] Manso, *Vita di Torquato Tasso*, 223–225.

[202] *Vita di Torquato Tasso*, 225.

would eventually serve as the poet's final resting place. Crucially, Cinzio made a point of visiting him ("andò a visitarlo") on his deathbed (a proactive gesture hinted at perhaps in *sponte* [*Mansus* 54]), and conferred on him a papal benediction ("& a recargli in nome del Pontefice la sua santa benedittione").[203] According to the *Vita*, the dying Tasso stated that this would serve as his coronation ("questa era quella coronatione"), his triumph "in a celestial Campidoglio" ("nel celestial Campidoglio").[204] Manso takes pains to signal the lugubrious nature of the deathbed scene, not least, the tear-drenched eyes of the Cardinal and of all the other bystanders ("le lagrime, le quali nell' uscir della stanza, egli e tutti gli altri circostanti sparsero per gli occhi copiosamente") ("the tears, which, upon leaving the room, he and all the other bystanders shed copiously from their eyes").[205] Tasso's death is followed on the same evening by the transportation of his body to the Church of San Onofrio, and by his "burial beneath marble, simple, and small" ("sotto un semplice, e picciol marmo seppellito"),[206] in anticipation of the erection of a more magnificent tomb. Manso proceeds to relate, however, that some ten years later, upon visiting Rome, and finding no such memorial in the Church, he took it upon himself to secure the agreement of all concerned "for the erection of a magnificent and splendid sepulcher" ("un magnifico, e splendido sepolcro innalzare").[207] He also claims responsibility for negotiating the simple epitaph *Hic iacet Torqatus Tassus*, so that foreigners and strangers ("i Peregrini, e gli stranieri"), who came from all over the world to see his tomb, would at least be able to locate the place where his ashes were buried ("potessero almeno il luogo ritrovare, dove fossero le ceneri di lui state riposte").[208] He concludes by remarking that it was only upon the death of Cardinal Cinzio that his successor, Cardinal Bonifazio Bevilacqua Aldobrandini, saw to the construction of a proper tomb, with a new epitaph, embracing that aforementioned line from Ennius, now recast in the third person: *volitat vivus per ora virum*.[209]

Mansus, too, has a deathbed scene, albeit an envisaged one: that of the speaker himself. Milton may well be a *iuvenis peregrinus* (26), daring

---

[203] *Vita di Torquato Tasso*, 230–231.

[204] *Vita di Torquato Tasso*, 231.

[205] *Vita di Torquato Tasso*, 233.

[206] *Vita di Torquato Tasso*, 233.

[207] *Vita di Torquato Tasso*, 234.

[208] *Vita di Torquato Tasso*, 234–235.

[209] *Vita di Torquato Tasso*, 235. See 83.

in quasi-Ennian (and indeed quasi-Tassonian epitaphic) terms, to "fly through" (*volitare per* [29]) the cities of Italy, and, like Tasso, the recipient of gracious favors from Manso.[210] But in the poem's closing lines it is as a virtual *senex*, an old man "in the fullness of years" (*Annorumque satur* [86]), that he envisages himself. He is, moreover, one into whose poetic autobiography Tasso's final days seem to be re-inscribed.[211] As Milton writes his own deathbed scene, he presents an imagined scenario, in which his elderly self, not without a Tassonian awareness of the imminence of death, would be graced by the presence of someone who would stand by his bedside with tear-drenched eyes (*Ille mihi lecto madidis astaret ocellis* [87]). It will be enough for Milton to say to him as he stands there, "Take me to your care" (*Astanti sat erit si dicam "Sim tibi curae"* [88]). *Sat erit*, when viewed alongside the dying Tasso's words, seems to betray a reticent simplicity. This deathbed confidant would see to it that his limbs, loosened by livid death, were gently laid in a small urn (*Ille meos artus liventi morte solutos/Curaret parva componi molliter urna* [89–90]), the whole mirroring, at least at this point, that "semplice, e picciol marmo," which initially served to mark Tasso's tomb. But then in a climactic conclusion Milton envisages something more: a splendid and elaborate means of commemoration in the form of a laureate coronation that is both ekphrastic (*his features too* sculpted in marble: *et nostros ducat de marmore vultus* [91]; his hair bound with Paphian myrtle or Parnassian laurel: *Nectens aut Paphia myrti aut Parnasside lauri/Fronde comas* [92–93]),[212] and Tassonian in its celestial essence (*Ipse ego caelicolum semotus in aethera divum* [95] ["I myself, removed into the ethereal regions of the heaven-dwelling gods"]). As with Tasso, the envisaged triumph is a heavenly one, even if the ultimate applause is, ironically, self-applause (*aethereo plaudam mihi laetus Olympo* [100]). But perhaps not entirely so. Milton's final days are envisaged as the completion of "the span of a life not silent" (*non tacitae … tempora vitae* [85]). Viewed in the context of the poem's "brief lives," *non tacita … vita* may well signal a Miltonic desire to be remembered in biography, perhaps by someone such as Manso. The phrase also seems to

---

[210] See 117–118, 120–121.

[211] Revard, "Across the Alps," 60 (though without discussion of Manso's *Vita*), aptly observes: "He [Milton] imagines himself as an aged man—a man of his host Manso's years—though not of Manso's status. Rather he is like Manso's friend Tasso, the poet whose reputation Manso cherished and whose passage from life to death Manso supervised, as only a friend could."

[212] For an alternative, though not mutually exclusive, reading of these lines as a reworking of details of Manso's cenotaph to Marino, see 183–184.

embody an artistic aspiration voiced two years later, itself inspired by Milton's favorable reception "in the privat Academies of Italy":

> that by labour and intent study (which I take to be my portion in this life) joyn'd with the strong propensity of nature, I might perhaps leave something so written to aftertimes, as they should not willingly let it die.[213]

---

[213] Milton, *The Reason of Church-Government*, 37.

Chapter 5

Dialogus de Amicitia Scriptus: Dialogue(s) of Friendship

Milton's Tassonian self-fashioning in *Mansus* also manifests itself in regard to the multiple dialogical intertexts with which the poem engages. That it does so on a self-conscious level[1] is suggested by the privileged position afforded to Tasso's *Dialogo dell' Amicitia* in the Headnote to the poem.[2] Milton, however, cites only the work's subtitle. In fact, it was under the more formal title of *Il Manso, Overo Dell' Amicitia Dialogo* that the tract was published in Naples (1596)[3] and in Ferrara (1602),[4] its title page giving due prominence to the dedicatee by setting apart "IL MANSO" (in strong bold capitals and in a larger font) from the subtitle. It was by this shorthand title that the work came to be more commonly known. Hence it is described as "il Dialogo dell' Amicitia, ch'egli intitolò il Manso" ("the Dialogue on Friendship, which he entitled *Il Manso*") by both Manso in his *Vita di Torquato Tasso*,[5] and by Francesco De Pietri in his *Compendio*.[6] This precise method of entitling "Dialogues on Friendship" after the name of the friend concerned is explicated by Manso in his own "Del Dialogo Trattato,"

---

[1] Milton's alertness to the genre of the dialogue had revealed itself just a few months prior to his Neapolitan sojourn in his letter to Benedetto Buonmattei (dated 10 September 1638). Included in a generically based list recommended by him for incorporation in the Florentine's forthcoming Tuscan grammar is a request that he demonstrate *quis scriptis epistolis aut dialogis argutus aut gravis* ("who is shrewd or authoritative in writing epistles or dialogues"). See Milton, *Epistola Familiaris* 8, in *John Milton: Epistolae Familiares and Uncollected Letters*, ed. Haan, 116–139, at 128–129. See also 31.

[2] See 116.

[3] *Il Manso, Overo Dell' Amicitia Dialogo del Sig. Torquato Tasso. Al Molto Illustre Sig. Gio. Battista Manso* (Naples: Gio. Iacomo Carlino and Antonio Pace, 1596).

[4] *Il Manso, Overo Dell' Amicitia Dialogo del Sig. Torquato Tasso. Al Molto Illustre Sig. Gio. Battista Manso* (Ferrara: Vittorio Baldini, 1602).

[5] Manso, *Vita di Torquato Tasso*, 4. See 115.

[6] De Pietri, *Compendio*, 6. See 116.

included in the *Erocallia* (1628),⁷ one of the two volumes in all likelihood gifted by him to Milton.⁸ Here he situates Tassonian practice in *Il Manso* alongside ancient Greek and Latin precedent in, for example, Plato's Λύσις ἡ Περί Φιλίας (*Lysis Or On Friendship*), named after the boy Lysis, one of the dialogue's speakers, and in Cicero's *Laelius: De Amicitia* (*Laelius: On Friendship*), named after Gaius Laelius, likewise one of the work's interlocutors:

> Dalle persone intitolarono gran parte de loro Dialoghi non meno i Greci, e latini, che' Nostrali etiandio: ond'è che havendo Platone, e Cicerone e'l Tasso tutti, e tre scritto ciascun d'essi un Dialogo dell' Amicitia, il primo intitolò il suo il Liside, il secondo il Lelio e'l terzo il Manso, per la diversità delle persone da loro introdotte.⁹

> The Greeks and Latins, no less than our own writers, entitled a great majority of their Dialogues after individuals: hence has been the practice of Plato, Cicero, and Tasso, all three of whom have written a Dialogue of Friendship: the first entitled his *Lysis*, the second *Laelius*, and the third *Manso*, in accordance with the diversity of the individuals introduced by them.

Milton reserves that shorthand *Il Manso*, now appropriately in its Latinized form, for the title of his poem. As such, it differs conspicuously from the titles of his other Latin verses addressed to Italian individuals, governed, as they are, by the more customary *Ad* + accusative: *Ad Leonoram Romae Canentem*, *Ad Salsillum Poetam Romanum Aegrotantem*. *Mansus* thus serves not only to replicate Tasso's titular methodology, but also perhaps to signal the dialogical contexts of friendship at the heart of the poem itself.

The prominence afforded to Manso may also be an implicit acknowledgment of his privileged role as one of three "Interlocutori" of *Il Manso* (alongside Tasso [under the pseudonym of Forestiero] and Scipione Belprato [Manso's brother-in-law]). That the work was treasured by its dedicatee is evinced by the autograph manuscript extant in the British Library. This includes a letter of donation to the Library of the Monastery of San Onofrio at Rome (where Tasso was buried),¹⁰ dated 25 March 1613, and signed by Manso. Here he conveys his great esteem for the friendship of Tasso during his lifetime, a friendship, he says, that

---

⁷ Manso, *Erocallia*, 1033–1064: "Del Dialogo Trattato del Marchese della Villa." On the *Erocallia*, see Chapter 2.

⁸ See 36–40.

⁹ "Del Dialogo Trattato," at *Erocallia*, 1047.

¹⁰ See 151–152.

was attested by the published *Il Manso*, and, above all, by the fact that its author bequeathed to him the present manuscript.[11] His precious regard for that gift underlies his concluding remark that never until now has it been his wish that the work be separated from him ("da me separare"). The bond between the two also shines through Tasso's dedicatory letter to Manso, prefixed to the published work, in which he announces: "[n]ell' amicitia non si può far dono maggior dell' amicitia istessa" ("in friendship there is no greater gift than friendship itself").[12] The present book, he continues, is gifted and, as it were, consecrated as a pledge ("pegno") and image ("imagine") of friendship.[13] And in a series of five sonnets to Manso, also prefixed to the work[14] (and, as noted previously, included by Manso [among the "Poesie di Diversi"] in his *Poesie Nomiche*),[15] Tasso acknowledges the fact that the Neapolitan has been hailed by a host of contemporary poets. Thus, not unlike Milton's *haec quoque ... carmina* (1), his first sonnet is presented "tra mille al vero honor sacrati carmi,/Ch'a voi conviensi, e'n voi lodando alzarmi" ("among the thousand poems dedicated to true honor that have been assembled for you, and have arisen in your praise").[16] In his fourth sonnet he, like Milton, acclaims the gift of immortality bestowed upon Manso by virtue of the printed page, and indeed more:

> E'l nome vostro in bel metallo, ò in pietra

---

[11] BL Add MS 12046: "Quanto mi fu cara l'amicitia di Torquato Tasso mentr' egli visse ... oltretanto mi preggiai dopo la sua morte del testimonio ch'egli ni diede al mondo col dono, che mi fece di questo Dialogo dell' Amicitia" ("How dear to me was Torquato Tasso's friendship during his lifetime ... moreover, after his death, the praise that he afforded me by the testimony that he gave to the world with the gift of this Dialogue of Friendship that he bestowed upon me").

[12] Tasso, "Al Molto Illustre Signor Gio. Battista Manso," in *Il Manso*, sig. 2^r–2^v, at sig. 2^r. Text of *Il Manso* here, and throughout, is that of the 1602 Ferrara edition.

[13] *Il Manso*, sig. 2^r: "ho voluto donarle, e quasi consecrarle questo, quasi pegno, & imagine dell' amicitia espressa col mio stile qualunque ella si sia, ma assai simile a quella nobilissima forma, ch'io haveva conceputa nell' animo" ("This I wanted to give, and, as it were, consecrate, as a pledge and image of friendship, expressed with my own style, whatever that may be, but greatly resembling that noble form, which I had conceived in my mind").

[14] *Il Manso*, sig. 3^r–4^v.

[15] Manso, *Poesie Nomiche*, 257–259. A further sixth sonnet by Tasso (*incipit* "Dove i frondosi colli") occurs at 260. See also 85.

[16] *Il Manso*, sig. 3^r.

> Scriver si dee; non solo in mille carte.[17]

> And the gods have inscribed your name not just
> in one thousand pages, but in beautiful metal or
> in stone.

Manso's theoretical exegesis of "le forme de Dialoghi" in his "Del Dialogo Trattato" divides them into three distinct categories: "narrative," "rappresentative," and "miste."[18] It is to the last of these that he assigns "'l Manso del Tasso," a subcategory in which, we are told:

> l'Autore parte narra le cose da altrui dette sotto la sua medesima
> persona, e parte spogliandosene affatto introduce scenicamente
> gli altri favellatori, a ragionare.[19]

> the Author partly narrates the affairs of others spoken in the
> guise of his own persona, and partly introduces in a dramatic
> fashion other speakers to present reasoned arguments.

Assessing the multiple functions of the introduction to any dialogue, Manso emphasizes that it should outline the context of the circumstances attendant upon place, time, and the persons who have assembled for the debate ("contezza delle circostanze del luogo, del tempo, e delle persone ragunate à favellare"). Thus, it should describe the reasons ("le cagioni") or the accidents ("gli accidenti") that led to the coming together of the participants.[20] Here again he cites *Il Manso*:

> Cosi il Tasso nel Manso, nel quale dovendosi favellare
> dell'amicitia l'introduttione fù presa dall'haver ritrovato me con.
> D. Scipione mio Cognato leggere il tratto dell' Amicitia scritto
> da Plutarco.[21]

> Thus did Tasso in *Manso*, in which the need to hold a discussion
> about friendship was met by his introducing the scenario of his

---

[17] *Il Manso*, sig. 4ʳ (cf. *Poesie Nomiche*, 257). Cf. *Mansus* 8: *aeternis inscripsit nomina chartis* ("he inscribed your name in his eternal pages"), where the agent of immortalization is now Tasso himself. See 82–85.

[18] "Del Dialogo Trattato," at *Erocallia*, 1050.

[19] "Del Dialogo Trattato," at *Erocallia*, 1051.

[20] "Del Dialogo Trattato," at *Erocallia*, 1052.

[21] "Del Dialogo Trattato," at *Erocallia*, 1055. Cf. *Il Manso*, 2: "una tra l'altre volte il ritrovai con l'operette di Plutarco d'avanti, e con Don Scipione Belprato suo cognato" ("one of the other times I found him with the aforementioned work of Plutarch, and in the company of his kinsman, Signor Scipione Belprato").

> having found me with Signor Scipione, my kinsman, reading the tract on Friendship written by Plutarch.

The Headnote to *Mansus* is atypically meticulous in its itemization of time, place, and circumstance.[22] Uniquely, it subsumes its English author into the "brief life" of the Neapolitan inscribed therein: the reference to the hospitality which Milton received, in return for which, and in advance of his departure from Naples, he sent Manso the present poem.[23]

Il Manso opens with an encomium of its dedicatee, now praised for, inter alia, his conversational skills ("tanta affabilità nella conversatione"),[24] and, especially, for his literary scholarship as evinced by his "reading of excellent books" ("nella lettione de gli ottimi libri"), and by his ability to clarify "the more obscure passages" ("luoghi più oscuri") of philosophy and of history. In this regard he resembles those who travel upon a well-known path, and, with no need of a guide, serve instead to show the way to others.[25] One particular talent is Manso's ability to cast a fresh eye, as it were, upon the subjects that attract his interest, and to do so in a manner akin to that of a foreigner, expatiating on knowledge ("a guisa di Signore, che di peregrino si spatia nelle scienze"), and immersing himself in the quest for arts and disciplines ("nel cerchio dell'arti, e delle discipline"). In all of this, the Tassonian Manso is both a scholar forever in search of knowledge, and an individual who possesses a high mental acumen ("l'acume dell'ingegno").[26] Such terms of praise, it should be noted, are not very far removed from those bestowed upon Milton himself by the Florentine Antonio Francini:

> Di bella gloria amante
> Milton dal Ciel natio per varie parti
> Le peregrine piante
> Volgesti a ricercar scienze, ed arti
> (37–40).[27]

> Milton, lover of beautiful glory,
> you turned your wandering feet
> away from your native sky, and
> through various regions in search
> of sciences and arts.

---

[22] On the multiple functions of the headnote in Milton's 1645 *Poemata*, see 113.

[23] See 114.

[24] Tasso, *Il Manso*, 1.

[25] *Il Manso*, 2.

[26] *Il Manso*, 2.

[27] Milton, *Poemata*, 6–7; Lewalski and Haan, 110–111, 417.

In *Mansus*, it could be argued, they are indeed shared by Milton and his addressee. On the one hand, that Tassonian equation of Manso with a traveling "peregrino" finds a parallel in the Miltonic self-description as a *iuvenis peregrinus* (26), who has journeyed from the icy north; on the other, the Italian poet's encomium of Manso's "l'acume del' ingegno" is matched by Milton's praise of his *Ingeniumque vigens, et adultum mentis acumen* (77) ("flourishing intellect and mature sharpness of mind"). In this reading, Tasso's encomium of Manso and the lauded qualities itemized therein are subdivided in *Mansus* to describe first the poem's author, and then its addressee. This method of self-appropriation, and indeed of self-applause, albeit implicit at this point, rears its head more conspicuously as the poem progresses.

5.1 *Amicitia, Benevolentia, Concordia*

Central to a more rounded understanding of *Mansus* and of its multiple dialogical intertexts are the arguments on the nature of friendship ("amicitia") posited by Tasso in *Il Manso*. That tract assumes a place of its own within a miniature genre of dialogues devoted exclusively to the theme of friendship. This is best epitomized by Plato's Λύσις ἢ Περί Φιλίας,[28] a tradition followed, yet imaginatively reinterpreted, by Cicero

---

[28] See David Bolotin, *Plato's Dialogue on Friendship: An Interpretation of the Lysis, with a New Translation* (Ithaca, NY: Cornell University Press, 1979); *Plato's Lysis*, eds. Terry Penner and Christopher Rowe (Cambridge: Cambridge University Press, 2005). On Plato's treatment of friendship, see, among others, Donald Norman Levin, "Some Observations Concerning Plato's *Lysis*," in *Essays in Ancient Greek Philosophy*, vol. I, eds. John P. Anton and George L. Kustas (Albany: State University of New York Press, 1971), 236–258; Julia Annas, "Plato and Aristotle on Friendship and Altruism," *Mind* 86 (1977): 532–554; James Haden, "Friendship in Plato's *Lysis*," *Review of Metaphysics* 37 (1983): 327–356; Aristide Tessitore, "Plato's *Lysis*: An Introduction to Philosophic Friendship," *The Southern Journal of Philosophy* 28 (1990): 115–132; Samuel Scolnicov, "Friends and Friendship in Plato: Some Remarks on the *Lysis*," *Scripta Classica Israelica* 12 (1993): 67–74; F. J. Gonzalez, "Plato's *Lysis*: An Enactment of Philosophical Kinship," *AP* 15 (1995): 69–90; Catherine Pickstock, "The Problem of Reported Speech: Friendship and Philosophy in Plato's *Lysis* and *Symposium*," *Telos* 123 (2002): 35–65; Eugene Garver, "The Rhetoric of Friendship in Plato's *Lysis*," *Rhetorica* 24 (2006): 127–146; Mary P. Nichols, "Friendship and Community in Plato's *Lysis*," *The Review of Politics* 68 (2006): 1–19; Frisbee Sheffield, "Plato on Love and Friendship," in *The Cambridge Companion to Ancient Ethics*, ed. Christopher Bobonich (Cambridge: Cambridge University Press, 2017), 86–102; José Antonio Giménez, "Friendship, Knowledge and Reciprocity in *Lysis*," *Apeiron* 53 (2020): 315–337.

in his *Laelius: De Amicitia*.[29] It also draws on a tradition of ancient theorizing on friendship,[30] not least by Aristotle in his *Nicomachean Ethics*.[31] From the outset Tasso, as Forestiero, maximizes the potential for

---

[29] See Cicero, *De Amicitia*, in *Cicero: Laelius, On Friendship (Laelius De Amicitia) & The Dream of Scipio (Somnium Scipionis)*, ed. J. G. F. Powell (Warminster: Aris and Phillips, 1990), 1–118. On Cicero's depiction of friendship, see Arthur L. Keith, "Cicero's Idea of Friendship," *SRev* 37 (1929): 51–58; T. N. Habinek, "Towards a History of Friendly Advice: The Politics of Candor in Cicero's *De Amicitia*," *Apeiron* 23 (1990): 165–185; John Gruber-Miller, "Exploring Relationships: *Amicitia* and *Familia* in Cicero's *De Amicitia*," *CW* 103 (2009): 88–92; Thornton C. Lockwood, "Defining Friendship in Cicero's *De Amicitia*," *AP* 39 (2019): 409–426.

[30] There is a vast literature on the nature and theorizing of friendship in the classical and postclassical worlds. See, among others, P. A. Brunt, "'Amicitia' in the Late Roman Republic," *PCPS* 11 (1965): 1–20; A. W. Price, *Love and Friendship in Plato and Aristotle* (Oxford: Clarendon Press, 1989); Richard Saller, "Patronage and Friendship in Early Imperial Rome: Drawing the Distinction," in *Patronage in Ancient Society*, ed. Andrew Wallace-Hadrill (London: Routledge, 1989), 49–62; Roy Porter and Sylvana Tomaselli, *The Dialectics of Friendship* (London: Routledge, 1989); Michael Pakaluk, ed., *Other Selves: Philosophers on Friendship* (Indianapolis: Hackett, 1991); Neera Kapur Badhwar, ed., *Friendship: A Philosophical Reader* (Ithaca, NY: Cornell University Press, 1993); David Konstan, *Friendship in the Classical World* (Cambridge: Cambridge University Press, 1997); James O. Grunebaum, *Friendship: Liberty, Equality, and Utility* (Albany: State University of New York Press, 2003); Bennett W. Helm, *Love, Friendship, and the Self* (Oxford: Oxford University Press, 2010); C. A. Williams, *Reading Roman Friendship* (Cambridge: Cambridge University Press, 2012); Preston King and Heather Devere, eds., *The Challenge to Friendship in Modernity* (London: Routledge, 2012); *Thinking About Friendship: Historical and Contemporary Philosophical Perspectives*, ed. Damian Caluori (Basingstoke: Palgrave Macmillan, 2013); Brown, *Friendship and its Discourses*.

[31] See Harris Rackham, ed. and trans., *Aristotle: The Nicomachean Ethics*, (Cambridge, MA: Harvard University Press, 1926); H. H. Joachim, *Aristotle: The Nicomachean Ethics: A Commentary*, ed. D. A. Rees (Oxford: Clarendon Press, 1951); Michael Pakaluk, trans., *Aristotle: Nicomachean Ethics, Books VIII and IX* (Oxford: Clarendon Press, 1998). On Aristotle's treatment of friendship, see W. W. Fortenbaugh, "Aristotle's Analysis of Friendship: Function and Analogy, Resemblance, and Focal Meaning," *Phronesis* 20 (1975): 51–62; John M. Cooper, "Aristotle on the Forms of Friendship," *Review of Metaphysics* 30 (1976): 619–648; John M. Cooper, "Friendship and the Good in Aristotle," *PR* 86 (1977): 290–315; A. D. M. Walker, "Aristotle's Account of Friendship in the *Nicomachean Ethics*," *Phronesis* 24 (1979): 180–196; Paul Schollmeier, *Other Selves: Aristotle on Personal and Political Friendship* (Albany: State University of New York Press, 1994); Suzanne Stern-Gillet, *Aristotle's Philosophy of Friendship* (Albany: State University of New York Press, 1995); Lorraine Smith Pangle, *Aristotle and the Philosophy of Friendship* (Cambridge: Cambridge University Press, 2003).

scrutiny and interrogation afforded by his dialogistic methodology.[32] Seeking to differentiate between the friend and the flatterer,[33] he argues that the flatterer aims to please, whereas the friend aims to be of use. But as a whole the work moves far beyond this to present a thorough exegesis of "amicitia" itself, and of the many forms that it may assume. Here Tasso is careful to point out the essential correlation between "amicitia" and "benevolenza," viewing them as virtually synonymous: "Diremo adunque che l'amicitia è benevolenza" ("We will therefore say that friendship is goodwill").[34] Stressing the reciprocal nature of goodwill ("benevolenza reciproca"),[35] he proceeds to proclaim:

> nell'amicitia conviene, che la benevolenza sia reciproca, tante adunque sotto le specie dell'amicitie quante degli amori.[36]
>
> in friendship it is fitting that goodwill be mutual; the forms of friendships, therefore, are as many as are those of love.

And ancient precedent is never far away. After all, according to Aristotle, "it is only when it is mutual that such goodwill is termed friendship" (εὔνοιαν γὰρ ἐν ἀντιπεπονθόσι φιλίαν εἶναι),[37] while, in Cicero's view, if one were to remove goodwill (*benevolentia*) from friendship (*amicitia*), the very name of friendship would be gone (*sublata enim benevolentia*

---

[32] On Tasso's use of the dialogue form in general, see, among others, Guido Baldassarri, "L'Arte del Dialogo in Torquato Tasso," *ST* 20 (1970): 5–46; Franco Pignatti, "I *Dialoghi* di Torquato Tasso e La Morfologia del Dialogo Cortigiano Rinascimentale," *ST* 36 (1988): 7–43; Virginia Cox, "Rhetoric and Politics in Tasso's *Nifo*," *SS* 30 (1989): 3–98; Stefano Prandi, "Sul Dibatto Critico Attorno ai *Dialoghi* di T. Tasso," *LI* 42 (1990): 460–466; Virginia Cox, *The Renaissance Dialogue: Literary Dialogue in its Social and Political Contexts, Castiglione to Galileo* (Cambridge: Cambridge University Press, 1992), 93–96.

[33] Tasso, *Il Manso*, 3: "Della differenza tra l'amico, e l'adulatore, e come l'uno dall'altro sia conosciuto" ("On the difference between the friend and the flatterer, and how one is recognized from the other"). For classical treatments of the distinction, see Plutarch, "How to Distinguish a Flatterer from a Friend," in *Plutarch: Essays*, trans. Robin Waterfield (London: Penguin Books, 1992), 61–112; Cicero, *De Amicitia* 25.95, 26.99.

[34] *Il Manso*, 33.

[35] *Il Manso*, 33.

[36] *Il Manso*, 35.

[37] Aristotle, *Nicomachean Ethics* 8.2.4. Text is that of *Aristotle: The Nicomachean Ethics*, trans. Rackham.

amicitiae nomen tollitur).³⁸ Friendship, in fact, is nothing other than an accord in all things, human and divine, conjoined with goodwill and affection (*est enim amicitia nihil aliud nisi omnium divinarum humanarumque rerum cum benevolentia et caritate consensio*).³⁹ It is the existence of mutual goodwill (*mutua benevolentia*) between two friends that affords them essential peace in this world.⁴⁰

The Headnote to *Mansus* highlights the *summa benevolentia* ("the greatest of goodwill") that Milton received from his Neapolitan host.⁴¹ Then, via an emphatic *itaque* ("in consequence"),⁴² it depicts the composition of the present poem, and its dispatch to its addressee as a reciprocal gesture made in return for such hospitality: *Ad hunc itaque hospes ille ... hoc carmen misit* ("*In consequence*, that guest [Milton] ... sent this poem to him [Manso]").⁴³ Indeed, hospitality itself, according to Tasso (citing Aristotle), constituted a form of *amicitia*:

> fra queste amicitie Aristotele ne i libri a Nicomaco pone quella de
> gli Hospiti & de gli Albergatori.⁴⁴
>
> Among these friendships Aristotle, in his books to Nicomachus
> places that of Hosts and of Innkeepers.

Tasso also emphasizes the link between "amicitia" ("friendship") and "concordia" ("concord"): "fra l'anime beate sia somma amicitia, e somma concordia" ("between blessed souls there should be the utmost friendship and the utmost concord").⁴⁵ As an instance of a particularly notable friendship between persons of different rank and circumstance,⁴⁶ he cites that between Petrarch and King Robert of Naples. This, he states "senza dubbio fù perfetta amicitia, perche fra loro fù la concordia di tutte le opinioni" ("constituted without doubt a perfect form of friendship

---

³⁸ Cicero, *De Amicitia* 5.19. Text is that of *Cicero: Laelius, On Friendship (Laelius De Amicitia)*, ed. Powell.

³⁹ *De Amicitia* 6.20.

⁴⁰ *De Amicitia* 6.22.

⁴¹ See 114.

⁴² See *OLD*, s.v. 1: "(expr. result or inference) Since that is (was) the case, accordingly, in consequence, (and) so."

⁴³ Emphasis is mine.

⁴⁴ Tasso, *Il Manso*, 36. Cf. Aristotle, *Nicomachean Ethics* 8.3.4, 8.12.1.

⁴⁵ *Il Manso*, 26.

⁴⁶ On friendship between people of unequal status, see Cicero, *De Amicitia* 19.69–70.

because they shared a concord in relation to all of their opinions").[47] *Concordia* is likewise integral to Milton's conception of *amicitia*. Having described Manso in the Headnote as *Tassi amicissimus*,[48] he summarizes the nature of his friendship with the Italian poet as a *felix concordia* (7), thereby developing the Tassonian correlation between "amicitia" and "concordia" into a bond that is both intimate and quasi-heroic in essence. This he does by evocation of Ovid's description (in an itemized list of heroes) of the relationship between Theseus and Perithous at *Metamorphoses* 8.303: *et cum Pirithoo, felix concordia, Theseus* (the noun *concordia* occurring here in its poetical sense of "an intimate friend").[49] Anthony Low posits an interesting suggestion:

> in view of the preoccupation of *Mansus* with friendship and death ... one wonders if Milton did not intend Manso to recall not only the immediate context of Ovid's line but also the fate of the famous pair.[50]

It emerges, in fact, that *Il Manso* had actually cited the bond between the heroic pair as indicative of the necessary fortitude ("fortezza") attendant upon particularly close forms of "amicitia":

> Ma la fortezza è più necessaria, ove è maggiore amicitia, come ci dimostra ... l'essempio di Theseo e di Piritoo, e di Achille, e di Patroclo.[51]

> But fortitude is more necessary where the friendship is greater, as is shown ... by the example of Theseus and Perithous, and Achilles and Patroclus.

Such fortitude, however, came at a cost. Upon descending to Hades in order to carry off Persephone, Theseus and Perithous were both chained to a bench. Theseus, with the help of Hercules, managed to escape, but Perithous failed to do so. It was a fate cited by Horace (*Odes* 4.7) as an instance of the inevitability of death, and of the essentially rigorous laws of the Underworld. In Horace, Theseus, himself now dead, still cannot free his friend (*nec Lethaea valet Theseus abrumpere caro/vincula*

---

[47] *Il Manso*, 84.

[48] See 114.

[49] See Lewis and Short, s.v. *concordia* I.b (citing, as its sole example, this precise Ovidian verse): "Poet., meton. (abstr. pro concr,) *an intimate friend*."

[50] Low, "*Mansus*: In Its Context," 109.

[51] *Il Manso*, 73–74.

Perithoo [4.7.27–28]) from an imprisonment which, in the words of Michael Putnam, "means the end of the individuality that humans possess while still alive in their sublunar environment."[52] Horace's poem, moreover, is addressed to a certain Torquatus, probably the lawyer, and son of the consul L. Manlius Torquatus,[53] who is warned that not even his birth, eloquence, and piety can save him from death: *non, Torquate, genus, non te facundia, non te/restituet pietas* (4.7.23–24). It is a warning that evinces, as Putnam capably puts it, the "very loss of individuality that follows upon the end of our day. ... In death we become formless continuities, forgetting and forgotten."[54] In *Mansus*, by contrast, *felix concordia* possesses intimations of a shared immortality. This is achievable because of the act of another Torquatus, so to speak. Now, in a reversal of agency it is Tasso himself who can indeed enable his friend to partake in a life everlasting, since he has inscribed Manso's name in his eternal pages (8), most likely a twofold reference to *Gerusalemme Conquistata* 20, and to *Il Manso* itself.

5.2 *Amicitia, Pietas, Fama*

Amicitia also operates on two, more explicit, levels in *Mansus*: in (1) the posthumous piety that Manso showed to Marino by the erection of a cenotaph in his honor: *Nec manes pietas tua cara fefellit amici* (15) ("And your loving devotion did not fail your *friend's* spirit"), further discussed in Chapter 6;[55] and (2) the Miltonic desire for a friend (such as Manso), who might pay similar respects to his departed self: *O mihi si mea sors talem concedat amicum,/Phoebaeos decorasse viros qui tam bene norit* (78–79) ("O if my fate would grant me a *friend* such as this, one who knows so well how to glorify the followers of Phoebus").[56] That contracted perfect infinitive *decorasse* (79) is evocative of *Torquati decus* (50), and the eternal fame, which, Milton had predicted, Manso will win because of his personal and literary affinities with such a celebrated poet:

---

[52] See Michael C. J. Putnam, "Horace, *Carm.* 4.7 and the Epic Tradition," *CW* 100 (2007): 355–362, at 360.

[53] See Michael C. J. Putnam, "Horace to Torquatus: *Epistle* 1.5 and *Ode* 4,7," *AJP* 127 (2006): 387–413, at 387.

[54] Putnam, "Horace to Torquatus," 403.

[55] See 175–184.

[56] Emphasis is mine.

> Fortunate senex, ergo quacunque per orbem
> Torquati decus et nomen celebrabitur ingens,
> Claraque perpetui succrescet fama Marini,
> Tu quoque in ora frequens venies plausumque virorum,
> Et parili carpes iter immortale volatu.
>
> (*Mansus* 49–53)

> And so, fortunate old man, wherever throughout the world are celebrated the glory and the powerful name of Torquato, and wherever is augmented the famous reputation of the deathless Marino, you too will frequently be on the lips and in the applause of men, and in a flight such as theirs will you press along the journey of immortality.

Low draws a comparison between this passage and Milton's previously articulated "reservations" in *Lycidas* about his own inherent desire for fame ("That last infirmity of Noble mind").[57] Reading into the lines "a similar attitude now," he regards the nature of the immortality assigned to Manso as "purely classical and literary."[58] This somewhat simplistic interpretation overlooks the subtle nuances attendant upon Milton's presentation of Manso's fame and subsequent immortality as intrinsically linked to, and the consequence of, his association with Tasso and Marino. These nuances come to the fore when the passage is examined in relation to an important discussion of "fama" in *Il Manso*.

In response to Manso's question "E chi non conosce il vostro merito, e la fama?" ("And who does not know your merit and your fame?"),[59] Tasso, as Forestiero, proffers a telling retort:

> La fama è bugiarda anzi che nò, laonde coloro che sono conosciuti per fama mi paiono simili a quelle imagini, che non son ritratte dal naturale, ma da un' altra pittura.[60]

> Fame is deceitful for the reason that those who are known by fame seem to me to resemble those images that are painted not from nature but from another picture.

---

[57] *Lycidas* 71. Contrast, however, 78–84: "Fame is no plant that grows on mortal soil,/Nor in the glistering foil/Set off to th' world, nor in broad rumour lies,/But lives and spreds aloft by those pure eyes,/And perfet witnes of all-judging Jove;/As he pronounces lastly on each deed,/Of so much fame in Heav'n expect thy meed." See William G. Riggs, "The Plant of Fame in *Lycidas*," *MS* 4 (1972): 151–161.

[58] Low, "*Mansus*: In Its Context," 114.

[59] *Il Manso*, 3.

[60] *Il Manso*, 3–4.

Crucially, however, he continues by professing his wish to be known not by fame alone, but by virtue of his associated friendship with Manso:

> Sin hora adunque non mi conosce chi per fama mi conosce, ma io direi di voler essere conosciuto per vostro amico.[61]
>
> Thus far, the person who knows me by reputation, does not actually know me, but I would say that it is my wish that I be known as your friend.

Mansus foretells the fulfillment of this Tassonian desideratum, but it does so with reference to, and from the perspective of, the other party (indeed parties) involved. Thus, Milton predicts, Manso's future *fama* will be guaranteed and indeed validated because of his past association with both Tasso and Marino. One senses, too, a not dissimilar aspiration on Milton's part. As noted earlier, his self-fashioning in the poem's closing lines is as one who has seen to its conclusion the span of "a life not silent" (*non tacitae ... vitae* [85]).[62] Indeed, this rather oddly expressed Miltonic desideratum is not very far removed from Tasso's proclamation to Manso:

> Non è segno d'adulatione il lodar le cose degne di loda, *ma di nemistà, ò malignità il tacerle*: però io non temo tanto il nome di adulatore lodandovi, quanto quello di malevolo, e di invidioso *tacendo de' vostri meriti*, & di quelli de' vostri nobilissimi progenitori.[63]
>
> It is not a sign of flattery to praise things worthy of praise, *but it is a sign of hostility or of malice to keep silent about them*. Yet I do not so much fear the name of flatterer by praising you as I do that of one who is malevolent and envious *by maintaining a silence about your merits*, and of those of your most noble ancestors.

Il Manso concludes in a glowing hymn to "Amicitia," a hymn significantly proclaimed by Manso himself:

> Tu giusta, Tu pietosa, Tu santa, Tu Celeste insieme, e Terrena, Mortale & immortale, humana & divina, risguarda questo mondo terrano.[64]

---

[61] *Il Manso*, 4.

[62] See 153–154.

[63] *Il Manso*, 5. Emphasis is mine.

[64] *Il Manso*, 85.

> You are just, you are pious, you are holy, you combine the Celestial and the Earthly, the Mortal and the immortal, the human and the divine, as you behold this earthly world.

In the envisaged apotheosis with which *Mansus* concludes, Milton, removed into the ethereal regions of the heaven-dwelling gods (*Ipse ego caelicolum semotus in aethera divum* [95]) assumes a not dissimilar perspective (*Secreti haec aliqua mundi de parte videbo* [97] ["I will behold these things from some remote region of the universe"]), but the hymn that he offers is one of self-applause. *Plaudam mihi* (100) is directly antithetical to the "applause of men" (*plausum ... virorum* [52]), which, Milton had predicted, Manso would undoubtedly win. At the same time, it is not necessarily at odds with the Tassonian view of *amicitia*. Rather, it seems, at least implicitly, to both acknowledge and conform to Forestiero's express misgivings as to whether any individual really ought to possess the desire to be exalted by his friends ("dubitare se l'huomo debba desiderare l'essaltatione de gli amici").[65]

5.3 Manso: *Et Amicus et Pater*

Editors, scholars, and biographers have duly observed the quasi-filial stance adopted by Milton in *Mansus*.[66] Likewise, they have noted links between the poem and *Ad Patrem*, from which Milton appropriates almost verbatim two separate verses. Not, however, without some puzzlement and consequential misreadings. Parker, for example, pointing out that "lines 6 and 43 of *Mansus* are apparently borrowed from *Ad Patrem* 102 and 46," contextualizes the whole in relation to Milton's later statement about the circumstantial and practical difficulties, the "scarcity of books and conveniences," purportedly encountered by him when composing poetry in the course of his Italian sojourn,[67] only to continue: "One might expect even more of such borrowing."[68] Atypically, he does some disservice to Milton's methodology and to the merits of what is arguably a carefully perfected poem (evident perhaps in the ideal round number of 100 lines). Bush, by contrast, aptly remarks that "[i]t would be wholly in Milton's way, in the writing of such a poem about poetry as

---

[65] *Il Manso*, 83.

[66] The is well defined by Low as "an unexpected, almost filial intimacy." See Low, "*Mansus*: In Its Context," 107.

[67] Milton, *The Reason of Church-Government*, 37.

[68] Parker, *Biography*, ed. Campbell, II, 827.

Mansus, to recall phrases from *Ad Patrem*, whatever its date."[69] Similarly, the nature and possible motivation behind the obvious points of contact between the two poems have been misrepresented by scholars, largely as a consequence of an overemphasis upon the belief that Milton is somehow seeking to "challenge" his addressee or to offer a poetic self-defense. Thus, Low remarks:

> The evidence of the poem suggests that in *Mansus* Milton acts very like a son challenging a father who has threatened to reject him, and that he hopes through the sheer accomplishment of his poem and the persuasiveness of its nuances to impel recognition from this man who loved poetry, to bridge the gap of sectarian difference between them.[70]

Lewalski, while making the pertinent observation that "Milton takes on the role of a worthy son respectfully asserting his worth to another father ('Manse pater' l. 25)," overstretches the issue by describing both "father" figures as people "who might not accept him as a poet or value his poetry," and continuing "As in 'Ad Patrem,' the son hopes the brilliance and elegance of his poem and his skillful rhetorical address will make his case to a man who demonstrably did and does value poetry."[71]

Read in the context of *Il Manso*, Milton's appropriation of lines from *Ad Patrem* seems less surprising. Among the many types of friendship explicated by Tasso is that described by Aristotle in his *Nicomachean Ethics* as existing between parties of unequal age and status. Such, for example, is "the friendship between father and son, and generally between an older person and a younger" (πατρὶ πρὸς υἱὸν καὶ ὅλως πρεσβυτέρῳ πρὸς νεώτερον). Here:

> the friendship between parents and children will be enduring and equitable, when the children render to the parents the services due to the authors of one's being, and the parents to the children those due to one's offspring.[72]

---

[69] Douglas Bush, "The Date of Milton's *Ad Patrem*," *MP* 61 (1964): 204–208, at 205. Bush considers various dates proposed for Milton's poem (1631–1632, 1634, 1637) and argues in favor of the earliest date.

[70] Low, "*Mansus*: In Its Context," 108–109.

[71] Lewalski, *Life*, 112.

[72] Aristotle, *Nicomachean Ethics* 8.7.2. Text and translation are those of Rackam at *Aristotle: Nicomachean Ethics*, 477–479. Contrast, however, Cicero, *De Amicitia*, where, in the words of Arthur Keith, "[o]f affection of son for father, father for son, or man for woman, not a word is said." See Keith, "Cicero's Idea of Friendship," 57.

Similarly, according to Tasso, the possible friendship between a father and son can facilitate a potential equivalence between the two parties, largely in consequence of mutual respect and the rendering of dignified duty:

> dell' amicitie alcune sono fra gli eguali, altre fra gli ineguali ... & queste sono tra il padre e'l figliuolo, tra il marito e la moglie, & tra il prencipe e'l soggetto ... i padri danno a figliuoli, quel che a figliuolo è conveniente, i figliuoli allo'ncontro concedono a i padri quel che è debito, & come in ciascuna di queste amicitie sia l'amore, è amore con dignità è convenevolezza ... in questa guisa nella disuguaglianza si fa l'egualità.[73]

> Some friendships exist among equals, others among unequals ... and these are between father and son, between husband and wife, and between prince and subject. ... Fathers give to sons what is proper to a son; sons, on the contrary, concede to fathers what is due and, since in each of these friendships there exists love, a love that is characterized by both dignity and courtesy, ... in this way equality arises in cases of inequality.

The father/son relationship implicit in *Mansus* is characterized by this quasi-Tassonian sense of equivalence between two like-minded parties (*Nos etiam* [30, 38]),[74] and by the dutiful acknowledgment of the merits of a *pater* (25) and *senex* (49, 70) by a *iuvenis* (26), who is also an implied *filius*. As Aristotle proclaimed:

> Honour also is due to parents, as it is to the gods ... we should pay to all our seniors the honour due to their age, by rising when they enter, offering them a seat, and so on.[75]

A closer examination of the two verbal parallels in particular and, more generally, of the respective contexts in which they occur, suggests not a random plundering, as it were, of verses from an earlier poem, but their imaginative redeployment as a means of establishing an intertextual dialogue between the two works and their respective addressees. It is one, moreover, that moves beyond the purely verbal to extol and, indeed, defend shared poetic traditions and networks. In this reading, *Mansus* evinces not so much a sense of emulation or self-justification on Milton's

---

[73] *Il Manso*, 65.

[74] See 89. On the possible friendship that can exist between like-minded men of virtue, see also Cicero, *De Amicitia* 5.18, 14.50, 18.65, 20.74; Aristotle, *Nicomachean Ethics* 8.3.6.

[75] Aristotle, *Nicomachean Ethics* 9.2.8–9.

part, as an implicit alignment of, and "dialogue" between, two septuagenarian *patres*[76] (suggested by the invocation of Manso as *Manse pater* [25]), to whom a "son," in both a literal and literary sense, renders respectful thanks. Dialogue, after all, in the words of Jon Snyder "operates as a fictional mise-en-scène of speaking characters."[77]

In the first instance, Milton voices his hope about the envisaged efficacy of his Latin encomiastic talents (*si nostrae tantum valet aura Camoenae* [5] ["if the breath of our Camena has power so great"]), having already contextualized *Mansus* in the poem's opening line (*Haec quoque ... carmina*) alongside other verse tributes to Manso, in all likelihood, the cluster of Italian encomia appended to the latter's *Poesie Nomiche*.[78] If his hope is realized, his Latin poem, he predicts, will enable Manso to sit among the ivies and laurels of victory (*Victrices hederas inter laurosque sedebis* [6]). The line is in effect a very pointed reworking of Milton's self-referential statement in *Ad Patrem* concerning his *own* elite membership of a coterie of learned poets, and his acknowledgment of the rewards that may ensue, privileges afforded him by the gift of education bestowed upon him by his father. These, Milton states, will ensure that he (Milton junior) will sit among the ivies and laurels of victory (*Victrices hederas inter laurosque sedebo* [*Ad Patrem* 102]). In *Mansus*, therefore, an authorial prediction about his own poetic fate (*sedebo*) has been dutifully gifted, as it were, from speaker to addressee (*sedebis*), from an English son to an Italian poetic father.

The second echo pertains to Milton's defense in *Mansus* of the traditions of British poetry. Poeticizing the learning of the Druids, he depicts them singing the praises of heroes, and their exploits worthy of imitation (*Heroum laudes imitandaque gesta canebant* [43]).[79] The line reworks what is in effect another defense: *Ad Patrem*'s retrospective

---

[76] Manso's dates are now generally accepted as 1567–1645. For controversy over the date of his birth, see Riga, *Giovan Battista Manso*, 13–14, who provides convincing evidence of a birth date of August 1567. This means that at the time of the poem's composition (ca. January 1639) Manso was 71 years of age, while Milton senior (1562–1647) was 76.

[77] Snyder, *Writing the Scene of Speaking*, 49. On the Renaissance dialogue in general, see, among others, David Marsh, *The Quattrocento Dialogue: Classical Tradition and Humanist Innovation* (Cambridge, MA: Harvard University Press, 1980); Peter Burke, "The Renaissance Dialogue," *RS* 3 (1989): 1–12; Raffaele Girardi, *La Società del Dialogo: Retorica e Ideologia nella Letteratura Conviviale del Cinquecento* (Bari: Adriatica, 1989); Cox, *The Renaissance Dialogue*, passim; *Printed Voices: The Renaissance Culture of Dialogue*, ed. Dorothea Heitsch and Jean-François Vallée (Toronto: University of Toronto Press, 2004).

[78] See Chapter 3.

[79] See 129–133.

vision of poetry in general, and of the role of the epic bard in particular. Proclaiming to his father the validity of his poetic vocation, Milton describes the age-old tradition of the *vates* (44), who would assume his customary seat before the festive banquets and sing his epic song: *Heroumque actus imitandaque gesta canebat* (*Ad Patrem* 46). The phraseology is evocative of Vida, *De Arte Poetica* 1.544: *post epulas laudes heroum et facta canentes* ("those who sing after their banquets the glories and deeds of heroes"), a work with which *Ad Patrem* engages on several intertextual levels as a means of establishing its addressee as an ideal Renaissance educator.[80] The echo in *Mansus* thus serves to reinforce Milton's proud defense of a long-standing epic tradition in England, articulated this time to an Italian academic father, so to speak, one whose own pedagogical interests had manifested themselves most conspicuously in his establishment of the Neapolitan Collegio dei Nobili.[81]

Potential echoes of *Ad Patrem* (frequently via Vida's *De Arte Poetica*) also operate on a thematic level: the invocation of Clio as Muse of history/biography,[82] the celebration of the powers of *carmen* through quasi-hymnic repetition of the noun,[83] and the emphasis on its Orphic ability to stupefy and beguile the world of nature.[84] It is worth noting too that in *Mansus* the Orphic power of *carmen* is depicted as the product of Apollo, who, in an attempt to avoid the din of the "clamorous herdsmen" (*clamosos ... vitare bubulcos* [59]), retreated (*cessit* [60]) to the famous cave of the gentle Chiron (*Nobile mansueti cessit Chironis in antrum* [60]). The potential pun on Manso's name (in *mansueti ... Chironis* [60]), his implicit identification with a leading mythological educator (Chiron),[85] and the association of effective song with withdrawal, amid

---

[80] See Estelle Haan, "Milton's Latin Poetry and Vida," *HL* 44 (1995): 282–304, at 283–292.

[81] See 11.

[82] In *Ad Patrem* 13–15, Milton's poetic wealth is depicted as having been provided by *aurea Clio* (14) ("golden Clio"). Masson, *Poetical Works*, III, 527, explicates the validity of Milton's reference to Clio, the muse of history: "what he is to say about his Father is strictly true." In *Mansus* 24–25, Milton wishes Manso a long and healthy life in the name of Clio and Apollo.

[83] See the lengthy hymn to *carmen* at *Ad Patrem* 24–55, with which cf. the recurring leitmotif in *Mansus*: *haec ... carmina* (1), *stupefecit carmine* (12), *carminibus* (46), *mulcenturque novo maculosi carmine lynces* (69), *revocabo in carmina reges* (80). Cf. also Vida, *De Arte Poetica* 1.532–556. See Haan, "Milton's Latin Poetry and Vida," 290–292.

[84] *Ad Patrem* 52–55; *Mansus* 65–69. Cf. Vida, *De Arte Poetica* 1.552–553. See Haan, "Milton's Latin Poetry and Vida," 290–291.

[85] See 89–91.

the *otium* afforded by a pastoral *locus amoenus*, merit comparison with Milton's account in *Ad Patrem* of a privilege afforded him by another educator, so to speak: his own father. Thus, we are told, John Milton, Sr. enabled his son to escape the dull clamorings (*insulsis ... clamoribus* [72]) of the courts of law in favor of literary seclusion amid deep retreats and the leisurely delights of the Aonian bank (*Me ... secessibus altis/Abductum Aoniae iucunda per otia ripae* [74–75]).[86] In all of this, the textual evidence seems to suggest an expectation on Milton's part that his addressee would recognize such points of comparison. Perhaps indeed he had shown *Ad Patrem* to Manso or had even performed it, in Manso's presence, before the Accademia degli Oziosi.[87]

Speaking of the Renaissance dialogue in general, Virginia Cox remarks:

> by duplicating its primary communication with a fictional double, the dialogue has the effect of calling attention to the art of communication itself. ... In the dialogue, ... the act of persuasion is played out before us, and we cannot simply absorb the message without reflecting on the way in which it is being sent and received.[88]

In this regard *Mansus*, it could be argued, proffers a poetic theory of friendship that is informed by the ethos and substance of Tasso's work,[89] but the poem also moves beyond this by establishing a series of intertextual (and intratextual) "dialogues" of its own between "doubles" that are both fictional and very real.

---

[86] Milton's lines echo Vida, *De Arte Poetica* 1.290–292; 1.486–495, on which see Haan, "Milton's Latin Poetry and Vida," 287–288.

[87] Certainly, *Ad Patrem* would have served as an ideal tool for Milton's showcasing before Italian academicians of his classical education, his multilingualism, and his poetic vocation. On Milton's possible performance of this poem in the academies of Italy, see Haan, *From Academia to Amicitia*, 26–28.

[88] Cox, *The Renaissance Dialogue*, 5–6.

[89] My discussion moves significantly beyond that of W. Scott Howard, "Companions with Time: Milton, Tasso, and Renaissance Dialogue," *The Comparatist* 28 (2004): 5–28, which overlooks *Mansus* and its Tassonian intertext.

Chapter 6

Dulciloquus ... Marinus:
Marino Re-Membered

Encomium, biography, and dialogue are certainly key forms of celebration, commemoration, and communication. There are, however, other ways of honoring poets and friends. This is nowhere more evident than in the multiple types of "monuments" that lie at the heart of *Mansus*. At times these are iconographical: cenotaphs both real (of Marino) and imagined (of Milton); at others, they are literary: the poetic afterlife of a work (Marino's *L'Adone*) as characterized by reader response on the part of audiences, past and present, that range from wider Italian communities to Milton himself. Afterlives can also be linguistic, not least in the potential "re-membering" of Marinesque "concettismo" in a neo-Latin voice that is both mannered and vibrantly new.

6.1 *Angelus Ipse Fores*: Milton in St. Angelo a Foro

Iconographical commemoration in *Mansus* seems to take us back full circle to that climactic prediction uttered by Manso in his encomium of Milton: *Angelus ipse fores*.[1] It is a phrase that may possess a hitherto unnoticed material significance by virtue of its potentially punning allusion to Manso's domestic chapel of St. *Angelo a Foro*.[2] In this reading, the wordplay on "angel" (in *Angelus*/"St. Angelo") and on "forum" (in *fores*/"Foro") seems particularly apposite. In Bede, after all, it was the Roman forum that had provided the location for the encounter between Gregory and the quasi-angelic youths for sale.[3] Manso's chapel,

---

[1] See 46. Emphasis is mine.

[2] Emphasis is mine.

[3] See *Bede's Ecclesiastical History*, eds. Colgrave and Mynors, 132: *Dicunt quia die quadam, cum advenientibus nuper mercatoribus multa venalia in forum fuissent conlata, multi ad emendum confluxissent, et ipsum Gregorium inter alios advenisse, ac vidisse inter alia pueros venales* ("They say that one day, when merchants had recently come together, many items had been brought to the *forum* for sale, and that,

which had been constructed beneath his palace, derived its name from the fact that it was located on the site of an ancient Neapolitan forum (the present-day Piazza dei Girolamini).[4] Thus, as Carlo De Lellis attests:

> E Questa, una Cappella eretta da Gio: Battista Manso Marchese di Villa, e chiamollo à Foro, per essere situata nel luogo ove anticamente era il foro, cioè il mercato della Città, onde questo quartiero di mercato vecchio ancor si chiama.[5]

> This is a Chapel erected by Gio. Battista Manso, Marquis of Villa, and named "à Foro" in accordance with its location in the place where the forum formerly existed, that is, the market of the City, whence this ancient quarter is still called the market quarter.

Here Manso had recently seen the completion of a cenotaph of Marino, a memorial that merits careful scrutiny, not only in terms of its status as a material indicator of Manso's unfailing sense of duty (*pietas* [15]) toward a deceased friend (*manes ... amici* [15]), but also, and especially, in that it is undoubtedly the monument that was viewed by Milton, and described by him in *Mansus*:

> Ille itidem moriens tibi soli debita vates
> Ossa tibi soli supremaque vota reliquit.
> Nec manes pietas tua cara fefellit amici:
> Vidimus arridentem operoso ex aere poetam.
> (*Mansus* 13–16)

> Likewise, when he was dying, it was to you alone that that bard left his bones, as was their due; to you alone, his final wishes. And your loving devotion did not fail your friend's spirit: we have seen the poet smiling from elaborate bronze.

Milton contextualizes the whole alongside an acknowledgment of the fact that it was to Manso alone that Marino, upon his death bed, entrusted his funeral arrangements, a bequest and privilege tellingly signaled in the

---

amongst others, there had arrived Gregory himself, and that he had seen, among other things, boys who were for sale"). Emphasis is mine.

[4] The palace in question was partially destroyed after Manso's death. See Vincenzo Cerino, *Il Real Monte Manso di Scala nella Storia della Città della Nobiltà Napoletana* (Naples: Rolando, 2009), 68–69.

[5] Carlo De Lellis, *Parte Seconda Overo Supplimento a Napoli Sacra di D. Cesare d'Engenio Caracciolo* (Naples: Roberto Mollo, 1654), 77.

emphatic repetition of *tibi soli* (13–14).[6] Manso had in fact been granted privileged access to the dying poet in the Spring of 1625, to whom he had offered continued support and assistance in his final days,[7] and by whom he was named as executor,[8] this last fact encapsulated perhaps in *supremaque vota reliquit* (14). Because Marino's death (on 26 March 1625) coincided with the liturgical celebrations of Easter week, his funeral arrangements had to be rescheduled. Hence his body was placed temporarily in the Church of the Holy Apostles, before being transferred to Manso's private chapel of St. Angelo a Foro. And it was Manso who subsequently ensured his friend's final resting place in the Church of the Holy Apostles.[9] That he did so not without a struggle is evident from records extant in the Archivio Stato del Monte Manso di Scala in Naples:

> Dopo la cui morte [del Marino] esso Marchese mandò il corpo del Cavaliere nella Chiesa di Santi Apostoli non ostante che da Principi sopremi gli fusse fatta gagliardissima instanza in contrario.[10]
>
> After the death [of Marino], the Marquis sent the body of the Count to the Church of The Holy Apostles, despite the fact that he was given a very strong ruling to the contrary by the highest Authorities.

The staunch Archbishop Decio Carafa, clearly ill-disposed to having a banned author laid to rest in the actual church, and stating that such an honor pertained to a saint and not to a member of the laity, preferred to have him buried in the adjoining cemetery, in what he envisaged as a low-key and swiftly executed night-time procedure.[11] Notwithstanding such opposition, on the night of 3 April Marino's body was transferred from Manso's private chapel to the actual Church of the Holy Apostles,

---

[6] See also 74–75.

[7] See Luigi Guarini, *Notizie della Morte, Sepoltura, e Tomba del Cavalier Marini* (Naples: A. Coda, 1817); Giorgio Fulco, "Il Sogno di una 'Galeria': Nuovi Documenti dul Marino Collezionista," *Antologia di Belle Arti* 3 (1979): 84–99; Denman, "A Gift Text of Hispano-Neapolitan Diplomacy," 685.

[8] See Riga, *Giovan Battista Manso*, 50. For an inventory of Marino's goods in the Summer of 1625, a few months after his death, see Giorgio Fulco, *La "Meravigliosa" Passione: Studi sul Barocco Tra Letteratura ed Arte* (Rome: Salerno, 2001), 83–117.

[9] See De Lellis, *Supplimento a Napoli Sacra*, 78: "riposandosi il corpo del Cavalier Marino nel Cimiterio della Chiesa di SS. Apostoli" ("laying to rest the body of Count Marino in the Cemetery of the Church of the Holy Apostles").

[10] ASMMS, An/23, doc. num. 3. See Riga, *Giovan Battista Manso*, 52.

[11] See Riga, *Giovan Battista Manso*, 50–51, and sources cited therein.

where he was buried.[12] And, doubtless in consequence of Manso's proactive endeavors, there assembled a large number of titled lords to escort the funeral cortege, thereby confirming Manso's huge efforts to protect the dignity and the image of the deceased, irrespective of the opposition of Neapolitan clergy.[13] It is an image that would be celebrated with sumptuous formality by the Roman Accademia degli Umoristi on the first anniversary of his death.[14]

Manso's efforts, however, went far beyond the fulfillment of a poet's burial request. Sixth months after Marino's death he was already hard at work making arrangements for what would be a very personal commemoration of his friend in a very private space. Thus, on 3 October 1625 he secured monies for the erection, in his domestic chapel of St. Angelo a Foro, of an extravagant marble cenotaph in Marino's honor. It was crowned by a bronze bust of the poet, beautifully crafted by Bartolomeo Bertaglia (more commonly known as Bartolomeo Viscontini),[15] after a clay model by the French sculptor, Christophe Cochet.[16] This is the bust and the associated cenotaph that were viewed

---

[12] See Miranda, *Una Quiete Operosa*, 220–221; Riga, *Giovan Battista Manso*, 50–51. On Marino's Neapolitan funeral, see Floriana Conte, *Tra Napoli e Milano. Viaggi di Artisti nell' Italia del Seicento I. Da Tanzio da Varallo a Massimo Stanzione* (Florence: Edifir, 2012), 205–268.

[13] See Riga, *Giovan Battista Manso*, 51.

[14] See Clizia Carminati, *Vita e Morte del Cavalier Marino. Edizione e Commento della Vita di Giovan Battista Baiacca, 1625, e della Relazione della Pompa Funerale Fatta dall' Accademia degli Umoristi di Roma, 1626* (Bologna: Emil di Odoya, 2011), 38–39. Members of the Umoristi composed verse threnodies in Marino's honor.

[15] See Franco Strazzullo, *La Chiesa dei SS. Apostoli a Napoli* (Naples: Arte Tipografica, 1959), 97; Elio and Corrado Catello, *La Cappella del Tesoro di San Gennaro* (Naples: Edizione del Banco di Napoli, 1977), 194.

[16] ASBN, Banco di S. Giacomo, g.m. 108 records (for 3 October 1625): "Al dottor marchese Villa D. 20. E per lui a Cristofaro Coscetto, francese, disse se li pagano in conto di D. 50 per il modello di creta del quondam Cavaliero Marino che li haverà da fare e delli modelli delli due cavalli marini, conforme appare cautela stipolata a 30 Settembre per Notar Loise Ferro de Napoli da farsi de tutta l'opra de quatro e di scoltura per servizio del tumulo del detto quondam cavaliero Marino come in detta cautela si conviene" ("To Dr Marquis of Villa 20 ducats, and, via him, to Cristophe Cochet, Frenchman, for the said payment of the sum of 50 ducats for the clay model of the late Count Marino, which he will have them make, and for the models of the two sea horses, in compliance with the caveat stipulated on 30 September by the Notary Loise Ferro of Naples, that the construction of the entire work of the quarter-stone and of the sculpture should be for the service of a cenotaph of the said late Count Marino as befits the said caveat"). See Gazzara, "Giovan Battista Manso," 56, 67. A later bank record (dated 3 September 1627) reveals that Manso also secured the

by Milton.[17] Several contemporary and later descriptions survive. Thus, Francesco de Pietri, writing in 1634, remarks:

> Ne la Capella dell'Angelo sotto il Palagio del Monte di Manso è il vivo capo di metallo del poeta Gio. Battista Marino Napolitano di rara maestria, opera di Barlolomeo Viscontini Milanese.[18]

> In the Chapel of Angelo, beneath the Palace of Manso's Monte, there is a living metal bust of the Neapolitan poet Gio. Battista Marino, of rare craftsmanship, the work of Bartolomeo Viscontini of Milan.

Giuseppe Battista notes that Manso "l'onorò eziandio d'una statua di bronzo in fino al petto dentro la cappella della sua propria casa" ("even honored him by building a bronze bust within the chapel of his own house").[19] It is described by De Lellis as a "true-to-life" ("al naturale") likeness of Marino, "who, when dying, left the Marquis of Villa as his executor."[20] It was Manso, in turn, who "l'eresse in questa Cappella un magnifico tumulo" ("erected in this chapel a magnificent cenotaph.")[21] Crucially, De Lellis proceeds to transcribe the original inscription:

---

services of Santillo Filosa for a work of art likewise envisaged for his private chapel: "Al Marchese di Villa ducati 14 e per esso a Santillo Filosa in parte di ducati 36 per lo prezzo di un quadro per la capella di S. Angelo sotto le case di lor Monte, quale avrà da essere alto palmi 12 e longo palmi 8 conforme ad disegno fatto da esso Santillo Filosa" ("To the Marquis of Villa 14 ducats and, via him, to Santillo Filosa the sum of 36 ducats for the price of a painting for the chapel of St. Angelo under the houses of their Monte, which should be 12 palms in height and 8 palms in width, conforming to the design made by the same Santillo Filosa") (Banco della Pietà, giorn. 156, f. 153). See Franco Strazzullo, "Documenti Inediti per la Storia dell' Arte a Napoli," *Il Fuidoro* 1 (1954): 143–145, at 145; Gazzara, *Giovan Battista Manso*, 56, 67.

[17] See Haan, "'Coelum non Animum Muto?'" 136–137. Cedric Brown, while not identifying the bust or the chapel, rightly remarks: "Milton was presumably taken to the church—his poem is as it were written in front of that bust." See Brown, *Friendship and Its Discourses*, 86.

[18] Francesco de Pietri, *Dell'Historia Napolitana Libri Due* (Naples: Gio. Domenico Montanaro, 1634), 210.

[19] BUG, MS A.VIII.11, f. 183^v.

[20] De Lellis, *Supplimento a Napoli Sacra*, 78: "Si vede in questa Cappella l'effigie al naturale del Principe della Lirica Italiana poesia, dico del Cavalier Gio: Battista Marino, che morendo lasciò herede il Marchese di Villa" ("In this Chapel you can see the true-to-life effigy of the Prince of Italian Lyric poetry, namely, Count Gio. Battista Marino, who, when dying, left the Marquis of Villa as his executor").

[21] De Lellis, *Supplimento*, 78.

Ioanni Baptistae Marino, Partenopaeo Maroni,
Aequestri Ordine ab Allobrogum Duce,
Senatorio censu à Rege Francorum,
Laurea ab omnium Orbis Terrarum plausu
Insignito, Impertito, Redimito,
Post Illustrem quinque lustrium
Europae lustrationem,
Natales ad lares, quasi ad tumulum reverso,
Ossibus tanto cum phaenore patria restitutis,
Nato CIƆIƆLXVIIII.
Denato CIƆIƆCXXV.
Io: Baptista Manso Villensium Marchio ex testamento
Haeres.
Merenti Vati,
Moerenti voto,
Quisquis ades,
Redde Marino debitum mari tributum,
Flumen lacrimarum.[22]

To Giovanni Battista Marino, the Virgil of Parthenope, of the Order of Knights, conferred upon him by the Duke of Savoy,[23] in accordance with the Senatorial roll decreed by the King of France; to one distinguished, and girt with Laurel in accordance with the applause of the whole World, who, after his illustrious traversal of Europe for five periods of five years, has returned to his native dwelling, as if to a tomb, his bones having been reinstated in his homeland with so great a profit.
Born 1569.
Died 1625.
Giovanni Battista Manso, Marquis of Villa,
His Executor.

---

[22] De Lellis, *Supplimento a Napoli Sacra*, 78. I have altered punctuation, and emended *reverse* to *reverso*, and *Moerenti Vati* to *Merenti Vati*, as in the original source, an epitaph by Francesco De Pietri. See *I Problemi Accademici* (at "Errori della Stampa," s.v. "In finè del Problema XLI. nel Funerale del Cavalier Marino"), where it is described as "il seguente mio Epitafio." This, presumably earlier, version contains several variants, including *Hospes* for *Quisquis ades*. I have also emended *CIƆIƆLXXIII* (1573) to *CIƆIƆLXVIIII* (1569, the established date of Marino's birth). Bartolomeo Chioccarelli describes the monument as "of marble" (*marmoreo tumulo*), and the bust as a "bronze statue" (*Statua ex aere conflata*), and transcribes the inscription (albeit with further inaccuracies). See Bartolomeo Chioccarelli, *De Illustribus Scriptoribus qui in Civitate et Regno Neapolis ab Orbe Condito ad Annum usque MDCXXXXVI Floruerunt* (Naples: V. Orsini, 1780), I: 312–313.

[23] Don Carlo Emanuele I, who awarded Marino a knighthood (the Order of Saints Maurice and Lazarus) in 1609.

> Whoever is present,
> Render onto Marino, a deserving poet,
> in a prayer of grief
> a tribute due to the sea,
> a river of tears.

Likewise, according to Lorenzo Crasso's *Elogio* of Manso, published in 1666: "l'onorò eziandio d'una mezza Statua di rame situata dentro la Capella di sua casa con una bellissima inscrizione" ("he even honored him [Marino] with a bronze Bust located inside the Chapel of his house together with a most beautiful inscription").[24] But, contrary to Crasso's belief that the bust was subsequently lost,[25] a belief echoed by scholars,[26] it emerges that, despite the vicissitudes of time and circumstance, it did in fact survive. Although indeed lost after Manso's death in 1645 and the subsequent demolition of his house and chapel, it was found in 1682, at which date, and in compliance with Manso's will,[27] it was transported to the Monastery of Sant'Agnello Maggiore in Caponapoli.[28] When this Monastery was suppressed, it was transferred in 1813 (upon the order of King Jochim Murat) to the Church of S. Domenico Maggiore, and placed upon a new plinth (with a new inscription) where it can be seen today.[29]

The monument as viewed by Milton, probably in late December 1638 or January 1639, had in fact seen completion only very recently, on a date whose *terminus ante quem* can be determined as 25 November

---

[24] Crasso, *Elogii d'Huomini Letterati*, I: 311.

[25] Crasso, *Elogii d'Huomini Letterati*, I: 311: "e d'amendue, o nascoste ò rotte da mano maligna, s'è fatta perdita" ("the loss has occurred of both, either through concealment or destruction by an evil hand").

[26] See, for example, Celano, *Delle Notitie*, 97; Angelo Borzelli, *Storia della Vita e delle Opere di Giovan Battista Marino* (Naples: Artigianelli, 1927), 196–198.

[27] Manso, in his will (dated 28 November 1638), stating that Marino had appointed him as his executor, assigned 1000 ducats to the Bank of S. Giacomo for the purpose of constructing a sepulcher in Marino's honor. See Manfredi, *Gio. Battista Manso*, 258.

[28] Celano, *Delle Notitie*, I, 278, II, 109. At this point a new plaque, bearing a new inscription, was substituted for the one in Manso's chapel. The plaque bears the date of that year (1682). The inscription (by Tommaso Cornelio) states that the Rectors of Monte di Manso built the monument. In reality, they had done little more than transport and reinstate it. On Tommaso Cornelio (1614–1684), a physician, scientist, philosopher, founder of the Neapolitan Accademia degli Investiganti, and author of several works, most notably, *Progymnasmata Physica* (Venice: Francesco Baba, 1663), see Vittor Ivo Comparato, "Cornelio, Tommaso," *DBI* 29 (1983): 136–140.

[29] See John Murray, *A Handbook for Travellers in Southern Italy* (London: John Murray, 1878), 123.

1638.³⁰ In its final state it comprised a bronze bust of Marino, crowned with a laurel wreath (which eventually became detached, probably in the course of its two subsequent journeys and reinstatement in the Monastery and the Church of San Domenico). Floriana Conte, who has closely inspected the bust now in the Church of San Domenico, remarks that the current cenotaph is very different from the original design: the bust is incomplete, lacking the laurel wreath mentioned in a contract between Manso and Viscontini³¹ (on the left-hand side of the head and on its crown, holes indicate the support points for this missing piece). We are fortunate to know (from extant contracts between Manso and the artists responsible for the finished work)³² other (now lost) sculptural details that Milton would have seen.³³ These included two Sirens of white marble (the work of Giovan Marco Vitale),³⁴ probably, as Conte suggests, turned toward the smiling poet, and perhaps stretching out to him representations of his literary output,³⁵ and two bronze sea horses (the work of Viscontini). These last, as Andrea Bacchi suggests, may have been intended to grace Vitale's two white marble statues.³⁶ Alternatively, as argued by Conte, they may have rested on either side of

---

³⁰ See Conte, *Tra Napoli e Milano*, 221.

³¹ ASMMS, An/15, ff. 16ʳ–17ᵛ, at 16ʳ: "consistente in testa, corona et petto, di bronzo" ("consisting of a bronze head, crown, and chest"). See Conte, *Tra Napoli e Milano*, 412.

³² For a transcription of the relevant contracts, see Conte, *Tra Napoli e Milano*, 411–420 (Appendices 13–19).

³³ For an excellent analysis of the cenotaph's details, see Conte, *Tra Napoli e Milano*, 227–234.

³⁴ See Conte, *Tra Napoli e Milano*, 217–218. On 30 October 1625 Vitale received 40 ducats for "due statue de marmore bianco" ("two statues of white marble") associated with the execution of Marino's monument. See Elio Catello, "Marmi, Bronzi, Argenti et Stucchi," in *Seicento Napoletano*, ed. Pane, 343–362, especially 362. Catello notes a payment on 31 October 1625 to Domenico Agliani of 160 ducats "per tutta l'opra de quarto del tumulo del cavalier Marino che have promesso fare" ("for all the work of the quarter-stone of Count Marino's cenotaph that they promised to do"). See also Andrea Bacchi, "Un Esempio Precoce di *Speaking Likeness* tra Vouet e Bernini: Il *Giovanni Battista Marino* di Cochet in San Domenico a Napoli," *Nuovi Studi: Rivista di Arte Moderna* 14 (2008): 121–125.

³⁵ Conte, *Tra Napoli e Milano*, 228.

³⁶ See Bacchi, "Un Esempio Precoce," 121. These, now lost, sea horses are clearly visible in an engraving of 1697. See Pompeo Sarnelli, *Guida de' Forastieri, Curiosi di Vedere e d'Intendere Le Cose Più Notabili della Regal Città di Napoli, e del suo Amenissimo Distretto* (Naples: Giuseppe Roselli, 1697), 162.

the base of the cenotaph, serving as supports for the entire structure.[37] The sculpted epitaph by Manso, now lost (albeit preserved in De Lellis's rough transcription), was perhaps placed horizontally at the base of the sarcophagus.[38] It is characterized by its abundantly extravagant wordplay: *Marino/Maroni*; *illustrem/lustrium/lustrationem*; *merenti/moerente*; *vati/voto*; *Marino/mari*.[39] The anagrammatic *Maroni* serves to present Marino as a second Virgil,[40] while *Partenopaeo* signals his Neapolitan identity by association with Parthenope, one of the Sirens in Greek mythology, whose body was said to have been washed ashore near Naples, and given a tomb there.[41] It is an adjective that assumes additional force, given the fact that the cenotaph, as viewed by Milton, incorporated two Sirens of white marble.

Some of these aforementioned features seem to recur, in a transmuted form, in the closing lines of *Mansus*. Now, however, they are appropriated to describe *Milton's* envisaged memorial to his deceased self, and the daring apotheosis with which the poem concludes. Thus *Laurea ... Insignito* ("girt ... with Laurel") is reconfigured in *Nectens ... Parnasside lauri/Fronde comas* (92–93) ("binding my hair in ... the leaf of Parnassian laurel"), while *omnium Orbis Terrarum plausu* ("with the applause of the whole World") becomes self-applause: *aethereo plaudam mihi laetus Olympo* (100) ("I will joyfully applaud myself on heavenly Olympus").[42] And might the adverbial *serenum*, qualifying Milton's envisaged act of smiling (*serenum/Ridens* (98–99) ["serenely smiling"]), itself tellingly evocative of the poem's earlier description of Marino in the bust in question (*arridentem ... poetam* [16] ["the smiling poet"]), punningly and even linguistically recreate those now lost Sirens ("Serene" in their Italian form)? In all of this, Milton the *Anglus*, Milton the possible *Angelus*, is aspiring to receive posthumous honors already won by the Italian Marino in St. Angelo a Foro. If so, the whole may develop that potentially punning phrase in Manso's Latin encomium:

---

[37] See Conte, *Tra Napoli e Milano*, 232, and ibid., 232 (Figure 122) for her sketch of the putative monument as a whole.

[38] Conte, *Tra Napoli e Milano*, 227.

[39] With the "Marino"/*mare* pun, cf. De Pietri, *I Problemi Accademici*, sig. b4^r (*Proemio*): *Diceris a Mare* ("You are named after the sea"), and the ensuing verse explication.

[40] For the "Marino"/"Maroni" anagrammatic wordplay, see, for example, the *Poesie di Diversi* appended to Marino's *Della Lira ... Parte Terza*, at 318, 345, 348.

[41] See 5–6.

[42] On Miltonic self-applause, cf. *Prolusio* VI, discussed at 59–60.

Angelus ipse fores.[43] Indeed, Milton's smiling countenance with its associated blushing is in itself quasi-angelic in essence, anticipating, as it does, Raphael in *Paradise Lost*, possessed of "a smile that glowed/ Celestial rosy red."[44] This is reinforced by the gesture of applause (100), evocative, as suggested earlier, of the heavenly hosts of *Elegia Tertia* (59).[45] This, in combination with the potentially punning *serenum* (98), is suggestive of the "angela sirena," an oxymoronic symbol (denoting both salvation and perdition) of a hybrid angel/Siren holding a large crown, evident among some of the earliest engravings associated with Manso's own Accademia degli Oziosi,[46] and possibly the invention of De Pietri himself.[47]

6.2 L'Adone Re-Membered

Mansus also demonstrates a Miltonic alertness to Marino's posthumous literary reputation. It does so in its periphrastic synopsis (11–12) of *L'Adone*, its reception, and some of the features that had come to characterize the Marinesque style. Marino's poem, a luscious recasting of the myth of Venus and Adonis, had seen publication in a sumptuous edition in Paris in 1623, followed by a second edition in Venice in 1626. Marrying a labyrinthine plot with a linguistic inventiveness that assumes

---

[43] Emphasis is mine.

[44] *Paradise Lost* 8. 618–619. On the angelic smile and blush, see 62, and Haan, *From Academia to Amicitia*, 135.

[45] See 63.

[46] See Giovanni Pietro d'Alessandro, *Academiae Ociosorum Libri Tres* (Naples: Giovanni Battista Gargani & Lucrezio Nuccio, 1613), 7, where the hybrid symbol introduces Francesco De Pietri's Latin epigram on the Accademia degli Oziosi. See De Miranda, *Una Quiete Operosa*, 55; De Miranda, "'À de Vagues Desseins L'Homme est Toujours en Proie': L'Accademia degli Oziosi e i Suoi Antagonisti tra Riti Fondativi e Costruzione d'Identità," in *Naples, Rome, Florence: Une Histoire Comparée des Milieux Intellectuels Italiens (XVIIe–XVIIIe Siècles)*, eds. Jean Boutier, Brigitte Marin, Antonella Romano (Rome: École Française de Rome, 2005), 89–104, at 91. See also Lodovico Tesauro's commendatory verses, prefixed to Marino, *La Musica, Diceria Seconda* in *Dicerie Sacre* (Venice: Giacomo Violati, 1615), 100: "Del Mar de le Sirene in sù l'arena/Nacque un' altra Sirena;/E questa il canto hor canta/D'una Sirena santa,/Che le Sirene angeliche confonde" ("Upon the sand of the sea of the Sirens there was born another Siren, and this one sings the song of a holy Siren which confounds the angelic Sirens").

[47] See De Miranda, *Una Quiete Operosa*, 55. The invention may have been prompted by Plato's allocation of a Siren to each of the celestial spheres in the myth of Er. See Plato, *Republic* 10. 616–617.

a variety of captivating forms, the work exudes a baroque extravagance, signaled by glittering description, artifice, repetition, paronomasia, and etymological play,[48] and by a narrative technique that is, in the words of Carlo Caruso, "dominated by surprising and unexpected turns of events."[49] Characterized by the self-conscious manipulation of words as sounds,[50] and by an interest in, and emphasis upon, sensuality,[51] Marino's linguistic methodology, as Maria Loh observes, "draws attention to form, to the language itself, rather than the content or subject matter."[52] The whole elicited from its contemporary readers what can only be described as something of a shock reaction.[53] This was provoked by its imaginative recourse to the technique of "meraviglia"/"wonder"/"the marvelous,"[54] or, as Giuseppe Mazzotta puts it:

> an esthetic effect produced by the poet's eloquence: it is a technique of shocking the audience with the deployment of unexpected and extraordinary devices.[55]

Likewise, in the words of Paolo Cherchi, "meraviglia" denotes "that shocking sense of wonderment, of surprising dazzle we experience in

---

[48] See, among others, Enrico Canevari, *Lo Stile del Marino nell' Adone* (Pavia: Giuseppe Frattini, 1901); Francesco Croce, "Nuovi Compiti della Critica del Marino e del Marinismo," *La Rassegna della Letteratura Italiana* 61 (1957): 459–473; Mirollo, *Poet of the Marvelous*, 115–120; Francesco Guardiani, *La Meravigliosa Retorica dell' 'Adone' di G.B. Marino* (Florence: Olschki, 1989).

[49] Carlo Caruso, *Adonis: The Myth of the Dying God in the Italian Renaissance* (London: Bloomsbury, 2013), 57.

[50] See Mirollo, *Poet of the Marvelous*, 139.

[51] See Elizabeth Cropper, "The Petrifying Art: Marino's Poetry and Caravaggio," *Metropolitan Museum Journal* 26 (1991): 193–212.

[52] See Maria H. Loh, *Titian Remade: Repetition and The Transformation of Early Modern Italian Art* (Los Angeles: Getty Research Institute, 2007), 136.

[53] The poem, as Loh observes, "predictably shocked less-sophisticated readers with its antilinear plot, incessant digression and repetition, indulgent language play, outrageous eroticism, and undisguised pastiches." See Loh, *Titian Remade*, 135.

[54] On "meraviglia," see, among others, Antonio Franceschetti, "Il Concetto di *Meraviglia* nelle Poetiche della Prima Arcadia," *LI* 21 (1969): 62–88; Susanna N. Peters, "'Metaphor and Meraviglia': Tradition and Innovation in the *Adone* of G. B. Marino," *Lingua e Stile* 7 (1972): 321–341; Paolo Cherchi, "Marino and the Meraviglia," in *Culture and Authority in the Baroque*, eds. Ciavolella and Coleman, 63–72. See also Mirollo, *Poet of the Marvelous*, 166–174.

[55] Giuseppe Mazzotta, *The New Map of the World: The Poetic Philosophy of Giambattista Vico* (Princeton, NJ: Princeton University Press, 1999), 109.

front of a number of creations and techniques that stress the unusual, the irregular, the bizarre, and the witty."[56]

Despite Marino's attested belief that "the marvelous was the poet's very purpose" ("E del poeta il fin la meraviglia"),[57] a viewpoint that finds precedent in a whole series of defenders of its creative potential,[58] his exuberant style was regarded by some of his contemporaries as leading to confusion and ambiguity. Even as far back as 1614, Lodovico Tesauro had found it necessary to publish a defense of Marino's style.[59] But it was the appearance of *L'Adone* in 1623 that generated a particularly heated debate. Shortly after Marino's death in 1625, Tommaso Stigliani[60] penned a vitriolically pedantic account of the poem's purported literary and linguistic shortcomings. This saw publication in Venice in 1627 as *Dello Occhiale*.[61] Among Stigliani's criticisms were the poem's length, and its verbal superfluity ("troppo più copia di parole"),[62] a linguistic excess, which, in his view, denoted an "asiatic style" ("stile ... asiatico"), marked by "an extremely redundant loquacity" ("ridontantissima

---

[56] Cherchi, "Marino and the Meraviglia," 63.

[57] Marino, Fischiata XXXIII, in *La Murtoleide Fischiate* (Venice: Joseph Stamphier, 1619), 35. See G. G. Ferrero, ed., *Marino e i Marinisti* (Milan: Ricciardi, 1954), 627; Emanuele Tesauro, "Metafora Settima di Oppositione," in *Il Cannocchiale Aristotelico, o Sia Idèa dell'Arguta et Ingegnosa Elocutione* (Bologna: Gioseffo Longhi, 1675), 294–305. For various interpretations of Marino's line, see Guido Pedrojetta, "Marino e La Meraviglia," in *Interpretazione e Meraviglia*, ed. Giuseppe Galli (Pisa: Giardini, 1994), 95–105; Alessandro Martini, "La Practica Mariniana," in ibid., 107–119.

[58] See Jacopo Mazzoni, *Della Difesa della Commedia del Divino Poeta Dante* (Bologna: Alessandro Benacci, 1572); Francesco Robortello, *In Librum Aristotelis De Arte Poetica Explicationes* (Florence: L. Torrentinus, 1548); Francesco Patrizi, *La Deca Ammirabili* (Ferrara: Vittorio Baldini, 1587). See, in general, Baxter Hathaway, *Marvels and Commonplaces: Renaissance Literary Criticism* (New York: Random House, 1968).

[59] *Ragioni del Conte Lodovico Tesauro in Difesa d'Un Sonetto del Cavalier Marino* (Bologna: Vittorio Benacci, 1614). For Tesauro's praise of Marino, see also 184.

[60] On Stigliani, see Mario Menghini, *Tommaso Stigliani: Contributo alla Storia Letteraria del Secolo XVII* (Modena: E. Sarasino, 1892); Ottavio Besomi, "Tommaso Stigliani: Tra Parodia e Critica," *SS* 13 (1972): 5–73.

[61] Tommaso Stigliani, *Dello Occhiale Opera Difensiva Del Cavalier Fr. Tomaso Stigliani. Scritta in Risposta al Cavalier Gio. Battista Marini* (Venice: Pietro Carampello, 1627). On Stigliani's criticism of Marino's linguistic exuberance, see Franco Croce, *Tre Momenti del Barocco Letterario Italiano* (Florence: Sansoni, 1966), 104–108. On his rivalry with Marino in general, see Emilio Russo, *Studi su Tasso e Marino* (Rome and Padua: Antenore, 2005), chapters 3–5.

[62] *Dello Occhiale*, 73.

loquacità") that he regarded as intolerable.⁶³ Nonetheless, Marino did not lack his posthumous supporters. Vigorous defenses of the poem and of the Marinesque style were swift to appear, themselves generating a literary and linguistic debate on *L'Adone* in particular and on seicento poetics in general.⁶⁴ Thus 1629 saw the publication of the *Occhiale Appannato* by the Oziosi academician Scipione Errico,⁶⁵ and the *Difesa dell'Adone* by the Umoristi academician Girolamo Aleandro, Jr.⁶⁶ These were followed in 1630 by the *L'Uccellatura* of Nicola Villani (published under the pseudonym Vincenzo Foresi).⁶⁷ Aleandro, in what was, in effect, the official response of the Marinisti (his *Difesa* having been

---

⁶³ *Dello Occhiale*, 92. It is worth remarking that Milton, speaking (on 26 March 1627) of the style of his own neo-Latin prose, had, in fact, lauded the liberating potential afforded him by the "asiatic style" of oratory, contrasting its essential floridity with the more simple Attic style. See Milton, *Epistola Familiaris* 1 (to Thomas Young): *oratione libera, immo potius si fieri posset, Asiatica verborum exuberantia* ("in a free oration, or rather, if it were possible, in an Asiatic abundance of words") in *John Milton: Epistolarum Familiarium Liber Unus and Uncollected Letters*, ed. Haan, 38–48, at 40–41, 45.

⁶⁴ For useful discussion of the debate, see, among others, Franco Croce, "Giambattista Marino," in *I Classici Italiani nella Storia della Critica*, ed. Walter Binni, 2 vols. (Florence: La Nuova Italia, 1955), II. 47–90; Franco Croce, *Tre Momenti*, 108–109, 115–128; Susanna N. Peters, "The Quarrel of the 'Adone': A Chapter in the History of Seventeenth-Century Italian Poetic Theory" (PhD thesis: Johns Hopkins University, 1968); Pierantonio Frare, "La 'Nuova Critica' della Meravigliosa Acutezza," in *Storia della Critica Letteraria in Italia*, ed. Giorgio Baroni (Turin: UTET, 1997), 223–277, at 242–247; Sanam Nader-Esfahani, "Knowledge and Representation Through Baroque Eyes: Literature and Optics in France and Italy ca. 1600–1640" (PhD thesis: Harvard University, 2016), 136–175.

⁶⁵ Scipione Errico, *L'Occhiale Appannato. Dialogo ... nel Quale Si Difende L'Adone del Cavalier Gio. Battista Marino, Contra L'Occhiale del Cavalier Tomaso Stigliani* (Naples: Giuseppe Matarozzi, 1629). On Errico, see Rosario Contarino, "Errico, Scipione," *DBI* 43 (1993): 261–265; *Scipione Errico: Le Guerre di Parnaso*, ed. Gino Rizzo (Lecce: Argo, 2004), xi–lvi. See also Riga, *Giovan Battista Manso*, 59.

⁶⁶ Girolamo Aleandro, *Difesa dell' Adone Poema del Cav. Marini* (Venice: Giacomo Scaglia, 1629). On Girolamo Aleandro, Jr. (1574–1629), a prominent member of the Roman Accademia degli Umoristi (where his academic name was "Aggirato"), and secretary to Cardinals Ottavio Bandini and Francesco Barberini, see Alberto Asor Rosa, "Aleandro, Girolamo, il Giovane," *DBI* 2 (1960): 135–136.

⁶⁷ Nicola Villani, *L'Uccellatura di Vincenzo Foresi all' Occhiale del Cavaliere Fra. Tomaso Stigliani contro l'Adone del Cavalier Gio. Battista Marini, e alla Difesa di Girolamo Aleandro* (Venice: Antonio Pinelli, 1630). Over a decade later Angelico Aprosio would publish his *L'Occhiale Stritolato di Scipio Glareano, per Riposta al Signor Cavalier Tommaso Stigliani*, in *Il Burrato: Replica di Carlo Galistoni al Molino del Signor Carlo Stigliani* (Venice: Taddeo Pavoni, 1642), 157–214.

commissioned by the Lincean academician Claudio Achillini),[68] openly censures Stigliani as "il quale havendo crudelmente lacerato il Poema del Marini" ("one who has cruelly torn to shreds the Poem of Marino").[69] And he does so with forensic scrutiny, carefully responding to each of Stigliani's charges in a methodology aptly described by Elizabeth Cropper as "Aristotelian."[70] Thus, for example, in response to Stigliani's criticism of *L'Adone*'s lack of linguistic purity and its consequential "barbarism" ("barbarismo")[71] Aleandro rises to Marino's defense, countering the charge by drawing attention to the diversity of Greek dialects evident in Homeric epic.[72]

That Milton was probably aware of the controversy sparked by *L'Adone*, and, indeed, of the intricate complexities attendant upon the Stigliani/Aleandro row is suggested in a number of ways. His alertness to literary and linguistic debates while upon Italian soil, conspicuously evident in his Latin writings pertaining to that period,[73] can only have been enhanced by conversations with Italian academicians, Manso included. Indeed, the Neapolitan seems to have played a minor role of his own in the aforementioned row, displaying his loyalty to the literary Marino by opposing and attempting to suppress Stigliani's various attacks. Thus, when Stigliani, in his *Il Mondo Nuovo*, lampooned Marino as a "pescihuom" ("fish-man"), roaming the seas, and rapaciously preying upon and imitating everything that he encountered,[74] Manso, according to Stigliani's own testimony, bought up and burned more than 300 copies of the work![75] Furthermore, as Giuseppe Battista relates, it was Manso who had eventually vetoed Stigliani's endeavors to secure

---

[68] See Nader-Esfahani, *Knowledge and Representation*, 141.

[69] *Difesa dell' Adone*, 2.

[70] See Elizabeth Cropper, *The Domenichino Affair: Novelty, Imitation, and Theft in Seventeenth-Century Rome* (New Haven CT: Yale University Press, 2005), 167.

[71] *Dello Occhiale*, 75–77.

[72] *Difesa dell' Adone*, 55–56.

[73] See 29–34, 76–77.

[74] Tommaso Stigliani, *Il Mondo Nuovo* (Piacenza: Alessandro Bazacchi, 1617), 480–481 (XVI: 34–35). Marino made sure to retaliate in verses that may not be unrelated to *Mansus* itself. See 205.

[75] Stigliani made the claim in a letter (dated 15 September 1630) to Domenico Molin. See Stigliani, *Lettere* (Rome: Angelo Bernabo, 1664), 163–174, at 172: "Marchese Manso in Napoli … hà comperi in più tempi più di trecento Mondi Nuovi, e bruciatigli" ("The Marquis Manso … has on more than one occasion bought more than three hundred *New Worlds*, and burned them").

membership of the Oziosi.⁷⁶ There are reasons too why Milton may have been drawn to Aleandro's *Difesa*, not least because the neo-Latin writings of this Italian humanist had already attracted his attention over a decade earlier. This is attested by a series of striking verbal and thematic echoes of Aleandro's Latin *epicedium* on the Neapolitan humanist and mentor of Galileo, Giovanni Vincenzo Pinelli (*In Obitum Io. Vincentii Pinelli*)⁷⁷ in Milton's *In Obitum Praesulis Eliensis*, lamenting the death (on 5 October 1626) of Nicolas Felton, Bishop of Ely.⁷⁸

Mansus, according to Mirollo, "praises Marino lavishly."⁷⁹ Closer inspection, however, suggests a critique that is rather more calibrated, measured, and even somewhat qualified:

---

⁷⁶ See Giuseppe Battista's letter (dated 29 January 1652) to Angelico Aprosio, in Gino Rizzo, "Lettere di Giuseppe Battista al Padre Angelico Aprosio," *SS* 38 (1997): 267–318, at 287: "Questi volendo onorarlo per dimostrargli segno di cortesia, avea determinato di riceverlo nella nostra Accademia degli Oziosi, e comunicandomi cotal sua determinazione, gli risposi che io non giudicava cosa convenevole onorare chi con pubbliche scritture avea strapazzato a tortor il Cavalier Marino, Principe della nostra Accademia. Il perché piacendo il mio senso al mentovato Signore, mutò egli parere e rimase lo Stigliani escluso" ("The latter [Manso], wishing to honor him by showing him a sign of courtesy, had determined to receive him into our Accademia degli Oziosi, and when he communicated his resolve to me, I replied that I did not think it appropriate to honor those, who with public writings had torn to shreds the Count Marino, Prince of our Academy. He, because he agreed with my viewpoint concerning the aforementioned gentleman, changed his opinion, and Stigliani remained excluded"). See also Riga, *Giovan Battista Manso*, 63.

⁷⁷ Aleandro's poem had seen print in Paolo Gualdo, *Vita Ioannis Vincentii Pinelli, Patricii Genuensis* (Augsburg: Markus Welser, 1607), 125–126 (where it is followed by a further *epicedium* by a certain Henricus Bantheus Anglus [127–128]). It was subsequently included among Aleandro's Latin poems published, with those of Girolamo, Giambattista, and Cornelio Amalteo, his maternal grandfather and uncles, at Venice in 1627. See *Trium Fratrum Amaltheorum Hieronimi, Io. Baptistae, Cornelii Carmina: Accessere Hieronymi Aleandri Iunioris Amaltheorum Cognati Poematia* (Venice: Andrea Muschio, 1627), at 241–243. Giovanni Vincenzo Pinelli (1535–1601) was a Neapolitan humanist, botanist, collector of scientific instruments, and a bibliophile in possession of a huge library.

⁷⁸ See Milton, *In Obitum Praesulis Eliensis*, at *Poemata*, 56–58; Lewalski and Haan, 180–185. Both *epicedia*, for example, contain a simile, in which the soul's release from the body is compared to the assumption of Elijah into Heaven, with the occurrence of the identical phrase *vates ut olim* at the beginning of a line and at exactly the same point (line 49) in each poem. For further discussion of this, and of further points of contact between the two poems, see Estelle Haan, "Milton and Two Italian Humanists: Some Hitherto Unnoticed Neo-Latin Echoes in *In Obitum Procancellarii Medici* and *In Obitum Praesulis Eliensis*," *N&Q* 44 (1997): 176–181, at 179–181.

⁷⁹ Mirollo, *Poet of the Marvelous*, 10.

> Mox tibi dulciloquum non inscia Musa Marinum
> Tradidit: ille tuum dici se gaudet alumnum,
> Dum canit Assyrios divum prolixus amores,
> Mollis et Ausonias stupefecit carmine nymphas
> *(Mansus* 9–12)

> Next, the Muse, not without knowledge, entrusted to you the sweetly-speaking Marino; he rejoiced in being called your foster-child as he proclaimed in verbose song the Assyrian love-affairs of the gods, and stunned the Ausonian nymphs with the smoothness of his strains.

Milton's albeit brief description of Marino's style and of the effect of *L'Adone* upon its readers serves to summarize, encapsulate, perhaps even to weigh up both sides of the familiar argument. This is evinced by prudent choice of adjectives (*dulciloquus* [9] *prolixus* [11], *mollis* [12]) and verb (*stupefecit* [12]). *Dulciloquus* ("sweetly-speaking") merits comparison with the posthumous praise, which, according to Flavio Fieschi, was lavished upon Marino by the Accademia degli Umoristi. Thus the "sweetness of his song" ("dolcezza del canto") renders Marino "a new Orpheus," one who is in turn aligned with the academy's own *impresa* (a cloud raining upon the earth) and associated motto: *redit agmine dulci*.[80] Initially, then, Milton seems to situate himself in the anti-Stiglianesque camp, so to speak, alongside those supporters who lauded his linguistically dulcet style. On the other hand, his choice of the adjective *prolixus*[81] is certainly not without a potentially pejorative undertone. As such, it is describable as quasi-Stiglianesque in essence, evoking perhaps that charge of "loquacità" leveled against a work, whose

---

[80] See Flavio Fieschi, "All' Illustrissimo e Reverendissimo Signor D. Girolamo Colonna," in *Relazione della Pompa Funerale*, appended to Carminati, *Vita e Morte del Cavalier Marino*, 137–155, at 138: "il quale con la dolcezza del canto, a guisa di novo Orfeo, non le fere, ma gli animi allettò de i maggiori principi del mondo ... Era similmente la catedra vestita e bruno, e sopra quella la nuvola, impresa generale dell'Accademia, che il salso umore avendo dalle marine onde succhiato, dolce e soave il rende" ("he who with the sweetness of song, like a modern Orpheus, enticed not the wild beasts, but the minds of the greatest Princes of the world ... Likewise, the *cathedra* was draped in brown, and above this there was a cloud, the general emblem of the Academy, which having absorbed the salty water from the waves of the sea, renders it sweet and pleasant"). For discussion of the *impresa* and motto of the Accademia degli Umoristi, and their possible evocation in Milton's *Ad Salsillum*, see Haan, *John Milton's Roman Sojourns*, 75–84. See also 33.

[81] Cf. *OLD*, s.v. *prolixus*, 1d: "(of writings) lengthy, copious."

extreme length (20 cantos, comprising almost 41,000 verses), style, digressions, and generic mix render it, in the words of Mirollo, "more like a luxuriant growth than a poem,"[82] the whole "resembling," as Carlo Caruso puts it, "a disproportionate, gigantic epyllion."[83] Milton's very generalized summation of the poem's subject matter as "the Assyrian love-affairs of the gods" (*Assyrios divum ... amores* [11])[84] could (through that genitive plural *divum*) easily take its place alongside Stigliani's censure of what he believed to be the poem's superfluity of deities (citing Adonis, Venus, Mars, Vulcan, Falsirena, among others), and their assumption of roles very distinct from those enacted by their classical counterparts.[85] This, in his view, was one of the reasons why the work "is not a single poetic entity, but a concatenation of poems" ("non è un solo poema, ma un groppo di poemi ammassati insieme").[86] Milton, in short, seems to be offering a balanced critique. Moreover, the two seemingly polar opposites (*dulciloquus/prolixus*) are qualified and even reconciled by a further adjective: *mollis*. In its sense "(of speech, verse, rhet. style, etc.) free from harshness, smooth,"[87] this adjective can be read as an acknowledgment of what Frank Warnke has termed the "auditory smoothness" of Marino's Italian verse,[88] or, as Mirollo puts it, "his *versi molli* manner."[89] Alternatively, in its sense of "effeminate in appearance or behaviour, womanish,"[90] and especially when viewed in the context of a poet stupefying with his verse (*stupefecit carmine* [12])[91] an Italian

---

[82] Mirollo, *Poet of the Marvelous*, 72.

[83] Caruso, *Adonis: The Myth of the Dying God*, 49.

[84] As noted by Bush, *Variorum*, I: 271: "Adonis, whose Babylonian prototype was Tammuz or Thammuz, was the son ... of Myrrha and her father Cinyras, king of Cyprus," while "Venus was identified with the Semitic Astarte or Ashtoreth."

[85] *Dello Occhiale*, 19–20.

[86] *Dello Occhiale*, 20. For Aleandro's refutation of the charge (again by recourse to Homeric precedent), see *Difesa dell' Adone*, 6.

[87] *OLD*, s.v. 8b. Cf. Ovid, *Epistulae ex Ponto* 1.5.14: *sed non fit fato mollior ille* [sc. *versus*] *meo*; Velleius Paterculus 1.7.1: *mollissima dulcedine carminum*; Persius, *Satires* 1.63: *carmina molli ... numero fluere*.

[88] Frank J. Warnke, "Marino and the English Metaphysicals," *SR* 2 (1955): 160–175, at 174.

[89] Mirollo, *Poet of the Marvelous*, 198–199.

[90] *OLD*, s.v. 15. Cf. Cicero, *De Oratore* 3.41: *Mollis vox aut muliebris*.

[91] Cf. *OLD*, s.v. *stupefacio*: "To stun (a person or his senses) with amazement, fear, etc., daze stupefy." On the "stupefying" potential of poetry over its female audience, cf. Propertius, *Elegiae* 2.13.7: *sed magis ut nostro stupefiat Cynthia versu* ("so that Cynthia may be all the more stupefied by my verse").

audience depicted herein as female (*Ausonias ... nymphas* [12]),[92] it contrasts sharply with Aleandro's account of *L'Adone*'s effect upon an essentially male readership. In his view, those poetic features criticized by Stigliani serve rather to "sweetly intoxicate with wonder the heart of every noble gentleman" ("il cuore d'ogni galant huomo di nobil maraviglia dolcemente inebriano").[93] Cedric Brown, commenting on Milton's lines, astutely wonders whether the description is "a bit mischievous," remarking that "[i]t is not clear that Marino's style was to Milton's own taste, always figured as masculine."[94] But perhaps it is not simply a matter of taste. Milton's association of a *mollis poeta* with a stupefied female audience can fruitfully be read in relation to the meaning and connotations of "effeminate" in the seventeenth century. As Roger Freitas observes:

> Whereas today describing a man as effeminate might imply homosexual leanings, the same term in the seventeenth century connotated too great a taste for *women*. ... Thus, a man who succumbed too much to the pleasures of the flesh, whose existence revolved too much around women, was considered in danger of losing his masculine nature and even physical strength. By the same principle, a man who presented a rather feminine demeanor—like the boy or castrato—was considered predisposed to becoming ensnared in the womanish pursuits of love.[95]

Indeed, Marino's description of Adone himself (his long golden hair, clear white skin, blushing cheeks, bright eyes, ivory neck),[96] while seemingly denoting a paragon of male beauty, is equally applicable to a woman.[97] The whole assumes additional force when considered in the context of seicento charges leveled against *L'Adone*. After all, Stigliani was far from reticent in his scathing remark concerning the deities of the

---

[92] As noted by Bush, *Variorum*, I: 56, "Ausonia was a common poetical name for Italy derived from the Ausones, the primitive inhabitants of the middle and lower part of the country (Virgil, *G*. 2.385: *Ausonii, Troia gens missa*)."

[93] *Difesa dell' Adone*, 32–33.

[94] Brown, *Friendship and its Discourses*, 85.

[95] Roger Freitas, "An Erotic Image of the Castrato Singer," in *Italy's Eighteenth Century: Gender and Culture in the Age of the Grand Tour*, eds. Paula Findlen, Wendy Wassyng Roworth, and Catherine M. Sama (Stanford, CA: Stanford University Press, 2009), 203–215, at 205.

[96] See *L'Adone*, I.41–43.

[97] See Freitas, "An Erotic Image," 206.

poem as "tutte lascive, tutte innamorate, e tutte *effemminate*" ("all lascivious, all in love, and all effeminate").[98]

Stigliani had included among the prerequisites of any story line the condition that it should be marvelous in itself and generate "meraviglia" in the minds of its listeners. This it could achieve by virtue of the occurrence of "the unexpected, the new, and the diverse" ("inaspettate, nuove e diverse").[99] Hand in hand with the marvelous was "the augmentation of passions but, especially, of delight" ("accrescitiva delle passioni, ma spezialmente del diletto."[100] *L'Adone*, he believed, failed in all these respects, largely on account of its "vulgarità," its mundanity ("cose mondane"), and its plagiarism "furto."[101] Over a decade later (in a letter of 4 March 1636) he complained about the quasi-Marinesque expectations of contemporary readers, forever vacillating between a desire for excellence, then a longing for wonders ("maraviglie"), "stupefactions" ("stupori"), and, finally, a quest for astonishment:

> Un tempo i lettori si contentarono d'una lettura non cattiva. Poi volsero eccellenza. Appresso disiderarono maraviglie. Ed oggi cercano stupori, ma dopo avergli trovati gli anno anco in fastidio, ed aspirano a trasecolamenti, ed a strabiliazioni.[102]

> At one time, readers were content with a reading that was not bad. Then they inclined toward excellence. Next, they yearned for wonders. And today they are looking for stupefactions, but after having found them, they are still annoyed, and aspire to bewilderment and astonishment.

The sense of "stupore" and of "meraviglia" aroused by Marino in his contemporary readership is aptly encapsulated in Milton's *stupefecit* (12). And perhaps not without a passing jibe at Stigliani, who, criticizing Marino's failure to state causation, had denounced as an illogical conceit the depiction (in *L'Adone* II. 87) of the stupefaction of "Stupor" itself at the sight of beauty:

---

[98] *Dello Occhiale*, 68.

[99] *Dello Occhiale*, 47.

[100] *Dello Occhiale*, 48.

[101] *Dello Occhiale*, 48–50.

[102] Stigliani, *Lettere*, 116–128, at 124.

> Non rende ragione, come verbigrazia avendo detto, che lo Stupore istesso stupiva d'una certa gran bellezza (il che non è maraviglia essendo questo il suo proprio ufficio) non soggiunge la causa.[103]
>
> He does not give a reason, such as when, for example, having said that Stupor itself was stupefied by a certain great beauty (which is not a marvel in that this is its proper function), he fails to supply the cause.

To this Aleandro presented the counter challenge that Stigliani had misunderstood the nuances of the conceit, whereby a personified "Stupor," now overcome by its own stupefying essence, is, in fact, moving far beyond its usual "ufficio" ("function").[104] In *Mansus*, and by a transfer of agency, the power of stupefying resoundingly pertains to Marino, to his poem, and, ultimately, to Marinism itself.

6.3 Marino and Two Italian Academies

But if *stupefecit carmine* (12) conveys the effect of Marino's poetry upon his readership, so too does it anticipate the later description in *Mansus* (59–69) of the stupefying power of Apollo's *carmen* in the course of his withdrawal to Chiron's cave. The passage is worth revisiting, especially in regard to its allegorical potential. As suggested earlier, the whole may subtly allude to a Miltonic performance before the Oziosi.[105] It is not impossible, however, that it also allegorizes the reception frequently afforded Marino by Manso in his home, and, by association, his participation in that same academy. That both interpretations are not mutually exclusive is enhanced, I would argue, by the essential polyvocalism of the lines. Noteworthy in this regard is the Ovidian language in which Marino as protegeé of Manso was earlier cast: *ille tuum dici se gaudet alumnum* (10) ("he rejoiced in being called your foster-child"),[106] evoking, as it does, Ovid's account in *Metamorphoses* 2 of the care afforded the youthful Asclepius by none other than Chiron himself (*semifer interea divinae stirpis alumno/laetus erat mixtoque oneri gaudebat honore* [*Metamorphoses* 2.633–634] ["meanwhile the centaur was rejoicing in his foster-child of heavenly stock, glad at the combined sense of responsibility and honor"]). Significantly, however,

---

[103] *Dello Occhiale*, 99.

[104] *Difesa dell Adone*, 84–85.

[105] See 89–92.

[106] Cf. *OLD*, s.v. *alumnus*, 3: "A ward, protégé, 'charge'."

Milton has transferred the emotion of associated joy from tutor to tutee.[107] It is a joy that is independently attested. Prefixed to Manso's *Erocallia* is a "Lettera dal Cavalier Gio. Battista Marino All'Autore" (dated 16 March 1625), in which Marino effusively describes the intellectual experiences that Manso's wisdom and learning afforded him "sotto l'ombra della sua casa" ("beneath the shade of his home").[108] He proceeds to recount the essential "protettione" that Manso provided for him in the course of his recovery from great misfortunes, and expresses gratitude for his assistance in his studies right from his youth up to these, his final years.[109] Certainly Manso afforded Marino refuge at a time of vicious opposition to his literary output, acting as one of the poet's hosts upon his return to Naples in 1624. More formally, the allegory may embrace Marino's own role as "principe" of the Accademia degli Oziosi (a prestigious honor, conferred upon him in 1624), and his associated academic performances. Milton may also be drawing upon anecdotal evidence to this effect from both Manso himself and from his still unpublished manuscript *Vita di Giambattista Marino*, of which he was interestingly aware.[110]

Of particular note is the envisaged soothing (*mulcenturque* [69]) of *maculosi ... lynces* (69) ("spotted lynxes") by the novelty of Apollo's song (*novo ... carmine* [69]). Although the effects of the Orphic power of music are quite conventional, its taming of spotted lynxes is, by comparison, less common. Milton's line may owe some debt to Euripides, *Alcestis* 570ff., where lynxes are charmed by Apollo's lyre, while he is shepherding the flocks of Admetus. More precise, its phraseology conflates two Virgilian intertexts: *stupefactae carmine lynces* (*Eclogue* 8.3) ("lynxes stunned by music"), and *maculosae tegmine lyncis* (*Aeneid* 1.323) ("the spotted skin of the lynx").[111] Robert Coleman, commenting on the first Virgilian reference, aptly observes that lynxes "do not belong to the Italian or Sicilian countryside."[112] Milton's lynxes, by contrast, may well pertain to a contemporary Italian world, a subtle nod, perhaps, to an exclusively scientific academic community, now envisaged as captivated and won over by the "novelty" ("novità") of Marino's poetry (*novo ... carmine* [69]).

---

[107] For further discussion, see Haan, *From Academia to Amicitia*, 150–152.

[108] *Erocallia*, sig. b1^r.

[109] *Erocallia*, sig. b1^r.

[110] See 122–124.

[111] Cf. Bush, *Variorum*, I: 277.

[112] *Vergil: Eclogues*, ed. Coleman, 227.

The year 1603 had seen the foundation, by Federico Cesi, of the Roman Accademia Nazionale dei Lincei.[113] Famed for its relentless devotion to scientific, mathematic, and physical research, it could boast of Galileo among its membership. Indeed, it was largely through the efforts of Stigliani (with the assistance of several other Lincei academicians) that Galileo's *Saggiatore* had been seen through the press in Rome in 1623.[114] The choice of "lynx" as the academy's name was intended to encapsulate the scrutiny which its members applied to scientific matters. After all, the lynx, according to Pliny, possessed the keenest sight of all quadrupeds.[115] Thus, as Francesco Stelluti observed:

> questo Signore ... per esser la Lince impresa della nostra Accademia, havendo questa eletta, acciò ne sia uno stimulo, e sprone continuo di ricordarci dell' acutezza della vista, non de gli occhi corporali, ma della mente, necessaria per le naturali contemplazioni, che professiamo; e tanto più dovendosi in queste procurare di penetrar l'interno delle cose, per conoscere le loro cause, & operazioni della natura, ch'interiormente lavora, come con bella similitudine dicesi che la Lince faccia col suo sguardo, vedendo non solo quel ch'è di fuori; ma anche ciò che dentro s'asconde.[116]
>
> This Gentleman [Cesi] ... chose the Lynx as the emblem of our Academy so that it might be a stimulus and a continuous spur to remind us of the acuteness of vision, not of corporeal eyes, but of those of the mind, necessary for the contemplation of nature that we profess; and it being all the more necessary in those matters to

---

[113] See Maylender, *Storia*, II, 430–503.

[114] Stigliani, however, had precociously altered the Galilean text by inserting his own name among poets who included scientific speculation in their writings. Thus, he had embellished Galileo's citation of the example of Dante ("come tra i nostri antichi fece Dante nella sua *Commedia*") to read "come tra i nostri antichi fece Dante nella sua *Commedia*, e come tra' moderni ha fatto il Cavalier Stigliani nel suo *Mondo Nuovo*." See Cropper, *The Domenichino Affair*, 167.

[115] Pliny, *Naturalis Historia* 28.122.

[116] Francesco Stelluti, *Persio Tradotto in Verso Sciolto* (Rome: Giacomo Mascardi, 1630), 37. See also Paolo Galluzzi, *The Lynx and the Telescope: The Parallel Worlds of Cesi and Galileo*, trans. Peter Mason (Leiden: Brill, 2017), 33. On the suitability of the academy's nomenclature, cf. Masson *Life*, I, 715: "In calling themselves 'the Lynxes,' the mathematicians and physical philosophers of Italy had selected a happy symbol. It was as if they proclaimed that it was in *their* constitution still to see when it might be dark to others, and that *their* occupation of penetrating the recesses of nature, seizing facts that eluded the common search, and holding them as if in permanent excruciation within the fangs of their definite relations of magnitude, weight, and number, might be carried on when poets were asleep, metaphysicians jaded, painters poor and meretricious, and orators without employment."

> penetrate the interior nature of things, in order to know their cause and the operations of nature, which works internally, since, in the words of the beautiful simile, the lynx acts with its glance, seeing not only what is outside, but also what lies hidden within.

According to the *Gesta Lyncaeorum*, the name of the academy was derived from "the animal endowed with the keenest of sight" (*animalium omnium oculatissimus*),[117] and also contained resonances of the Lycaeum, a Platonic academy.[118] As such, its nomenclature was one by which, in the words of Paolo Galluzzi, "the spirit that animated its founders" was "perfectly expressed."[119] While precedent can be found in Della Porta's choice of the lynx as the emblem of his *Magiae Naturalis* (Naples, 1589),[120] its adoption by the Lincei was undoubtedly inspired by the myth of Lynceus, an Argonaut famed for his keen-sightedness.[121] Crucially, however, that keen-sightedness was expanded quite specifically by the Lincei to epitomize microscopic scrutiny.[122]

Milton's choice of the adjective *maculosus* (69) to describe the lynxes, itself denoting "(of animals, etc.) Variegated, spotted, or striped,"[123] may assume additional significance when examined in the

---

[117] *Gesta Lyncaeorum* in Biblioteca dell'Accademia dei Lincei e Corsiniana, Rome: Archivio Linceo 3, f. 3ʳ.

[118] *Gesta Lyncaeorum*, f. 6ʳ.

[119] Galluzzi, *The Lynx and the Telescope*, 31.

[120] Giambattista Della Porta, *Magiae Naturalis Libri Viginti* (Naples: Horatius Salvianus, 1589). See William Eamon, "Medicine as a Hunt: Searching for Secrets of the New World," in *Renaissance Futurities: Science, Art, Invention*, eds. Charlene Villaseñor Black and Mari-Tere Álvarez (Oakland: University of California Press, 2020), 100–117, at 103.

[121] Cf. Horace, *Satires* 1.2.90–91; Seneca, *De Beneficiis* 4.27.3. See also the associated Latin adjective *lynceus* ("resembling Lynceus [in keenness of sight])" (*OLD*). Cf. Cicero, *Epistulae ad Familiares* 9.2.2. Writing to Leonard Philaras in 1654, Milton, in a moving letter itemizing details of his blindness, would tellingly conclude by self-appropriating the myth of Lynceus: *Teque, mi Philara, quocunque res ceciderit, non minus forti et confirmato animo quam si Lynceus essem valere iubeo* ("As for you, my Philaras, whatever may come to pass, I bid you farewell with a mind no less brave and resolute than if I were Lynceus"). See Milton, *Epistola Familiaris* 15, in *John Milton: Epistolarum Familiarium Liber Unus and Uncollected Letters*, ed. Haan, 233–246, at 238–239, 246.

[122] See C. H. Lüthy, "Atomism, Lynceus, and the Fate of Seventeenth-Century Microscopy," *Early Science and Medicine* 1 (1996): 1–27.

[123] See *OLD*, s.v. 2a. Cf., for example, Virgil, *Aeneid* 1.323: *maculosae tegmine lyncis*; Baptista Mantuanus, *Eclogue* 6. 27: *maculosaque tergora lyncis* ("the lynx's spotty hide").

context of criticisms leveled against *L'Adone* itself, and, not least, against Stigliani's diatribe, and the methodology of Lyncean scrutiny which that tract had explicitly employed. *Maculosus* in its primary sense of "Covered with stains or blotches, spotted, blotted"[124] is the adjective used by Pliny to describe the moon.[125] The noun *macula* had functioned as a virtual leitmotif in Galileo's *Sidereus Nuncius* (1610), a volume interestingly hailed by Manso, himself an avid follower of the new science,[126] in a letter to the astronomer dated just five days after the work's publication.[127] Thus the Italian astronomer had seen hitherto unobserved *maculae* on the moon,[128] and had used the positioning of bright and dark borders of the *maculae* to distinguish between concave and convex irregularities of the lunar surface, or, as Milton would later describe it:

> the moon, whose orb
> Through optic glass the Tuscan artist views
> At evening from the top of Fesole,
> Or in Valdarno, to descry new lands,
> Rivers or mountains in her spotty globe.
> (*Paradise Lost* 1. 287–291)[129]

---

[124] See *OLD*, s.v. 1.

[125] Pliny, *Naturalis Historia* 2.42.

[126] See Riga, *Giovan Battista Manso*, 15–32; Cocco, *Watching Vesuvius*, 54.

[127] On 18 March 1610 Manso wrote from Naples to Galileo in Padua, expressing his good fortune in having been born in the age of such discoveries, and hailing Galileo as a modern Atlas ("nuovo Atlante") and, as it were, a new Colombus ("quasi novello Colombo"). See *Le Opere di Galileo Galilei*, ed. Antonio Favaro, 20 vols. (Florence: G. Barbèra, 1890–1909), X, 296 (Letter 275). At around the same time Manso addressed to Paolo Beni a letter replete with a sense of wonderment at Galileo's invention of the telescope, and its ability to extend the range of human vision. See *Le Opere di Galileo Galilei*, X, 291–296 (Letter 274). Then on 8 June 1610 Manso wrote again to Galileo, announcing that his astronomical discoveries were long awaited by the entire city of Naples. See *Le Opere di Galileo Galilei*, X, 371 (Letter 329). For the three letters, see also Riga, *Giovan Battista Manso*, 172–179, and, for further discussion, Barbara Bartocci, "Paolo Beni and Galileo Galilei: The Classical Tradition and the Reception of The Astronomical Revolution," *Rivista di Storia della Filosofia* 71 (2016): 423–452.

[128] Galileo, *Sidereus Nuncius* (Venice: Tommaso Baglioni, 1610), sig. 7^v: *hae [maculae] vero a nemine ante nos observatae fuerunt* ("but these spots have never been observed by anyone before me").

[129] For an excellent discussion of the role of Galileo in Milton's epic, see Neil Harris, "Galileo as Symbol: The 'Tuscan Artist' in *Paradise Lost*," *Annali dell' Istituto e Museo di Storio della Scienza di Firenze* 10 (1985): 3–29. See also, among others, Roy Flannagan, "Art, Artists, Galileo and Concordances," *MQ* 20 (1986): 103–105; Donald Friedman, "Galileo and the Art of Seeing," in *Milton in Italy*, ed. Di Cesare,

Galileo was also the first astronomer to direct a telescope toward the sun.[130] There, too, he discovered spots ("macchie solari") announced in three eponymous letters: *Istoria e Dimostrazioni Intorno alle Macchie Solari e Loro Accidenti* (1613),[131] whose title page showcases the academy's emblem: the spotted lynx encircled within a wreath, the whole topped by a crown. Here we are told that "le macchie vedute non sono illusioni dell' occhiale" ("the spots seen are not illusions produced by glasses"),[132] in a work unsurprisingly peppered by the noun "macchia" in its singular and plural forms,[133] and by the associated adjective "macchiato."

The idea lies at the very heart of Stigliani's eponymous *Occhiale*, the "Eye-glass," a quasi-Galilean lens through which he scrutinized *L'Adone*,[134] finding therein flaws described as "macchiasi di bassezza" ("stains of baseness"),[135] and a "style" ("stile") that is "macchiato" ("blemished").[136] The work's title and methodology had provoked censure on the part of Aleandro, who turns the whole upon its head.[137] If detection of the poem's shortcomings necessitates recourse to a magnifying lens in a manner comparable to Galileo's use of the telescope to observe sunspots, then the poem must emulate the luminosity of the sun itself. Thus, in a section entitled "Del Titolo del Libro," he proclaims:

159–174; Amy Boesky, "Milton, Galileo, and Sunspots: Optics and Certainty in *Paradise Lost*," *MS* 34 (1996): 23–43; Maura Brady, "Galileo in Action: The 'Telescope' in *Paradise Lost*," *MS* 44 (2005): 129–152; Justin Clemens, "Galileo's Telescope in John Milton's *Paradise Lost*: The Modern Origin of the Critique of Science as Instrumental Rationality?" *Filozofski Vestnik* 33 (2012): 163–194.

[130] See Richard S. Westfall, "Science and Patronage: Galileo and the Telescope," *Isis* 76 (1985): 11–30; Mario Biagioli, *Galileo's Instruments of Credit: Telescopes, Images, Secrecy* (Chicago: The University of Chicago Press, 2006); Pietro Greco, *Galileo Galilei: The Tuscan Artist* (Cham, Switzerland: Springer, 2018).

[131] Galileo, *Istoria e Dimostrazioni Intorno alle Macchie Solari e Loro Accidenti* (Rome: Giacomo Mascardi, 1613).

[132] *Istoria e Dimostrazioni*, 12.

[133] "Macchia" (37 occurrences); "macchie" (178 occurrences).

[134] See Sanam Nader-Esfahani, "The Critical Occhiale: Lenses, Readers, and Critics in the Polemic Regarding Marino's *L'Adone*," *RS* 35 (2021): 170–187.

[135] *Dello Occhiale*, 94.

[136] *Dello Occhiale*, 429: "Egli professa e pretende d'avere in esso poema altissimo stile (dove per verità l'hà mezano se ben macchiato)" ("He professes and claims to be in possession, in that poem, of an extremely lofty style [when, in truth it has a style that is average and greatly blemished]").

[137] See Jonathan Unglaub, *Poussin and the Poetics of Painting: Pictorial Narrative and the Legacy of Tasso* (Cambridge: Cambridge University Press, 2006), 137.

> O pure s'ha à dire, che se per entro all'Adone vi sono diffetti, vengano questi coperti dal gran splendore delle sue bellezze; si che per rintracciarneli v'abbisogni un occhiale, nella guisa c'ha fatto il Galilei per iscoprire le macchie Solari. Ma sicome ci resta per dubbio, se possano macchie haver luogo in quel luminoso corpo, o pure altra cosa sia, che per la gran lontananza faccia frode alla nostra veduta, cisì non può essere così agevole all' Occhiale Stiglianesco il far credere, che l'Adone macolato sia nella maniera, ch' egli pretende.[138]

> Or it has to be said that if there are defects within *L'Adone*, these are covered by the great splendor of its beauties; so that to track them down you need glasses, in the way Galileo did to discover sun spots. But as it remains a matter of doubt as to whether stains can occupy a place in that luminous body, or whether otherwise, due to the great distance, it deceives our view, it cannot be so easy for the Eye-glass of Stigliani to make us believe that *L'Adone* is spotted in the manner that he claims.

In its pejorative sense *maculosus* can also denote "Stained with infamy or disgrace, disreputable, foul."[139] Milton's phrase may thus subtly attribute to the Lynceans, now on a moral and methodological level, both the astronomical *maculae* discovered by its leading member, Galileo, and the literary and linguistic *maculae* that Stigliani claimed to have uncovered in *L'Adone* itself.[140]

Central to the quasi-Orphic effect of the described performance in *Mansus* is the novelty of its song (*novo ... carmine* [69]). Here Mirollo's gloss of the term "novità" is particularly pertinent:

> NOVITÀ: freshness, newness, novelty, innovation; and since *nuovo* also connotes the extraordinary and the surprising, *novità* is usually very close to *meraviglia*.[141]

---

[138] *Difesa dell'Adone*, sig. A10ʳ.

[139] *OLD* s.v. 3. Cf. Cicero, *Epistulae ad Atticum* 1.16.3; Tacitus, *Historiae* 1.7, 2.30.

[140] Milton's claim that in the course of his Italian journey he visited Galileo (see *Areopagitica* [London: s.n., 1644], 24), although much contested, is probably true. It is worth remarking too that in *Paradise Lost*, Galileo and his discovery of sunspots are depicted in an essentially Satanic context: "There lands the fiend, a spot like which perhaps/Astronomer in the sun's lucent orb/Through his glazed optic tube yet never saw" (*Paradise Lost* 3. 588–590). For a reading of the Satan/Galileo link in *Paradise Lost* as a possible repudiation of Galileo's enterprise, see Joan M. Webber, *Milton and His Epic Tradition* (Seattle: University of Washington Press, 1979), 142–143. For a perceptive discussion, see Stephen B. Dobranski, *Milton's Visual Imagination: Imagery in "Paradise Lost"* (Cambridge: Cambridge University Press, 2015), 105–107.

[141] Mirollo, *Poet of the Marvelous*, 119.

The proclaimed "novelty" of *L'Adone* was a much-contested issue. In his "Discours" prefixed to the first edition, Jean Chapelain, as if preempting subsequent criticism, had taken particular care to situate the poem's novelty in its diversity ("la Diversité), its new ideas ("son Idée nouvelle"), and its incorporation of the marvelous ("la Merveille").[142] In short, according to Chapelain, Marino invented a new type of heroic poem.[143] Stigliani, however, had countered this by accusing Marino of plagiarism, not least from his own *Il Mondo Nuovo*.[144] Aleandro capably responded,[145] saluting instead "la varietà de' pensieri, la novità de' concetti, e la nobilta e delicatezza della dicitura" ("the variety of thoughts, the novelty of concepts, and the verbal delicacy")[146] pervading Marino's poem.

6.4 *Mansus* and Marinesque "Concettismo"

These last terms of praise, it might be argued, are, in the end, equally applicable to *Mansus*, not least in regard to its linguistic appropriation of some of the stylistic features of Marinesque "concettismo," and in its possible engagement with *L'Adone*. One potential signifier is provided by Milton's use of the adverb *molliter* to describe the envisaged honors bestowed upon his deceased self: *Ille meos artus liventi morte solutos/Curaret parva componi molliter urna* (89–90) ("He would see to it that my limbs, loosened by livid death, were gently laid in a small urn"). The adverb draws the discerning reader back to the description of Marino's style as *mollis* (12),[147] on which occasion the substantive use of the adjective functions as a virtual synonym for the Italian poet himself. In short, the placing of *molliter* within Milton's small urn suggests a self-alignment with Marino, and an associated aspiration for posthumous

---

[142] See "Lettre ou Discours de M. Chapelain," at *L'Adone*, sig. bi^r–biv^v.

[143] See Cropper, *The Domenichino Affair*, 164. Caruso, *Adonis: The Myth of the Dying God*, 63, pertinently regards Chapelain's "Discours" as "principally aim[ing] to vindicate the legitimacy of the poem's novelty in terms of its unusual combination of disparate styles." Cf. Unglaub, *Poussin and the Poetics of Painting*, 134: "Chapelain attributes everything that is novel about the poem—whether its figurative language, its amorous subject, or its wealth of subsidiary episodes—to the fact that it embodies a new type of epic: *le poem de paix*."

[144] *Dello Occhiale*, 104.

[145] *Difesa dell' Adone*, 29–30.

[146] *Difesa dell' Adone*, 69.

[147] See 191–193.

commemoration "in a manner that is *mollis*." Might this also operate on a linguistic level in *Mansus*?

"Concettismo," subsequently termed "Marinism," this last not without pejorative implications, was a literary technique that indulged in wordplay, keen wit and acuity ("arguzia"), metaphors, paradoxes, and ingenious conceits.[148] It is a technique that permeates *L'Adone*, in, for example, such verbal play as "L'idea"/"la dea" (II.155), "lusinghre"/ "lusinghiero" (III.151), "Sospira"/"spira" (XII.9), and "sforza"/"forza" (VIII.48).[149] As Paolo Cherci puts it, "words in their materiality are the [poem's] content."[150] Throughout, as Mirollo notes, Marino displays his ability to "manipulate words as though they were bits of mosaic or musical notes,"[151] and his "keen sense of sonority and sound pattern."[152] Something similar seems to be at play in *Mansus*, especially in its quasi-baroque wordplay on:

a) proper names:

> *Baptista* [titulus] / *lustratio* ["baptism"]: *miti lustrarit lumine Phoebus* (71)
> *Mansus* [titulus] / *mansuetus* (60)[153]
> *Mansus* [titulus] / *manus* / χείρ / Chiron (60)
> *Manse* (1, 2) / *manes* [anagrammatic] (15)
> *Manse* (1, 2) /"names" [macaronic and anagrammatic] / *nomina* (8)
> *Manse tuae* (1) / *mansuetae* [anagrammatic]
> *Tasso* (7) / *habitasse* (54)
> *Cynthius* (55) / Cinzio
> *lynces* (69) / Accademia dei Lincei
> *Saxon*[*icus*] (84) / *saxum* (66, 84)

b) adjectives:

> *solus* (13–14) / *sol*
> *iuvenis* (26) / "giovane" / Giovanni / *Ioannes* / John
> *nobilis* (60) / Collegio dei Nobili
> *mansueti* (60) / *Manse tui* [anagrammatic] / *Mansus* [titulus]

---

[148] See 185–186.

[149] See Mirollo, *Poet of the Mavelous*, 138–139.

[150] Paolo Cherchi, "The Seicento: Poetry, Philosophy and Science," in *The Cambridge History of Italian Literature*, eds. Peter Brand and Lino Pertile (Cambridge: Cambridge University Press, 2007), 301–317, at 307.

[151] Mirollo, *Poet of the Marvelous*, 132.

[152] Mirollo, *Poet of the Marvelous*, 198.

[153] For a similarly marinesque inclination toward wordplay on Manso's name (and formal title) see the Italian tributes in his honor discussed at 93–96.

c)   nouns:

>   *decus* (50) / *decorasse* (79)
>   *frons-frontis* (76) / *frons-frondis*

and in the employment of the alliterative *M* (frequently at the beginning of the line):

>   *Manse* (1, 2, 25)
>   *Mecaenatis* (4)
>   *Mox ... Musa Marinum* (9)
>   *Mollis* (12)
>   *manes* (15)
>   *Minervae* (21)
>   *Mycalen* (22)
>   *Missus* (26)
>   *Misimus* (41)
>   *Mulcenturque ... maculosi* (69)
>   *Magnanimos* (83).

Sometimes the wordplay is more implicit, as in the case of the possible evocation of the Accademia degli Oziosi and its motto (*Non Pigra Quies*)[154] in the poem's depiction of pastoral *otium* (59–64) and in the Miltonic prediction of eternal repose: *At ego secura pace quiescam* (93).

Central to the effect of "meraviglia" elicited by *L'Adone* is the ability to confound the very senses that the poem purportedly celebrates. For example, the "garden" Cantos (VI–VIII), though carefully divided into five separate sections, one for each of the senses, oscillate continuously between them.[155] Thus, as Adonis beholds an abundance of flowers in "The Garden of Pleasure," he is "blinded" by the "scents" around him (VI.122). Later (VII.18–31), the description of songbirds (VII.18–31), as Slawinski remarks, "dwells less on sound than on their coloured plumage and airy flight ... confounding the senses." In the Garden of Smell it is the scentless passion-flower that is extolled above all the others, while "the celebration of taste begins with a description of trees whose fruits are not edible (VII.100)."[156] *Mansus* celebrates a rich sensuality, conveyed in luxuriantly sonorous sibilants. Now, however, the

---

[154] See 85.

[155] See Maurice Slawinski, "The Poet's Senses: G.B. Marino's Epic Poem *L'Adone* and the New Science," *CC* 13 (1991): 51–81. See also Estelle Haan, "Marvell's Latin Poetry and the Art of Punning," in *The Oxford Handbook of Andrew Marvell*, eds. Martin Dzelzainis and Edward Holberton (Oxford: Oxford University Press, 2019), 463–480, at 476–480.

[156] Slawinski, "The Poet's Senses," 61.

speaker has indeed "heard" the sound of birdsong (*obscuras noctis <u>sensisse</u> per umbras* [31]). The garden of pleasure enjoyed by Apollo is seductive in its foliage, conveyed in equally seductive language (*Irriguos inter saltus frondosaque tecta* [61]). On the other hand, sensation is tellingly displaced, as in the inability of a cliff to "feel" the weight of its forests (*nec <u>sentit</u> solitas, immania pondera, silvas* [67]).[157] In both instances the agent is music/poetry. Marinesque music, and its stupefying effect (*stupefecit* [12]) upon the senses, an effect implicitly aligned with "meraviglia," is thus replicated in the quasi-Orphic powers attributed to Apollo's *<u>novum</u> ... <u>carmen</u>* (69) This is mirrored by a Miltonic "novità," now showcased in neo-Latin verse, whereby the reader (or listener), I would argue, is (in an appropriation of Stanley Fish's terminology)[158] "surprised by syntax."[159] A few examples will suffice:

a) the poem's syntactical self-consciousness as it plays itself backwards through the reverse iteration of line openings/adverbs:

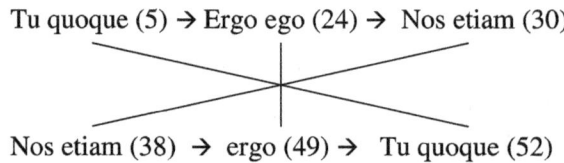

Tu quoque (5) → Ergo ego (24) → Nos etiam (30)

Nos etiam (38) → ergo (49) → Tu quoque (52)

b) the visual affinity, in *Ergo ego* (24), between the Latin adverb and pronoun, an affinity offset by their somewhat jarring and even jingling juxtaposition;

c) the potential assimilation, on a phonological level, of aspects of the Italian vernacular in the sonorities of the poem's *Latinitas*: in, for example:
> *dulciloquum* (9) / "dolceloquente"
> *tota mente* (98) / "totalmente."

Such assimilation may move beyond the linguistic to embrace Milton's national and poetic self-fashioning. As a *iuvenis ... peregrinus*

---

[157] Emphasis is mine.

[158] Stanley Fish, *Surprised by Sin: The Reader in Paradise Lost* (Basingstoke: Macmillan, 1997).

[159] For discussion of syntactical surprise in *Paradise Lost*, see Haan, *Bilingualism and Biculturalism*, 167–198.

(26), sent from the northern skies (*Hyperboreo ... ab axe* [26]),[160] he is possessed of a far-distant Muse, one depicted in language suggestive of a bird, which, though improperly nourished in an icy climate,[161] has ventured to fly (*volitare* [29]) through the cities of Italy. The implied sense of alterity, of a bird who might otherwise seem out of place in Italy's literal and literary climate, is, however, countered by Milton's later proclamation: he too (*Nos etiam* [30]) has heard swans singing (*modulantes ... cygnos* [30]), but this time, the river is his native Thames (32).[162] He has heard such song amid night's dark shadows (*obscuras noctis ... per umbras* [31]). Bush, commenting on this rather enigmatic phrase, remarks: "Milton seems to suggest the slow or recent rise of English poetry in comparison with that of Italy."[163] Not necessarily. Rather, the very coexistence of swans and surrounding shadows seems both to echo and to reconfigure a key scene in *L'Adone*.

In *L'Adone*, Canto IX, Venus and Adonis witness a competition between a flock of rivaling swans. These represent Greek, Latin, and Italian poets, the last periphrastically including Petrarch, Dante, Sannazaro, and Tasso. Suddenly out of the shadows a would-be swan makes his unwelcome appearance. This is none other than Stigliani himself, "a deformed and ruffled owl" ("difforme e rabbuffato un Gufo" [IX, 183]), a companion of shade and of night ("e del' ombre campagno, e della notte" [IX, 184]). Venus can only spurn the profundity of darkness, both literal and metaphorical, from which he has emerged, asking him: "From what deep and dark night-time hollow have you rashly emerged into the day?" ("Da qual profonda, e tenebrosa buca/Nottula temeraria, al giorno uscisti?" [IX, 185]). Scornfully interrogating him about his origins and purpose, she denounces him as a son of Envy, questioning with sardonic rebuke his wish to be transformed into a swan ("vuoi trasformarti in Cigno?" [IX, 185]). Manso is asked not to spurn (*nec ... aspernabere*) the Miltonic *Musa ... imprudens* (27–29),

---

[160] Cf. Milton, *In Quintum Novembris* 95: *Hyperboreo gens barbara nata sub axe* ("a barbarous nation born beneath the Hyperborean sky").

[161] At *Mansus* 37 the British are described as suffering *brumalem ... Boöton* ("wintry Bootes"), a reference to the northern constellation, the Bear-keeper/Waggoner (with which, cf. *Elegia* 5.35–36: *Iamque Lycaonius plaustrum caeleste Boötes/Non longa sequitur fessus ut ante via* ["And now Lyconian Bootes does not wearily pursue the heavenly wagon in a long journey as previously"]). On Milton's association of the cold northern climate with darkness and the dearth of poetical inspiration, see Fink, "Milton and the Theory of Climatic Influence"; Revard, *The Tangles of Neaera's Hair*, 217–218.

[162] See the discussion at 97–104.

[163] Bush, *Variorum*, I, 273.

not least because England has already produced her own flock of talented swans. Among these is one who has recently been welcomed upon Italian shores. After all, as *Mansus* capably demonstrates, literary swans, both ancient and modern, both Latin and Italian, both English and Neapolitan, can majestically swim together. Or, as the poet of *Paradise Lost* would later proclaim:

> Others on silver lakes and rivers bathed
> Their downy breast; the *swan* with archèd neck
> Between her white wings *mantling* proudly, rows
> Her state with oary feet.
>   (*Paradise Lost* 7. 437–440)[164]

---

[164] Emphasis is mine. Cf. the association of swan ("cigno") with Manso and a punning "mantle" ("manto"), at *Poesie Nomiche*, 273, 298, for discussion of which, see 95, 97.

APPENDIX

Mansus[1]

Ioannes Baptista Mansus Marchio Villensis, vir ingenii laude, tum litterarum studio, nec non et bellica virtute apud Italos clarus in primis est. Ad quem Torquati Tassi dialogus exstat de Amicitia scriptus; erat enim Tassi amicissimus; ab quo etiam inter Campaniae principes celebratur in illo poemate cui titulus Gerusalemme Conquistata, lib. 20:

> "*Fra cavalier magnanimi e cortesi*
> *Risplende il Manso ...* "

Is auctorem Neapoli commorantem summa benevolentia prosecutus est, multaque ei detulit humanitatis officia. Ad hunc itaque hospes ille antequam ab ea urbe discederet, ut ne ingratum se ostenderet, hoc carmen misit.

Haec quoque, Manse, tuae meditantur carmina laudi
Pierides; tibi, Manse, choro notissime Phoebi,
Quandoquidem ille alium haud aequo est dignatus honore
Post Galli cineres et Mecaenatis Etrusci.
Tu quoque, si nostrae tantum valet aura Camoenae,   5
Victrices hederas inter laurosque sedebis.
    Te pridem magno felix concordia Tasso
Iunxit, et aeternis inscripsit nomina chartis.
Mox tibi dulciloquum non inscia Musa Marinum
Tradidit: ille tuum dici se gaudet alumnum,   10
Dum canit Assyrios divum prolixus amores,
Mollis et Ausonias stupefecit carmine nymphas.
Ille itidem moriens tibi soli debita vates
Ossa tibi soli supremaque vota reliquit.
Nec manes pietas tua cara fefellit amici: 15
Vidimus arridentem operoso ex aere poetam.
Nec satis hoc visum est in utrumque, et nec pia cessant
Officia in tumulo; cupis integros rapere Orco,
Qua potes, atque avidas Parcarum eludere leges:
Amborum genus et varia sub sorte peractam   20
Describis vitam moresque et dona Minervae,
Aemulus illius Mycalen qui natus ad altam
Rettulit Aeolii vitam facundus Homeri.

---

[1] Text is that of *Poems of Mr. John Milton, Both English and Latin* (London: Humphrey Moseley, 1645), at *Poemata*, 72–76. I have modernized orthography and punctuation, and normalized accents and redundant capitals.

Manso[2]

Giovanni Battista Manso, Marquis of Villa, is a man more famous than any other among the Italians, not only for the reputation of his genius and his pursuit of literary studies, but also for his bravery in war. There is extant a dialogue on Friendship, which Torquato Tasso addressed to him; for he was a very good friend of Tasso, by whom he is also celebrated among the princes of Campania in that poem which is entitled The Conquest of Jerusalem, book 20:

> *"Among great-hearted and courteous knights*
> *Manso is resplendent ..."*

When the author was sojourning in Naples, he attended him with the greatest of goodwill, and conferred on him many kind services. In consequence, that guest, before his departure from that city, sent him this poem in order that he might not appear ungrateful.

These verses too, Manso, do the Pierians compose in your praise: for you, Manso, very well known to the choir of Phoebus, inasmuch as he has deemed no one else worthy of equal distinction since the death of Gallus and Etruscan Maecenas. You too, if the breath of our Camena has power so great, will sit among the ivies and laurels of victory.

In the past a happy bond of friendship joined you to the mighty Tasso, and he inscribed your name in his eternal pages. Next, the Muse, not without knowledge, entrusted to you the sweetly-speaking Marino; he rejoiced in being called your foster-child as he proclaimed in verbose song the Assyrian love-affairs of the gods, and stunned the Ausonian nymphs with the smoothness of his strains. Likewise, when he was dying, it was to you alone that that bard left his bones, as was their due; to you alone, his final wishes. And your loving devotion did not fail your friend's spirit: we have seen the poet smiling from elaborate bronze. But it did not seem to you that this was enough for them both, nor did your dutiful services cease at the grave: you longed to snatch them unharmed from Orcus, as far as you were able, and to cheat the greedy laws of the Fates: you record in writing the ancestry of both, and their lives lived under varying fortunes, their characters, and their gifts for Minerva, rivaling that man born near lofty Mycale, who eloquently related the life of Aeolian Homer.

---

[2] Translation is mine.

  Ergo ego te Clius et magni nomine Phoebi,
Manse pater, iubeo longum salvere per aevum   25
Missus Hyperboreo iuvenis peregrinus ab axe.
Nec tu longinquam bonus aspernabere Musam,
Quae nuper gelida vix enutrita sub Arcto
Imprudens Italas ausa est volitare per urbes.
Nos etiam in nostro modulantes flumine cygnos 30
Credimus obscuras noctis sensisse per umbras,
Qua Thamesis late puris argenteus urnis
Oceani glaucos perfundit gurgite crines;
Quin et in has quondam pervenit Tityrus oras.
  Sed neque nos genus incultum nec inutile Phoebo, 35
Qua plaga septeno mundi sulcata Trione
Brumalem patitur longa sub nocte Boöten.
Nos etiam colimus Phoebum, nos munera Phoebo
Flaventes spicas et lutea mala canistris
Halantemque crocum (perhibet nisi vana vetustas) 40
Misimus, et lectas Druidum de gente choreas.
(Gens Druides antiqua sacris operata deorum
Heroum laudes imitandaque gesta canebant.)
Hinc quoties festo cingunt altaria cantu
Delo in herbosa Graiae de more puellae   45
Carminibus laetis memorant Corineïda Loxo
Fatidicamque Upin, cum flavicoma Hecaërge,
Nuda Caledonio variatas pectora fuco.
  Fortunate senex, ergo quacunque per orbem
Torquati decus et nomen celebrabitur ingens, 50
Claraque perpetui succrescet fama Marini,
Tu quoque in ora frequens venies plausumque virorum,
Et parili carpes iter immortale volatu.
Dicetur tum sponte tuos habitasse penates
Cynthius, et famulas venisse ad limina Musas. 55
At non sponte domum tamen idem et regis adivit
Rura Pheretiadae caelo fugitivus Apollo
(Ille licet magnum Alciden susceperat hospes);
Tantum ubi clamosos placuit vitare bubulcos
Nobile mansueti cessit Chironis in antrum,   60
Irriguos inter saltus frondosaque tecta,
Peneium prope rivum. Ibi saepe sub ilice nigra

And so, father Manso, I, a young foreigner sent from the Hyperborean sky, wish you, in the name of Clio and of the mighty Phoebus, a long and healthy life. Do not, in your goodness, be scornful of a Muse, who has traveled a long distance, and who, though poorly nourished beneath the icy Bear, has recently ventured in her rashness to fly through the cities of Italy. We, too, believe that we have heard swans singing in our river amid night's dark shadows, where the silver Thames with pure urns soaks her green locks in Ocean's wide waters. Indeed, even Tityrus once reached these shores.

But we are a people neither uncultured nor useless to Phoebus, one enduring wintry Bootes for long nights in that region of the universe furrowed by the seven-fold Triones. We, too, worship Phoebus; to Phoebus we have sent gifts of golden ears of corn, rosy apples in baskets, the fragrant crocus (unless the proclamations of ancient lore be in vain), and choirs chosen from the Druid race. (The Druids, an ancient race, well versed in the rituals of the gods, used to sing the praises of heroes, and their exploits worthy of imitation.) Hence as often as Greek girls in grassy Delos encircle the altars in festive song according to custom, they commemorate in joyful song Loxo, daughter of Corineus, and prophetic Upis, together with Hecaerge of the golden tresses, their bare breasts colorfully painted with Caledonian woad.

And so, fortunate old man, wherever throughout the world are celebrated the glory and the powerful name of Torquato, and wherever is augmented the famous reputation of the deathless Marino, you too will frequently be on the lips and in the applause of men, and in a flight such as theirs will you press along the journey of immortality. Then it will be said that Cynthius has dwelt of his own accord in your home, and that the Muses have come like handmaids to your threshold; but it was not of his own accord that that same Apollo, a fugitive from heaven, approached the home and farm of the royal son of Pheres (even though the latter had been an hospitable host to mighty Hercules); but when he wished to avoid the clamorous herdsmen, he withdrew into the famous cave of the gentle Chiron, amid the well-watered pastures and leafy dwellings beside the river Peneus. It was there, beneath

Ad citharae strepitum blanda prece victus amici
Exilii duros lenibat voce labores.
Tum neque ripa suo barathro nec fixa sub imo   65
Saxa stetere loco; nutat Trachinia rupes,
Nec sentit solitas, immania pondera, silvas;
Emotaeque suis properant de collibus orni,
Mulcenturque novo maculosi carmine lynces.

    Diis dilecte senex, te Iuppiter aequus oportet   70
Nascentem, et miti lustrarit lumine Phoebus
Atlantisque nepos; neque enim nisi carus ab ortu
Diis superis poterit magno favisse poetae.
Hinc longaeva tibi lento sub flore senectus
Vernat, et Aesonios lucratur vivida fusos,   75
Nondum deciduos servans tibi frontis honores,
Ingeniumque vigens, et adultum mentis acumen.

    O mihi si mea sors talem concedat amicum,
Phoebaeos decorasse viros qui tam bene norit,
Si quando indigenas revocabo in carmina reges   80
Arturumque etiam sub terris bella moventem,
Aut dicam invictae sociali foedere mensae
Magnanimos heroas, et (o modo spiritus adsit!)
Frangam Saxonicas Britonum sub Marte phalanges.
Tandem ubi non tacitae permensus tempora vitae,   85
Annorumque satur cineri sua iura relinquam,
Ille mihi lecto madidis astaret ocellis;
Astanti sat erit si dicam "Sim tibi curae."
Ille meos artus liventi morte solutos
Curaret parva componi molliter urna;   90
Forsitan et nostros ducat de marmore vultus,
Nectens aut Paphia myrti aut Parnasside lauri
Fronde comas, at ego secura pace quiescam.
Tum quoque, si qua fides, si praemia certa bonorum,
Ipse ego caelicolum semotus in aethera divum,   95
Quo labor et mens pura vehunt atque ignea virtus,
Secreti haec aliqua mundi de parte videbo
(Quantum fata sinunt), et tota mente serenum
Ridens purpureo suffundar lumine vultus,
Et simul aethereo plaudam mihi laetus Olympo.   100

a dark oak tree, that he would be overcome by the winsome entreaties of his friend and would often alleviate exile's cruel hardships by singing in accompaniment to the resounding lyre. Thereupon neither riverbanks nor rocks, lodged in the lowest ravine, remained in their places; the Trachinian cliff nodded, and did not feel the familiar weight of its massive woodland, and mountain ashes were uprooted and hastened down their own hills, while spotted lynxes were soothed by the novelty of his song.

Old man, beloved of the gods, Jupiter must have favored you at birth, and Phoebus and the grandson of Atlas must have looked upon you with kindly glance, for no one, unless dear to the heavenly gods from his birth, is afforded the chance to befriend a mighty poet. Hence your lengthy old age is Spring-like beneath a lingering blossom and, in its vigor, enjoys the profits of Aeson's spindles, preserving the glories of your brow not yet fallen, your intellect flourishing, and the sharpness of your mind mature.

O if my fate would grant me a friend such as this, one who knows so well how to glorify the followers of Phoebus, if ever I summon back into verse our native kings, and Arthur instigating wars even under the ground; or if I tell of great-souled heroes of a table rendered invincible by the bond of fellowship, and (if only the breath of inspiration be present!) I shatter the Saxon phalanxes in a British war; then at last when I have measured out the span of a life not silent, and in the fullness of years have paid to the ashes the dues that are theirs, he would stand before my bed with tear-drenched eyes; it will be enough if I say to him as he stands there: "Take me to your care." He would see to it that my limbs, loosened by livid death, were gently laid in a small urn. Perhaps he would have my features too depicted in marble, binding my hair in Paphian myrtle or in the leaf of Parnassian laurel, but I shall rest safely in peace. Then also, if faith exists anywhere, if the rewards for the righteous are assured, I myself, removed into the ethereal regions of the heaven-dwelling gods, whither toil, purity of heart, and fiery virtue conduct, will behold these things from some remote region of the universe (as far as the fates allow) and smiling with complete serenity of mind, my face will be suffused with blushing radiance, while at the same time I will joyfully applaud myself on heavenly Olympus.

BIBLIOGRAPHY

1. MANUSCRIPTS

CAMBRIDGE
Trinity College
MS R.3.4.

FLORENCE
Biblioteca Marucelliana
MS A.36.

Biblioteca Nazionale Centrale
MS Magliabecchiana Cl. IV, cod. 61.
MS Magliabecchiana Cl. IX, cod. 60.

GENOA
Biblioteca Universitaria
MS A.VIII.11.

HARVARD
Houghton Library
MS Sumner 84.

LONDON
British Library
Add MS 4320.
Add MS 12046.
Egerton MS 1635.
Harl. Misc. (v. 33).

NAPLES
Biblioteca Nazionale
MS Brancacciana V.D.14.
MS Vind. lat.72.
MS XIII. C.82.
MS XIII. F.63.

Monte Manso di Scala
ASMMS, An/9.
ASMMS, An/15.
ASMMS, An/23.

Museo dell' Archivio Storico Banco
ASBN, Banco di S. Giacomo, g.m. 108.

NEW YORK
Public Library
MSSCol 2011(John Milton Papers, 1647-1882).

OXFORD
Bodleian Library
MS Rawl.D.121, 150.

ROME
Biblioteca Apostolica Vaticana
Barb.lat. 2181.

Biblioteca dell'Accademia dei Lincei e Corsiniana
Archivio Linceo 3.

English College
Pilgrim Book.

2. **MILTON: TEXTS**

MILTON, John. *A Maske Presented at Ludlow Castle, 1634* (London: Humphrey Robinson, 1637).
———. *An Apology Against a Pamphlet Call'd A Modest Confutation of the Animadversions Upon the Remonstrant Against Smectymnuus* (London: John Rothwell, 1642).
———. *Areopagitica: A Speech of Mr. John Milton for the Liberty of Unlicenc'd Printing* (London: s.n., 1644).
———. *Commonplace Book*. In *The Complete Works of John Milton: Volume XI*, ed. William Poole (Oxford: Oxford University Press, 2019).
———. *Complete Poems and Major Prose*, ed. Merrit Y. Hughes (New York: Odyssey, 1957).
———. *Complete Prose Works*, eds. D. M. Wolfe et al., 8 vols. (New Haven, CT: Yale University Press, 1953–1982).
———. *Complete Shorter Poems*, ed. John Carey (London: Longman, 1968; rev. 1997).
———. *De Doctrina Christiana*. In *The Complete Works of John Milton: Volume VIII: De Doctrina Christiana*, eds. John K. Hale and J. Donald Cullington, 2 vols. (Oxford: Oxford University Press, 2012).
———. *Epistolarum Familiarium Liber Unus and Uncollected Letters*, ed. Estelle Haan, Supplementa Humanistica Lovaniensia XLIV (Leuven: Leuven University Press, 2019).

———. *Epistolarum Familiarium Liber Unus Quibus Accesserunt Eiusdem Iam Olim in Collegio Adolescentis Prolusiones Quaedam Oratoriae* (London: Brabazon Aylmer, 1674).

———. *Latin Writings: A Selection*, ed. and trans. John K. Hale (Assen: Van Gorcum and Tempe, AZ: Medieval and Renaissance Texts and Studies, 1998).

———. *Of Education* (London: s.n., 1644).

———. *Paradise Lost*, ed. Alastair Fowler (London: Longman, 1998).

———. *Paradise Regained*. In *The Complete Works of John Milton: Volume II: The 1671 Poems: Paradise Regain'd and Samson Agonistes*, ed. Laura Lunger Knoppers (Oxford: Oxford University Press, 2008).

———. *Poems ... Both English and Latin, Compos'd at Several times* (London: Humphrey Moseley, 1645).

———. *Poetical Works*, ed. David Masson, 3 vols. (London: Macmillan, 1874).

———. *Pro Populo Anglicano Defensio Secunda. Contra Infamem Libellum Anonymum cui Titulus, Regii Sanguinis Clamor ad Coelum Adversus Parricidas Anglicanos* (London: Thomas Newcomb, 1654).

———. *Samson Agonistes*. In *The Complete Works of John Milton: Volume II: The 1671 Poems: Paradise Regain'd and Samson Agonistes*, ed. Laura Lunger Knoppers (Oxford: Oxford University Press, 2008).

———. *Shorter Poems*. In *The Complete Works of John Milton: Volume III: The Shorter Poems*, eds. Barbara Kiefer Lewalski and Estelle Haan (Oxford: Oxford University Press, 2012; rev. 2014).

———. *The History of Britain* (London: James Allestry, 1670).

———. *The Latin Poems*, ed. Walter MacKellar (New Haven, CT: Yale University Press, 1930).

———. *The Poems*, ed. Thomas Keightley, 2 vols. (London: Chapman and Hall, 1859).

———. *The Poems*, eds. John Carey and Alastair Fowler (London: Longman, 1968).

———. *The Reason of Church-Government Urg'd Against Prelaty. In Two Books* (London: John Rothwell, 1641).

———. *The Works*, eds. Frank A. Patterson et al., 18 vols. (New York: Columbia University Press, 1931–1940).

3. MILTON: COMMENTARIES

BUSH, Douglas. *A Variorum Commentary on the Poems of John Milton: Volume I: The Latin and Greek Poems* (New York: Columbia University Press, 1970).

4. MILTON: BIOGRAPHIES AND BIOGRAPHICAL RESOURCES

CAMPBELL, Gordon. *A Milton Chronology* (London: Macmillan, 1997).
CAMPBELL, Gordon, and Thomas N. CORNS. *John Milton: Life, Work, and Thought* (Oxford: Oxford University Press, 2008).
DARBISHIRE, Helen, ed. *The Early Lives of Milton* (London: Constable & Co., 1932).
FRENCH, J. M., ed. *The Life Records of John Milton*, 5 vols. (New Brunswick, NJ: Rutgers University Press, 1949–1958).
LEWALSKI, Barbara K. *The Life of John Milton: A Critical Biography* (Oxford: Blackwell, 2000).
MASSON, David. *The Life of John Milton: Narrated in Connexion with the Political, Ecclesiastical, and Literary History of his Time*, 7 vols. (London: Macmillan, 1859–1894).
MCDOWELL, Nicholas. *Poet of Revolution: The Making of John Milton* (Princeton, NJ: Princeton University Press, 2020).
PARKER, W. R. *Milton: A Biography*, 2 vols. (Oxford: Oxford University Press, 1968; revised ed., Gordon Campbell, 1996).

5. OTHER PRIMARY TEXTS AND ANTHOLOGIES

Academia Tenuta da Fantastici a 12 di Maggio 1655. In Applauso della S[anti]tà di N[ostro] S[ignore] Alesandro VII (Rome: Vitale Mascardi, 1655).
ALAMANNI, Luigi. *Versi e Prose*, ed. Pietro Raffaelli, 2 vols. (Florence: Le Monnier, 1859).
ALDROVANDI, Ulisse. *Ornithologiae Hoc Est De Avibus Historiae Libri XII* (Bologna: Francesco de Franceschi, 1599).
ALEANDRO, Girolamo. *Difesa dell' Adone Poema del Cav. Marini* (Venice: Giacomo Scaglia, 1629).
——————. *Sopra l'Impresa de gli Accademici Humoristi Discorso ... Detto nella Stessa Accademia* (Rome: Giacomo Mascardi, 1611).
Applausi Poetici alle Glorie della Signora Leonora Baroni, ed. Francesco Ronconi (Bracciano: Giovanni Battista Cavario, 1639).
APROSIO, Angelico. *L'Occhiale Stritolato di Scipio Glareano, per Riposta al Signor Cavalier Tommaso Stigliani*, in *Il Burrato: Replica di Carlo Galistoni al Molino del Signor Carlo Stigliani* (Venice: Taddeo Pavoni, 1642), 157–214.
ARIOSTO, Ludovico. *Orlando Furioso* (Venice: Felice Valgrisi, 1603).
ARISTOTLE. *Nicomachean Ethics, Books VIII and IX*, trans. with comm. Michael Pakaluk (Oxford: Clarendon Press, 1998).
——————. *The Nicomachean Ethics*, trans. Harris Rackham (Cambridge, MA: Harvard University Press, 1926).
ASCHAM, Roger. *The Scholemaster* (London: John Daye, 1570).
BACCO, Enrico. *Il Regno di Napoli Diviso in Dodici Provincie* (Naples: G. G. Carlino and C. Vitale, 1609).

BAIACCA, Giovan Battista. *Vita del Cavalier Maroni*, ed. Clizia Carminati, in *Vita e Morte del Cavalier Marino. Edizione e Commento della Vita di Giovan Battista Baiacca, 1625, e della Relazione della Pompa Funerale Fatta dall' Accademia degli Umoristi di Roma, 1626* (Bologna: Emil di Odoya, 2011), 63–134.

BATTISTA, Giuseppe. *Epigrammatum Centuria Prima* (Venice: Baba, 1659).

——. *Le Giornate Accademiche* (Venice: Combi & La Noù, 1673).

BEDE. *Ecclesiastical History*, eds. Bertram Colgrave and R. A. B. Mynors (Oxford: Clarendon Press, 1969).

——. *Historiae Ecclesiasticae Gentis Anglorum Libri V*, in *Rerum Britannicarum*, 147–280.

BIONDO, Flavio. *Italia Illustrata* (Rome: Johannes Philippus de Lignamine, 1474).

BOCCACCIO, Giovanni. *Vita di Dante Alighieri* (Rome: Francesco Priscianese, 1544).

BOUCHARD, Jean-Jacques. *Journal II: Voyage dans Le Royaume de Naples; Voyage dans La Campagne de Rome* (Turin: Giappichelli, 1976).

BRAUN, Georg, and Frans HOGENBERG. *Civitates Orbis Terrarum* (Cologne: Bertram Bochholtz, 1599).

BUONMATTEI, Benedetto. *Della Lingua Toscana ... Libri Due* (Florence: Zanobi Pignoni, 1643).

——. *Delle Cagioni della Lingua Toscana* (Venice: Alessandro Polo, 1623).

——. *Introduzione alla Lingua Toscana* (Venice: Giovanni Salis, 1626).

BURMAN, Pieter, ed. *Anthologia Veterum Latinorum Epigrammatum et Poematum sive Catalecta Poetarum Latinorum in VI Libros Digesta* (Amsterdam: Schouten, 1759–1763).

——, ed. *Sylloges Epistolarum a Viris Illustribus Scriptarum*, 5 vols. (Leiden: Samuel Luchtmans, 1727).

CAMOLA, Giacomo Filippo. *Breve Racconto della Vita del Sig. Cavalier Marino Descritta dal Sig. Giacomo Filippo Camola, Academico Humorista, detto L'Infecondo* (Rome: Mascardi, 1633).

CAMPANILE, Giuseppe. *Prose Varie ... Divise in Funzioni Accademiche* (Naples: Luc' Antonio di Fusco, 1666).

CAPACCIO, Giulio Cesare. *Neapolitanae Historiae ... Tomus Primus* (Naples: Io. Iacobus Carlinus, 1607).

Carmina Illustrium Poetarum Italorum, ed. G. G. Bottari, 11 vols. (Florence: Giovanni Gaetano Tartini and Sante Franchi, 1719–1726).

CELANO, Carlo. *Delle Notitie del Bello, dell'Antico, e del Curioso della Città di Napoli*, 10 vols. (Naples: Giacomo Raillard, 1692).

CHAUCER, Geoffrey. *The Workes*, ed. Thomas Speght (London: Adam Islip, 1602).

CHIARO, Francesco. *Vita di Marino*, appended to *La Strage degli Innocenti* (Naples: Ottavio Beltrano, 1632).

CHIOCCARELLI, Bartolomeo. *De Illustribus Scriptoribus qui in Civitate et Regno Neapolis ab Orbe Condito ad Annum usque MDCXXXXVI Floruerunt* (Naples: V. Orsini, 1780).

CICERO. *De Amicitia*. In *Cicero: Laelius, On Friendship (Laelius De Amicitia) & The Dream of Scipio (Somnium Scipionis)*, ed. J. G. F. Powell (Warminster: Aris and Phillips, 1990), 1–118.

CLÜVER, Philip. *Italia Antiqua* (Leiden: Elsevier, 1624).

CONTI, Natale. *Mythologiae, Sive Explicationis Fabularum Libri Decem* (Lyon: Petrus Landrus, 1602).
CORNELIO, Tommaso. *Progymnasmata Physica* (Venice: Francesco Baba, 1663).
CRASSO, Lorenzo. *Elogii d'Huomini Letterati*, 2 vols. (Venice: Combi & La Noù, 1666).
D'ALESSANDRO, Giovanni Petro. *Academiae Ociosorum Libri Tres* (Naples: Giovanni Battista Gargani & Lucrezio Nuccio, 1613).
DANIELE, Francesco. *La Vita di Francesco de' Pietri Giureconsulto e Storico Napoletano* (Naples: Simoniana, 1803).
DANTE, Alighieri. *Divina Comedia*, ed. Bernardino Daniello (Venice: Pietro da Fino, 1568).
DE LELLIS, Carlo. *Discorsi delle Famiglie Nobili del Regno di Napoli*, 3 vols. (Naples: G. F. Paci, 1663).
———. *Parte Seconda Overo Supplimento a Napoli Sacra di D. Cesare d'Engenio Caracciolo* (Naples: Roberto Mollo, 1654).
DELLA PORTA, Giambattista. *Magiae Naturalis Libri Viginti* (Naples: Horatius Salvianus, 1589).
DE PIETRI, Francesco. *Compendio della Vita di Torquato Tasso Scritta da Gio. Battista Manso* (Naples: Gio. Domenico Roncagliolo, 1619).
———. *Dell'Historia Napolitana Libri Due* (Naples: Gio. Domenico Montanaro, 1634).
———. *I Problemi Accademici ... ove Le Più Famose Quistioni Proposte nell' Illustrissima Accademia de gli Otiosi di Napoli* (Naples: Francesco Savio, 1642).
DE PISE, Marcellino. *Moralis Encyclopaedia Id Est Scientiarum Omnium Chorus*, 4 vols. (Lyon: Laurentius Anisson, 1656).
DE ROSA, Carlo Antonio. *Ritratti Poetici di Alcuni Uomini Antichi e Moderni del Regno di Napoli* (Naples: Cartiera del Fibreno, 1834).
DE TORO, Miguel Martinez. *Declaración de la Lei Única c. Si Quis Imperatori Maledixerit y Fren de Maldicientes* (Naples: Roberto Mollo, 1640).
DIACONUS, Paulus. *Sancti Gregorii Magni Vita*. In *Patrologia Latina*, ed. Migne, LXXV (1862), 42–60.
DI FALCO, Benedetto. *Descrittione de I Luoghi Antichi di Napoli e del Suo Amenissimo Distretto* (Naples: Francesco Sugganappo, 1549).
DI GREGORIO, Maurizio. *Rosario delle Stampe de' Tutti i Poeti, e Poetesse, Antichi, e Moderni, Cinquecento di Numero Tomo Ottavo, del Giardino de Tutte le Scienze* (Naples: G. G. Carlino, 1614).
DORIA, Paolo Mattia. *Massime del Governo Spagnolo a Napoli*, ed. Vittorio Conti (Naples: Guida, 1973).
DRAYTON, Michael. *Poly-Olbion* (London: Humphrey Lownes, 1612).
DU MOULIN, Pierre. *Regii Sanguinis Clamor ad Coelum Adversus Parricidas Anglicanos* (The Hague: Adrian Vlacq, 1652).
ELIOT, John. *Ortho-Epia Gallica. Eliots Fruits for the French* (London: John Wolfe, 1593).
ERRICO, Scipione. *L'Occhiale Appannato. Dialogo ... nel Quale Si Difende L'Adone del Cavalier Gio. Battista Marino, Contra L'Occhiale del Cavalier Tomaso Stigliani* (Naples: Giuseppe Matarozzi, 1629).

ERYTHRAEUS, Ianus Nicius. *Pinacotheca Imaginum Illustrium, Doctrinae vel Ingenii Laude, Virorum*, 3 vols. (Cologne: Iodocus Kalcovius 1648).
EVELYN, John. *Diary*, ed. E. S. De Beer, 6 vols. (Oxford: Clarendon Press, 1955).
FABRICIUS, Johannes Albert. *Conspectus Thesauri Literarii Italiae* (Hamburg: Christ. Wilh. Brandt, 1730).
FERRO, Giovanni. *Teatro d'Imprese*, 2 vols. (Venice: Giacomo Sarzina, 1623),
FIAMMA, Gabriel. *Le Vite de' Santi*, 4 vols. (Venice: Domenico Farri, 1602).
FRANCO, Nicolò. *Dialoghi Piacevolissimi* (Venice: Altobello Salicato, 1539).
———. *Dialogo ... Dove Si Ragiona delle Bellezze* (Venice: Antonio Gardane, 1542).
———. *Hisabella* (Naples: Giovanni Sultzbach and Mattia Cancer, 1535).
GADDI, Jacopo. *De Scriptoribus Non Ecclesiasticis, Graecis, Latinis, Italicis Tomus Secundus* (Lyon: Jean Pierre Chancel, 1649).
GAETANI, Filippo. *La Schiava* (Naples: Tarquinio Longo, 1613).
GALILEI, Galileo. *Istoria e Dimostrazioni Intorno alle Macchie Solari e Loro Accidenti* (Rome: Giacomo Mascardi, 1613).
———. *Le Opere*, ed. Antonio Favaro, 20 vols. (Florence: G. Barbèra, 1890–1909).
———. *Sidereus Nuncius* (Venice: Tommaso Baglioni, 1610).
GANDERSHEIM, Roswitha of. *Opera Hrosvitae Illustris Virginis et Monialis Germanae Gente Saxonica Ortae Nuper a Conrado Celte Inventa* (Nuremburg: Sodalitas Celtica, 1501).
GENTILI, Scipio. *Solymeidos Libri Duo Priores de Torquati Tassi Italicis Expressi* (London: John Wolfe, 1584).
GENUINO, Girilamo. *Metamorphoses Nominum, sive Metatheses Litterarum, sive Anagrammata in Quinque Libros Divisa* (Rome: Mascardi, 1635).
GIMMA, Giacinta. *Elogi Accademici della Società degli Spensierati di Rossano,* (Naples: Carlo Troise, 1703).
GIOVIO, PAOLO. *Regionum et Insularum atque Locorum Descriptiones: videlicet Britanniae, Scotiae, Hyberniae, Orchadum, item Moscoviae et Larii Lacus* (Basel: Petrus Perna, 1578).
GIUSTINIANI, Bernardo. *De Origine Urbis Venetiarum Rebusque ab Ipsa Gestis Historia* (Venice, 1492).
GUALDO, Paolo. *Vita Ioannis Vincentii Pinelli, Patricii Genuensis* (Augsburg: Markus Welser, 1607).
GUARINI, Luigi. *Notizie della Morte, Sepoltura, e Tomba del Cavalier Marini* (Naples: A. Coda, 1817).
HARDING, John. *The Chronicle* (London: Richard Grafton, 1543).
HERBERT, Edward. *Autobiography* (Strawberry Hill: s.n., 1764).
HERODOTUS. *The Histories*, trans. A. D. Godley, 4 vols. (Cambridge MA: Harvard University Press, 1920–1925).
HEYLYN, Peter. *Mikrokosmos. A Little Description of the Great World* (Oxford: John Lichfield and William Turner, 1625).
HOLLAND, Hugh. *Pancharis* (London, V[alentine] S[immes], 1603).
HOLSTENIUS, Lucas. *Demophili Democratis et Secundi, Veterum Philosophorum Sententiae Morales* (Rome: Mascardus, 1638).

―――――. *Porphyrii Philosophi Liber de Vita Pythagorae* (Rome: Typis Vaticanis, 1630).
HOMER. *Opera*, ed. Demetrius Chalcondylas (Florence: Bernardo and Nero Nerli, 1488).
―――――. *Opera* (Venice: Aldus Manutius, 1504).
Il Teatro delle Glorie della Signora Adriana Basile (Venice; rpt Naples: s.n., 1628).
KIRCHER, Athanasius. *Oedipi Aegyptiaci Tomus Secundus. Gymnasium sive Phrontisterion Hieroglyphicum in Duodecim Classes Distributum* (Rome: Vitale Mascardi, 1653).
LANDOR, Walter Savage. *The Works*, 2 vols. (London: Edward Moxon, 1846).
LELAND, John. *Assertio Inclytissimi Arturii Regis Britanniae* (London: Reyner Wolfe, 1544).
―――――. Κύκνειον Ἆσμα. *Cygnea Cantio* (London: Reyner Wolfe, 1545).
―――――. *Principum ac Illustrium Aliquot et Eruditorum in Anglia Virorum, Encomia, Trophaea, Genethliaca et Epithalamia a Ioanne Lelando Antiquario Conscripta* (London: Thomas Orwin, 1589).
LITHGOW, William. *The Totall Discourse of the Rare Adventures and Painefull Peregrinations of Long Nineteene Yeares Travayles from Scotland to the Most Famous Kingdomes in Europe, Asia and Affrica* (London: Nicholas Okes, 1632).
LOREDANO, Giovan Francesco. *Lettere*, 2 vols. (Bologna: Gioseffo Longhi, 1674).
―――――. *Vita del Cavalier Marino* (Venice: Giacomo Sarzina, 1633).
MANSO, Giovanni Battista. *Enciclopedia* (MS).
―――――. *Erocallia Overo dell'Amore e della Bellezza Dialoghi XII* (Venice: Evangelista Deuchino, 1628).
―――――. *I Paradossi overo D'Amore Dialoghi* (Milan: Girolamo Bordoni, 1608).
―――――. "Lettera ... in Materia del Vesuvio." *Archivio Storico per le Provincie Napoletane*, vol. 14, fasc. 3 and 4 (Naples 1889), 503–504.
―――――. *Poesie Nomiche* (Venice: Francesco Baba, 1635).
―――――. *Vita di Giambattista Marino* (MS: lost).
―――――. *Vita di Torquato Tasso* (Venice: Evangelista Deuchino, 1621).
―――――. *Vita di Torquato Tasso* (Rome: Francesco Cavalli, 1634).
―――――. *Vita di Torquato Tasso*, ed. Bruno Basile (Rome: Salerno Editrice, 1995).
―――――. *Vita, Virtù, e Miracoli Principali di S. Patricia Vergine* (Naples: Gio. Iacomo Carlino, 1611).
MANTUANUS, Baptista. *Fastorum Libri Duodecim* (Cologne: Maternus Cholinus, 1561).
MARINO, Giambattista. *Della Lira ... Parte Terza* (Venice: Giovanni Battista Ciotti, 1616).
―――――. *Dicerie Sacre* (Venice: Giacomo Violati, 1615).
―――――. *L'Adone* (Paris: Oliviero di Varano, 1623).
―――――. *La Murtoleide Fischiate* (Venice: Joseph Stamphier, 1619).
―――――. *La Strage degli Innocenti* (Naples: Ottavio Beltrano, 1632).
MAZZONI, Jacopo. *Della Difesa della Commedia del Divino Poeta Dante* (Bologna: Alessandro Benacci, 1572).
MONMOUTH, Geoffrey of. *De Origine et Gestis Regum Britanniae Libri XII*, in *Rerum Britannicarum*, 1–92.
―――――. *Historia Regum Britannie V: Gesta Regum Britannie*, ed. and trans. Neil Wright (Cambridge: D. S. Brewer, 1991).

———. *The History of the Kings of Britain*, ed. Michael D Reeve, trans. Neil Wright (Woodbridge, Suffolk: The Boydell Press, 2007).

MORMILE, Giuseppe. *Descrittione del Amenissimo Distretto della Città di Napoli* (Naples: Tarquinio Longo, 1617).

MORYSON, Fynes. *An Itinerary Written by Fynes Morison Gent. First in the Latine Tongue, and Then Translated by Him into English: Containing His Ten Yeeres Travell Through the Twelve Dominions of Germany, Bohmerland, Sweitzerland, Netherland, Denmarke, Poland, Italy, Turky, France, England, Scotland, and Ireland* (London: John Beale, 1617).

MUNDAY, Anthony. *The English Romayne Lyfe, 1582*, ed. G. B. Harrison (Edinburgh: Edinburgh University Press, 1966).

MURRAY, John. *A Handbook for Travellers in Southern Italy* (London: John Murray, 1878).

NEMESIANUS. *Hirtengedichte Aus Spätrömischer und Karolingischer Zeit: Marcus Aurelius Olympius Nemesianus, Severus Sanctus Endelechius, Modoinus, Hirtengedicht Aus Dem Codex Gaddianus*, ed. Dietmar Korzeniewski (Darmstadt: Wissenschaftliche Buchgesellschaft, 1976).

———. *Oeuvres*, ed. Pierre Volpilhac (Paris: Les Belles Lettres, 1975).

———. *The Eclogues and Cynegetica*, ed. Heather J. Williams (Leiden: Brill, 1986).

———. *The Eclogues of Calpurnius and Nemesianus*, ed. Charles Haines Keene (Hildesheim: Georg Olms, 1969).

———. *The Eclogues of Nemesian and the Einsiedeln Manuscript*, ed. J. B. Pearce (San Antonio, TX: Scylax Press, 1992).

PADIGLIONE, Carlo. *Le Legge dell'Accademia degli Oziosi in Napoli Ritrovate nella Biblioteca Brancacciana* (Naples: F. Giannini, 1878).

PATRIZI, Francesco. *La Deca Ammirabili* (Ferrara: Vittorio Baldini, 1587).

PLATO. *Lysis*, eds. Terry Penner and Christopher Rowe (Cambridge: Cambridge University Press, 2005).

PLUTARCH. *Essays*, trans. Robin Waterfield (London: Penguin Books, 1992).

Poesie de' Signori Accademici Fantastici di Roma (Rome: Grignano, 1637).

POLIZIANO, Angelo Ambrogini. *Prose Volgari Inedite e Poesie Latine e Greche Edite e Inedite*, ed. Isidore del Lungo (Hildesheim: Georg Olms, 1976).

RAYMOND, John. *An Itinerary Contayning a Voyage, Made through Italy, in the Yeare 1646, and 1647* (London: Humphrey Moseley, 1648).

RENNES, William of. *Gesta Regum Britannie*. In *The Historia Regum Britannie of Geoffrey of Monmouth V: Gesta Regum Britannie*, ed. and trans. Neil Wright (Cambridge: D. S. Brewer, 1991).

Rerum Britannicarum, id est Angliae, Scotiae, Vicinarumque Insularum ac Regionum Scriptores Vetustiores ac Praecipui (Heidelberg: Commelinus, 1587).

REUSNER, Nicolaus. *De Italia, Regione Europae Nobilissima Libri Duo* (Strasbourg: Bernardus Iobinus, 1585).

ROBINSON, Richard, trans. *A Learned and True Assertion of the Original, Life, Actes, and Death of the Most Noble, Valiant, and Renoumed Prince Arthure, King of Great Brittaine ... Collected and Written of Late Yeares in Lattin, by the Learned English Antiquarie of Worthy Memory John Leyland* (London: John Wolfe, 1582).

ROBORTELLO, Francesco. *In Librum Aristotelis De Arte Poetica Explicationes* (Florence: L. Torrentinus, 1548).
SANDYS, George. *A Relation of a Journey Begun in Anno Domini 1610*, (London: William Barrett, 1615).
——————. *Travels, Containing an History of the ... Turkish Empire* (London: William Barrett, 1615).
SANNAZARO, Iacopo. *Opera Omnia* (Lyons: Seb. Gryphius, 1536).
SARNELLI, Pompeo. *Guida de' Forastieri, Curiosi di Vedere e d'Intendere Le Cose Più Notabili della Regal Città di Napoli, e del suo Amenissimo Distretto* (Naples: Giuseppe Roselli, 1697).
SCARAMUCCIA, Angelita. *Discorso Historico ... sopra l'Origine, e Rovina di Ricinia, e dell' Edificatione, ed Avenimenti di Monte Cassiano* (Loreto: Paolo and Giovanni Battista Serafini, 1638).
——————. *Gli Amor Concordi* (Macerata: Pietro Salvioni, 1618).
——————. *Il Belisario* (Rome: Lodovico Grignano, 1635).
——————. *Il Garbuglio* (Macerata: Pietro Salvioni, 1624).
——————. *La Damigella* (Rome: Pietro Salvioni 1631).
——————. *La Schiava di Cipro* (Macerata: Pietro Salvioni, 1624).
——————. *La Vagante di Egitto* (Rome: Pietro Salvioni, 1631).
SCOPPA, Lucio Giovanni. *Parthenopei in Varios Authores Collectanea* (Naples: Sigismondo Mayr, 1507).
SELDEN, John. *Opera Omnia*, ed. David Wilkins, 3 vols. (London: John Walthoe, 1726).
SERASSI, Pierantonio. *La Vita del Tasso* (Rome: Pagliarini, 1785).
SEVILLE, Isidore of. *Etymologiarum Libri XX*, in *Patrologia Latina*, ed. Migne, LXXXII (1850), 73–1054.
SHAKESPEARE, William. *Comedies, Histories, & Tragedies* (London: Isaac Iaggard and Ed. Blunt, 1623).
SILVEYRA, Miguel. *El Macabeo Poema Heroico* (Naples: Egidio Longo, 1638).
SPENSER, Edmund. *The Faerie Queene*, ed. A. C. Hamilton (Oxford: Routledge, 2013).
——————. *The Shorter Poems*, eds. William A. Oram, Einar Bjorvand, Ronald Bond, Thomas H. Cain, Alexander Dunlop, and Richard Schell (New Haven, CT: Yale University Press, 1989).
SPERELLI, Alessandro. *Paradossi Morali* (Venice: Paolo Baglioni, 1666).
STELLUTI, Francesco. *Persio Tradotto in Verso Sciolto* (Rome: Giacomo Mascardi, 1630).
STIGLIANI, Tommaso. *Dello Occhiale Opera Difensiva Del Cavalier Fr. Tomaso Stigliani. Scritta in Risposta al Cavalier Gio. Battista Marini* (Venice: Pietro Carampello, 1627).
——————. *Il Mondo Nuovo* (Piacenza: Alessandro Bazacchi, 1617).
——————. *Lettere* (Rome: Angelo Bernabo, 1664).
TASSO, Torquato. *Apologia in Difesa della Sua Gierusalemme Liberata* (Mantua: Francesco Osana, 1585).
——————. *Delle Lettere Familiari*, 2 vols. (Bergamo: Comino Ventura, 1588).
——————. *Di Gerusalemme Conquistata del Sig. Torquato Tasso Libri XXIIII* (Rome: Guglielmo Facciotti, 1593).

———. *Discorsi ... dell'Arte Poetica; et in Particolare del Poema Heroico* (Venice: Giulo Vassalini, 1587).

———. *Gerusalemme Conquistata: Ms. Vind.Lat.72 della Biblioteca Nazionale di Napoli*, ed. Claudio Gigante (Alessandria: Edizioni dell'Orso, 2010).

———. *Gerusalemme Liberata* (Parma: Erasmo Viotti, 1581).

———. *Il Manso, Overo Dell' Amicitia Dialogo del Sig. Torquato Tasso. Al Molto Illustre Sig. Gio. Battista Manso* (Naples: Gio. Iacomo Carlino and Antonio Pace, 1596).

———. *Il Manso, Overo Dell' Amicitia Dialogo del Sig. Torquato Tasso. Al Molto Illustre Sig. Gio. Battista Manso* (Ferrara: Vittorio Ballini, 1602).

———. *Le Lettere*, ed. Cesare Guasti, 5 vols. (Florence: Felice Le Monnier, 1853–1855).

———. *Le Sette Giornate del Mondo Creato* (Viterbo: Girolamo Discepolo, 1607).

TERENCE. *Comoediae Sex cum Interpretatione Donati et Calphurnii et Commentario Perpetuo*, ed. Arn. Henr. Westerhoven (The Hague: Isaac van der Kloot, 1732).

TESAURO, Emanuele. "Metafora Settima di Oppositione." In *Il Cannocchiale Aristotelico, o Sia Idèa dell'Arguta et Ingegnosa Elocutione* (Bologna: Gioseffo Longhi, 1675), 294–305.

TESAURO, Lodovico. *Ragioni del Conte Lodovico Tesauro In Difesa d'Un Sonetto del Cavalier Marino* (Bologna: Vittorio Benacci, 1614).

TILBURY, Gervase of. *Otia Imperialia: Recreation for an Emperor*, ed. and trans. S. E. Banks and J. W. Binns (Oxford: Clarendon Press, 2002).

TRISSINO, Giangiorgio. *Tutte Le Opere*, 2 vols. (Verona: Jacopo Vallarsi, 1729).

Trium Fratrum Amaltheorum Hieronimi, Io. Baptistae, Cornelii Carmina: Accessere Hieronymi Aleandri Iunioris Amaltheorum Cognati Poematia (Venice: Andrea Muschio, 1627).

TURLER, Hieronymus. *De Peregrinatione et Agro Neapolitano Libri II ... Omnibus Peregrinantibus Utiles ac Necessarii ac in Eorum Gratiam Nunc Primum Editi* (Strasbourg: Bernardus Iobinus, 1574).

VALLANS, William. *A Tale of Two Swanns. Wherein Is Comprehended the Original and Increase of The River Lee* (London: Roger Ward, 1590).

VERMIGLI, Peter Martyr. *In Librum Iudicum ... Commentarii* (Zurich: Christophorus Froschoverus, 1565).

VILLANI, Nicola. *L'Uccellatura di Vincenzo Foresi all' Occhiale del Cavaliere Fra. Tomaso Stigliani contro l'Adone del Cavalier Gio. Battista Marini, e alla Difesa di Girolamo Aleandro* (Venice: Antonio Pinelli, 1630).

VIRGIL. *Aeneidos Liber Secundus*, ed. R. G. Austin (Oxford: Clarendon Press, 1964).

———. *Bucolica et Georgica*, ed. Jean Luis De la Cerda (Cologne: Bernhard Wolter, 1628).

———. *Eclogues*, ed. Robert Coleman (Cambridge: Cambridge University Press, 1977).

———. *Opera*, ed. F. A. Hirtzel (Oxford: Clarendon Press, 1942).

———. *Priores Sex Libri Aeneidos Argumentis, Explicationibus, Notis Illustrati*, ed. Jean Luis De La Cerda, (Lyon: Horatius Cardon, 1612).

———. *The Pastoral Poems: The Text of the Eclogues*, trans. E. V. Rieu (Baltimore: Penguin, 1967).

Vitae Vergilianae Antiquae, eds. Giorgio Brugnoli and Fabio Stok (Rome: Istituto Poligrafico e Zecca dello Stato, 1997).
Vocabulario degli Accademici della Crusca (Venice: Giovanni Alberti, 1612).
WEBBE, Edward. *Chief Master Gunner, His Travailes. 1590*, ed. Edward Arber (London: Alex Murray & Son, 1869).
WILSON, Thomas. *The Arte of Rhetorique, for the Use of All Suche as are Studious of Eloquence, Set Forthe in Englishe* (London: Ihon Kingston, 1560).

6. WORKS OF REFERENCE

A Latin Dictionary, eds. C. T. Lewis and Charles Short (Oxford: Clarendon Press, 1955).
A Transcript of the Registers of the Worshipful Company of Stationers from 1640–1708, ed. G. F. Briscoe, 3 vols. (London: s.n. 1913–1914).
Diccionario de Historia de España, ed. Germán Bleiberg, 3 vols. (2nd ed. Madrid: Alianza, 1968–1969).
Dizionario Biografico degli Italiani, 100 vols. (Rome: Istituto dell' Enciclopedia Italiana, 1960–2020).
Glossarium Mediae et Infimae Latinitatis, eds. Charles de Fresne Du Cange et al. (Niort: L. Favre, 1883–1887).
Neue Deutsche Biographie, ed. Historische Kommission bei der Bayrischen Akademie der Wissenschaften (Berlin: Duncker und Humblot, 1953–).
Oxford Dictionary of National Biography, 60 vols. (Oxford: Oxford University Press, 2004).
Oxford Latin Dictionary, ed. P. G. W. Glare (Oxford: Clarendon Press, 1968–1982).
Patrologia Latina Cursus Completus. Series Latina, ed. J-P. Migne, 221 vols. (Paris: Garnier Frères, 1844–1864).
Paulys Realencyclopädie der Classischen Altertumwissenschaft, eds. Georg Wissowa, Wilhelm Kroll, Karl Mittelhaus, and Konrat Ziegler, 85 vols. (Stuttgart: A. Druckenmüller, 1893–1978).
Storia delle Accademie d'Italia, ed. Michele Maylender, 5 vols. (Bologna: L. Capelli, 1926–1930).

7. SECONDARY LITERATURE

ACKRILL, John L. "Aristotle on Eudaimonia." *Proceedings of the British Academy* 60 (1974): 339–359.
AHL, Frederick. "Amber, Avalon, and Apollo's Singing Swan." *American Journal of Philology* 103 (1982): 373–411.
ALLODOLI, Ettore. *Giovanni Milton e l'Italia* (Prato: Vestri & Spighi, 1907).
ALMAGIÀ, Roberto. *L'Opera Geografica di Luca Holstenio*, Studi e Testi 102 (Vatican City: Biblioteca Apostolica Vaticana, 1942).

ALPERS, Paul J. *The Singer of The Eclogues: A Study of Virgilian Pastoral* (Berkeley: University of California Press, 1979).
ANNAS, Julia. "Plato and Aristotle on Friendship and Altruism." *Mind* 86 (1977): 532–554.
ANTON, John P., and George L. KUSTAS, eds. *Essays in Ancient Greek Philosophy*, vol. I, (Albany: State University of New York Press, 1971).
ARNOTT, W. Geoffrey. "Swan Songs." *Greece & Rome* 24 (1977): 149–153.
ARZALLUZ, Iñigo Ruiz, Alejandro Martínez SOBRINO, M.ª Teresa Muñoz García DE ITURRSOPE, Iñaki Ortigosa EGIRAUN, and Enara San Juan MANSO, eds. *Estudios de Filología e Historia en Honor del Profesor Vitalino Valcárcel*, 2 vols. (Vitoria-Gasteiz: Universidad del País Vasco, 2014).
ASTARITA, Tommaso, ed. *A Companion to Early Modern Naples* (Leiden: Brill, 2013).
BACCHI, Andrea. "Un Esempio Precoce di *Speaking Likeness* tra Vouet e Bernini: Il *Giovanni Battista Marino* di Cochet in San Domenico a Napoli." *Nuovi Studi: Rivista di Arte Moderna* 14 (2008): 121–125.
BADHWAR, Neera Kapur, ed. *Friendship: A Philosophical Reader* (Ithaca, NY: Cornell University Press, 1993).
BAKER, Stewart A. "Sannazaro and Milton's Brief Epic." *Comparative Literature* 20 (1968): 116–132.
BALDASSARRI, Guido. "L'Arte del Dialogo in Torquato Tasso." *Studi Tassiani* 20 (1970): 5–46.
BALDI, Agnello. "La 'Fenice Rinascente' di Tommaso Gaudiosi e La Traduzione Letteraria nel Seicento Italiano." *Studi Secenteschi* 18 (1977): 127–144.
BARCHIESI, Alessandro. "Masculinity in the 90's: The Education of Achilles in Statius and Quintilian." In *Roman and Greek Imperial Epic*, ed. Paschalis, 47–75.
BARONI, Giorgio, ed. *Storia della Critica Letteraria in Italia* (Turin: UTET, 1997).
BARTOCCI, Barbara. "Paolo Beni and Galileo Galilei: The Classical Tradition and the Reception of The Astronomical Revolution." *Rivista di Storia della Filosofia* 71 (2016): 423–452.
BASILE, Bruno. "La Più Antica Biografia del Tasso." *Italianistica: Rivista di Letteratura Italiana* 24 (1995): 525–539.
———. "Tasso Traduttore: La Versione Poetica del 'De Ave Phoenice' dello Pseudo-Lattanzio nel 'Mondo Creato.'" *Lettere Italiane* 31 (1979): 342–405.
———, ed. *La Fenice: Da Claudiano a Tasso* (Rome: Carocci, 2004).
BATES, Catherine, ed. *A Companion to Renaissance Poetry* (Oxford: Wiley Blackwell, 2018).
BELLI, Carolina. "La Fondazione del Collegio dei Nobili di Napoli." In *Chiesa, Assistenza e Società*, ed. Russo, 183–280.
BELLI, Pietro, ed. *Palazzo Donn' Anna: Storia, Arte e Natura* (Turin: Allemandi, 2017).
BENET, Diana Treviño. "The Escape From Rome: Milton's Second Defense and a Renaissance Genre." In *Milton in Italy*, ed. Di Cesare, 29–49.
BERGER, Harry, Jr. "The Aging Boy: Paradise and Parricide in Spenser's *Shepheards Calender*." In *Poetic Traditions*, eds. Mack and Lord, 25–46.
BESOMI, Ottavio. "Tommaso Stigliani: Tra Parodia e Critica." *Studi Secenteschi* 13 (1972): 5–73.

BIAGIOLI, Mario. *Galileo's Instruments of Credit: Telescopes, Images, Secrecy* (Chicago: The University of Chicago Press, 2006).
BIDDLE, Martin. *King Arthur's Round Table: An Archaeological Investigation* (Woodbridge: The Boydell Press, 2000).
BINNI, Walter, ed. *I Classici Italiani nella Storia della Critica*, 2 vols. (Florence: La Nuova Italia, 1955).
BLACK, Charlene Villaseñor, and Mari-Tere ÁLVAREZ, eds. *Renaissance Futurities: Science, Art, Invention* (Oakland: University of California Press, 2020).
BLACK, John. *Life of Torquato Tasso with An Historical and Critical Account of His Writings*, 2 vols. (Edinburgh: John Murray, 1810).
BLOM, F. J. "Lucas Holstenius (1596–1661) and England." In *Studies in Seventeenth-Century English Literature, History and Bibliography*, eds. Janssens and Aarts, 25–39.
BLOOM, Harold. *The Anxiety of Influence: A Theory of Poetry* (Oxford: Oxford University Press, 1973).
BOBONICH, Christopher, ed. *The Cambridge Companion to Ancient Ethics* (Cambridge: Cambridge University Press, 2017).
BOEHM, Friedrich. *Lustratio, Paulys Realencyclopädie der Classischen Altertumwissenschaft* 13 (1927): 2029–2039.
BOEHM, Laetitia, and Ezio RAIMONDI, eds. *Università, Accademie e Società Scientifiche in Italia e in Germania dal Cinquecento al Settecento* (Bologna: Il Mulino, 1981).
BOESKY, Amy. "Milton, Galileo, and Sunspots: Optics and Certainty in *Paradise Lost*." *Milton Studies* 34 (1996): 23–43.
BOLD, John, and Edward CHANEY, eds. *English Architecture Public and Private: Essays for Kerry Downes* (London: Hambleton Press, 1993).
BOLOTIN, David. *Plato's Dialogue on Friendship: An Interpretation of the Lysis, with a New Translation* (Ithaca, NY: Cornell University Press, 1979).
BORZELLI, Angelo. *Giovan Battista Manso Marchese di Villa* (Naples: Federico & Ardia, 1916).
———. *Storia della Vita e delle Opere di Giovan Battista Marino* (Naples: Artigianelli, 1927).
BOTTKOL, Joseph McG. "The Holograph of Milton's Letter to Holstenius." *Publications of the Modern Language Association of America* 68 (1953): 617–627.
BOUTIER, Jean, Brigitte MARIN, and Antonella ROMANO, eds. *Naples, Rome, Florence: Une Histoire Comparée des Milieux Intellectuels Italiens (XVIIe–XVIIIe Siècles)* (Rome: École Française de Rome, 2005).
BOYD, Barbara Weiden. "Arms and the Man: Wordplay and the Catasterism of Chiron in Ovid *Fasti* 5." *American Journal of Philology* 122 (2001): 67–80.
BRADNER, Leicester. "Milton's *Epitaphium Damonis*." *Times Literary Supplement* (18 August 1932): 581.
BRADY, Maura. "Galileo in Action: The 'Telescope' in *Paradise Lost*." *Milton Studies* 44 (2005): 129–152.
BRAND, C. P. "Stylistic Trends in the *Gerusalemme Conquistata*." In *Italian Studies Presented to E.R. Vincent*, eds. Brand, Foster, and Limentani, 136–153.
———. *Torquato Tasso: A Study of the Poet and of his Contribution to English Literature* (Cambridge: Cambridge University Press, 1965).

BRAND, C. P., Kenelm FOSTER, and Uberto LIMENTANI, eds. *Italian Studies Presented to E.R. Vincent on his Retirement from the Chair of Italian at Cambridge* (Cambridge: W. Heffer, 1962).
BRAND, Peter, and Lino Pertile, eds. *The Cambridge History of Italian Literature* (Cambridge: Cambridge University Press, 2007).
BRASWELL, Bruce. "Apollo at Chiron's Cave: A Note on Milton's 'Mansus,' 59–60." *Arethusa* 3 (1970): 197–203.
BRAZEAU, Bryan. "Who Wants to Live Forever? Overcoming Poetic Immortality in Torquato Tasso's *Gerusalemme Conquistata*." *Modern Language Notes* 129 (2014): 42–61.
BRESCIANI, Antonio. "L'Ebreo di Verona: Racconto Storico dall'Anno 1846 all'Anno 1849." *Civiltà Cattolica* II (1851): 157–158.
BROMWICH, Rachel, A. O. H. JARMAN, and Brynley F. ROBERTS, eds. *The Arthur of the Welsh: The Arthurian Legend in Medieval Welsh Literature* (Cardiff: University of Wales Press, 1991).
BROOKES, Ian. "The Death of Chiron: Ovid, *Fasti* 5.379–414." *Classical Quarterly* 44 (1994): 444–450.
BROWN, Cedric C. *Friendship and Its Discourses in the Seventeenth Century* (Oxford: Oxford University Press, 2016).
BROWN, Phyllis R., and Stephen L. WAILES, eds. *A Companion to Hrotsvit of Gandersheim (fl. 960)* (Leiden: Brill, 2013).
BROWN, Phyllis R., Linda A. MCMILLIN, and Katharina M. WILSON, eds. *Hrotsvit of Gandersheim: Contexts, Identities, Affinities, and Performances* (Toronto: University of Toronto Press, 2004).
BRUNT, P.A. "'Amicitia' in the Late Roman Republic." *Proceedings of the Cambridge Philological Society* 11 (1965): 1–20.
BURKE, Peter. "The Renaissance Dialogue." *Renaissance Studies* 3 (1989): 1–12.
BUSH, Douglas. "The Date of Milton's *Ad Patrem*." *Modern Philology* 61 (1964): 204–208.
BYER, Silvia Giovanardi. "Celestial Crusades and Wars in Heaven: The Biblical Epics of the Late 1500s" (PhD thesis, University of North Carolina, Chapel Hill, 2008).
CAIRNS, Francis. *Sextus Propertius: The Augustan Elegist* (Cambridge: Cambridge University Press, 2006).
CALARESU, Melissa, and Helen HILLS, eds. "Introduction: Between Exoticism and Marginalization: New Approaches to Naples." In *New Approaches to Naples*, eds. Calaresu and Hills, 1–8.
———, eds. *New Approaches to Naples c.1500–c.1800: The Power of Place* (London: Routledge, 2016).
CALITTI, Floriana C. "Manso, Giovan Battista." *Dizionario Biografico degli Italiani* 69 (2007): 148–152.
CALUORI, Damian, ed. *Thinking About Friendship: Historical and Contemporary Philosophical Perspectives* (Basingstoke: Palgrave Macmillan, 2013).
CAMPBELL, Gordon. "Milton and the Lives of the Ancients." *Journal of the Warburg and Courtauld Institutes* 47 (1984): 234–238.
———. "Milton's Spanish." *Milton Quarterly* 30 (1996): 127–132.
CANEVARI, Enrico. *Lo Stile del Marino nell' Adone* (Pavia: Giuseppe Frattini, 1901).

CAPUANO, Giovanni. *Viaggiatori Britannici a Napoli tra '500 e '600* (Salerno: Pietro Laveglia, 1994).
CARLEY, James P. "John Leland." In *The Spenser Encyclopedia*, eds. Hamilton et al., 433.
———. "John Leland's 'Cygnea Cantio': A Neglected Tudor River Poem." *Humanistica Lovaniensia* 32 (1983): 225–241.
———. "Leland, John (c. 1503–1552), Poet and Antiquary." *Oxford Dictionary of National Biography* (Oxford: Oxford University Press, 2004). http//www.oxforddnb.com
———. "Polydore Vergil and John Leland on King Arthur: The Battle of the Books." *Interpretations* 15 (1984): 86–100.
———. "The Manuscript Remains of John Leland, 'The King's Antiquary.'" *Text: Transactions for the Society for Textual Scholarship* 2 (1985): 111–120.
CARLEY, James P., and Felicity RIDDY, eds. *Arthurian Literature XVI* (Cambridge: Brewer, 1998).
CARMINATI, Clizia. "Loredan, Giovan Francesco." *Dizionario Biografico degli Italiani* 65 (2005): 761–770.
CARRIÓ-INVERNIZZI, Diana. "Royal and Viceregal Art Patronage in Naples (1500–1800)." In *A Companion to Early Modern Naples*, ed. Astarita, 383–404.
CARUSO, Carlo. *Adonis: The Myth of the Dying God in the Italian Renaissance* (London: Bloomsbury, 2013).
CATELLO, Elio. "Marmi, Bronzi, Argenti et Stucchi." In *Seicento Napoletano*, ed. Pane, 343–362.
CATELLO, Elio, and Corrado CATELLO. *La Cappella del Tesoro di San Gennaro* (Naples: Edizione del Banco di Napoli, 1977).
CERINO, Vincenzo. *Il Real Monte Manso di Scala nella Storia della Città della Nobiltà Napoletana* (Naples: Rolando, 2009).
CESERANI, Giovanna. *Italy's Lost Greece: Magna Graecia and the Making of Modern Archaeology* (Oxford: Oxford University Press, 2012).
CHANEY, Edward. "Inigo Jones in Naples." In *English Architecture Public and Private*, eds. Bold and Chaney, 31–53.
———. *The Evolution of the Grand Tour: Anglo-Italian Cultural Relations since the Renaissance* (London: Frank Cass, 1998).
———. "The Grand Tour and Beyond: British and American Travellers in Southern Italy, 1545–1960." In *Oxford, China and Italy*, eds. Chaney and Ritchie, 133–160.
———. *The Grand Tour and the Great Rebellion: Richard Lassels and "The Voyage of Italy" in the Seventeenth Century* (Geneva: Slatkine, 1985).
CHANEY, Edward, and Neil RITCHIE, eds. *Oxford, China and Italy: Writings in Honour of Sir Harold Acton on His Eightieth Birthday* (London: Thames and Hudson, 1985).
CHANKOWSKI, Véronique. *Athènes et Délos à L'Époque Classique: Recherches sur L'Administration du Sanctuaire d'Apollon Délien* (Paris: De Boccard, 2008).
CHENEY, Patrick. "'Novells of His Devise': Chaucerian and Virgilian Career Paths in Spenser's *Februarie* Eclogue." In *European Literary Careers*, eds. Cheney and De Armas, 231–267.

CHENEY, Patrick, and Frederick A. DE ARMAS, eds. *European Literary Careers: The Author from Antiquity to the Renaissance* (Toronto: University of Toronto Press, 2002).
CHERCHI, Paolo. "Marino and the Meraviglia." In *Culture and Authority in the Baroque*, eds. Ciavolella and Coleman, 63–72.
——————. "The Seicento: Poetry, Philosophy and Science." In *The Cambridge History of Italian Literature*, eds. Brand and Pertile, 301–317.
CIAVOLELLA, Massimo, and Patrick COLEMAN, eds. *Culture and Authority in the Baroque* (Toronto: University of Toronto Press, 2005).
CINQUEMANI, A. M. *Glad to Go for a Feast: Milton, Buonmattei, and the Florentine Accademici* (New York: Peter Lang, 1998).
CLEMENS, Justin. "Galileo's Telescope in John Milton's *Paradise Lost*: The Modern Origin of the Critique of Science as Instrumental Rationality?" *Filozofski Vestnik* 33 (2012): 163–194.
COCCO, Sean. *Watching Vesuvius: A History of Science and Culture in Early Modern Italy* (Chicago: University of Chicago Press, 2013).
COCHRANE, E. W. *Tradition and Enlightenment in the Tuscan Academies 1690–1800* (Chicago: University of Chicago Press, 1961).
COLOMBO, Michele. "Benedetto Buonmattei e La Questione della Lingua nel Primo Seicento." *Aevum* 77 (2003): 615–634.
COMPARATO, Vittor Ivo. "Cornelio, Tommaso." *Dizionario Biografico degli Italiani* 29 (1983): 136–140.
——————. "Società Civile e Società Letteraria nel Primo Seicento: L'Accademia degli Oziosi." *Quaderni Storici* 23 (1973): 359–388.
CONDEE, Ralph W. "*Mansus* and the Panegyric Tradition." *Studies in the Renaissance* (1968): 174–192.
——————. *Structure in Milton's Poetry: From the Foundation to the Pinnacles* (University Park: Pennsylvania State University Press, 1974).
——————. "The Structure of Milton's 'Epitaphium Damonis.'" *Studies in Philology* 62 (1965): 577–594.
CONTARINO, Rosario. "Errico, Scipione." *Dizionario Biografico degli Italiani* 43 (1993): 261–265.
CONTE, Floriana. *Tra Napoli e Milano. Viaggi di Artisti nell' Italia del Seicento I. Da Tanzio da Varallo a Massimo Stanzione* (Florence: Edifir, 2012).
COOK, Brendan. *Pursuing Eudaimonia: Re-Appropriating the Greek Philosophical Foundations of the Christian Apophatic Tradition* (Newcastle upon Tyne: Cambridge Scholars Publishing, 2013).
COOPER, Helen. "Milton's King Arthur." *Review of English Studies* 65 (2014): 252–265.
COOPER, John M. "Aristotle on the Forms of Friendship." *Review of Metaphysics* 30 (1976): 619–648.
——————. "Friendship and the Good in Aristotle." *Philosophical Review* 86 (1977): 290–315.
CORNS, Thomas N. "Milton and the Limitations of Englishness." In *Early Modern Nationalism and Milton's England*, eds. Loewenstein and Stevens, 205–216.
CORTHELL, Ronald, and Thomas N. CORNS, eds. *Milton and Catholicism* (Notre Dame, IN: University of Notre Dame Press, 2017).

Cox, Virginia. "Rhetoric and Politics in Tasso's *Nifo*." *Studi Secenteschi* 30 (1989): 3–98.

———. *The Renaissance Dialogue: Literary Dialogue in its Social and Political Contexts, Castiglione to Galileo* (Cambridge: Cambridge University Press, 1992).

Croce, Francesco. "Nuovi Compiti della Critica del Marino e del Marinismo." *La Rassegna della Letteratura Italiana* 61 (1957): 459–473.

Croce, Franco. "Giambattista Marino." In *I Classici Italiani*, ed. Binni, II: 47–90.

———. *Tre Momenti del Barocco Letterario Italiano* (Florence: Sansoni, 1966).

Cropper, Elizabeth. *The Domenichino Affair: Novelty, Imitation, and Theft in Seventeenth-Century Rome* (New Haven, CT: Yale University Press, 2005).

———. "The Petrifying Art: Marino's Poetry and Caravaggio." *Metropolitan Museum Journal* 26 (1991): 193–212.

Curtius, Ernst Robert. *European Literature and the Latin Middle Ages* (London: Routledge, 1953).

Darbishire, Helen. "The Chronology of Milton's Handwriting." *The Library* 14 (1934): 229–235.

Davis, Gregson. *Parthenope: The Interplay of Ideas in Vergilian Bucolic* (Leiden: Brill, 2012).

De Divitiis, Gigliola Pagano. *English Merchants in Seventeenth-Century Italy*, trans. Stephen Parkin (Cambridge: Cambridge University Press, 1990).

De Filippis, Michele. "Anecdotes in Manso's 'Vita di Tasso' and Their Sources." *University of California Publications in Modern Philology* 18 (1936): 443–502.

———. "G. B. Manso's *Enciclopedia*." *University of California Publications in Modern Philology* 20 (1937): 239–288.

———. "Milton and Manso: Cups or Books?" *Publications of the Modern Language Association of America* 51 (1936): 745–756.

De Iturrospe, M.ª Teresa Muńoz García. "Some Classical Patterns in John Milton's Latin Funerary Compositions." In *Estudios de Filología e Historia*, eds. Arzalluz et al., II, 727–736.

De Michele, Giuseppe. "Nicolò Franco. Biografia con Documenti Inediti." *Studi di Letteratura Italiana* 11 (1915): 61–154.

De Miranda, Girolamo. "'À de Vagues Desseins L'Homme est Toujours en Proie': L'Accademia degli Oziosi e i Suoi Antagonisti tra Riti Fondativi e Costruzione d'Identità." In *Naples, Rome, Florence*, eds. Boutier, Marin, and Romano, 89–104.

———. *Una Quiete Operosa: Forma e Pratiche dell'Accademia Napoletana degli Oziosi 1611–1645* (Naples: Fridericiana Editrice Universitaria, 2000).

Denman, Thomas. "A Gift Text of Hispano-Neapolitan Diplomacy: Giovan Battista Manso's *Erocallia* (1628)." *History of European Ideas* 42 (2016): 683–693.

———. "Giovan Battista Manso and the Politics of Publishing *I Paradossi* (1608) and *Erocallia* (1628)." Paper presented at the 60th Annual Meeting of the Renaissance Society of America in New York on 27–29 March 2014.

DI BIASE, Carmine G., ed. *Travel and Translation in the Early Modern Period* (Amsterdam and New York: Rodopi, 2006).

DI CESARE, Mario A., ed. *Milton in Italy: Contexts, Images, Contradictions* (Binghamton, NY: Medieval and Renaissance Texts and Studies, 1991).

DICKSON, Donald R., and Holly Faith NELSON, eds. *Of Paradise and Light: Essays on Henry Vaughan and John Milton in Honor of Alan Rudrum* (Newark: University of Delaware Press, 2004).

DI LIELLO, Salvatore. *Il Paesaggio dei Campi Flegrei: Realtà e Metafora* (Naples: Electa Napoli, 2005).

DOBRANSKI, Stephen B. *Milton's Visual Imagination: Imagery in "Paradise Lost"* (Cambridge: Cambridge University Press, 2015).

——————, ed. *Political Turmoil: Early Modern British Literature in Transition, 1623–1660* (Cambridge: Cambridge University Press, 2019).

DOMINIK, W. J., C. E. NEWLANDS, and K. GERVAIS, eds. *Brill's Companion to Statius* (Leiden: Brill, 2015).

DZELZAINIS, Martin, and Edward HOLBERTON, eds. *The Oxford Handbook of Andrew Marvell* (Oxford: Oxford University Press, 2019).

EAMON, William. "Medicine as a Hunt: Searching for Secrets of the New World." In *Renaissance Futurities*, eds. Black and Álvarez, 100–117.

EDWARDS, Karen L. "Raphael, Diodati." In *Of Paradise and Light*, eds. Dickson and Nelson, 123–141.

ENGELBACH, Lewis. *Naples and the Campagna Felice. In a Series of Letters Addressed to a Friend in England in 1802* (London: R. Ackermann, 1815).

EVERSON, Jane E., Denis V. REIDY, and Lisa SAMPSON, eds. *The Italian Academies 1525–1700: Networks of Culture, Innovation and Dissent* (Cambridge: Legenda, 2016).

FABRIS, Dinko. *Music in Seventeenth-Century Naples: Francesco Provenzale (1624–1704)* (Aldershot: Ashgate, 2007).

FERRERO, G. G, ed. *Marino e i Marinisti* (Milan: Ricciardi, 1954).

FIELD, Arthur. *The Origins of the Platonic Academy of Florence* (Princeton, NJ: Princeton University Press, 1988).

FINDLEN, Paula, Wendy Wassyng ROWORTH, and Catherine M. SAMA, eds. *Italy's Eighteenth Century: Gender and Culture in the Age of the Grand Tour* (Stanford, CA: Stanford University Press, 2009).

FINK, Z. S. "Milton and the Theory of Climatic Influence." *Modern Language Quarterly* 2 (1941): 67–80.

FIORELLI, Piero, ed. "Il 'Trattato della Pronunzia' di Benedetto Buommattei." *Studi Linguistici Italiani* 1 (1960): 109–161.

FIRPO, Luigi. "Campanella, Tommaso." *Dizionario Biografico degli Italiani* 17 (1974): 372–401.

FISH, Stanley. *Surprised by Sin: The Reader in Paradise Lost* (Basingstoke: Macmillan, 1997).

FISHER, Barbara M. *Noble Numbers, Subtle Words: The Art of Mathematics in the Science of Storytelling* (London: Associated University Presses, 1997).

FITZPATRICK, Mary Cletus. "Lactanti De Ave Phoenice" (PhD thesis, University of Pennsylvania, 1933).

FLANNAGAN, Roy. "Art, Artists, Galileo and Concordances." *Milton Quarterly* 20 (1986): 103–105.
FLETCHER, H. F. "The Seventeenth-Century Separate Printing of Milton's *Epitaphium Damonis*." *Journal of English and Germanic Philology* 61 (1962): 788–796.
FORTENBAUGH, W. W. "Aristotle's Analysis of Friendship: Function and Analogy, Resemblance, and Focal Meaning." *Phronesis* 20 (1975): 51–62.
FOWLER, W. W. *Lustratio*. In *Anthropology and the Classics*, ed. Marrett, 169–191.
FRANCESCHETTI, Antonio. "Il Concetto di *Meraviglia* nelle Poetiche della Prima Arcadia." *Lettere Italiane* 21 (1969): 62–88.
FRARE, Pierantonio. "La 'Nuova Critica' della Meravigliosa Acutezza." In *Storia della Critica Letteraria*, ed. Baroni, 223–277.
FREEMAN, James A. "Milton's Roman Connection: Giovanni Salzilli." *Milton Studies* 19 (1984): 87–104.
FREITAS, Roger. "An Erotic Image of the Castrato Singer." In *Italy's Eighteenth Century*, eds. Findlen, Roworth, and Sama, 203–215.
FRIEDMAN, Donald. "Galileo and the Art of Seeing." In *Milton in Italy*, ed. Di Cesare, 159–174.
FUCHS, Peter. "Holste, Lukas." *Neue Deutsche Biographie* 9 (1972): 548–550.
FULCO, Giorgio. "Il Sogno di una 'Galeria': Nuovi Documenti dul Marino Collezionista." *Antologia di Belle Arti* 3 (1979): 84–99.
————. *La "Meravigliosa" Passione: Studi sul Barocco Tra Letteratura ed Arte* (Rome: Salerno, 2001).
GALLI, Giuseppe, ed. *Interpretazione e Meraviglia* (Pisa: Giardini, 1994).
GALLUZZI, Paolo. *The Lynx and The Telescope: The Parallel Worlds of Cesi and Galileo*, trans. Peter Mason (Leiden: Brill, 2017).
GARCÍA, Encarnación Sánchez. "'Aplicossi a Render Immortal La Sua Memoria nel Regno': El Virrey Medina de las Torres en Nápoles (1636–1644)." In *La Nobleza y Los Reinos*, ed. Martínez, 361–394.
————. "Il Viceré Medina de Las Torres a Napoli: Decoro del Lignaggio e Avanguardia Culturale." In *Palazzo Donn' Anna*, ed. Belli, 39–69.
GARRISON, Irene Peirano. "The Tomb of Virgil Between Text, Memory, and Site." In *Tombs of the Ancient Poets*, eds. Goldschmidt and Graziosi, 265–280.
GARVER, Eugene. "The Rhetoric of Friendship in Plato's *Lysis*." *Rhetorica* 24 (2006): 127–146.
GAZZARA, Loredano. "Giovanni Battista Manso, Promotore delle Arti e della Cultura." In *Manso, Lemos, Cervantes: Letteratura*, ed. Mondola, 39–67.
GERI, Lorenzo. "La Funzione del Paratesto negli *Erocallia* (1628) di Giovan Battista Manso." *Linguistica e Letteratura* 32 (2007): 61–77.
GIANFRANCESCO, Lorenza. "From Propaganda to Science: Looking at the World of Academies in Early Seventeenth-Century Naples." *California Italian Studies* 3 (2012): 1–31.
GIGANTE, Claudio. *"Vincer Pariemi Più se Stessa Antica": La "Gerusalemme Conquistata" nel Mondo Poetico di Torquato Tasso* (Naples: Bibliopolis, 1996).
GIMÉNEZ, José Antonio. "Friendship, Knowledge and Reciprocity in *Lysis*." *Apeiron* 53 (2020): 315–337.

GIRARDI, Raffaele. *La Società del Dialogo: Retorica e Ideologia nella Letteratura Conviviale del Cinquecento* (Bari: Adriatica, 1989).
GIUSTINIANI, Lorenzo. *Breve Contezza delle Accademie Istitute nel Regno di Napoli* (Naples: s.n., 1801).
—————. "Lettera al ch. Signor D. Luigi Targioni intorno alla Vita, ed alle Opere di Gio. Battista Manso Napoletano Marchese di Villa." *Giornale Letterario di Napoli per Servire di Continuazione all'Analisi Ragionata de' Libri Nuovi* 60 (1796): 3–34.
GOLDSCHMIDT, Nora, and Barbara GRAZIOSI, eds. *Tombs of the Ancient Poets: Between Literary Reception and Material Culture* (Oxford: Oxford University Press, 2018).
GONZALEZ, F. J. "Plato's *Lysis*: An Enactment of Philosophical Kinship." *Ancient Philosophy* 15 (1995): 69–90.
GOODE, James. "Milton and Sannazaro." *Times Literary Supplement* (13 August 1931): 621.
GOTTFRIED, Rudolf. "Milton, Lactantius, Claudian, and Tasso." *Studies in Philology* 30 (1933): 497–503.
GRECO, Pietro. *Galileo Galilei: The Tuscan Artist* (Cham, Switzerland: Springer, 2018).
GRUBER-MILLER, John. "Exploring Relationships: *Amicitia* and *Familia* in Cicero's *De Amicitia*." *Classical World* 103 (2009): 88–92.
GRUNEBAUM, James O. *Friendship: Liberty, Equality, and Utility* (Albany: State University of New York Press, 2003).
GUARDIANI, Francesco. *La Meravigliosa Retorica dell' 'Adone' di G.B. Marino* (Florence: Olschki, 1989).
GURRERI, Clizia, and Ilaria BIANCHI, eds. *Le Virtuose Adunanze. La Cultura Accademica tra XVI e XVIII Secolo* (Avellino: Edizioni Sinestesie, 2014).
GUY-BRAY, Stephen. "How to Turn Prose into Literature: The Case of Thomas Nashe." In *Early Modern Prose Fiction*, ed. Liebler, 33–45.
HAAN, Estelle. *Both English and Latin: Bilingualism and Biculturalism in Milton's Neo-Latin Writings* (Philadelphia: American Philosophical Society, 2012).
—————. "'Coelum non Animum Muto'?: Milton's Neo-Latin Poetry and Catholic Italy." In *Milton and Catholicism*, eds. Corthell and Corns, 131–167.
—————. "England, Neo-Latin, and the Continental Journey." In *Political Turmoil*, ed. Dobranski, 322–338.
—————. *From Academia to Amicitia: Milton's Latin Writings and the Italian Academies* (Philadelphia: American Philosophical Society, 1998).
—————. "John Milton Among the Neo-Latinists: Three Notes on *Mansus*." *Notes & Queries* 44 (1997): 172–176.
—————. *John Milton's Roman Sojourns, 1638–1639: Neo-Latin Self-Fashioning* (Philadelphia: American Philosophical Society Press, 2020).
—————. "Marvell's Latin Poetry and the Art of Punning." In *The Oxford Handbook of Andrew Marvell*, eds. Dzelzainis and Holberton, 463–480.
—————. "Milton and Two Italian Humanists: Some Hitherto Unnoticed Neo-Latin Echoes in *In Obitum Procancellarii Medici* and *In Obitum Praesulis Eliensis*." *Notes & Queries* 44 (1997): 176–181.

―――――. "Milton's Latin Poetry and Vida." *Humanistica Lovaniensia* 44 (1995): 282–304.
―――――. "Pastoral." In *A Guide to Neo-Latin Literature*, ed. Moul, 163–179.
HABINEK, T. N. "Towards a History of Friendly Advice: The Politics of Candor in Cicero's *De Amicitia*." *Apeiron* 23 (1990): 165–185.
HADEN, James. "Friendship in Plato's *Lysis*." *Review of Metaphysics* 37 (1983): 327–356.
HADFIELD, Andrew. "Chorography, Map-Mindedness, Poetics of Place." In *A Companion to Renaissance Poetry*, ed. Bates, 485–497.
HAGEN, Margareth, Randi KOPPEN, and Margery Vibe SKEGEN, eds. *The Human and its Limits: Explorations in Science, Literature and the Visual Arts* (Oslo: Scandanavian Academic Press, 2012).
HALE, John K. *Milton's Cambridge Latin: Performing in the Genres, 1625–1632* (Tempe, AZ: Medieval and Renaissance Texts and Studies, 2005).
―――――. *Milton's Languages: The Impact of Multilingualism on Style* (Cambridge: Cambridge University Press, 1997).
HAMILTON, A. C., Donald CHENEY, David A. RICHARDSON, and William W. BARKER, eds. *The Spenser Encyclopedia* (Toronto: University of Toronto Press, 1990).
HANFORD, James Holly. "Milton and the Art of War." *Studies in Philology* 18 (1921): 232–266.
―――――. "The Chronology of Milton's Private Studies." *Publications of the Modern Language Association of America* 36 (1921): 251–314.
HANKINS, James. "The Myth of the Platonic Academy of Florence." *Renaissance Quarterly* 44 (1991): 429–475.
HARDIE, Philip. "Milton's *Epitaphium Damonis* and the Virgilian Career." In *Pastoral Palimpsests*, ed. Paschalis, 79–100.
―――――. *Rumour and Renown: Representations of Fama in Western Literature* (Cambridge: Cambridge University Press, 2012).
HARRIS, Ann Sutherland. *Seventeenth-Century Art and Architecture* (London: Laurence King Publishing, 2005).
HARRIS, Neil. "Galileo as Symbol: The 'Tuscan Artist' in *Paradise Lost*." *Annali dell' Istituto e Museo di Storio della Scienza di Firenze* 10 (1985): 3–29.
HARTWELL, Kathleen. *Lactantius and Milton* (Cambridge, MA: Harvard University Press, 1929).
HATHAWAY, Baxter. *Marvels and Commonplaces: Renaissance Literary Criticism* (New York: Random House, 1968).
HAY, Denys. *Polydore Vergil, Renaissance Historian and Man of Letters* (Oxford: Clarendon Press, 1952).
HEITSCH, Dorothea, and Jean-François VALLÉE, eds. *Printed Voices: The Renaissance Culture of Dialogue* (Toronto: University of Toronto Press, 2004).
HELM, Bennett W. *Love, Friendship, and the Self* (Oxford: Oxford University Press, 2010).
HENDRIX, Harald. "Topographies of Poetry: Mapping Early Modern Naples." In *New Approaches to Naples*, eds. Calaresu and Hills, 81–101.
―――――. "Virgil's Tomb in Scholarly and Popular Culture." In *Tombs of the Ancient Poets*, eds. Goldschmidt and Graziosi, 281–298.

HOWARD, W. Scott. "Companions with Time: Milton, Tasso, and Renaissance Dialogue." *The Comparatist* 28 (2004): 5–28.

HUGHES, Jessica, and Claudio BUONGIOVANNI, eds. *Remembering Parthenope: The Reception of Classical Naples From Antiquity To The Present* (Oxford: Oxford University Press, 2015).

IMPIERI, Eleonora. "Nicolo Franco, Prosatore e Poeta Tra Innovazione e Tradizione" (PhD thesis: University of Pisa, 2012).

IRVINE, Susan, and Winfried RUDOLF, eds. *Childhood and Adolescence in Anglo-Saxon Literary Culture* (Toronto: University of Toronto Press, 2018).

JANSSENS, G. A. M., and F. G. A. M. AARTS, eds. *Studies in Seventeenth-Century English Literature, History and Bibliography* (Amsterdam: Rodopi, 1984).

JAVITCH, David. "The Disparagement of Chivalric Romance for its Lack of Historicity in Sixteenth-Century Italian Poetics." In *Romance and History*, ed. Whitman, 187–199.

JERRAM, C. S. *The Lycidas and Epitaphium Damonis of Milton* (London: Longman, 1874).

JOACHIM, H. H. *Aristotle: The Nicomachean Ethics: A Commentary*, ed. D. A. Rees (Oxford: Clarendon Press, 1951).

JONES, Edward, ed. *Young Milton: The Emerging Author, 1620–1642* (Oxford: Oxford University Press, 2013).

JONES, P. F. "Milton and the Epic Subject from British History." *Publications of the Modern Language Association of America* 42 (1927): 901–909.

KALLENDORF, Craig. "Epic and Tragedy—Virgil, La Cerda, Milton." In *Syntagmatia*, eds. Sacré and Papy, 579–593.

KEANE, Catherine. *Figuring Genre in Roman Satire* (Oxford: Oxford University Press, 2006).

KEITH, Arthur L. "Cicero's Idea of Friendship." *Sewanee Review* 37 (1929): 51–58.

KENDRICK, T. D. *The Druids: A Study in Keltic Prehistory* (London: Methuen, 1927).

KING, Preston, and Heather DEVERE, eds. *The Challenge to Friendship in Modernity* (London: Routledge, 2012).

KIRKLAND, N. Bryant. "Herodotus and Pseudo-Herodotus in the *Vita Herodotea*." *Transactions of the American Philological Association* 148 (2018): 299–329.

KOEBNER, Richard. "'The Imperial Crown of This Realm': Henry VIII, Constantine the Great, and Polydore Vergil." *Bulletin of the Institute of Historical Research* 26 (1953): 29–52.

KOENIGSBERGER, H. G. "English Merchants in Naples and Sicily in the Seventeenth Century." *English Historical Review* 62 (1947): 304–326.

KONSTAN, David. *Friendship in the Classical World* (Cambridge: Cambridge University Press, 1997).

KOWLAZIG, Barbara. *Singing for the Gods: Performances of Myth and Ritual in Archaic and Classical Greece* (Oxford: Oxford University Press, 2007).

LAIRD, Andrew. "Dead Letters and Buried Meaning: Approaching the Tomb of Virgil." In *Tombs of the Ancient Poets*, eds. Goldschmidt and Graziosi, 253–264.

LAZZERI, Allessandro. *Intellettuali e Consenso nella Toscana del Seicento: L'Accademia degli Apatisti* (Milan: A. Giuffrè, 1983).

LEES, Jay T. "Hrotsvit of Gandersheim and the Problem of Royal Succession in the East Frankish Kingdom." In *Hrotsvit of Gandersheim*, eds. Brown, McMillin, and Wilson, 13–28.

LEMKE, Andreas. "Children and the Conversion of the Anglo-Saxons in Bede's *Historia Ecclesiastica Gentis Anglorum*." In *Childhood and Adolescence in Anglo-Saxon Literary Culture*, eds. Irvine and Rudolf, 120–138.

LEO, Russ. "Milton's Aristotelian Experiments: Tragedy, *Lustratio*, and 'Secret Refreshings' in *Samson Agonistes* (1671)." *Milton Studies* 52 (2011): 221–252.

LETTS, Malcolm. "Some Sixteenth-Century Travellers in Naples." *English Historical Review* 33 (1918): 176–196.

LEVIN, Donald Norman. "Some Observations Concerning Plato's *Lysis*." In *Essays in Ancient Greek Philosophy*, eds. Anton and Kustas, 236–258.

LEWALSKI, Barbara K. *Milton's Brief Epic: The Genre, Meaning, and Art of Paradise Regained* (Providence, RI: Brown University Press and Methuen, 1966).

LIEB, Michael. *Milton and the Culture of Violence* (Ithaca, NY: Cornell University Press, 1994).

LIEBLER, Naomi Conn, ed. *Early Modern Prose Fiction: The Cultural Poetics of Reading* (New York: Routledge, 2007).

LOCKWOOD, Thornton C. "Defining Friendship in Cicero's *De Amicitia*." *Ancient Philosophy* 39 (2019): 409–426.

LOEWENSTEIN, David, and Paul STEVENS, eds. *Early Modern Nationalism and Milton's England* (Toronto: University of Toronto Press, 2008).

LOH, Maria H. *Titian Remade: Repetition and The Transformation of Early Modern Italian Art* (Los Angeles: Getty Research Institute, 2007).

LOMBARDI, Carmela. *Enciclopedia e Letturatura: Retorica, Politica e Critica della Letturatura in Una Enciclopedia del Primo Seicento* (Arezzo: Mediateca del Barocco, 1993).

LOW, Anthony. "*Mansus*: In Its Context." *Milton Studies* 19 (1984): 105–126.

LÜTHY, C. H. "Atomism, Lynceus, and the Fate of Seventeenth-Century Microscopy." *Early Science and Medicine* 1 (1996): 1–27.

MACCOLL, Alan. "Richard White and the Legendary History of Britain." *Humanistica Lovaniensia* 51 (2002): 245–257.

MACK, Maynard, and George de Forest LORD, eds. *Poetic Traditions of the English Renaissance* (New Haven, CT: Yale University Press, 1982).

MANFREDI, Michele. *Gio. Battista Manso nella Vita e nelle Opere* (Naples: Jovene, 1919).

MARINO, John A. *Becoming Neapolitan: Citizen Culture in Baroque Naples* (Baltimore: Johns Hopkins University Press, 2011).

———. "Constructing the Past of Early Modern Naples: Sources and Historiography." In *A Companion to Early Modern Naples*, ed. Astarita, 11–34.

MARRETT, R. R., ed. *Anthropology and the Classics: Six Lectures Delivered before the University of Oxford* (Oxford: Clarendon Press, 1908).

MARSH, David. *The Quattrocento Dialogue: Classical Tradition and Humanist Innovation* (Cambridge, MA: Harvard University Press, 1980).

MARTIN, Catherine Gimelli. *Milton's Italy: Anglo-Italian Literature, Travel, and Religion in Seventeenth-Century England* (New York: Routledge, 2017).

MARTÍNEZ, Adolfo Carrasco, ed. *La Nobleza y Los Reinos: Anatomía del Poder en La Monarquía de España (Siglos XVI–XVII)* (Madrid: Iberoamericana Vervuert, 2017).

MARTINI, Alessandro. "La Practica Mariniana." In *Interpretazione e Meraviglia*, ed. Galli, 107–119.

MARX, Steven. "'Fortunate Senex': The Pastoral of Old Age." *Studies in English Literature* 25 (1985): 21–44.

MAZZOTTA, Giuseppe. *The New Map of the World: The Poetic Philosophy of Giambattista Vico* (Princeton, NJ: Princeton University Press, 1999).

MCDOWELL, Nicholas, and Nigel SMITH, eds. *The Oxford Handbook of Milton* (Oxford: Oxford University Press, 2009).

MCRAE, Andrew. "Early Modern Chorographies." In *The Oxford Handbooks Online* (Oxford: Oxford University Press, 2015). https://www.oxfordhandbooks.com/view/10.1093/oxfordhb/9780199935338.001.001/oxfordhb-9780199935338-e-102

MENGELKOCH, Dustin. "Statian *Recusatio*: Angelo Poliziano and John Dryden." In *Brill's Companion to Statius*, eds. Dominik, Newlands, and Gervais, 562–578.

MENGHINI, Mario. *Tommaso Stigliani: Contributo alla Storia Letteraria del Secolo XVII* (Modena: E. Sarasino, 1892).

MILETTI, Lorenzo. "Setting the Agenda: The Image of Classical Naples in Strabo's *Geography* and Other Ancient Literary Sources." In *Remembering Parthenope*, eds. Hughes and Buongiovanni, 19–38.

MILLER, Leo. "Milton and Holstenius Reconsidered: An Exercise in Scholarly Practice." In *Milton in Italy*, ed. Di Cesare, 573–587.

———. "Milton Dines at the Jesuit College: Reconstructing the Evening of October 30, 1638." *Milton Quarterly* 13 (1979): 142–146.

———. "The Italian Imprimaturs in Milton's *Areopagitica*." *Papers of the Bibliographical Society of America* 65 (1971): 345–355.

MINIERI RICCIO, Carlo. "Cenno Storico delle Accademie Fiorite nella Città di Napoli." *Archivio Storico per le Provincie Napoletane* 3 (1878): 745–758; 4 (1879): 163–178, 379–394, 519–536; 5 (1880): 131–157, 349–373, 578–612.

MIROLLO, James V. *The Poet of the Marvelous: Giambattista Marino* (New York: Columbia University Press, 1963).

MODESTINO, Carmine. *Della Dimora di Torquato Tasso in Napoli negli Anni 1588, 1592, 1594* (Naples: Vaglio, 1859).

MONDOLA, Roberto, ed. *Manso, Lemos, Cervantes: Letteratura, Arti e Scienza nella Napoli del Primo Seicento* (Naples: Tullio Pironti, 2018).

MONTAGU, Jennifer. *An Index of Emblems of the Italian Academies* (London: Warburg Institute, 1988).

MOORE, Olin H. "The Infernal Council." *Modern Philology* 16 (1918): 169–193.

MORANDO, Simona. "Passions as Limits and Resources in 17th Century Italian Literature: Giambattista Marino's *Adone* (1623)." In *The Human and its Limits*, eds. Hagen, Koppen, and Skagen, 255–270.

MORGAN, Vincent, and Christopher BROOKE. *A History of the University of Cambridge II: 1546–1750* (Cambridge: Cambridge University Press, 2004).

MOTTRAM, Stewart. *Ruin and Reformation in Spenser, Shakespeare, and Marvell* (Oxford: Oxford University Press, 2019).

MOUL, Victoria, ed. *A Guide to Neo-Latin Literature* (Cambridge: Cambridge University Press, 2017).

MURLEY, Clyde. "'Et Dona Ferentis.'" *Classical Journal* 22 (1927): 658–662.

MUTO, Giovanni. "Urban Structures and Population." In *A Companion to Early Modern Naples*, ed. Astarita, 35–61.

NADER-ESFAHANI, Sanam. "Knowledge and Representation Through Baroque Eyes: Literature and Optics in France and Italy ca. 1600–1640" (PhD thesis: Harvard University, 2016).

———. "The Critical Occhiale: Lenses, Readers, and Critics in the Polemic Regarding Marino's *L'Adone*." *Renaissance Studies* 35 (2021): 170–187.

NARDO, Anna K. "Academic Interludes in *Paradise Lost*." *Milton Studies* 27 (1991): 209–241.

NEWLANDS, Carole Elizabeth. *Playing with Time: Ovid and the Fasti* (Ithaca, NY: Cornell University Press, 1995).

NEWMAN, J. K. "Milton and the Pastoral Mode: The *Epitaphium Damonis*." *Illinois Classical Studies* 15 (1990): 379–397.

NG, Su Fang. "Milton, Buchanan, and King Arthur." *Review of English Studies* 70 (2019): 659–680.

NICHOLS, Mary P. "Friendship and Community in Plato's *Lysis*." *The Review of Politics* 68 (2006): 1–19.

NICOLSON, Marjorie. "Milton's Hell and the Phlegraean Fields." *University of Toronto Quarterly* 7 (1938): 500–513.

OLDCORN, Anthony. *The Textual Problems of Tasso's "Gerusalemme Conquistata"* (Ravenna, Italy: Longo, 1976).

OWEN, A. L. *The Famous Druids: A Survey of Three Centuries of English Literature on the Druids* (Oxford: Clarendon Press, 1962).

PACELLI, Vicenzo. "Affreschi Storici in Palazzo Reale." In *Seicento Napoletano*, ed. Pane, 158–179.

PAKALUK, Michael, ed. *Other Selves: Philosophers on Friendship* (Indianapolis: Hackett, 1991).

PANE, Roberto, ed. *Seicento Napoletano: Arte, Costumi, e Ambiente* (Milan: Edizioni di Comunità, 1984).

PANGLE, Lorraine Smith. *Aristotle and the Philosophy of Friendship* (Cambridge: Cambridge University Press, 2003).

PAPAIOANNOU, Sophia. *Epic Succession and Dissension: Ovid, Metamorphoses 13.623–14.582, and the Reinvention of the Aeneid* (Berlin: Walter de Gruyter, 2005).

PASCHALIS, Michael, ed. *Pastoral Palimpsests: Essays in the Reception of Theocritus and Virgil* (Herakleion: Crete University Press, 2007).

———, ed. *Roman and Greek Imperial Epic* (Herakleion: Crete University Press, 2005).

PEDROJETTA, Guido. "Marino e La Meraviglia." In *Interpretazione e Meraviglia*, ed. Galli, 95–105.

PETERS, Susanna N. "'Metaphor and Meraviglia': Tradition and Innovation in the *Adone* of G.B. Marino." *Lingua e Stile* 7 (1972): 321–341.

———. "The Quarrel of the 'Adone': A Chapter in the History of Seventeenth-Century Italian Poetic Theory" (PhD thesis: Johns Hopkins University, 1968).
PICKSTOCK, Catherine. "The Problem of Reported Speech: Friendship and Philosophy in Plato's *Lysis* and *Symposium*." *Telos* 123 (2002): 35–65.
PIGGOTT, Stuart. *The Druids* (London: Thames and Hudson, 1968).
PIGNATTI, Franco. "Franco, Nicolo." *Dizionario Biografico degli Italiani* 50 (1998): 202–206.
———. "I *Dialoghi* di Torquato Tasso e La Morfologia del Dialogo Cortigiano Rinascimentale." *Studi Tassiani* 36 (1988): 7–43.
———. "Nicolò Franco a Roma 1558–1570." *Archivio della Società Romana di Storia Patria* 121 (1998): 118–166.
PINCOMBE, Mike, and Cathy SHRANK, eds. *The Oxford Handbook of Tudor Literature, 1485–1603* (Oxford: Oxford University Press, 2009).
POOLE, William. "John Milton and Giovanni Boccaccio's *Vita di Dante*." *Milton Quarterly* 48 (2014): 139–170.
———. *Milton and the Making of Paradise Lost* (Cambridge, MA: Harvard University Press, 2017).
———. "'The Armes of Studious Retirement'? Milton's Scholarship, 1632–1641." In *Young Milton*, ed. Jones, 21–47.
PORTER, Roy, and Sylvana TOMASELLI. *The Dialectics of Friendship* (London: Routledge, 1989).
POTTER, Lois. *A Preface to Milton* (rev. ed., London: Routledge, 1986).
PRANDI, Stefano. "Sul Dibatto Critico Attorno ai *Dialoghi* di T. Tasso." *Lettere Italiane* 42 (1990): 460–466.
———. "Sulla 'Vita di Torquato Tasso' di Giambattista Manso." *Lettere Italiane* 47 (1995): 623–628.
PRICE, A. W. *Love and Friendship in Plato and Aristotle* (Oxford: Clarendon Press, 1989).
PUTNAM, Michael C. J. "Horace, *Carm*. 4.7 and the Epic Tradition." *Classical World* 100 (2007): 355–362.
———. "Horace to Torquatus: *Epistle* 1.5 and *Ode* 4,7." *American Journal of Philology* 127 (2006): 387–413.
———. *Virgil's Poem of the Earth: Studies in the Georgics* (Princeton, NJ: Princeton University Press, 1979).
RABBÅS, Øyvind. "*Eudaimonia*, Human Nature, and Normativity: Reflections on Aristotle's Project in *Nicomachean Ethics* Book I." In *The Quest for The Good Life*, eds. Rabbås et al., 88–112.
RABBÅS, Øyvind, Eyjólfur K. EMILSSON, Halvard FOSSHEIM, and Miira TUOMINEN, eds. *The Quest for The Good Life: Ancient Philosophers on Happiness* (Oxford: Oxford University Press, 2015).
RAYMOND, Joad. *Milton's Angels: The Early-Modern Imagination* (Oxford: Oxford University Press, 2010).
RESIDORI, Matteo. *L'Idea del Poema: Studio sulla Gerusalemme Conquistata di Torquato Tasso* (Pisa: Scuola Normale Superiore, 2004).

REVARD, Stella P. "Across the Alps—An English Poet Addresses an Italian in Latin: John Milton in Naples." In *Travel and Translation*, ed. Di Biase, 53–64.

———. *Milton and the Tangles of Neaera's Hair: The Making of the 1645 Poems* (Columbia: University of Missouri Press, 1997).

RICCIO, Martina. "Torquato Tasso nel Castello di Bisaccia. L'Amicizia con Giovan Battista Manso." *Riscontri* 1 (2018): 73–81.

RIETBERGEN, P. J. *Power and Religion in Baroque Rome: Barberini Cultural Policies* (Leiden: Brill, 2006).

RIGA, Pietro Giulio. "Alcune Note sulle Tendenze Letterarie nell' Accademia degli Oziosi di Napoli." In *Le Virtuose Adunanze*, eds. Gurreri and Bianchi, 159–171.

———. *Giovan Battista Manso e La Cultura Letteraria a Napoli Nel Primo Seicento: Tasso, Marino, Gli Oziosi* (Bologna: Emil di Odoya, 2018).

———. "Manso, Gli Oziosi e La Riflessione sulla Poesia Lirica Tra Paratesti ed Esegesi Accademica." In *Manso, Lemos, Cervantes*, ed. Mondola, 125–146.

———. "Scaramuccia, Angelita." *Dizionario Biografico degli Italiani* 91 (2018): 320–322.

RIGGS, William G. "The Plant of Fame in *Lycidas*." *Milton Studies* 4 (1972): 151–161.

RIZZO, Gino. "Lettere di Giuseppe Battista al Padre Angelico Aprosio." *Studi Secenteschi* 38 (1997): 267–318.

———, ed. *Scipione Errico: Le Guerre di Parnaso* (Lecce: Argo, 2004).

ROEBUCK, Thomas. "Milton and the Confessionalization of Antiquarianism." In *Young Milton*, ed. Jones, 48–71.

ROSA, Alberto Asor. "Aleandro, Girolamo, il Giovane." *Dizionario Biografico degli Italiani* 2 (1960): 135–136.

ROSENBERG, D.M. *Oaten Reeds and Trumpets: Pastoral and Epic in Virgil, Spenser, and Milton* (Lewisburg, PA: Bucknell University Press, 1981).

RUSSO, Carla, ed. *Chiesa, Assistenza e Società nel Mezzogiorno Moderno* (Galatina: Congedo, 1994).

RUSSO, Emilio. *Studi su Tasso e Marino* (Rome and Padua: Antenore, 2005).

RUTHERFORD, R. B. "Virgil's Poetic Ambitions in *Eclogue* 6." *Greece & Rome* 36 (1989): 42–50.

SACRÉ, Dirk, and Jan PAPY, eds. *Syntagmatia: Essays on Neo-Latin Literature in Honour of Monique Mund-Dopchie and Gilbert Tourney* (Leuven: Leuven University Press, 2009).

SALE, William. "The Hyperborean Maidens on Delos." *Harvard Theological Review* 54 (1961): 75–89.

SALLER, Richard. "Patronage and Friendship in Early Imperial Rome: Drawing the Distinction." In *Patronage in Ancient Society*, ed. Wallace-Hadrill, 49–62.

SCHOLLMEIER, Paul. *Other Selves: Aristotle on Personal and Political Friendship* (Albany: State University of New York Press, 1994).

SCHOONHOVEN, Henk. "Purple Swans and Purple Snow (Hor. *C.* IV 1, 10 and *Eleg. in Maec.* 62)." *Mnemosyne* 31 (1978): 200–203.

SCHWYZER, Philip. "John Leland and His Heirs: The Topography of England." In *The Oxford Handbook of Tudor Literature, 1485–1603*, eds. Pincombe and Shrank, 238–253.

SCIANATICO, Giovanna. *L'Arme Pietose. Studio sulla Gerusalemme Liberata* (Venice: Marsilio, 1990).

———. "*L'Idea del Perfetto Principe*": *Utopia e Storia nella Scrittura del Torquato Tasso* (Naples: Edizioni Scientifiche Italiane, 1998).

SCOLNICOV, Samuel. "Friends and Friendship in Plato: Some Remarks on the *Lysis*." *Scripta Classica Israelica* 12 (1993): 67–74.

SEIDER, Aaron M. "Genre, Gallus, and Goats: Expanding the Limits of Pastoral in *Eclogues* 6 and 10." *Vergilius* 62 (2016): 3–23.

SHAWCROSS, J. T. "One Aspect of Milton's Spelling: Idle Final 'E'." *Publications of the Modern Language Association of America* 78 (1963): 501–510.

———. "The Date of the Separate Edition of Milton's *Epitaphium Damonis*." *Studies in Bibliography* 18 (1965): 262–265.

SHEFFIELD, Frisbee. "Plato on Love and Friendship." In *The Cambridge Companion to Ancient Ethics*, ed. Bobonich, 86–102.

SHRANK, Cathy. *Writing the Nation in Reformation England, 1530–1580* (Oxford: Oxford University Press, 2004).

SIMIANI, Carlo. *La Vita e Le Opere di Nicolò Franco* (Turin: L. Roux, 1894).

SIMS-WALLACE, Patrick. "The Early Welsh Arthurian Poems." In *The Arthur of the Welsh*, eds. Bromwich, Jarman, and Roberts, 33–71.

SKARSTROM, A. W. "'Fortunate Senex': The Old Man, A Study of the Figure, His Function and His Setting" (PhD thesis: Yale University, 1971).

SLAWINSKI, Maurice. "The Poet's Senses: G.B. Marino's Epic Poem *L'Adone* and the New Science." *Comparative Criticism* 13 (1991): 51–81.

SMITH, H. Maynard, ed. *John Evelyn in Naples 1645* (Oxford: Blackwell, 1914).

SNYDER, Jon R. "Truth and Wonder in Naples circa 1640." In *Culture and Authority in the Baroque*, eds. Ciavolella and Coleman, 85–105.

———. *Writing the Scene of Speaking: Theories of Dialogue in the Late Italian Renaissance* (Stanford, CA: Stanford University Press, 1989).

STARKEY, David. "King Henry and King Arthur." In *Arthurian Literature XVI*, eds. Carley and Riddy, 171–196.

STEPHENS, Walter. "Reading Tasso Reading Vergil Reading Homer: An Archaeology of Andromache." *Comparative Literature Studies* 32 (1995): 296–319.

STERN-GILLET, Suzanne. *Aristotle's Philosophy of Friendship* (Albany: State University of New York Press, 1995).

STEVENS, Paul. "Archipelagic Criticism and Its Limits: Milton, Geoffrey of Monmouth, and the Matter of England." *The European Legacy* 17 (2012): 151–164.

———. "Milton and National Identity." In *The Oxford Handbook of Milton*, eds. McDowell and Smith, 342–363.

STOK, Fabio. "Why Was Virgil Called 'Parthenias'?" *Giornale Italiano di Filologia* 69 (2017): 157–170.

STRADLING, R. A. "A Spanish Statesman of Appeasement: Medina De Las Torres and Spanish Policy, 1639–1670." *The Historical Journal* 19 (1976): 1–31.

STRAZZULLO, Franco. "Documenti Inediti per la Storia dell' Arte a Napoli." *Il Fuidoro* 1 (1954): 143–145.

———. *La Chiesa dei SS. Apostoli a Napoli* (Naples: Arte Tipografica, 1959).

———. *L'Antica Via del Marzano a Villanove* (Naples: Arte Tipografica, 1994).

SULLIVAN, Karen. *The Danger of Romance: Truth, Fantasy, and Arthurian Fiction* (Chicago: The University of Chicago Press, 2018).

SUMMERS, David A. "Re-Fashioning Arthur in the Tudor Era." *Exemplaria* 9 (1997): 371–392.

SVENDSEN, Kester. *Milton and Science* (Cambridge, MA: Harvard University Press, 1956).

TERRY, Richard. *Poetry and the Making of the English Literary Past 1660–1781* (Oxford: Oxford University Press, 2001).

TESKEY, Gordon. *Delirious Milton: The Fate of the Poet in Modernity* (Cambridge, MA: Harvard University Press, 2006).

———. *Spenserian Moments* (Cambridge, MA: Harvard University Press, 2019).

TESSITORE, Aristide. "Plato's *Lysis*: An Introduction to Philosophic Friendship." *The Southern Journal of Philosophy* 28 (1990): 115–132.

TESTA, Simone. *Italian Academies and Their Networks, 1525–1700: From Local to Global* (Basingstoke: Palgrave Macmillan, 2015).

———. "Le Accademie Senesi e il Network Intellettuale della Prima Età Moderna in Italia (1525–1700): Un Progetto Online." *Bullettino Senese di Storia Patria* 117 (2010): 613–637.

TICKNOR, George. *History of Spanish Literature*, 3 vols. (London: John Murray, 1849).

TILLYARD, E. M. W. *Milton* (London: Chatto & Windus, 1930).

———. *The Miltonic Setting Past and Present* (Cambridge: Cambridge University Press, 1938).

TRAPP, J. B. *Essays on the Renaissance and the Classical Tradition* (Aldershot: Variorum, 1990).

———. "The Grave of Virgil." *Journal of the Warburg and Courtauld Institutes* 47 (1984): 1–31.

UNGLAUB, Jonathan. *Poussin and the Poetics of Painting: Pictorial Narrative and the Legacy of Tasso* (Cambridge: Cambridge University Press, 2006).

URBAN, David V. "The Lady of Christ's College, Himself A 'Lady Wise and Pure': Parabolic Self-Reference in John Milton's *Sonnet IX*." *Milton Studies* 47 (2008): 1–23.

VASOLI, Cesare. "Le Accademie fra Cinquecento e Seicento e il Loro Ruolo nella Storia della Tradizione Enciclopedica." In *Università, Accademie e Società Scientifiche in Italia*, eds. Boehm and Raimondi, 81–115.

VENUTI, Lawrence. *The Translator's Invisibility: A History of Translation* (London: Routledge, 1995).

VERDE, Paolo Carla. "Domenico Fontana a Napoli (1592–1607): Le Opere per La Committenza Vicereale Spagnola." *Anuario del Departamento de Historia y Teoría del Arte* 18 (2006): 49–78.

———. "L'Originario e Completo Progetto di Domenico Fontana per il Palazzo Reale di Napoli." *Quaderni dell' Istituto di Storia dell' Architettura* 42 (2003): 29–52.

VILLARI, Rosario. *La Rivolta Antispagnola a Napoli: Le Origini (1585–1647)* (Bari: Laterza, 1967).
WALKER, A. D. M. "Aristotle's Account of Friendship in the *Nicomachean Ethics*." *Phronesis* 24 (1979): 180–196.
WALLACE, Andrew. *The Presence of Rome in Medieval and Early Modern Britain* (Cambridge: Cambridge University Press, 2020).
WALLACE-HADRILL, Andrew, ed. *Patronage in Ancient Society* (London: Routledge, 1989).
WARNEKE, Sara. *Images of the Educational Traveller in Early Modern England* (Leiden: Brill, 1995).
WARNKE, Frank J. "Marino and the English Metaphysicals." *Studies in the Renaissance* 2 (1955): 160–175.
WEBBER, Joan M. *Milton and His Epic Tradition* (Seattle: University of Washington Press, 1979).
WESTFALL, Richard S. "Science and Patronage: Galileo and the Telescope." *Isis* 76 (1985): 11–30.
WHITMAN, Jon., ed. *Romance and History: Imagining Time From the Medieval to the Early Modern Period* (Cambridge: Cambridge University Press, 2015).
WILLIAMS, C. A. *Reading Roman Friendship* (Cambridge: Cambridge University Press, 2012).
WOODMAN, A. J. "The Position of Gallus in *Eclogue* 6." *Classical Quarterly* 47 (1997): 593–597.

INDEX NOMINUM ET LOCORUM

Abra, 104; *see also* Humber
Accademia
  degli Addormentati, *see s.v.* Naples
  degli Apatisti, *see s.v.* Florence
  degli Ardenti, *see s.v.* Naples
  degli Arditi, *see s.v.* Naples
  degli Armeristi, *see s.v.* Naples
  degli Assetati, *see s.v.* Naples
  degli Erranti, *see s.v.* Naples
  degli Incogniti, *see s.v.* Naples
  degli Incogniti, *see s.v.* Venice
  degli Incolti, *see s.v.* Naples
  degli Infuriati, *see s.v.* Naples
  degli Intronati, *see s.v.* Naples
  degli Investiganti, *see s.v.* Naples
  degli Oscuri, *see s.v.* Naples
  degli Oziosi, *see s.v.* Naples
  degli Scatenati, *see s.v.* Naples
  degli Svegliati, *see s.v.* Naples
  degli Svogliati, *see s.v.* Florence
  degli Umoristi, *see s.v.* Rome
  degli Uniti, *see s.v.* Naples
  dei Fantastici, *see s.v.* Rome
  dei Lunatici, *see s.v.* Naples
  dei Pigri, *see s.v.* Naples
  dei Rinomati, *see s.v.* Naples
  dei Segreti, *see s.v.* Naples
  dei Sicuri, *see s.v.* Naples
  dei Sireni, *see s.v.* Naples
  dei Volanti, *see s.v.* Naples
  del Cimento, *see s.v.* Naples
  del Colonna, *see s.v.* Naples
  della Crusca, *see s.v.* Florence
  de' Ravvivati, *see s.v.* Naples
  Fiorentina, *see s.v.* Florence
  Laurenziana, *see s.v.* Naples
  Nazionale dei Lincei, *see s.v.* Rome
  Partenia, *see s.v.* Naples
  Pontaniana, *see s.v.* Naples
Acetto, Torquato, 76
Achaeia, 131
Achelous, 5
Achilles, 81, 87, 89, 90, 92, 164
Achillini, Claudio, 188
Ackermann, Rudolph, 14
Admetus, 195
Adonis, 26, 81–83, 108, 184, 185, 191, 192, 203, 205
Aenaria, 2
Aeneas, 139, 143
Aeolia, 121
Aeschylus, 110
Aeson, 55, 56
Aesop, 107
Africa, 25
Agliani, Domenico, 182
Agnello Maggiori, Saint
  Monastery of, 181
Alamanni, Luigi, 37
Alba
  Duke of, *see* De Toledo y
    Pimental, Fernando Álvarez
Alberti
  Giovanni, 108
  Leandro, 6
Alcestis, 195
Alcon, 105
Aldrobrandini
  Bonifazio Bevilacqua, Cardinal, 152
  Cinzio Passeri, Cardinal, 150–152, 202
Aldrovandi, Ulisse, 72–73
Aleandro, Girolamo, Jr., 33, 187, 192, 194, 199, 200, 201
  Difesa dell' Adone, 187, 192, 194, 200, 201
  Sopra l'Impresa de gli Academici Humoristi, 33
Alessandro VII, Pope, *see* Chigi, Fabio
Alighieri, Dante, 17, 29, 186, 196, 205
  Divina Comedia, 29
Allestry, James, 48
Alps, 46, 103, 153
Amalteo
  Cornelio, 189
  Giambattista, 189
  Girolamo, 189
Amphion, 59
Amsterdam, 74
Anabasis, 34
Anchises, 143
Andrantonelli, Fulvio, 95
Andrewes, Lancelot, 63
Angela Sirena, 184
Angelo a Foro, Saint
  Chapel of,
    see s.v. Manso, domestic chapel
angels, 53, 59–63, 84, 85, 148, 175, 183–184
Anglo-Saxons, 49

Anisson, Laurentius, 33
Anjou
    Robert of, King, 163
Annwf, 142
Antonio Abate, Saint, 19
Antwerp, 47
Anversa, 120
Aonia, 77, 172
Apollo, 73, 77, 79, 80, 81, 89, 90, 95, 96, 99, 101, 110, 129, 130, 131, 132, 133, 147, 149, 150, 165, 172, 194, 195, 202, 204
Applausi Poetici alle Glorie della Signora Leonora Baroni (1639), 76
Aprosio, Angelico, 187, 189
Aquinas, Thomas, Saint, 62
Arabia, 68
Arcamone, Giacomo, 97
Arctus (Great/Little Bear), 102
Arge, 131
Argonauts, 89, 197
Ariosto, Ludovico, 29
    Orlando Furioso, 29
Aristotle, 87–88, 96, 110, 137, 160, 161, 162, 163, 169, 170, 186, 188
    Nicomachean Ethics, 161, 162, 163, 169, 170
Arnobius, 63
Artemis, 131
Arthur, King, 104, 120, 133–134, 138–149
    Round Table of, 120, 133–134, 144–146
Ascham, Roger, 102
Asclepius, 89, 90, 92, 194
Ashtoreth, *see* Astarte
Asia, 25
Asiatic (style of oratory), 186–187
Assyria, 82, 190, 191
Astarte, 191
Athena, 86
Athens, 103, 130
Atlas, 96, 198
Attic (style of oratory), 187
Augsburg, 189
Augustine of Hippo, Saint, 62
Augustinian Hermits, 11
Aurora, 72
Ausones, 192
Ausonia, 190, 192

Avalon, 110
Avoli
    family of, 125
Avon, 99
Aylmer, Brabazon, 60

Baba, Francesco, 10, 78, 181
Babylonia, 191
Bacchantes, 125
Bacchetta, Giovanni Pietro, 95, 97
Bacco, Enrico, 7
Baglioni
    Paolo, 33
    Tommaso, 198
Baldini, Vittorio, 155, 186
Balducci, Giovanni, 21
Bandini, Ottavio, Cardinal, 187
Bantheus, Henricus, 189
Baptism, 96
Barberini
    family of, 34
    Francesco, Cardinal, 4, 33, 34, 187
    Library of, 33
    Maffeo (Pope Urban VIII), 122
Bari, Saint Niccolò da, 19
Baroni, Leonora, 12, 35, 63, 76, 113, 125
Baroque, The, 23, 34, 185, 187
Barrett, William, 2, 24
Basile, Adriana, 35–36
Basingstoke, 140
Battista, Giuseppe, 78, 90, 110–111, 179, 188–189
    Epigrammatum Centuria Prima (1659), 78, 90
    Le Giornate Accademiche (1673), 110–111
Bazacchi, Alessandro, 188
Beale, John, 7
Bede, 47–48, 175–176
    Commentarius in Genesim, 47
    Historia Ecclesiastica, 47–48, 175–176
Belinus, 139
Belisarius, Flavius, 80, 135
Bel Prato
    Bernardino, 120
    Costanza, 119, 120
    family of, 119
    Scipione, 156, 158–159

Beltrano, Ottavio, 123
Bembo, Pietro, 15, 67
Benacci
    Alessandro, 186
    Vittorio, 186
Benedictines, Order of, 147
Beni, Paolo, 198
Berardelli, Alessandro, 67
Bergamo, 125, 135
Bernabo, Angelo, 188
Bernini, Gian Lorenzo, 182
Bertaglia, Bartolomeo, *see* Visconti, Bartolomeo
Biaguazzoni, Antonio, 78, 79, 95, 146
Bible, 23
    versions of,
        King James (Authorized Version), 62, 63
        Vulgate, 63
    books of,
        Genesis, 47
        Psalms, 62, 63
        Job, 31
        Matthew, 148
        Corinthians, 96
        Revelation, 62
Biffi, Giovanni Ambrosio, 80
Bilingualism, 3, 29, 30, 31, 78, 115, 204
Biondo, Flavio, 6
Bisaccio, 120
Blessed Virgin, Society of, 55
Blount, Edward, 99
Boccaccio, Giovanni, 29
    Vita di Dante, 29
Bochholtz, Bertram, 111
Bologna, 72, 123, 186
Bombardo, Domitio, 35
Bootes, 107
Bordoni, Girolamo, 41
Boreas, 132
Bouchard, Jean-Jacques, 9, 17
Bouillon, Godfrey of, 81, 118, 135
Bracciano, 76
Braun, George, 111
Brennus, 139
Brent, Nathan, 25
Bresciani, Antonio, 14
Breton, 148

Britain, 25, 61, 99, 103, 104, 105, 111, 130, 132, 140
Britons, 130, 132, 140, 143, 146, 148
Bruni, Antonio, 76
Brutus, 132, 139
Buchanan, George, 104, 140, 141, 147
Buonmattei, Benedetto, 29–31, 155
    Della Lingua Toscana ... Libri Due (1643), 30–31
    Delle Cagioni della Lingua Toscana (1623), 30
    Delle Lodi della Lingua Toscana (1623), 29
    Introduzione alla Lingua Toscana (1626), 30
    Trattato della Pronunzia (MS), 30
Burman, Pieter, 24, 74

Cacace, Giovanni Camillo, 73–74, 85–86, 97
Caesar, Julius, 78, 132, 133
Caledonia, 130
Callimachus, 31, 131–133
Calphurnius, Ioannes, 127
Calpurnius Siculus, Titus, 105, 106–107
Cam, 13
Cambridge
    University of, 13, 53, 54, 138
        Christ's College, 53, 60, 102
Camenae, 78, 80, 103, 171; *see also* Muses
Camola, Giacomo Filippo, 123
Campanella, Tommaso, 11, 52
Campania, 82
Campanile, Giuseppe, 67
Campidoglio, 124, 151, 152
Cancer, Mattia, 50
Capaccio, Giulio Cesare, 4
Caponapoli, 181
Capra, 2
Capua, Isabella of, 50–51
Caracciolo
    Battistello, 21
    Giovanni Battista, 8
    Giulio Cesare, 67, 80, 76
Carafa
    Decio, Archbishop, 177
    Pietro, Pope, 52

Carampello, Pietro, 186
Caravaggio, Michelangelo Merisi da, 8, 185
Caria, Giulio, 65, 70, 73
Carlino
 Giacomo, 4, 155
 Giovan Giacomo, 7, 65
Carrafa
 Fra Giulio, 88–89
 Luigi, 95
Carucciolo
 Annibale, 97
 Giulio, Duke, 94
Castalia, 86
Castelvetro, Lodovico, 137
Castiglione, Baldassare, 162
Catholicism, Roman, 23, 51, 53, 54, 60, 61, 63, 96, 102, 137, 140
Catullus, Gaius Valerius, 111
Cavalieri, Marcantonio, 19
Cavalli, Francesco, 124
Cavario, Giovanni Battista, 76
Celano, Carlo, 4, 181
Celtis, Conradus, 147
Celts, 101, 142
Cencovius, Stanislaus, 14
Cerdogni, Camillo, 47, 54
Cerenza, 115
Ceres, 44
Cervantes, Miguel de, 19, 67
Cesi, Federico, 196
Chalcis, 5, 36, 39
Chalcondylas, Demetrius, 128, 129
Chancel, Jean Pierre, 10
Chapelain, Jean, 201
Charlemagne, King, 135, 137
Chaucer, Geoffrey, 104–106, 107, 108
Cherubini, Antonio, 25
Chiaro, Francesco, 123
Chigi, Fabio, 33
Chioccarelli, Bartolomeo, 180
Chiron, 89–93, 172, 194, 202
Cholinus, Maternus, 83
Christ, Jesus, 96, 148
Christianity, 63, 96, 135
Ciamboli, Tomaso, 86
Cicero, 1, 31, 57, 83, 85, 110, 121, 160, 162, 169, 170, 191, 197
 De Amicitia, 156, 161, 162, 163, 169, 170

 De Officiis, 85
 De Oratore, 191
 Epistulae ad Familiares, 197
 Pro Cluentio, 121
 Somnium Scipionis, 118, 161
 Tusculanae Disputationes, 57, 83, 110, 118, 121, 156
Cifra, Antonio, 27
Cinyras, 191
Ciotti, Giovan Battista, 75
Circe, 102
Cito, Donato Antonio, 80
Civitella, 20
Claudian, Claudius, 38, 65, 66, 68, 69, 70, 71, 72, 73, 131
 De Consulatu Stilichonis, 70, 131
 De Raptu Proserpinae, 66
 Phoenix, 38, 65, 68, 70, 73
Clio, 90, 133, 172
Clüver, Philip, 7
Cochet, Christophe, 178, 182
Codner, David, 47, 134
Collegio dei Nobili, *see s.v.* Naples
Cologne, 55, 78, 83, 111
Colonna, Girolamo, 80, 190
Columbus, Christopher, 198
Columella, Lucius Junius Moderatus, 56
Combi, Sebastian, 111, 122
Comentati, Giovanni Battista, 79, 147
Commelinus, Johann, 48
Como, Lake, 111
Composti, Giovanni Battista, 95
Comus, 54
Concettismo, 201–202; *see also* Marinism
Constantine, the Great, 139
Conti, Natale, 6
Contrulla, 82
Cordon, Horatius, 145
Corezio, Belisario, 21
Corineus, 130, 132
Cornelio, Tommaso, 181
Cornwall, 132
Corydon, 15, 106, 107
Cotti, Giovanni Battista, 75
Counter Reformation, 137
Crasso, Lorenzo, 122, 181
Cuddie, 107–109
Cumae, 2

Index Nominum et Locorum

Cupid, 36–37, 42, 45, 74, 86
Cynthia, 191
Cynthius, 150, 202; *see also* Apollo
Cynthus, Mount, 150, 151
Cyprus, 191
Cyrene, 73

D'Alessandro, Giovanni Pietro, 184
D'Alife, Valeriano Seca Vescovo, 87
Damon, 113–114
D'Andrea, Onofrio, 93, 97, 110
Daniele, Francesco, 122
Daniello, Bernardino, 29
Dante, *see* Alighieri
Dardanus, 139
Dati, Carlo, 23–24, 25, 28, 38, 39, 47, 49, 91, 92, 114, 134
Daye, John, 102
De Castro, Pedro Fernández, 19, 57, 67
De Franceschi, Francesco, 73
De Guzmán, Ramiro Felipe, 19–21
Deira, 48
De La Cerda, Jean Luis, 78, 145
De Lellis, Carlo, 115, 176, 177, 179–180, 183
    Discorsi delle Famiglie Nobili (1663), 115
    Supplimento a Napoli Sacra (1654), 176, 177, 179–180
Del Fibreno, Cartiera, 122
Delians, 132
De Lignamine, Johannes Philippus, 6
Della Casa, Giovanni, 67
Della Marra, Hettore, 97
Della Porta, Giambattista, 197
Della Rovere
  family of, 118
  Francesco Maria II, 135
Del Mare, Giovanni, 105
Delos, 130–132, 151
De Medici
  family of, 118
  Piero, 129
Democrates, 34
Demophilus, 34
De Pietri, Francesco, 51, 72–73, 85, 93, 110, 115–116, 121, 122, 155, 179, 180, 183, 184
    Compendio della Vita di Torquato Tasso (1619), 115–116, 155
    I Problemi Accademici (1642), 51, 72–73, 85, 110, 183
De Pise, Marcellino, 33
De Rosa, Carlo Antonio, 122
De Rossi, Porzia, 126
D'Este
  family of, 118, 136
  Leonora, 124–125
De Toledo y Pimental, Fernando Álvarez, 20
De Toro, Miguel Martinez, 20–21
Deuchino, Evangelista, 1, 10
Diaconus, Paulus, 50
Di Costanzo, Angelo, 66, 76, 84
Di Donno, Ferdinando, 74, 75
Di Falco, Benedetto, 6, 12
Di Fusco, Luc' Antonio, 67
Di Gregorio, Maurizio, 65
Dio, Cassius, 129
Diodati, Charles, 7, 13, 36, 44, 68, 78–79, 84, 113, 114, 135
Dionysius I, ruler of Syracuse, 20
Dionysius, the Areopagite, 62
Di Scala
  family of, 66, 74
  Monte Manso, 122, 176, 177, 181, 182
Di Varano, Oliviero, 82
Domenichino (Zampieri, Domenico), 188, 201
Dominicans, Order of, 11, 52
Donatus, Aelius, 52, 127
Dorchester, 101
Dorylas, 145
Drayton, Michael, 99, 130, 133
Druids, 129, 130, 132–133, 171
Dryden, John, 90

Easter, 177
Edinburgh, 37
Egypt, 33, 68, 80, 82
Ekphrasis, 28, 36–37, 45, 68–75, 153
Elijah, 189
Eliot, John, 124
Elizabeth I, Queen, 99
Ely, 189
Emanuele, Carlo I, Duke, 180
Emmanuel, Vittor III, 122

Endelechius, Severus Sanctus, 105
England, 22, 34, 38, 47, 48, 49, 89, 98, 102, 104, 105, 111, 124, 134, 137, 138, 206
English
  Channel, 104
  language 24, 140
  merchants, 4
Englishness, 47, 103
Ennius, Quintus, 83, 152, 153
Er, myth of, 184
Errico, Scipione, 79, 95, 97, 187
Erythraeus, Janus Nicius, *see* Rossi, Vittorio
Etna, Mount, 142–143
Eton College, 7
Euripides, 31, 125, 195
Europe, 25, 67, 88, 180
Evelyn, John, 14–15, 17

Fabricius
  Georgius, 6
  Johannes Albert, 8
Faccioti, Guglielmo, 116
Facciuti, Donato, 87
Falese, Francesco, 75
Falsirena, 191
Farri, Domenico, 47
Felton, Nicolas, 189
Ferrara, 155, 157, 186
  Alfonso II, Duke of, 135
Ferro
  Giovanni, 33
  Loise, 178
Fiamma, Gabriel, 47
Fieschi, Flavio, 190
Fiesole, 198
Filosa, Santillo, 179
Flaccus, Valerius, 89
Florence, 2, 8, 23, 25, 28, 29, 30, 38, 39, 49, 91, 92, 119, 128, 134, 155, 159, 184, 185, 186, 198
  Accademia degli Apatisti, 2–3
  Accademia degli Svogliati, 2–3
  Accademia della Crusca, 108
  Accademia Fiorentina, 29
  Biblioteca Marucelliana, 3
  Biblioteca Nazionale Centrale, 3, 30
Fontana
  Domenico, 21
  Giulio Cesare, 20
Fontanella, Geronimo, 93
Foresi, Vincenzo, *see* Villani, Nicola
Forestiero, 156, 161, 166, 168; *see also* Tasso, Torquato
France, 22, 138, 149–150, 180, 187
Francini, Antonio, 22, 28, 29, 38, 47, 49, 91, 134, 159
Franco, Nicolò, 50–53
  Dialoghi Piacevolissimi (1539), 52
  Hisabella (1535), 50–53
Franks, 147–148
French, 20, 178
  language, 22
Frères, Garnier, 50
Freschoverus, Christophorus, 139
Fulgentius, Fabius Planciades, 114

Gaddi, Jacopo, 10, 36, 90
Gaddianus, Codex, 105
Gaetani, Filippo, 57
Galilei, Galileo, 162, 189, 196, 198–199, 200
  Istoria e Dimostrazioni Intorno alle Macchie Solari (1613), 199
  Saggiatore (1623), 196
  Sidereus Nuncius (1610), 198
Galistoni, Carlo, 187
Gallerati, Antonio, 80
Gallicini, Teofilo, 76
Gallus, Cornelius, 77, 79
Gandersheim, Roswitha of, 147
Gargani, Giovanni Battista, 184
Gaudiosi, Tommaso, 65
Geneva, 47, 54
Gennaro, Saint, 19, 23, 178
Genoa, 105, 179
  Biblioteca Universitaria, 179
Gentiles, 63
Gentili, Scipio, 124
Genuino, Girolamo, 93
Genuzio, Andre, 20
Germany, 139, 149–150
Gesualdo
  Alfonso, Cardinal, 10
  Carlo, 27
Giacomo, Saint, 178, 181
Gildas, Priscus, 48
Gimma, Giacinta, 33

Giovio, Paolo, 111
Giustiniani
    Bernardo, 7
    Lorenzo, 119
Glareano, Scipio, 187
God, 43, 48, 62
Gogmagon, 132
Góngora, Luis de, 21
Gonzaga
    family of, 118
    Ferrante I, 50
Gori, Anton Francesco, 3
Gorlois, 139
Goths, 135
Grafton, Richard, 144
Greece, 7, 22, 130, 131, 132
Greek
    history, 7
    language, 22, 34, 79, 143
Greeks, 156
Greenwich, 100, 101
Gregory XV, Pope, 47–52, 55, 175–176
Grignano, Lodovico, 32, 80
Grossi, Gennaro, 94, 95
Gualdo, Paolo, 189
Guasti, Cesare, 119
Gunpowder Plot, 23
Gwendolen, 132

Hades, 142, 164
Haemonia, 56
Hague, The, 54, 127
Hales, John, 7
Halicarnassus, 128
Harding, John, 144
Harvard,
    Houghton Library, 54
Heaven, 60, 63, 101, 109, 166, 189
Hebe, 86
Hebrew (language), 22
Hebrews, 96
Hecaerge, 130, 131, 132
Hector, 92
Heidelberg, 48
Heinsius, Nicolas, 24
Henry VIII, King, 101, 139, 143
Herbert, Edward, 25
Hercules, 46, 52, 60, 144

Herodotus, 72, 128–133
Heylyn, Peter, 7
Hogenburg, Frans, 111
Holland, Hugh, 99
Holstenius, Lucas, 33–34, 123, 143
    Demophili Democratis et Secundi ... Sententiae Morales (1638), 34
    Porphyrii Philosophi Liber de Vita Pythagorae (1630), 34
Homer, 31, 87, 90, 118, 121, 128–129, 134, 188
    Iliad, 90
Horace, 32, 57, 60, 79, 111, 137, 144, 164–165, 197
    Epistles, 144, 165
    Epodes, 57
    Odes, 79, 111, 164–165
    Satires, 60, 197
Humber, 104; *see also* Abra
Hybla, 106, 107
Hydropolis, 101; *see also* Dorchester
Hyperboreans, 83, 130–132, 205
Hyperoche, 131, 133

Iaggard, Isaac, 99
Igerne, 139
Ilithia, 131
Il Teatro delle Glorie della Signora Adriana Basile (1628), 35–36
India, 71
Ingegneri, Angelo, 151
Iobinus, Bernardus, 6, 12
Ionians, 131
Ireland, 111
Iris, 74
Isis, 103
Islip, Adam, 106
Italian
    academies, 3, 8–9, 46, 49, 122, 137, 154, 173, 175, 194–200
    history, 7
    journey, 4, 7, 9, 15, 29, 36, 54, 102, 104, 137, 168, 200
Italy, 15, 20, 22, 23, 28, 29, 32, 38, 42, 44, 46, 54, 83, 89, 102, 103, 105, 120, 125, 135, 143, 153, 173, 187, 191, 195, 196, 198, 205

James I, King, 99

Jason, 56
Jerusalem, 20, 21, 35, 62, 81, 82, 115–120, 124, 128, 136, 149–150, 165
Jesuits, Order of, 3–4, 11, 24
Jews, 63
John the Baptist, 96
Jones, Inigo, 9
Jonson, Ben, 99
Jupiter, 42, 80, 89, 95–96, 145, 166

Kalcovius, Iodocus, 55
Katabasis, 34
Kent, 107
Kingston, Ihon, 25
Kircher, Athenasius, 33
Kloot, Isaac van der, 127
Kyne, Melanopos of, 131

Lactantius, Lucius Caecilius Firmianus, 63, 68, 69
   De Ave Phoenice, 68, 69, 72
Laelius, Gaius, 156, 161
Landor, Walter Savage, 146
Landrus, Petrus, 6
La Noù, Giovanni, 111, 122
Laodice, 131, 133
Lassels, Richard, 4
Latin (language), 22, 26, 28, 34, 38, 47–48, 50, 58, 66, 78, 79, 115
Latium, 83
Lazarus, Saint, 180
Lee, 98, 99
Leiden, 24
Leland, John, 99–101, 103, 132, 139, 142
   Assertio Inclytissimi Arturii Regis Britanniae (1544), 139–140, 143–146, 147
   Commigratio Bonarum Literarum in Britanniam (1589), 103
   Cygnea Cantio (1545), 100–101, 132
   Synchrisis Cygnorum et Poetarum (1589), 99–100
Le Monnier, Felice, 119
Lemos, Count of, *see* De Castro, Pedro Fernández
Lethe, 73, 164
Lichfield, John, 7
Lithgow, William, 24, 25

Locus amoenus, 87–91, 173
Loffredo
   Cecco, 94
   family of, 118
   Vittoria, 118–119
Lombards, 135
Lombardy, 20
London, 98, 101, 111, 134, 139
   British Library, 17, 22, 33, 39, 156
   St. Anne Parish Church, Blackfriars, 36
   St. Paul's School, 103
Longhi
   Gioseffo, 123, 186
   Roberto, 186
Longo
   Egidio, 20
   Tarquinio, 4, 57
Loredano, Francesco, 123
Loreto, 80
Lotti, Giovanni, 33
Lownes, Humphrey, 99
Loxo, 130, 131, 132
Lucan, Marcus Annaeus, 132, 133
Lucca, 114
Luchtmans, Samuel, 24
Lucia, Saint, 19
Lucretius, Titus, 33, 57
Lucullus, Lucius Licinius, 1
Lycaeum, 197
Lycia, 131
Lycidas, 91
Lynceus, 197
Lyon, 6, 10, 33, 145
Lysis, 156, 160

Maccabeus, Judas, 21
Macedonia, 149–150
Macerata, 80
Maecenas, Gaius, 20, 77, 79, 111, 203
Manilius, Marcus, 56
Manso, Giovanni Battista
   Del Dialogo Trattato (1628), 44, 155–156, 158–159
   domestic chapel of, 26, 175–184
   Enciclopedia (MS), 41–42, 136
   Erocallia (1628), 10, 26, 36, 37, 38–40, 41–63, 84, 156, 195
   I Paradossi (1608), 41, 47, 78
   La Fenice, 70–72

Index Nominum et Locorum 255

Latin encomium of Milton, 25, 45, 46–54, 57, 61, 63, 84, 137, 148, 175, 183–184
Lettera ... in Materia del Vesuvio (MS), 23
Palace of, 176, 179
Poesie Nomiche (1635), 10, 18, 19, 26, 36, 38–40, 42, 65–111, 146, 157–158, 171, 206
Vita di Giambattista Marino (MS), 35, 122–124, 195
Vita di Torquato Tasso (1621), 1–2, 26, 35, 115–117, 119, 123, 124–128, 150–153
Vita, Virtù e Miracoli ... di S. Patricia (1611), 23, 47
Mantua, 95, 136
Mantuanus, Baptista, 83, 197
Manutius, Aldus, 129
Marenza, Luca, 27
Marinism, 26, 83, 85, 184, 186–188, 202–204; see also *Concettismo*
Marino, Giambattista, 26, 35, 41, 49, 74, 75, 76, 80–85, 88, 92, 93, 108, 113, 153, 165, 166, 167, 175–206
   Della Lira (1616), 75, 183
   L'Adone (1623), 26, 81–83, 108, 122, 175, 184–194, 199, 200, 201, 202, 203, 205
   La Strage degli Innocenti (1632), 123
   Letter to Manso (1625), 84
   Sonnets in praise of Manso, 85
Maro, *see* Virgil, Publius
Mars, 78, 80, 81, 133, 143, 146, 147, 191
Martial, Marcus Valerius, 81
Martinius, Christopher, 78
Marvell, Andrew, 98, 203
Mascardi
  Giacomo, 33, 123, 196, 199
  Vitale, 33, 93
Matarozzi, Giuseppe, 187
Maurice, Saint, 180
Mayr, Sigismondo, 6
Mazzoni, Jacopo, 137, 186
Mazzucci, Lelio, 97
Medea, 56
Mediterranean, 4
Mega, Francesco, 87, 97
Meles, 129, 134,
Meliboeus, 87–89, 106, 107
Mempricius, King, 138
Menalcas, 91
Meraviglia, 185–186, 191–194, 200, 203, 204
Mercury, 89, 96
Merlin, 139
Michiele, Pietro, 67
Milan, 20, 41, 105, 179
Milton
  Deborah, 22
  John,
    Manuscripts
      Trinity College, Cambridge MS R. 3.4., 102, 142
    poetry
      Ad Leonoram 1, 35, 63, 76, 156
      Ad Leonoram 2, 35, 76, 125, 156
      Ad Leonoram 3, 12, 35–36, 76, 156
      Ad Patrem, 22, 79, 113, 133, 168–173
      Ad Salsillum, 32–33, 83, 101–102, 113, 156, 190
      Comus, see Maske, A
      De Idea Platonica, 113
      Elegia Prima, 13, 16, 113, 139
      Elegia Secunda, 56
      Elegia Tertia, 60, 63, 184
      Elegia Quarta, 91
      Elegia Sexta, 78–79, 113
      Elegiarum Liber, 113
      Epitaphium Damonis, 10, 15, 36–37, 38–39, 45, 68–75, 104, 113, 114, 134, 135, 139, 141
      Il Penseroso, 109–110
      In Obitum Praesulis Eliensis, 113, 189
      In Obitum Procancellarii Medici, 113, 189
      In Quintum Novembris, 23, 113, 139, 205
      Latin epigrams on the Gunpowder Plot, 23
      Latin epigrams to Leonora Baroni, 76, 113
      Latin poetry, 3, 28, 49
      Lycidas, 37, 102, 133, 149, 166
      Maske, A, 5, 15, 39, 54, 82

Naturam Non Pati Senium, 113
Paradise Lost, 18, 22, 46, 51, 59, 62, 68, 75, 84, 85, 91–92, 116, 134, 184, 198, 199, 200, 204, 206
Paradise Regained, 16, 129
Poemata (1645), 16, 22, 23, 25, 28, 29, 32, 38, 40, 46, 47, 49, 76, 82, 113, 134, 189
Poems ... Both English and Latin (1645), 15, 16, 25
projected *Arthuriad*, 133–150
Samson Agonistes, 96
Sonnet 9, 53
Sylvarum Liber, 113
prose
  Apology for Smectymnuus, 38–39, 138
  Areopagitica, 28, 200
  Commonplace Book, 29, 48, 106, 138, 139, 144
  De Doctrina Christiana, 96
  Defensio Secunda, 1, 11, 16–17, 19, 22, 23–25, 54, 102
  Epistola Familiaris 1, 187
  Epistola Familiaris 7, 7, 44, 84, 102
  Epistola Familiaris 8, 29–31, 155
  Epistola Familiaris 9, 4, 33–34, 123–124, 143
  Epistola Familiaris 10, 23–24, 39, 92, 114
  Epistola Familiaris 15, 197
  Epistolarum Familiarium Liber Unus, 4, 7, 24, 29, 30, 31, 33, 39, 44, 84, 92, 123, 143, 155, 187, 197
  History of Britain, 48, 50, 140
  Latin prose, 28
  Of Education, 137
  Prolusiones, 13, 59–60
  Prolusio VI, 53, 59, 138, 147, 183
  Reason of Church-Government, 31, 46, 49, 135, 137, 154, 168
Milton, John, Sr., 168–173; see also Milton, John, *Ad Patrem*
Mincius, 134
Minerva, 121, 125, 127, 203

Misenus, 2
Mocia, Scipione, 97
Modena, 186
Modestino, Carmine, 119
Moduin, 105
Molin, Domenico, 188
Mollo, Roberto, 176
Monmouth, Geoffrey of, 47, 48, 132, 138–140, 144, 148
Montecassiano, 80, 83
Monteverdi, Claudio, 27
Mordred, 148
Mormile, Giuseppe, 5
Moryson, Fynes, 7, 14, 17, 24
Moscovia, 111
Moseley, Humphrey, 15, 25
Moulin, Pierre du, Jr., 54
  Regii Sanguinis Clamor (1652), 54
Moxon, Edward
Multilingualism, 147, 173
Munday, Anthony, 24
Murat, Jochim, King, 181
Murray, John, 21, 37
Muschio, Andrea, 189
Muses, 78, 83, 86, 102, 103, 106, 172, 190, 205
Mycale, 121, 203
Myrrha, 191

Naiads, 5, 35
Naples
  Accademia
    degli Addormentati, 8
    degli Ardenti, 8
    degli Arditi, 8
    degli Armeristi, 8
    degli Assetati, 8
    degli Erranti, 8
    degli Incogniti, 8
    degli Incolti, 8
    degli Infuriati, 8, 122
    degli Intronati, 8
    degli Investiganti, 8, 181
    degli Oscuri, 8
    degli Oziosi, 3, 8, 9, 23, 45, 51, 57, 65, 67, 72–74, 76, 78, 85–92, 93, 97–98, 103, 110, 115, 122, 126, 172, 184, 187, 189, 194–195, 203
    degli Scatenati, 8

degli Svegliati, 8
degli Uniti, 8
dei Lunatici, 8
dei Pigri, 8
dei Rinomati, 8
dei Segreti, 8
dei Sicuri, 8
dei Sireni, 8
dei Volanti, 8
del Cimento, 8
del Colonna, 8
de' Ravvivati, 8
Laurenziana, 8
Partenia, 8
Pontaniana, 8
Archivio di Stato, 122
Banco della Pietà, 179
Banco di San Giacomo e Vittoria, 178, 181
Biblioteca Nazionale, 23, 76, 119, 122, 136
Cave of the Sibyl, 9
Church of San Domenico Maggiore, 181, 182
Church of the Holy Apostles, 177, 178
Collegio dei Nobili, 11, 91, 202
Grotta di Posillipo, 9–10, 14
Museo dell' Archivio Storico Banco, 178
Palazzo Reale, 16, 19–21, 22
Phlegraean Fields, 9, 13, 17, 18
Piazza dei Girolamini, 176
Posillipo, 10, 12, 14
Pozzuoli, 2, 9, 18
Reale Biblioteca Borbonica, 122
Solfatara, 9, 17–18
tomb of Virgil, 1, 9–10, 14
topography of, 1–2, 4–7, 9–10, 27, 57
Vesuvius, Mount, 2, 11, 23, 52, 98, 198
Via Toledo, 17
Nashe, Thomas, 106
Navarrete, Antonio Pérez, 21
Neaera, 56, 60, 90
Nemesianus, Marcus Aurelius Olympius, 58, 105, 106, 107

Nerli
  Bernardo, 128, 129
  Nero, 128
Newcomb, Thomas, 1
New York, 24, 41
  Public Library, 24
Nonnus, *see* Panopolis
Northumberland
  Alla, King of, 48
Nuccio, Lucrezio, 184
Nuremburg, 148
Nymphs, 78

Oedipus, 33
Okes, Nicholas, 25
Olen, 131
Olympus, 59, 84, 149, 153
Onofrio
  Church of, *see s.v.* Rome
  Monastery of, *see s.v.* Rome
Opis, *see* Upis
Orcus, 121
Orkney Islands, 111
Orpheus, 59, 91, 172, 190, 195, 200, 204
Orsini, Vincenzo, 180
Orwin, Thomas, 100
Osana, Francesco, 136
Ostia, 20
Otto I, Emperor, 147
Ovid, 5, 16, 39, 56, 58, 61, 68, 69, 89, 90, 92, 93, 106, 110, 125, 164, 191, 194
  Amores, 68, 106
  Ars Amatoria, 58, 90
  Epistulae ex Ponto, 93, 106, 191
  Fasti, 90, 92, 93, 110
  Metamorphoses, 5, 39, 56, 61, 68, 89, 92, 110, 125, 164, 194
  Tristia, 110
Oxford, 7, 17, 29, 100
  Bodleian Library, 17, 29

Pace, Antonio, 155
Paci, Giovanni Francesco, 115
Padua, 186, 198
paganism, 47, 48, 51–52, 60, 63, 96, 148

Pagliarini, Marco, 119
Palomba, Arello Maria, 73
Pan, 95–96
Panopolis
  Nonnus of, 131
papacy, 24, 102, 148, 152
Paphos, 153
Parcae, 121
Paris (city), 47, 50, 82, 184
Parma, 81
Parnassus, 153, 183
Parthenias, 53
Parthenope, 5–6, 10, 12, 35, 54, 78, 87, 88, 180, 183
Paterculus, Velleius, 191
Patricia, Saint, 23, 47
Patrizi, Francesco, 186
Patroclus, 164
Pausanias, 131, 132
Pavia, 185
Pavoni, Taddeo, 187
Pegasus, 84
Pella, *see* Macedonia
Pendragon, Uther, 139
Peneus, 90
Pentheus, 125
Perithous, 164–165
Persephone, 164; *see also* Proserpina
Persius Flaccus, Aulus, 191
Peter, Saint, 51, 148
Petrarch, Francesco, 67, 114, 163, 205
Petrone, Vincenzo, 79, 146
Philaras, Leonard, 197
Philip
  II, King, 20
  IV, King, 41, 42
Phillips
  Edward, 22, 27
  John, 27
Phoebus, *see* Apollo
Piacenza, 188
Picus, 110
Pierians, 77
Pignatelli, Hettore, 95
Pignatello, Ascanio, 76
Pignoni, Zanobi, 30
Pindar, 31, 89
Pindus, Mount, 81
Pinelli
  Antonio, 187

Galeazzo Franco, 115
  Vincenzo, 189
Pipini, Tomaso, 94, 95
Pisa, 186
Plato, 8, 37, 42, 156, 160, 161, 184, 197
  Lysis, 156, 160
  Republic, 184
  Symposium, 160
Plautus, Titus Maccius, 121, 144
Pliny the Elder, 5, 57, 68, 69, 110, 132, 196, 198
Plutarch, 129, 158–159, 162
Poesie de' Signori Accademici Fantastici di Roma (1637), 32
Poesie di Diversi a Gio. Battista Manso (1635), 66, 79–98, 146, 157
Poliziano, Angelo, 89–90
Polo, Alessandro, 30
Pontano, Giovanni, 6
Pontes, 101; *see also* Reading
Porphyry, Pomponius, 34
Portuguese, 20–21
Posillipo, *see s.v.* Naples
Poussin, Nicolas, 199, 200
Pozzuoli, *see s.v.* Naples
Priscianese, Francesco, 29
Prochita, 2
Propertius, Sextus, 56, 61, 77, 106, 191
Proserpina, 44, 66
Protestantism, 46, 52–53, 60, 63, 102
Provano, Jacopo, 105
Provenzale, Francesco, 17
Pugliese, Vittoria, 119
Pythagoras, 34, 42, 61

Quintilian, Marcus Fabius, 31, 81
Quirinus, 78

Raillard, Giacomo, 4
Raphael (angel), 62, 68, 184
Raymond, John, 15
Reading, 101
Recanati, 80
Red Sea, 68
Rennes
  William of, 148
Reusner, Nicolaus, 6
Ricinia, *see* Recanati
Robert, King, *see s.v.* Anjou, Robert of

Robertello, Francesco, 186
Robinson
  Humphrey, 15
  Richard, 140
Roch, Saint, 83
Rome, 2, 4, 11, 12, 24, 25, 29, 32, 33, 34, 35, 47, 50, 63, 76, 78, 80, 83, 93, 101, 102, 105, 106, 116, 122, 123, 124, 125, 134, 143, 147, 149–150, 151, 152, 156, 161, 184, 188, 190, 196, 199
  Accademia degli Umoristi, 33, 101–102, 122, 178, 187, 190
  Accademia dei Fantastici, 32–33
  Accademia Nazionale dei Lincei, 188, 196, 202
  Biblioteca dell' Accademia dei Lincei e Corsiniana, 197
  English College, 3–4, 11
  Onofrio
    Church of, 152
    Monastery of, 151, 156
  Ponte Sant' Angelo, 52
  Vatican Library, 4, 33–34, 123
Romulus, 76; *see also* Quirinus
Roncagliolo, Gio. Domenico, 115
Ronconi, Francesco, 76
Roselli, Giuseppe, 182
Rossi, Vittorio, 55, 56
Rothwell, John, 31, 39
Rovitto, Ferrante, 74, 75, 97
Ruccelai, Cosimo, 37
Russo, Giovanni Battista, 35
Rutupiae, 139

Salicato, Altobello, 52
Salis, Giovanni, 30
Sallust, Gaius, 144
Salvianus, Horatius, 197
Salvioni, Pietro, 80
Salzilli, Giovanni, 25, 32–33, 47, 83, 101–102, 134
Sambiasi, Scipione, 77, 79
Sandys, George, 2, 24
Sannazaro, Iacopo, 1, 6, 15, 16, 82, 97, 98, 122, 205
  De Partu Virginis, 16
  Elegiae, 16
Santamaria, Andrea, 94
San Vitale, Countess, 125

Sarasino, Ernesto, 186
Sarnelli, Pompeo, 182
Sarocchi, Margherita, 94
Sarriano, Anello, 79, 95, 146
Sarzina, Giacomo, 33, 123
Satan, 18, 75, 200
Savio, Francesco, 51
Savoy
  Duke of, see Emanuele, Carlo I
Saxon, 101
Saxons, 133–134, 144, 146–149, 202
Sbarra, Ottavio, 85
Scaglia, Giacomo, 187
Scaliger, Joseph, 6
Scaramuccia, Angelita, 80–84
Schouten, Petrus, 74
Scipio Africanus, Publius Cornelius, 85, 118
Scoppa, Lucio Giovanni, 6
Scotland, 25, 48, 111
Scythia, 130, 131
Scythians, 78
Sebeto, 98, 134
Secundus (Greek philosopher), 34
Selden, John, 130
Selvaggio, Matteo, *see* Codner, David
Seneca the Younger, 56, 57, 197
  De Beneficiis, 197
  Hercules Furens, 57
  Hercules Oetaeus, 56
  Phaedra, 58
Serafini
  Giovanni Battista, 80
  Paolo, 80
seraphim, 62
Serassi, Pierantonio, 119
Seville
  Isidore of, 127, 147, 148
Shakespeare, William, 98, 99
Sibyl, 9, 145
Sicily, 195
Siculus, Diodorus, 133
Sidney, Philip, 98
Silenus, 77
Silius Italicus, Tiberius Catius Asconius, 6
Silvestris, Bernardus, 114
Silveyra, Miguel, 20–21
  El Macabeo, 20–21
Simancas

Archivo General de, 20
Simmes, Valentine, 99
Simoniana, 122
Sincerus, Actius, *see* Sannazaro, Iacopo
Sirens, 5, 6, 89, 183, 184
Solfatara, *see s.v.* Naples
Sophocles, 31
Soranzo, Giovanni, 79
Sorrento, 2
Southey, Robert, 146
Spain, 22, 42
Spanish, 4, 9, 19, 20, 21, 22, 94
Sparano, Simone, 93
Sparta, 149–150
Speght, Thomas, 106
Spenser, Edmund, 74, 98–99, 100, 105, 106, 107–109
   Prothalamion (1596), 99
   The Faerie Queene (1596), 74
   The Ruines of Time (1591), 98–99
   The Shepheardes Calender (1579), 105, 106, 107–109
Sperelli, Alessandro, 33
Stamphier, Joseph, 186
Statius
  Achilles, 6
  Publius Popinius, 57, 81, 92, 145
   Silvae, 92
   Thebaid, 57, 81, 145
Stella, Girolamo, 86, 95, 97
Stelluti, Francesco, 196
Stigliani
  Carlo, 187
  Tommaso, 186–188, 190–194, 196, 198, 199–201, 205
   Il Mondo Nuovo (1617), 188, 196, 201
   Occhiale (1627), 186–188, 199–201
Stordito, Estonne, 76, 79
Strabo, 5, 6
Strasbourg, 12, 47
Sugganappo, Francesco, 6
Sultzbach, Giovanni, 50
swans, 97–111
Symonds, Richard, 17, 33
Syriac (language), 22

Tacitus, Publius Cornelius, 121

Tamara, 104
Targioni, Luigi, 119
Tasso
  Bernardo, 125
  Torquato, 1–2, 10, 17, 21, 26, 31, 37, 38, 39, 42–43, 49, 52, 57, 62, 65, 68, 69, 72, 76, 80–85, 88, 94, 113–120, 121, 122, 124–128, 134, 135, 136, 137, 141, 146, 149, 150–153, 155–173, 199, 202, 205
   Gerusalemme Conquistata (1593), 35, 62, 82, 84, 115–120, 136, 149–151, 165
   Gerusalemme Liberata (1581), 20, 81, 124, 128, 136, 151
   Il Manso (1596), 26, 35, 84, 115, 116, 155–173
   Le Sette Giornate del Mondo Creato (1607), 65, 68, 72, 117, 128
  sonnets in praise of Manso, 85, 94, 157–158
Tassone, Ferrante, 135
Tempe, 90
Terence, 127
Tesauro
  Emanuele, 186
  Lodovico, 184, 186
Thames, 98–101, 103, 104, 105, 130, 134, 205
T(h)ammuz, 191
Thebes, 68, 125
Thenot, 107
Theocritus, 15, 37, 58
Theseus, 164
Thessaly, 56
Thule, 81
Thyrsis, 15, 91, 113
Tiber, 12
Tibullus, Albius, 61
Tilbury
  Gervase of, 142–143
Tityrus, 87–89, 98, 104–107, 108
Toland, John, 27–28
Tomis, 16
Toraldo, Don Vincenzo, 77
Torquatus, L. Manlius, 165
Torrentino, Lorenzo, 186
Torres, Medina de las, 19
Trenovantum, 101

Trissino, Gangiorgio, 37
Trivulzio, Cesare, 37
Troilus, 105
Troise, Carlo, 33
Trojan Horse, 127–128
Trojans, 127, 132, 139
Troy, 139, 141, 192
Tudor, House of, 100, 103, 143
Turkish Empire, 25
Turler, Hieronymus, 12–15
Turner, William, 7
Tuscan tongue, 29–31, 155
Tuscany, 8, 22, 29, 91, 114
Tyrrhanian Sea, 2

Ulysses, 134
Upis, 130, 131, 132
Urban VIII, Pope, *see* Barberini, Maffeo
Urbino, 135

Valdarno, 198
Vallans, William, 98
Vassalini, Giulio, 138
Vecchi, Horatio, 27
Venice, 1, 7, 10, 27, 28, 30, 33, 35, 41, 47, 52, 65, 75, 78, 108, 111, 122, 123, 124, 129, 138, 181, 184, 186, 187, 189, 198
    Accademia degli Incogniti, 123
Venosa, Prince of, *see* Gesualdo, Carlo
Ventura, Comino, 135
Venus, 42, 78, 82, 138, 184, 191, 205
Vergil, Polydore, 139–140, 143–144
Vermigli, Peter Martyr, 139
Verona, 14
Vesuvius, *see s.v.* Naples
Vicenza, 184
Vico, Giambattista, 185
Vida, Marco Girolamo, 61, 133, 172, 173
    De Arte Poetica, 61, 133, 172, 173
Villani, Nicola, 187
Violati, Giacomo, 184
Viotti, Erasmo, 81

Virgil, Publius, 6, 10, 14, 15, 31, 34, 37, 38, 53, 54, 61, 74, 77, 83, 84, 87–89, 97, 98, 104, 105, 106, 107, 108, 111, 114, 118, 127, 134, 141, 143, 144, 145, 147, 180, 183, 192, 195, 197
    Aeneid, 15, 34, 61, 110, 111, 127, 141, 143, 145, 147, 195, 197
    Eclogues, 15, 37, 77, 78, 87–89, 106, 195
    Georgics, 5, 15, 78, 83, 144, 147, 192
Visconti, Bernabo, 105
Viscontini, Bartolomeo, 178, 179, 182
Vitale
    Costantino, 7
    Giovan Marco, 181
Vittorelli, Andrea, 79
Vivo, Francesco, 86–87
Vlacq, Adrian, 54
Volpiano, 20
Vossius, Isaac, 24
Vouet, Simon, 182
Vulcan, 191

Wales, 140
Walthoe, John, 130
Ward
    John, 22
    Roger, 98
Webbe, Edward, 24
Welser, Markus, 189
White, Richard, 140
Wilson, Thomas, 25
Wolfe
    John, 124, 140
    Reyner, 100, 139
Wolter, Bernhard, 78
Wood, Anthony à, 27

Young, Thomas, 91, 187

Zephyr, 71
Zinani, Gabriel, 76
Zurich, 129

www.ingramcontent.com/pod-product-compliance
Lightning Source LLC
Chambersburg PA
CBHW080731300426
44114CB00019B/2551